People usually associate the team of Sanjo and Inada with our earlier series, *Dai's Big Adventure*. But we're working hard on *Beet the Vandel Buster*, always hoping to outstrip the success of *Dai*. Please give us your good will and favor.

And now, let volume 9, "Soul of the Saiga," begin!
— Riku Sanjo and Koji Inada

Author Riku Sanjo and artist Koji Inada were both born in Tokyo in 1964. Sanjo began his career writing a radio-controlled car manga for the comic **Bonbon**. Inada debuted with **Kussotare Daze!!** in **Weekly Shonen Jump**. Sanjo and Inada first worked together on the highly successful **Dragon Quest–Dai's Big Adventure**. **Beet the Vandel Buster**, their latest collaboration, debuted in **Monthly Shonen Jump** in 2002 and was an immediate hit, inspiring an action-packed video game and an animated series on Japanese TV.

BEET THE VANDEL BUSTER
VOL. 9
The SHONEN JUMP Manga Edition

STORY BY RIKU SANJO
ART BY KOJI INADA

Translation/Naomi Kokubo
Touch-Up & Lettering/Mark McMurray
Graphics & Cover Design/Andrea Rice
Editor/Shaenon K. Garrity

Managing Editor/Elizabeth Kawasaki
Director of Production/Noboru Watanabe
Vice President of Publishing/Alvin Lu
Vice President & Editor in Chief/Yumi Hoashi
Sr. Director of Acquisitions/Rika Inouye
Vice President of Sales & Marketing/Liza Coppola
Publisher/Hyoe Narita

Published by VIZ Media, LLC
P.O. Box 77064
San Francisco, CA 94107

SHONEN JUMP Manga Edition
10 9 8 7 6 5 4 3 2 1
First printing, April 2006

www.viz.com

THE WORLD'S
MOST POPULAR MANGA
SHONEN JUMP
www.shonenjump.com

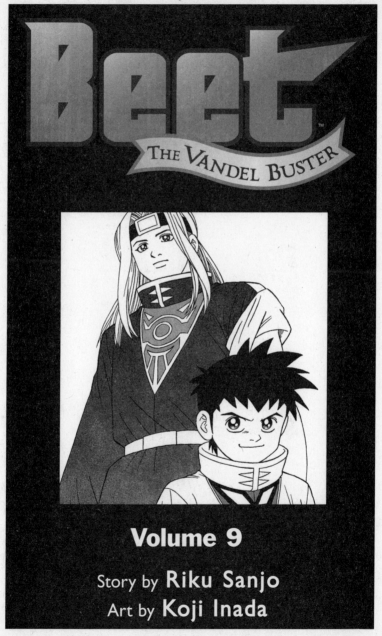

Beet
THE VANDEL BUSTER

Volume 9

Story by **Riku Sanjo**
Art by **Koji Inada**

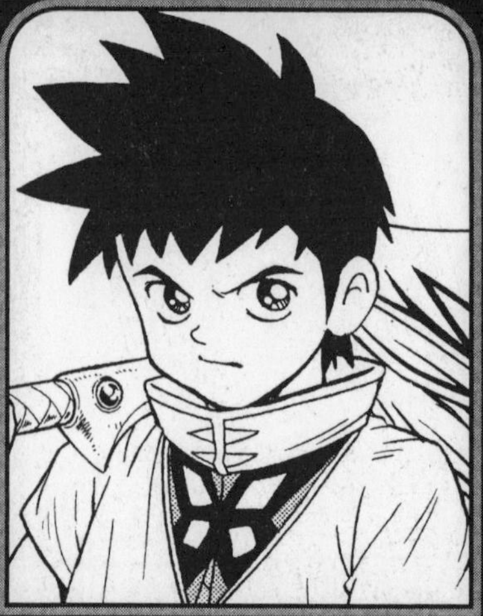

BEET
The hero of this story.
Believing in justice, he sets out on a journey to save the world. He received five Saiga weapons from the Zenon Warriors.

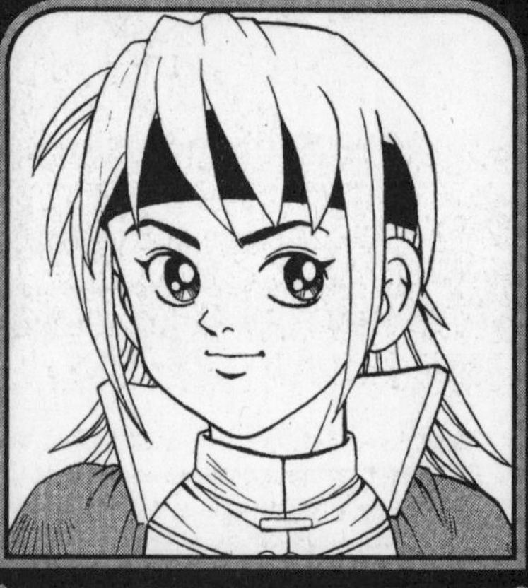

POALA
Beet's childhood friend has an unyeilding spirit. She joins Beet as the second of the Beet Warriors and sets out on his journey with him. She is skilled at Kenjutsu, the art of the samurai sword, as well as the Divine Attack.

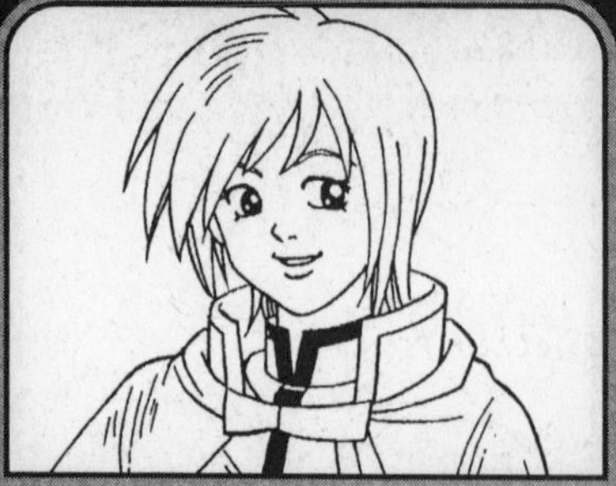

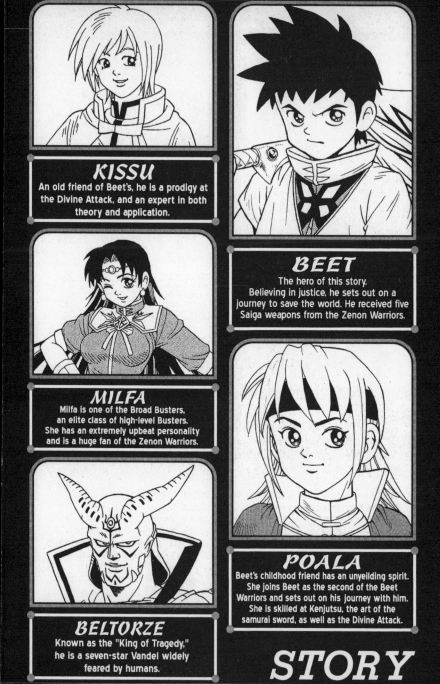

KISSU
An old friend of Beet's, he is a prodigy at the Divine Attack, and an expert in both theory and application.

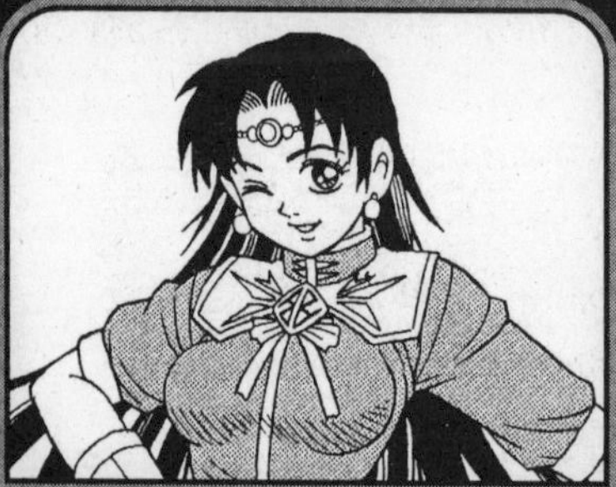

MILFA
Milfa is one of the Broad Busters, an elite class of high-level Busters. She has an extremely upbeat personality and is a huge fan of the Zenon Warriors.

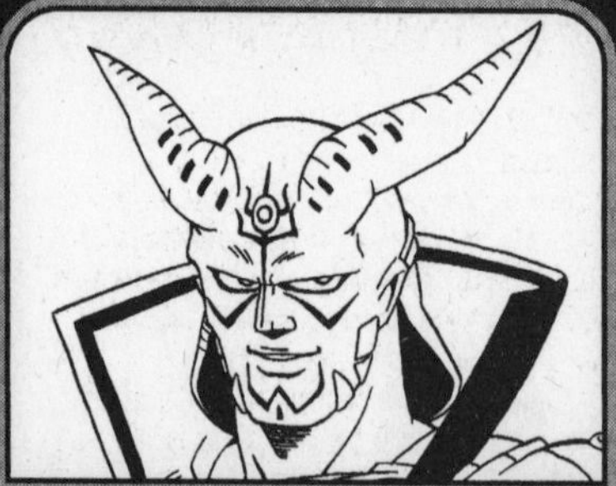

BELTORZE
Known as the "King of Tragedy," he is a seven-star Vandel widely feared by humans.

STORY

CHARACTERS

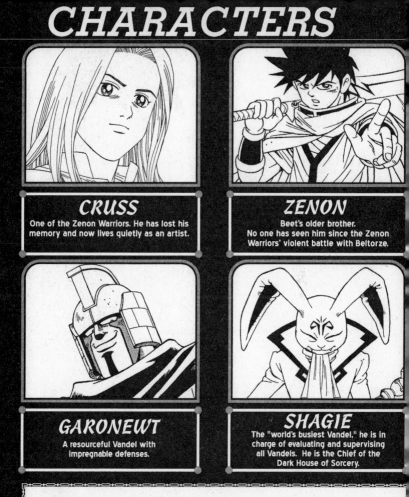

CRUSS
One of the Zenon Warriors. He has lost his memory and now lives quietly as an artist.

ZENON
Beet's older brother. No one has seen him since the Zenon Warriors' violent battle with Beltorze.

GARONEWT
A resourceful Vandel with impregnable defenses.

SHAGIE
The "world's busiest Vandel," he is in charge of evaluating and supervising all Vandels. He is the Chief of the Dark House of Sorcery.

"Vandels"... In this story, that's what we call evil creatures with magical powers. One day they appeared on the surface of the Earth, releasing monsters and destroying whole nations. People called this seemingly endless era "The Dark Age." Beet, a young boy who believes in justice, binds himself with a contract to become a Vandel Buster. Early in his career, Beet stumbles into a battle between the Zenon Warriors and a Vandel named Beltorze, where he suffers a fatal injury. He miraculously survives by receiving the Saiga of the Zenon Warriors.
Carrying on the Zenon Warriors' dream of peace, Beet sets out with his friends Poala and Kissu on a quest to destroy all Vandels. To atone for the crimes Kissu committed as a servant of the Vandels, the Beet Warriors agree to travel to Gransista, where the Vandel Buster headquarters are located, under Milfa's supervision. In Bekatrute, Beet discovers Cruss, one of the long-lost Zenon Warriors. A Vandel named Garonewt attacks the city, looking for Cruss--and repels all of Beet's attacks. At Beet's most desperate moment, Garonewt is sucked into a mysterious blackness...

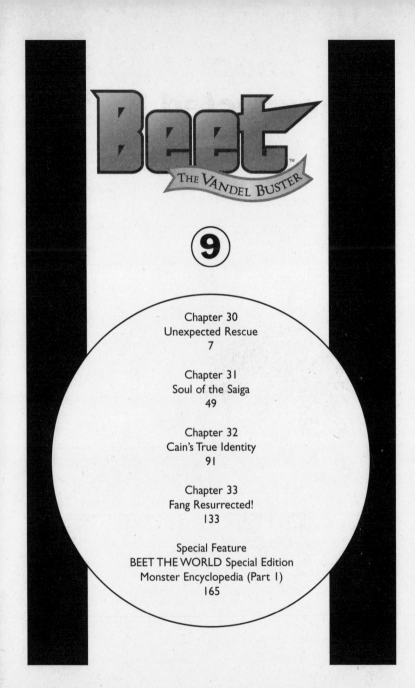

Beet
THE VANDEL BUSTER

9

Chapter 30: Unexpected Rescue

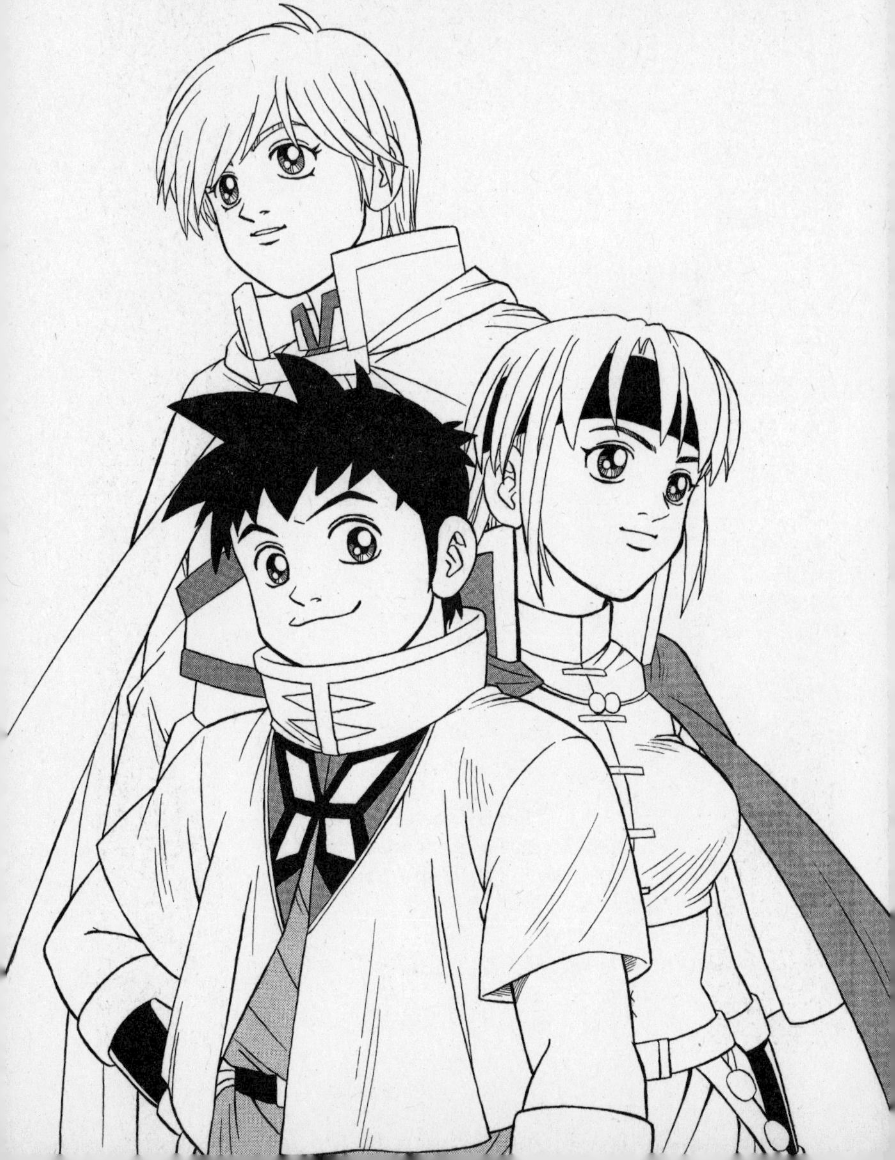

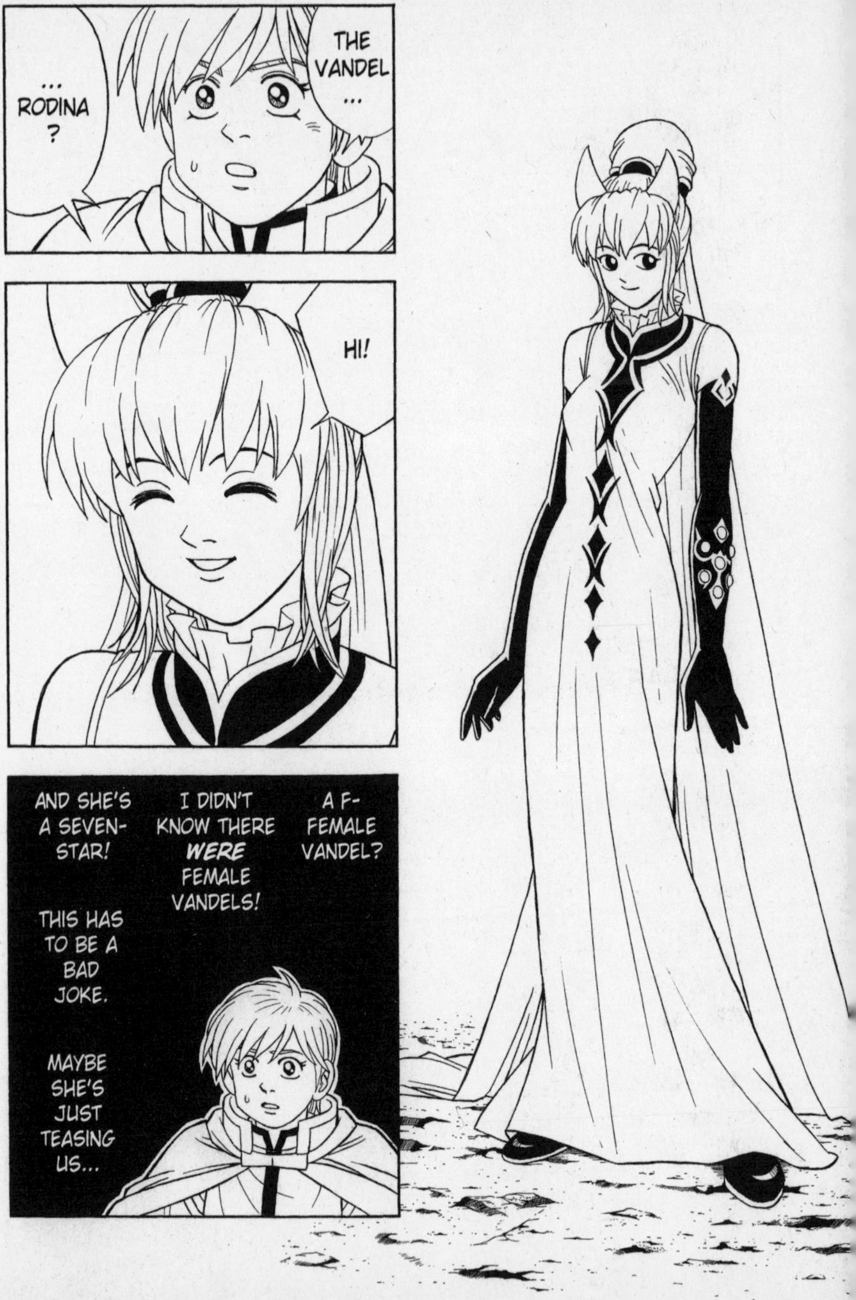
THE VANDEL ...
... RODINA ?
HI!
A F- FEMALE VANDEL?
I DIDN'T KNOW THERE WERE FEMALE VANDELS!
AND SHE'S A SEVEN-STAR!
THIS HAS TO BE A BAD JOKE.
MAYBE SHE'S JUST TEASING US...

READ THIS WAY

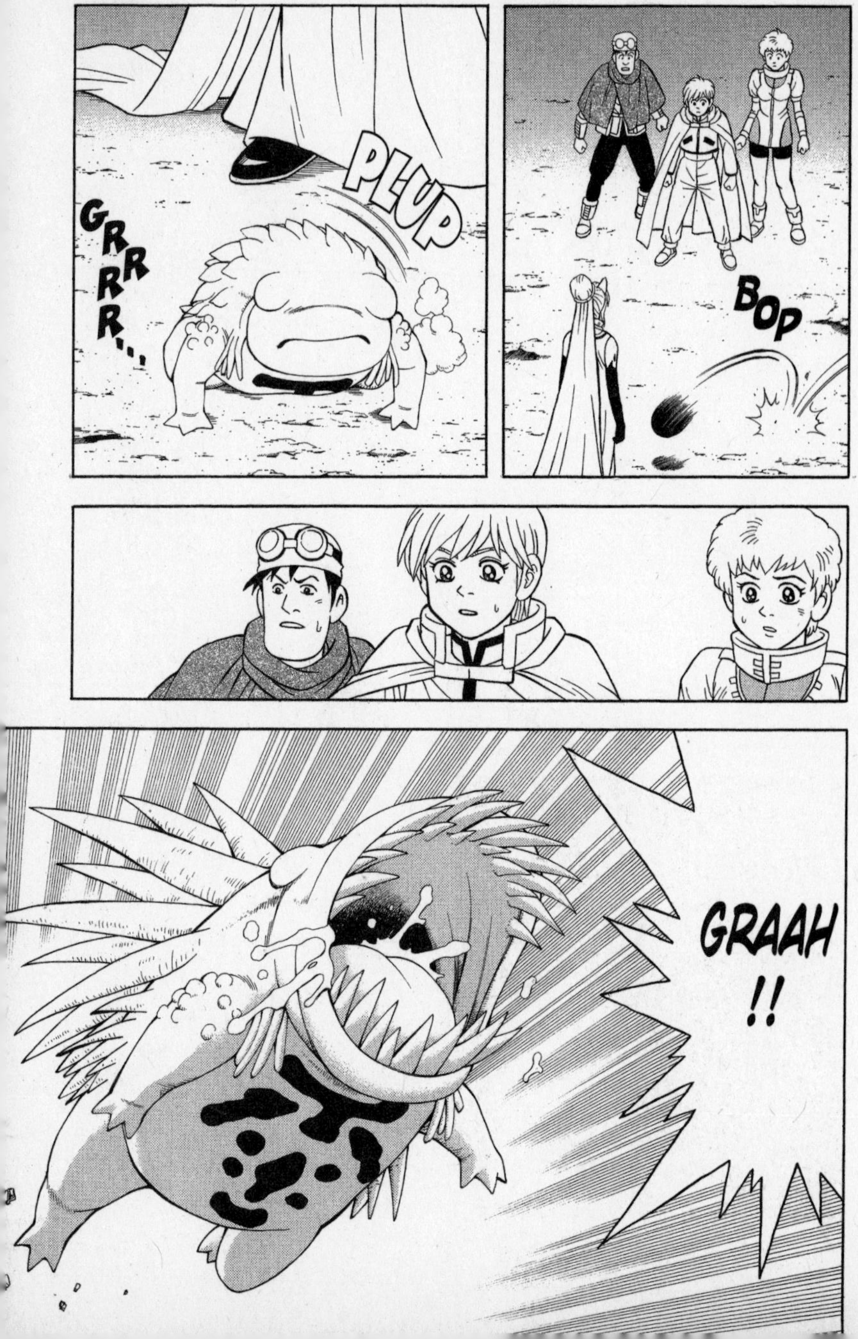
BOP
PLUP
GRRRR...
GRAAH!!

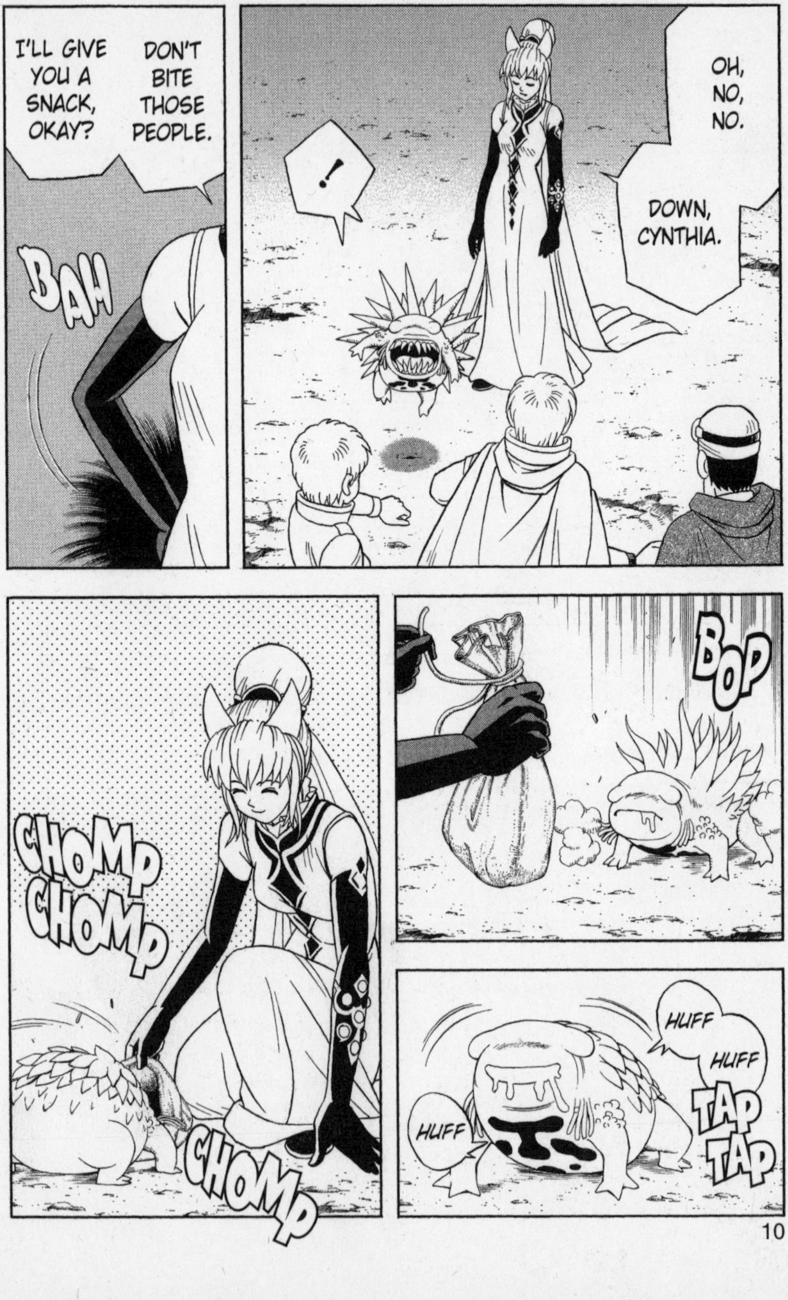
OH, NO, NO.
DOWN, CYNTHIA.
!
DON'T BITE THOSE PEOPLE.
I'LL GIVE YOU A SNACK, OKAY?
BAH
BOP
HUFF
HUFF
TAP TAP
HUFF
CHOMP CHOMP
CHOMP

READ THIS WAY

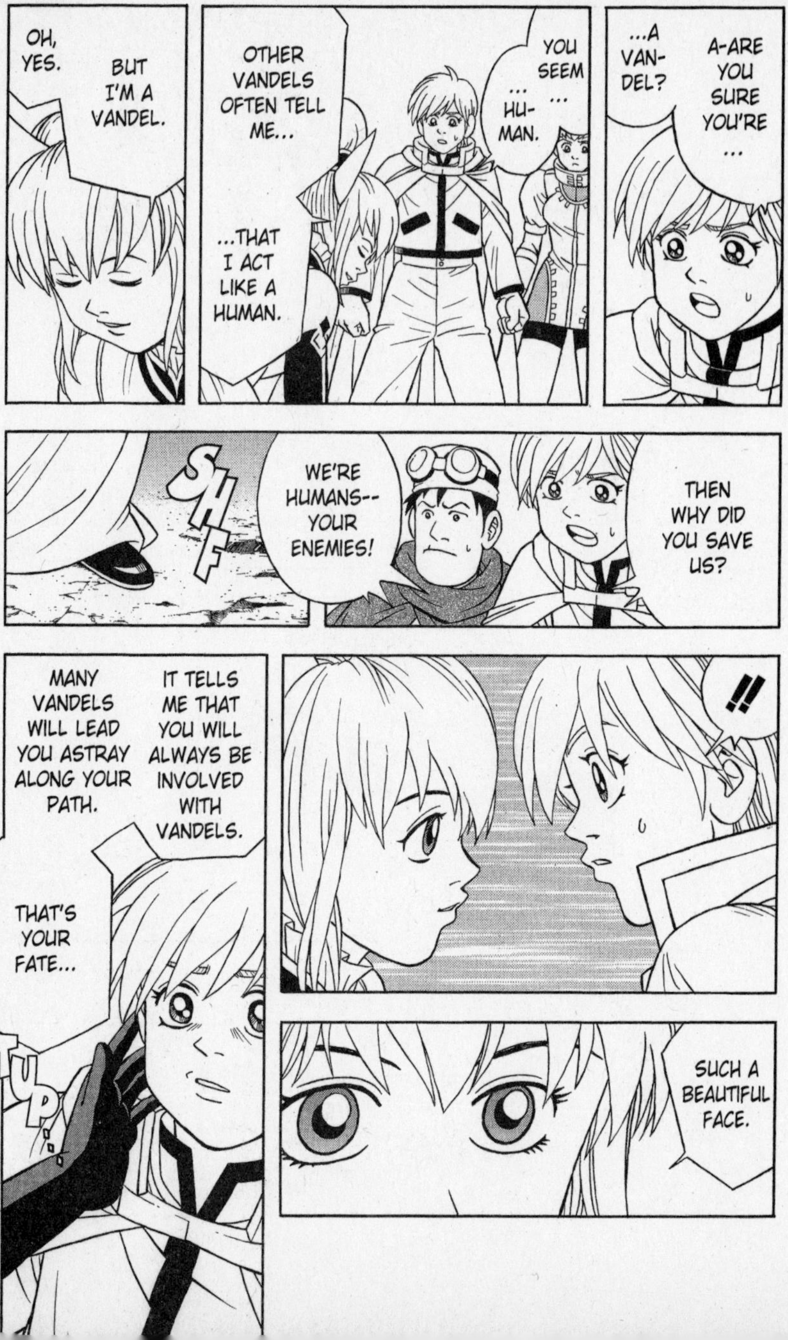
A-ARE YOU SURE YOU'RE ...
...A VAN-DEL?
YOU SEEM ...
... HU-MAN.
OTHER VANDELS OFTEN TELL ME...
...THAT I ACT LIKE A HUMAN.
OH, YES.
BUT I'M A VANDEL.
THEN WHY DID YOU SAVE US?
WE'RE HUMANS--YOUR ENEMIES!
SHF
!!
SUCH A BEAUTIFUL FACE.
IT TELLS ME THAT YOU WILL ALWAYS BE INVOLVED WITH VANDELS.
MANY VANDELS WILL LEAD YOU ASTRAY ALONG YOUR PATH.
THAT'S YOUR FATE...
TUP

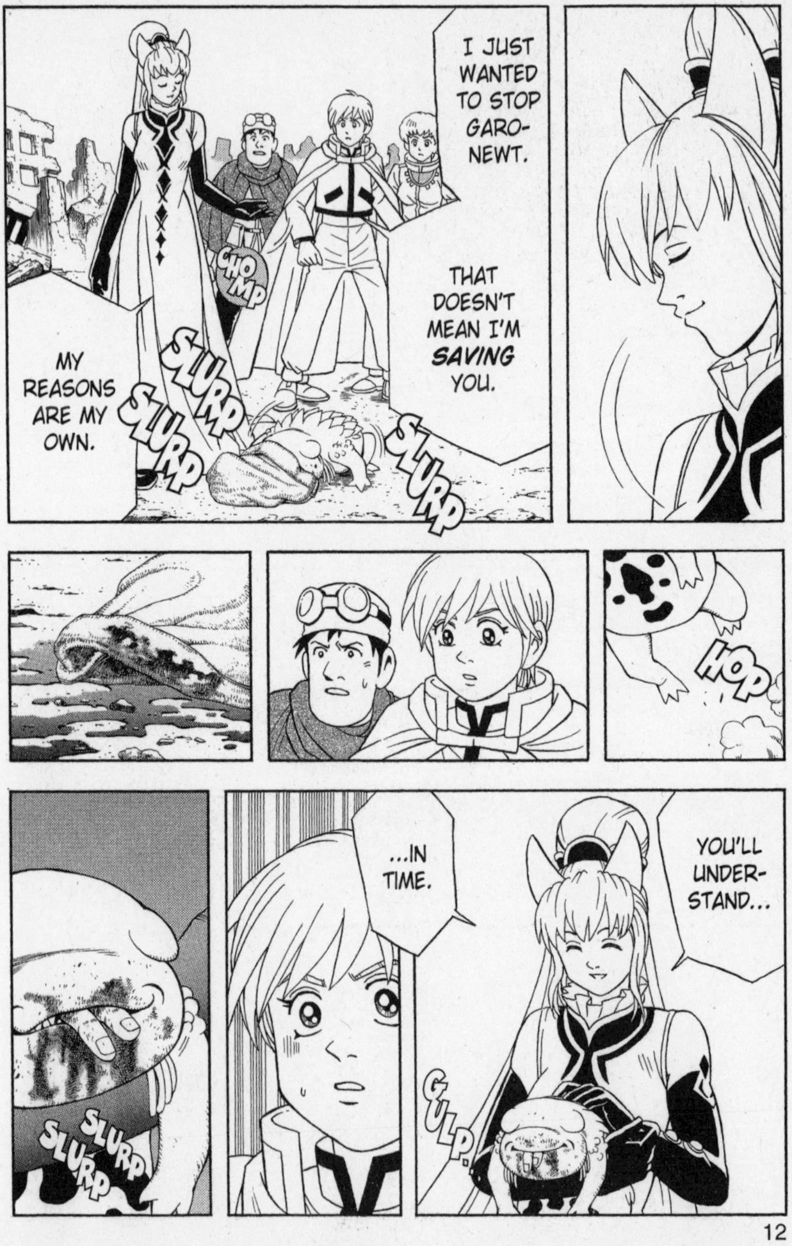
I JUST WANTED TO STOP GARO-NEWT.
THAT DOESN'T MEAN I'M *SAVING* YOU.
CHOMP
SLURP
SLURP
MY REASONS ARE MY OWN.
SLURP
HOP
YOU'LL UNDER-STAND...
...IN TIME.
GULP.
SLURP
SLURP

READ THIS WAY

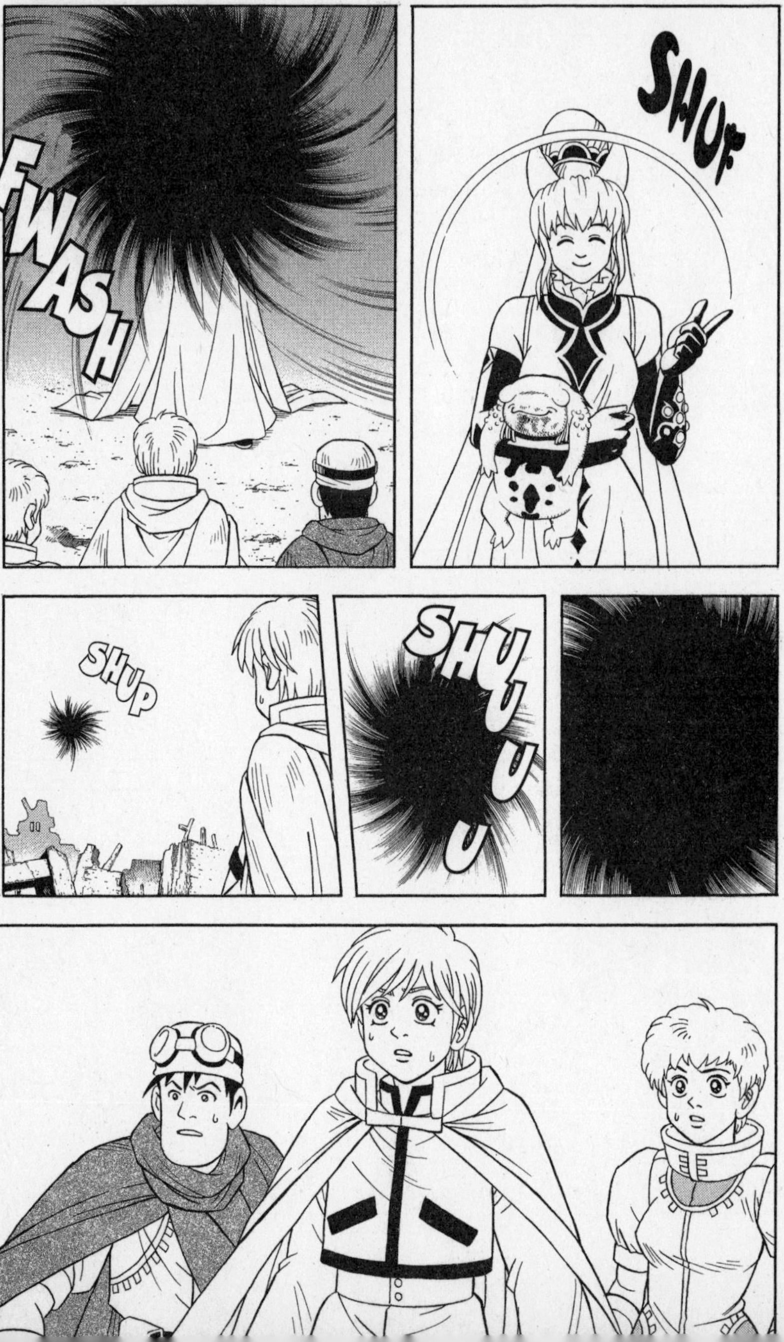
SHUF
FWASH
SHUUUU
SHUP

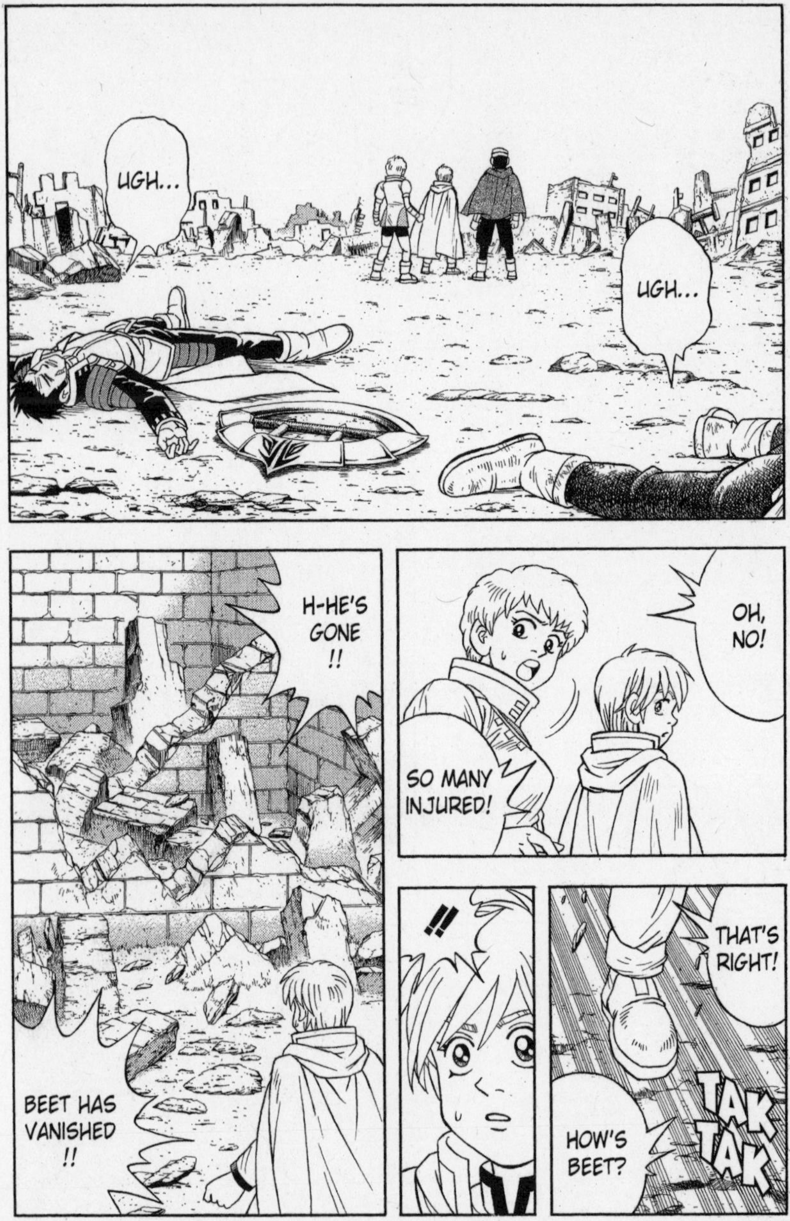
UGH...
UGH...
OH, NO!
SO MANY INJURED!
THAT'S RIGHT!
TAK TAK
HOW'S BEET?
!!
H-HE'S GONE !!
BEET HAS VANISHED !!

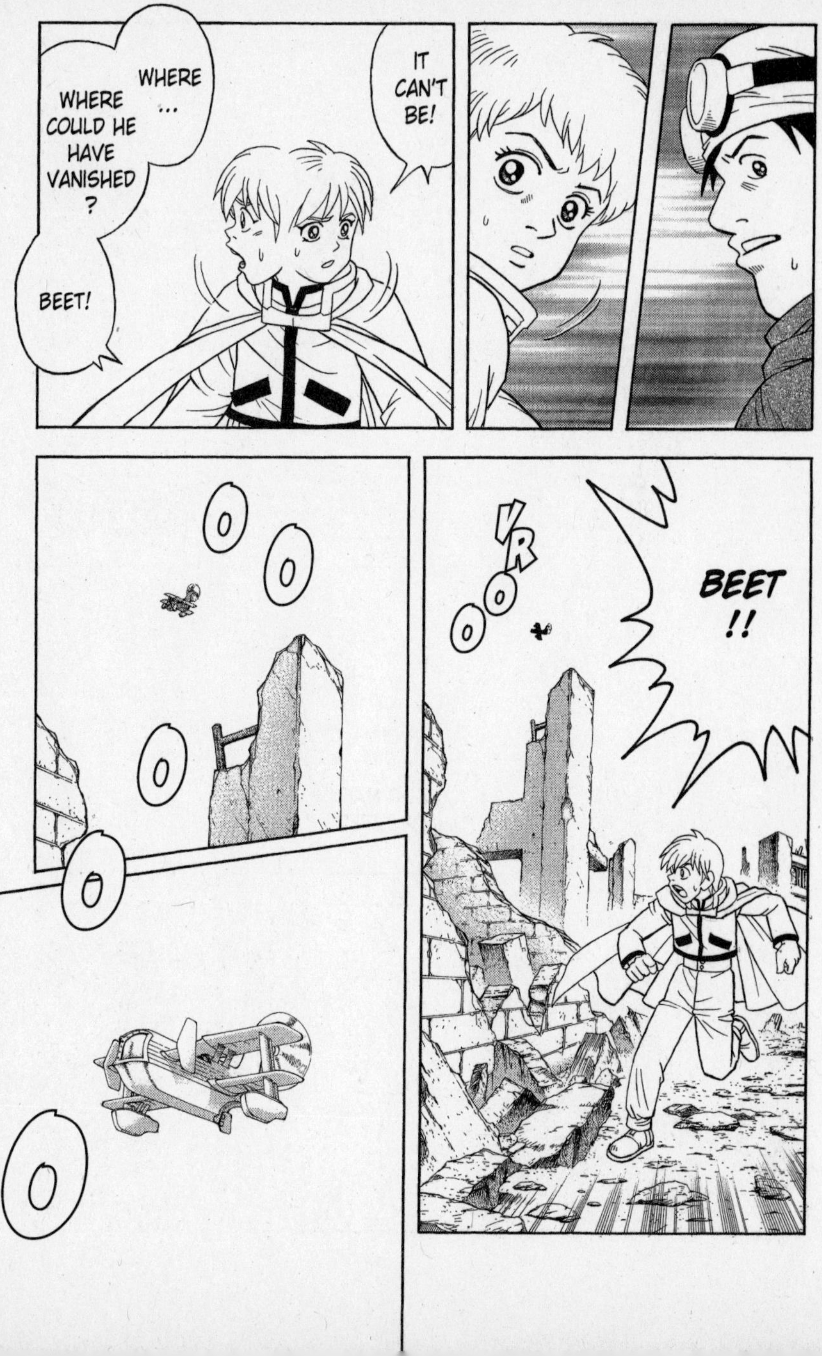
IT CAN'T BE!
WHERE ...
WHERE COULD HE HAVE VANISHED?
BEET!
BEET!!
VR
OO
OOOO
O

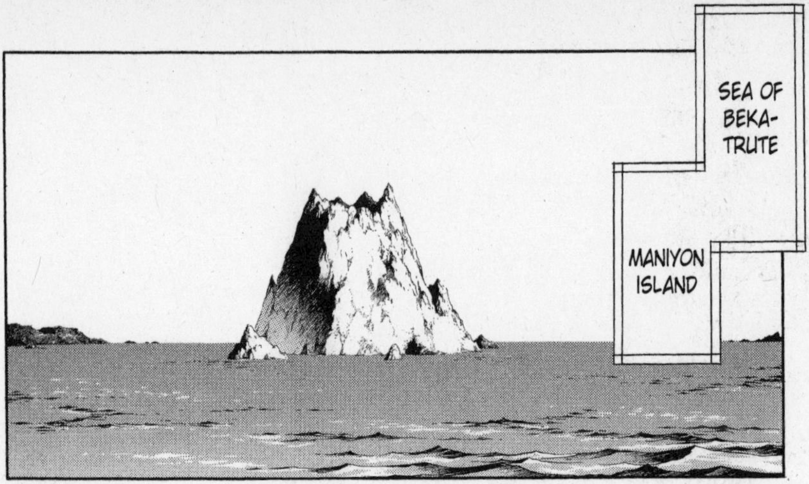
SEA OF BEKA-TRUTE
MANIYON ISLAND

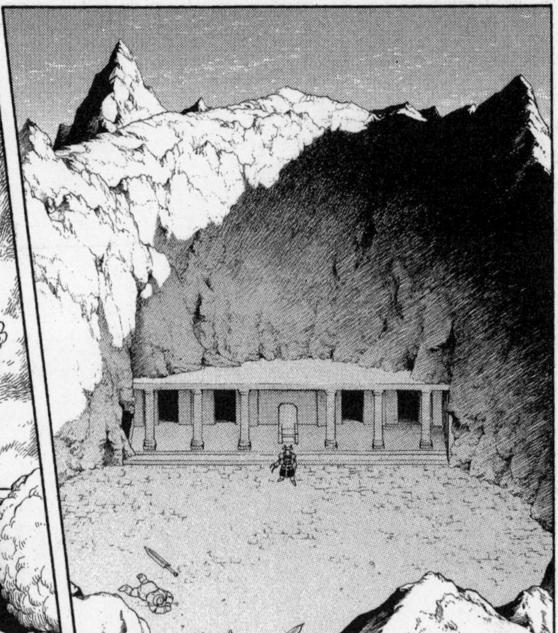

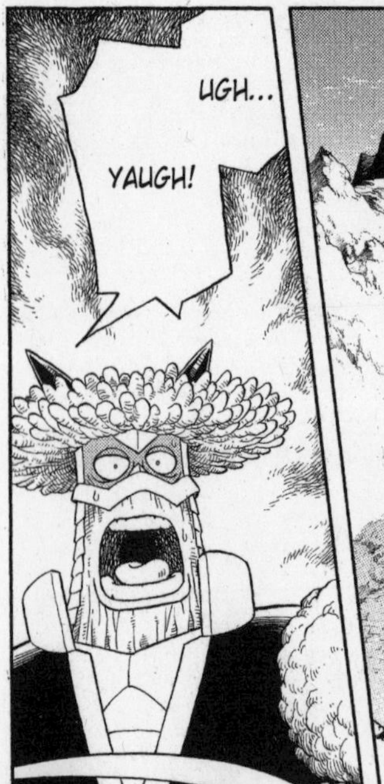
UGH...
YAUGH!

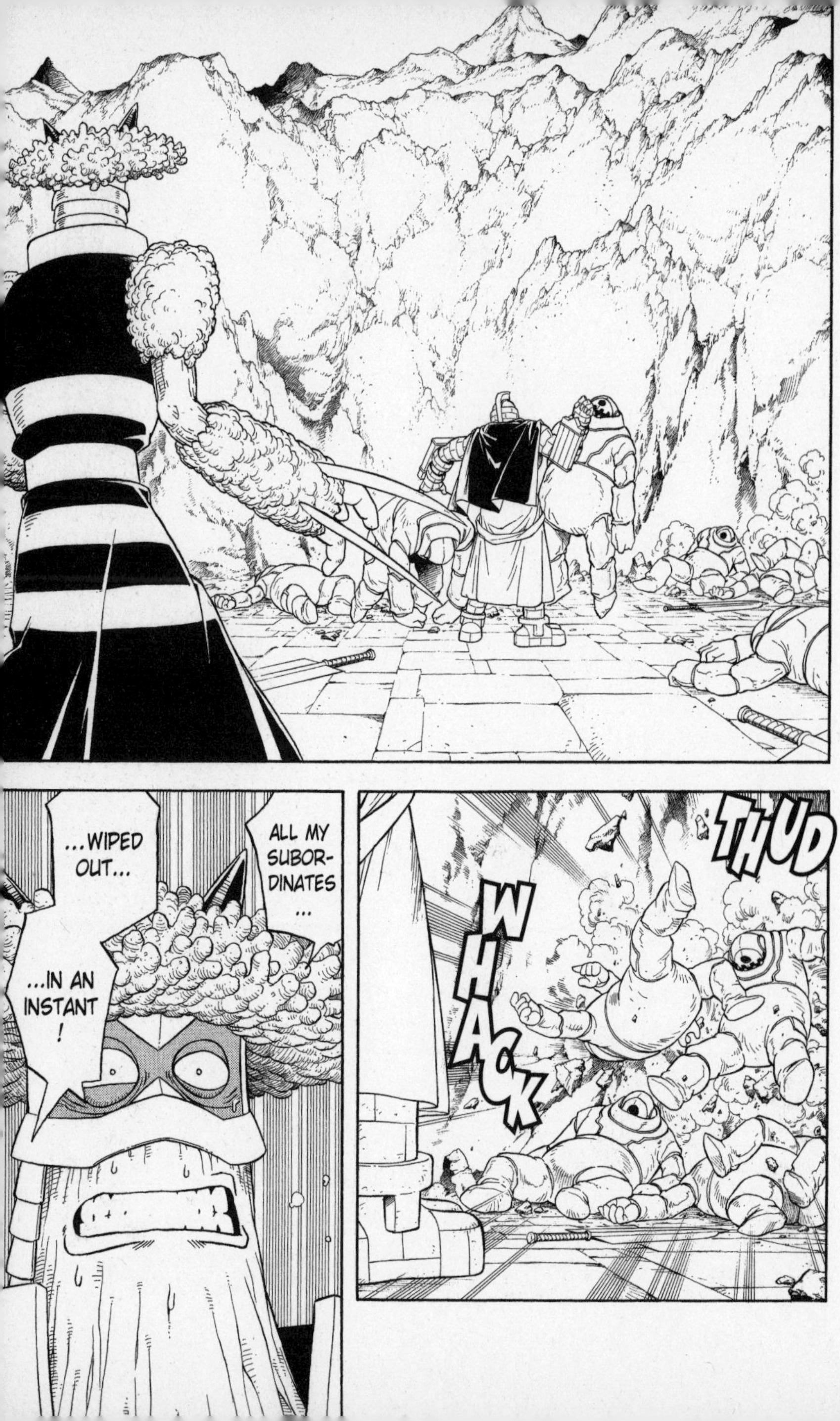
THUD
WHACK
ALL MY SUBORDINATES ...
...WIPED OUT...
...IN AN INSTANT!

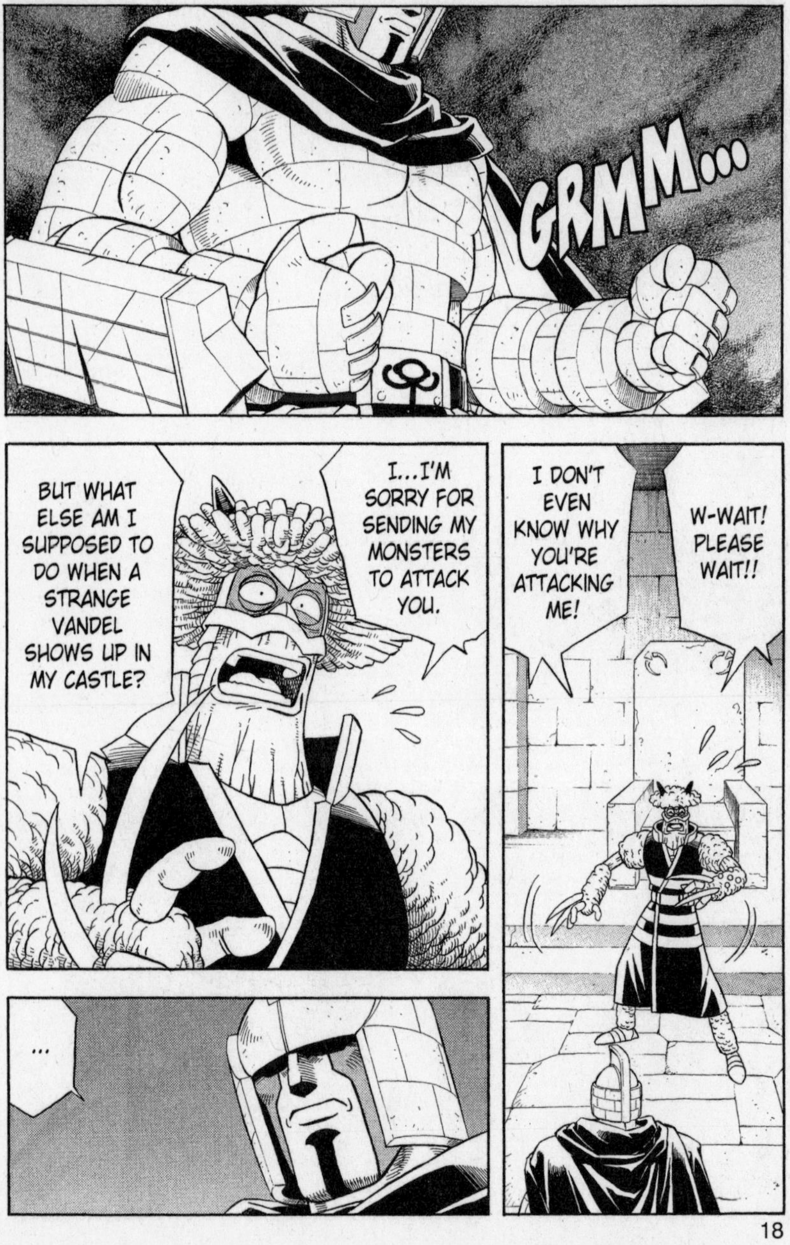
GRMM...
W-WAIT! PLEASE WAIT!!
I DON'T EVEN KNOW WHY YOU'RE ATTACKING ME!
I...I'M SORRY FOR SENDING MY MONSTERS TO ATTACK YOU.
BUT WHAT ELSE AM I SUPPOSED TO DO WHEN A STRANGE VANDEL SHOWS UP IN MY CASTLE?
...

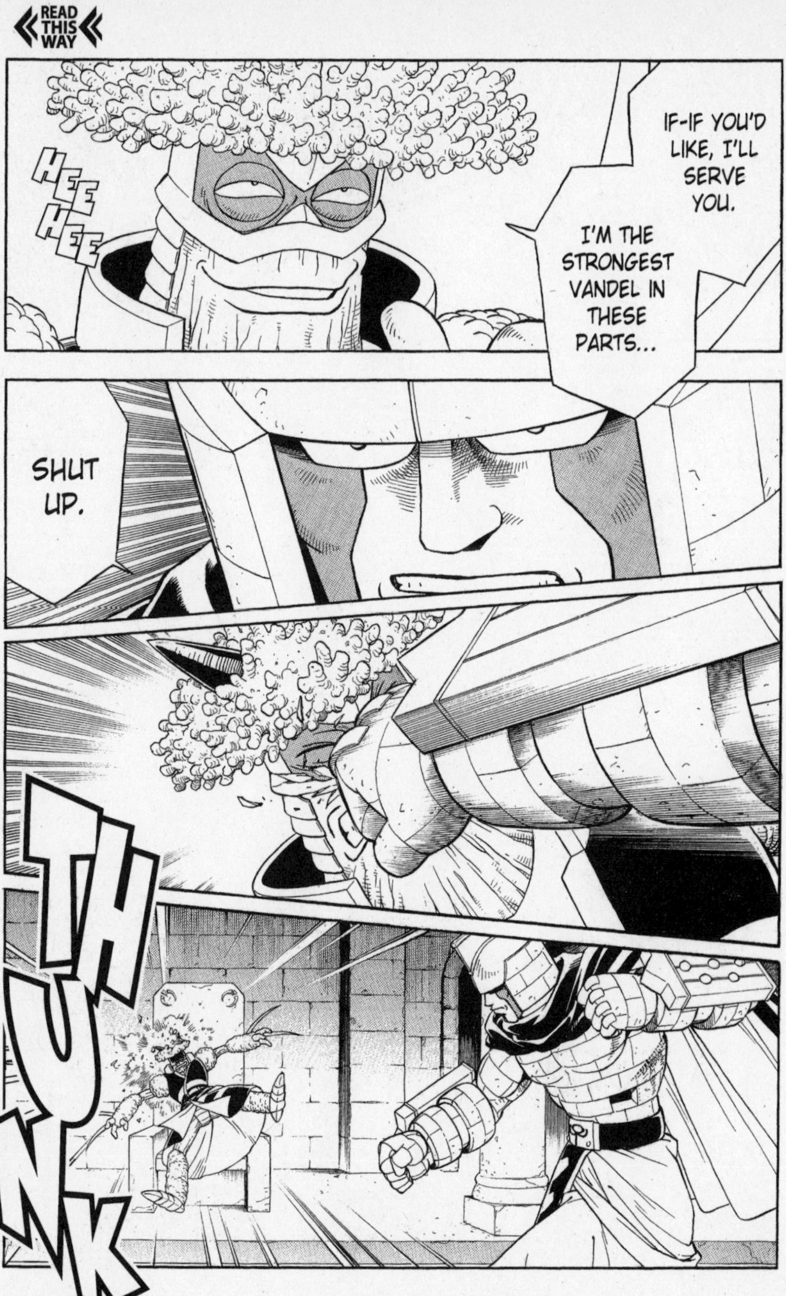

READ THIS WAY
IF-IF YOU'D LIKE, I'LL SERVE YOU.
I'M THE STRONGEST VANDEL IN THESE PARTS...
HEE HEE
SHUT UP.
THUNK

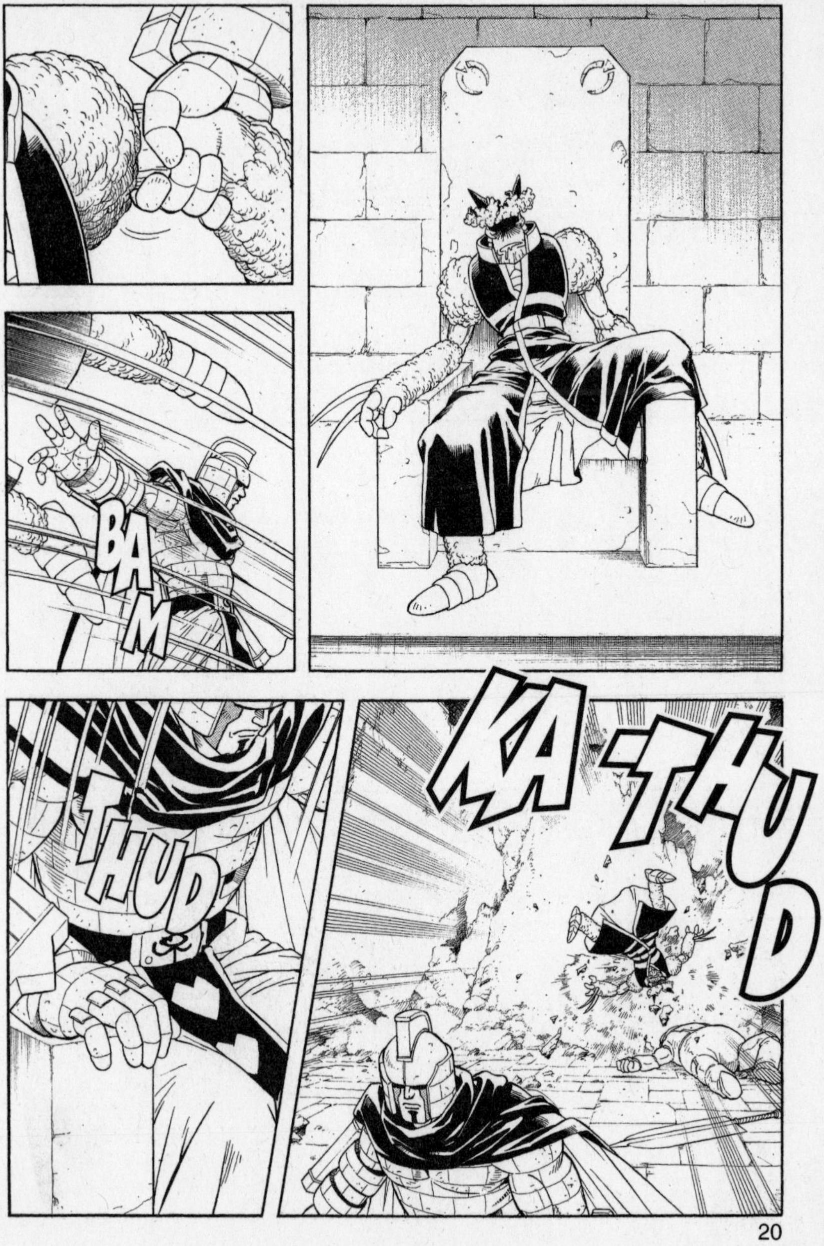
BAM
KA-THUD
THUD

READ THIS WAY

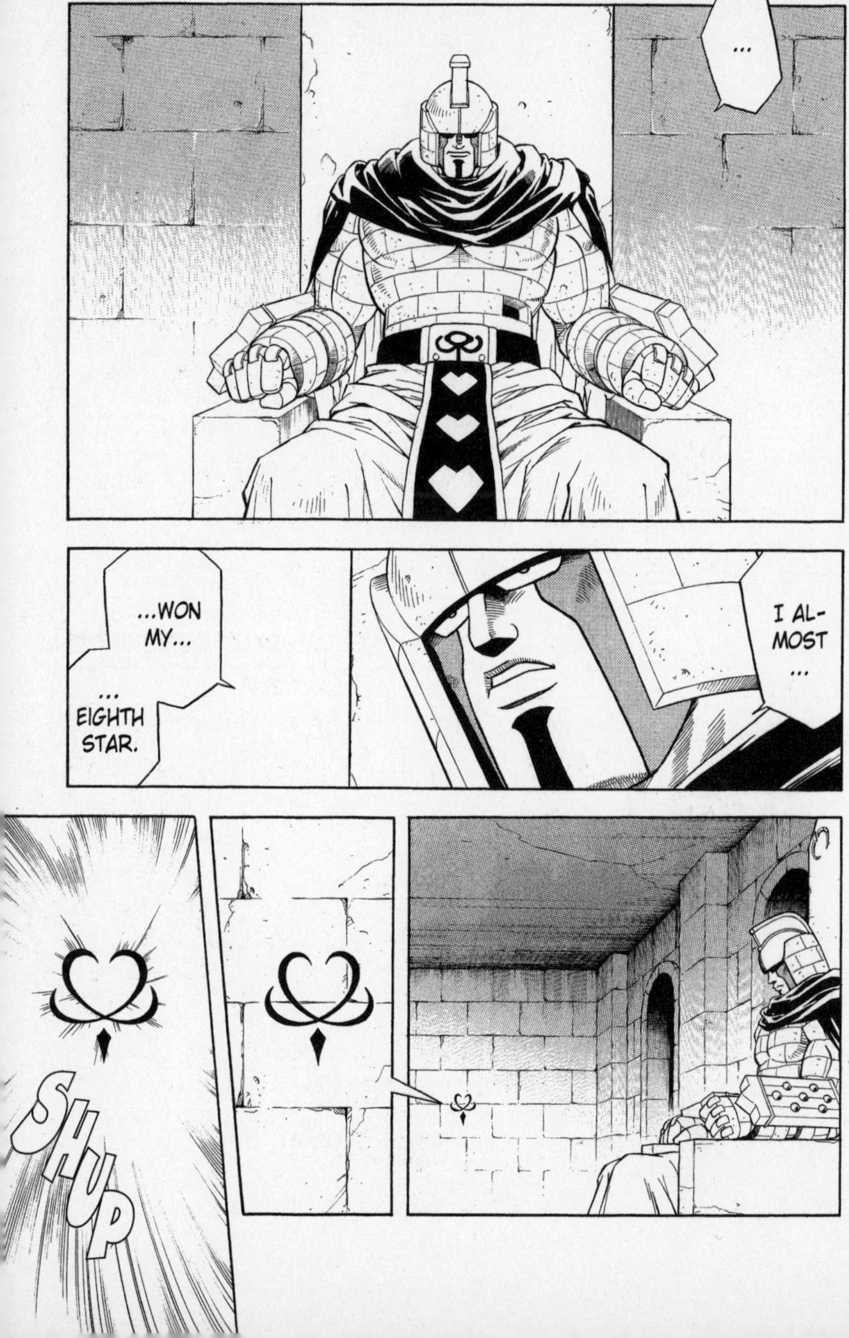
...
I AL-MOST ...
...WON MY...
... EIGHTH STAR.
SHUP

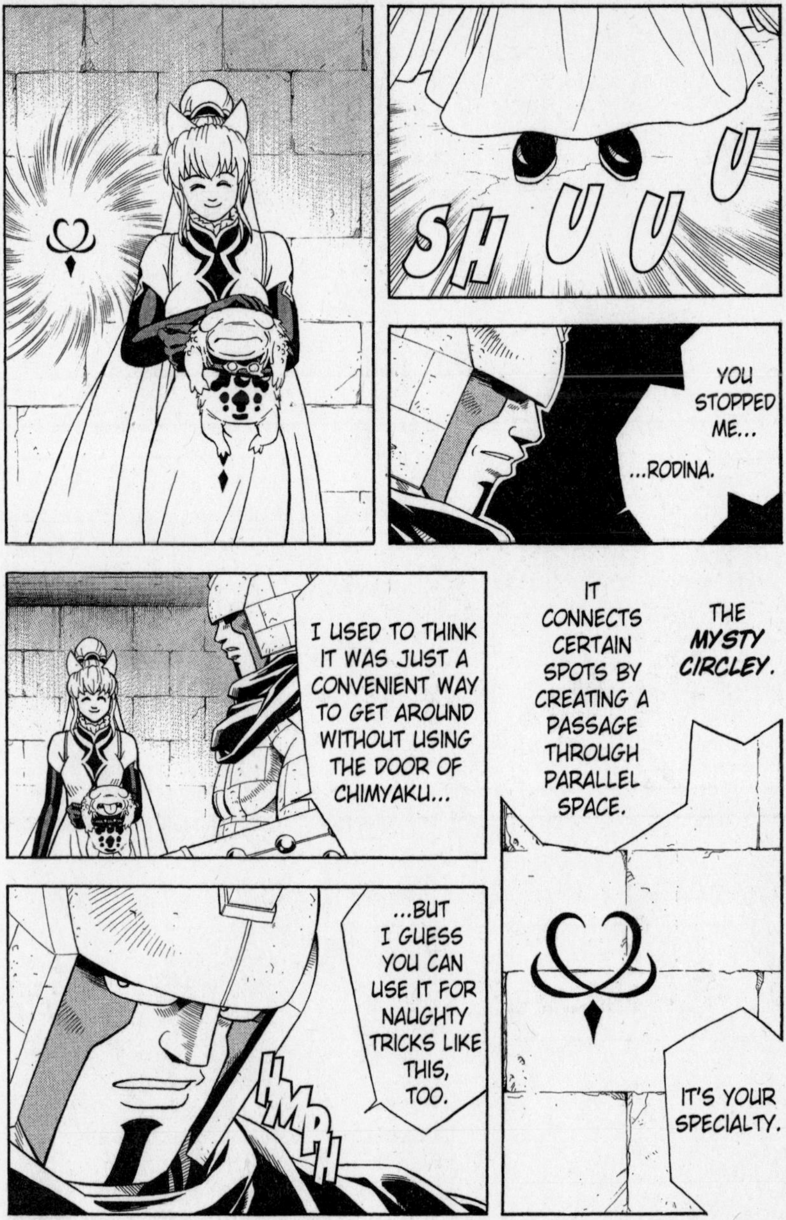
SHUUUU
YOU STOPPED ME...
...RODINA.
THE *MYSTY CIRCLEY*.
IT CONNECTS CERTAIN SPOTS BY CREATING A PASSAGE THROUGH PARALLEL SPACE.
IT'S YOUR SPECIALTY.
I USED TO THINK IT WAS JUST A CONVENIENT WAY TO GET AROUND WITHOUT USING THE DOOR OF CHIMYAKU...
...BUT I GUESS YOU CAN USE IT FOR NAUGHTY TRICKS LIKE THIS, TOO.
HMPH

READ THIS WAY

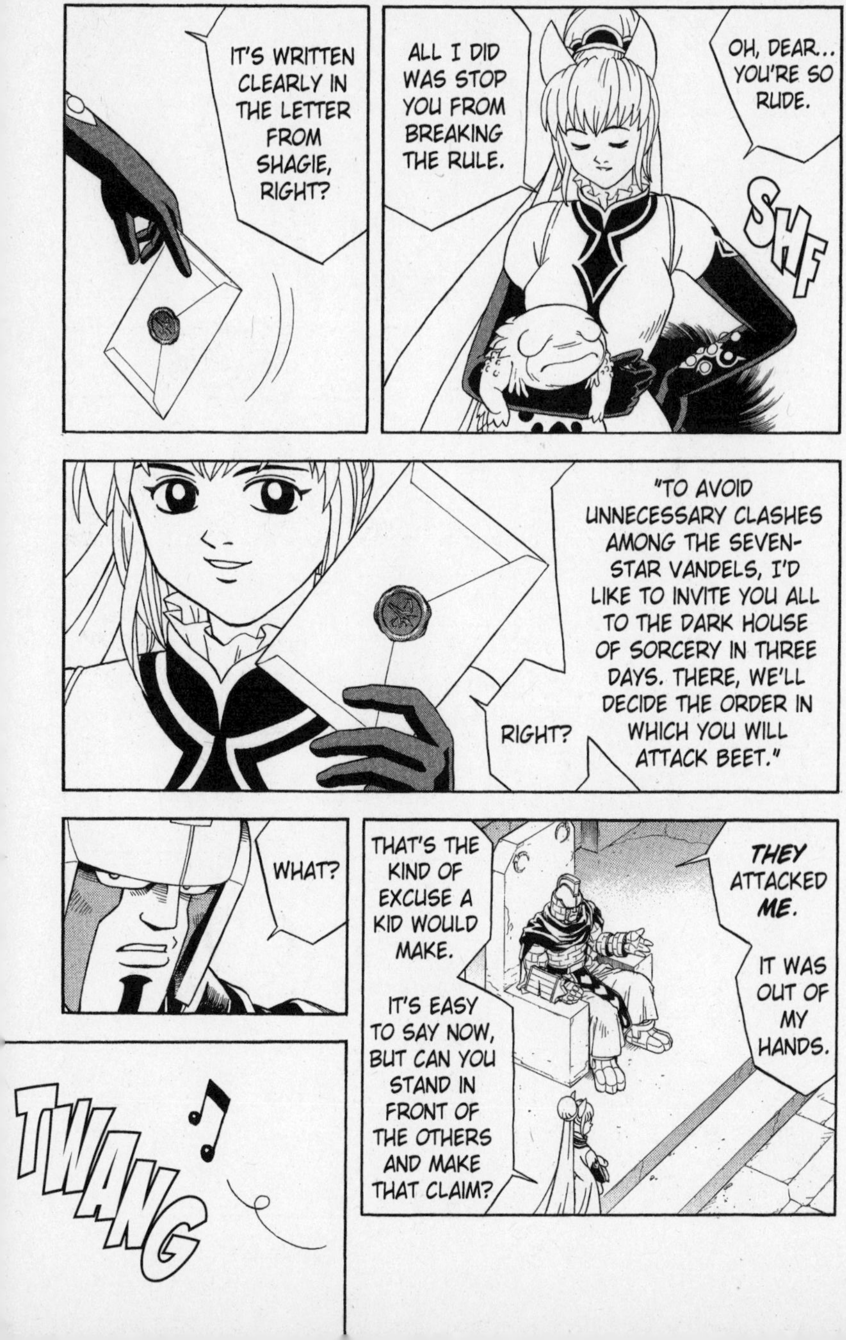

OH, DEAR... YOU'RE SO RUDE.
SHF
ALL I DID WAS STOP YOU FROM BREAKING THE RULE.
IT'S WRITTEN CLEARLY IN THE LETTER FROM SHAGIE, RIGHT?
"TO AVOID UNNECESSARY CLASHES AMONG THE SEVEN-STAR VANDELS, I'D LIKE TO INVITE YOU ALL TO THE DARK HOUSE OF SORCERY IN THREE DAYS. THERE, WE'LL DECIDE THE ORDER IN WHICH YOU WILL ATTACK BEET."
RIGHT?
THEY ATTACKED *ME*.
IT WAS OUT OF MY HANDS.
THAT'S THE KIND OF EXCUSE A KID WOULD MAKE.
IT'S EASY TO SAY NOW, BUT CAN YOU STAND IN FRONT OF THE OTHERS AND MAKE THAT CLAIM?
WHAT?
TWANG

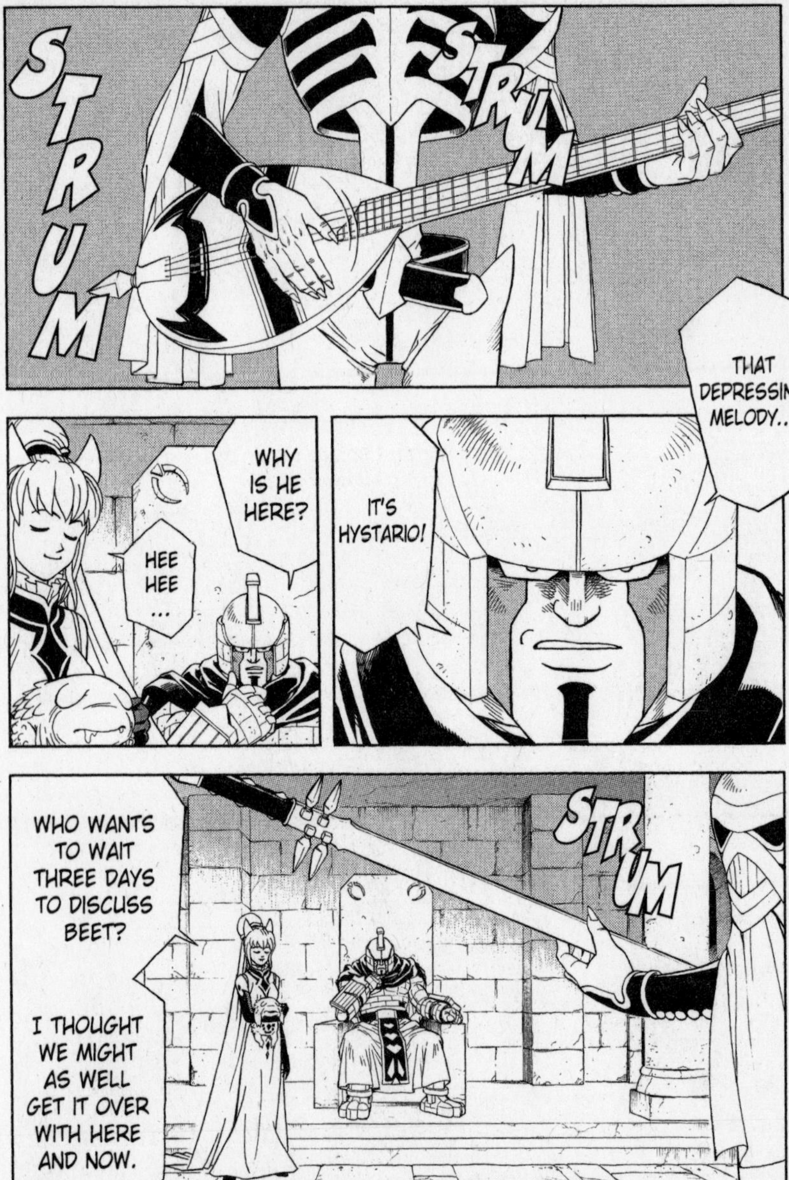
STRUM
STRUM
THAT DEPRESSING MELODY...
IT'S HYSTARIO!
WHY IS HE HERE?
HEE HEE ...
STRUM
WHO WANTS TO WAIT THREE DAYS TO DISCUSS BEET?
I THOUGHT WE MIGHT AS WELL GET IT OVER WITH HERE AND NOW.

READ THIS WAY

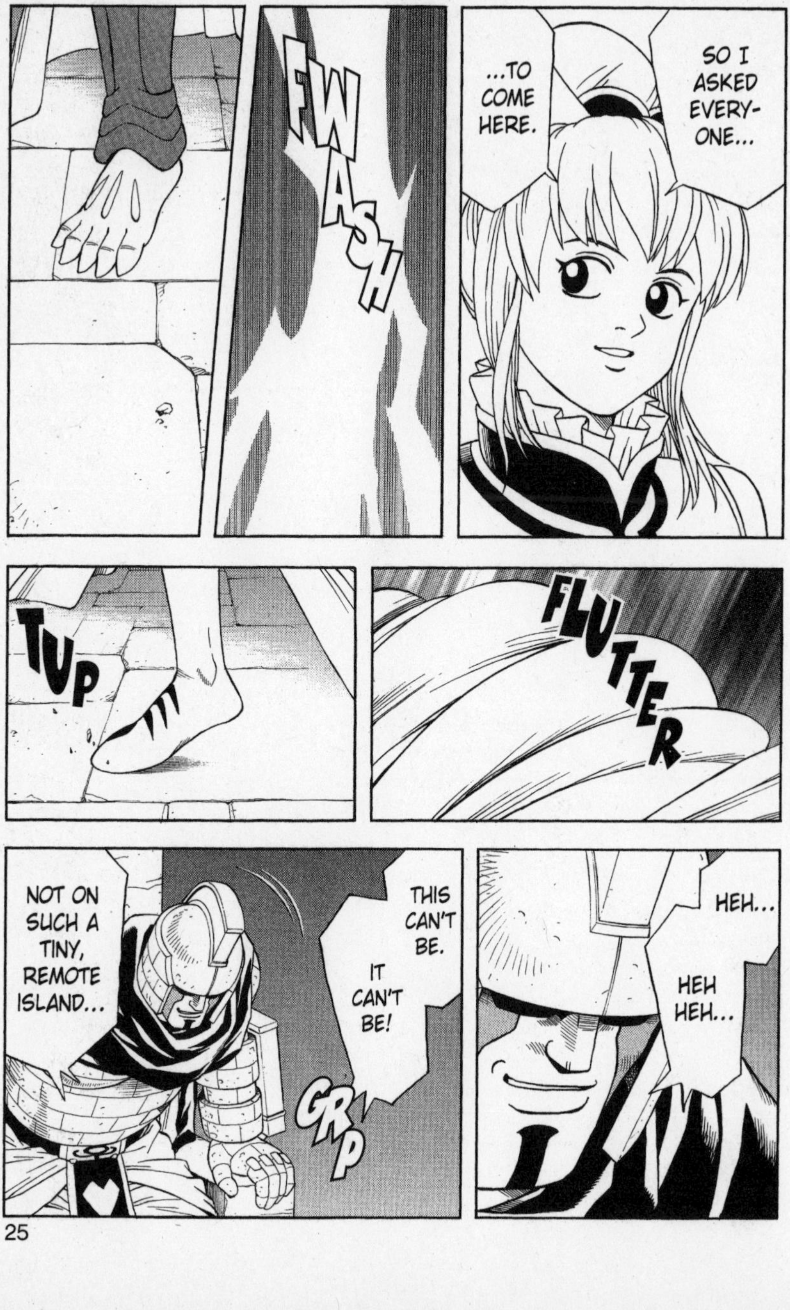
SO I ASKED EVERY-ONE...
...TO COME HERE.
FWASH
FLUTTER
TUP
HEH...
HEH HEH...
THIS CAN'T BE.
NOT ON SUCH A TINY, REMOTE ISLAND...
IT CAN'T BE!
GRP

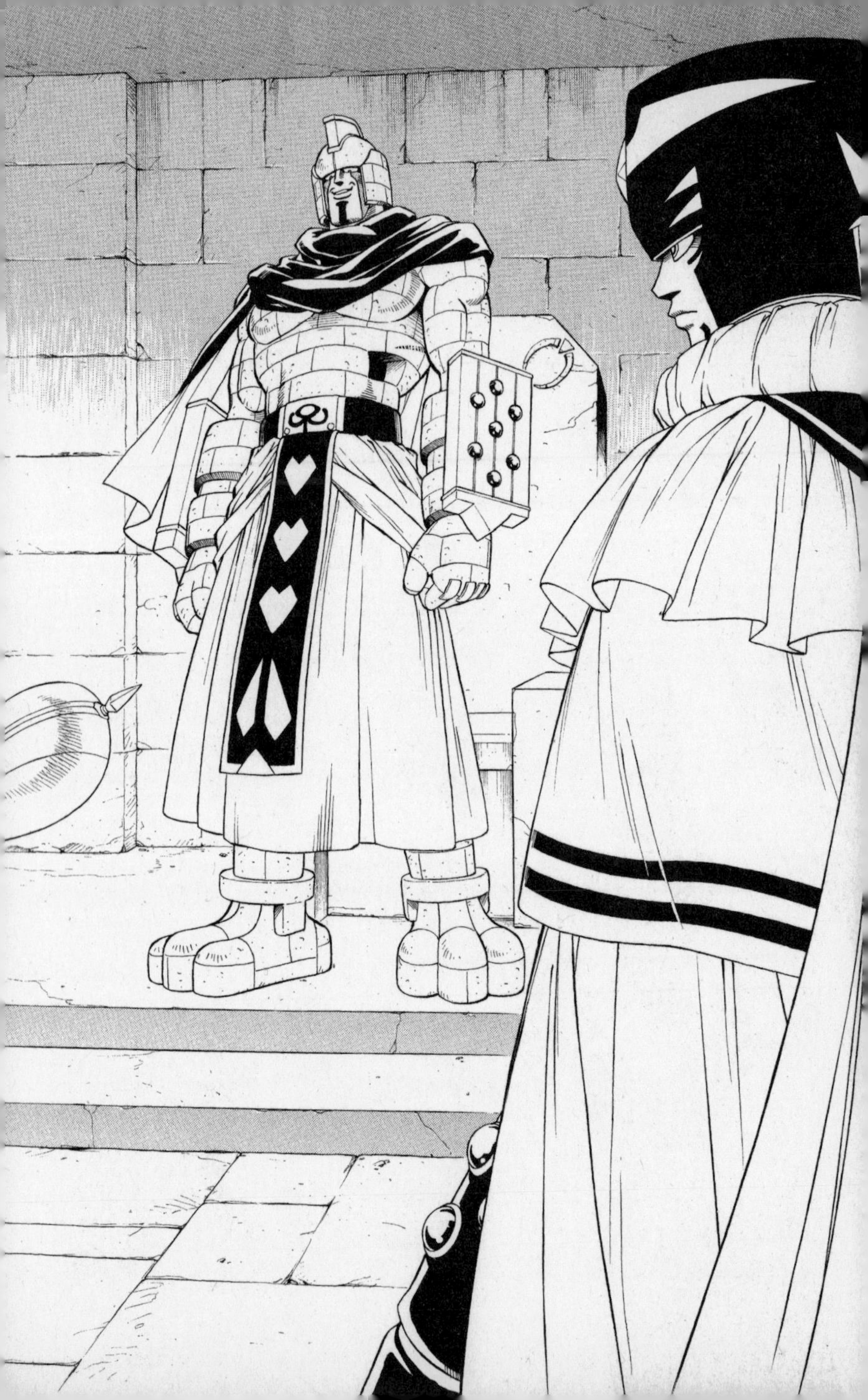

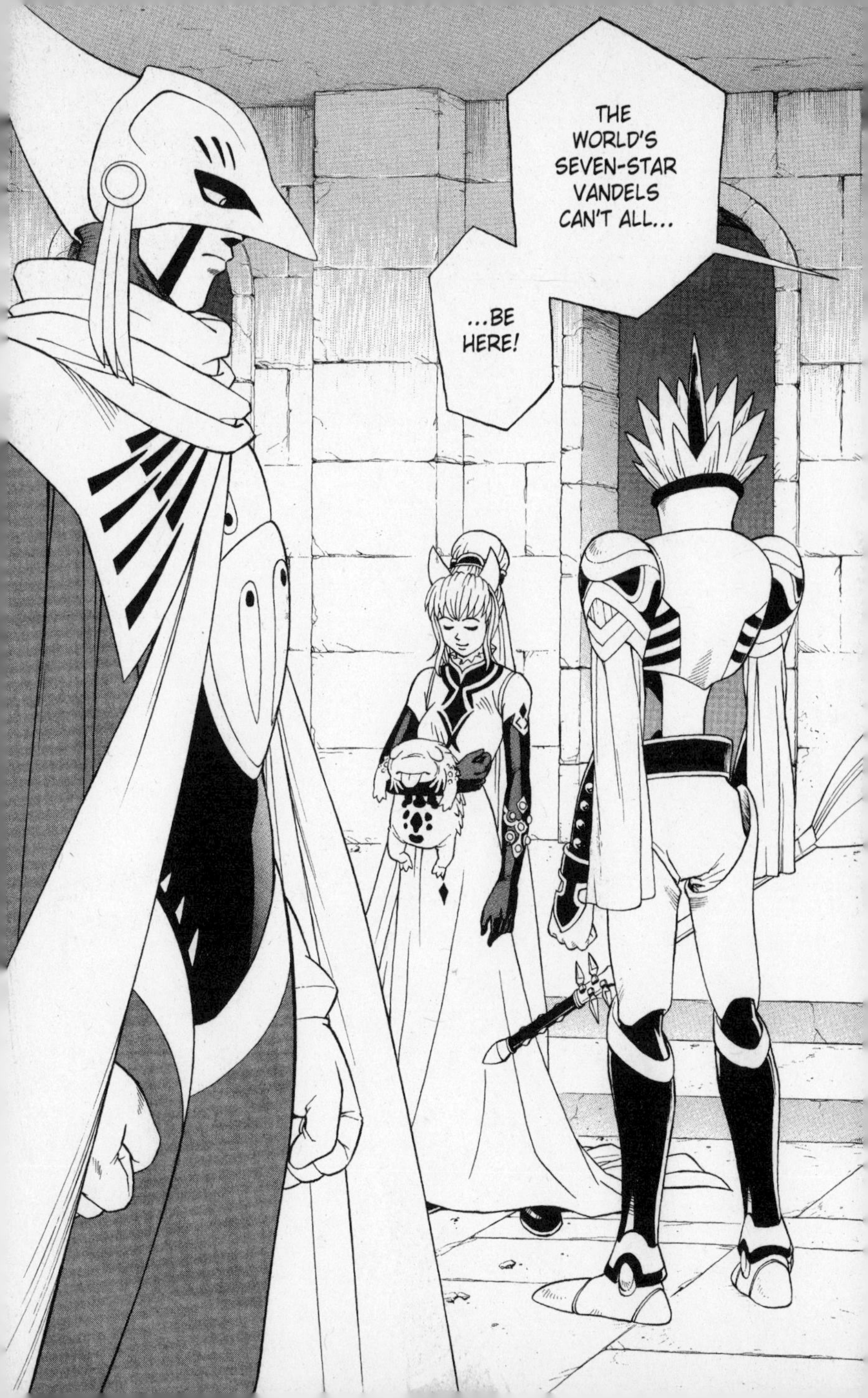
THE WORLD'S SEVEN-STAR VANDELS CAN'T ALL...
...BE HERE!

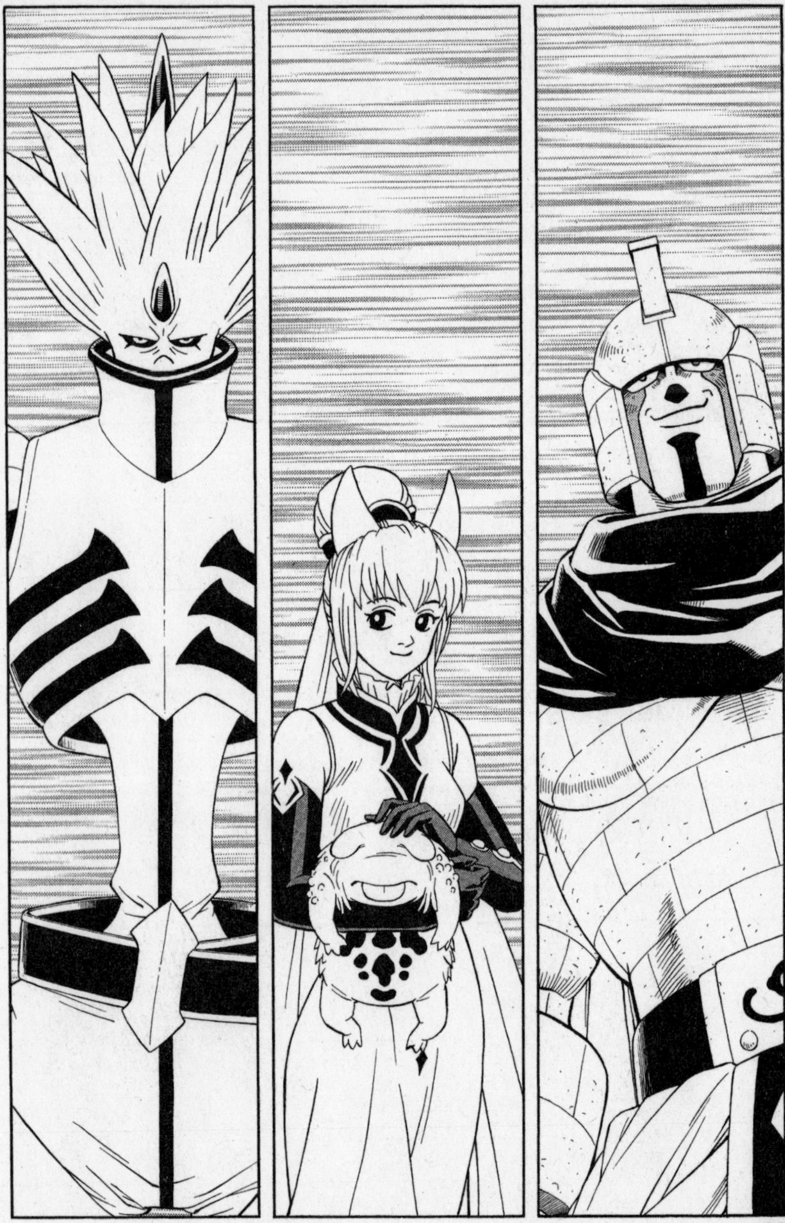

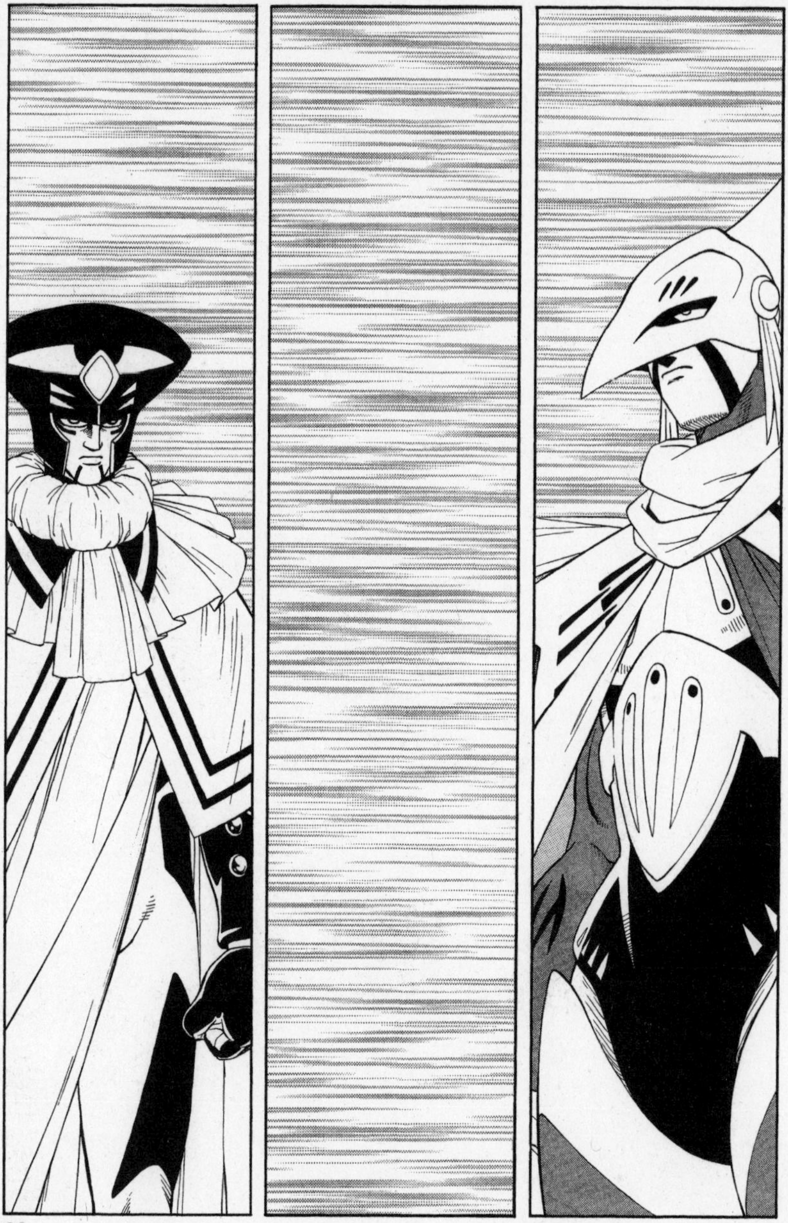

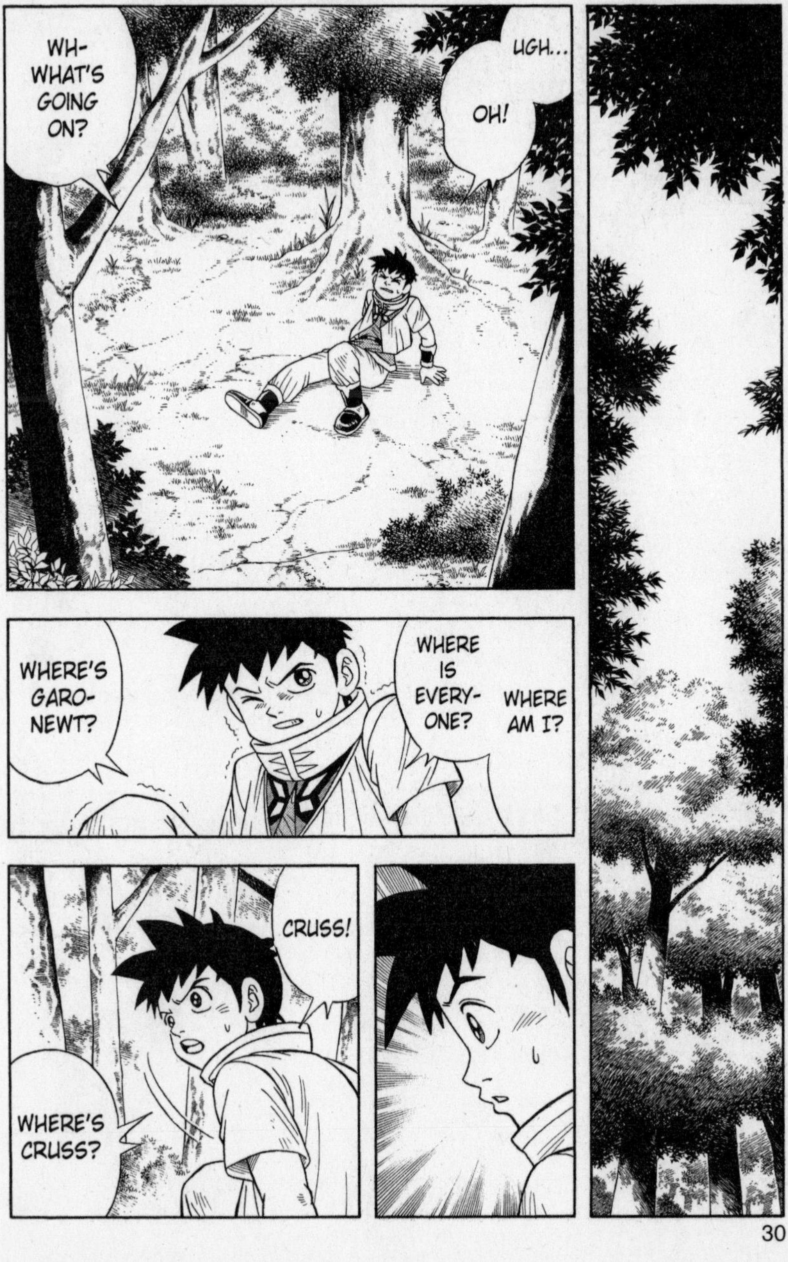
UGH...
OH!
WH- WHAT'S GOING ON?
WHERE AM I?
WHERE IS EVERY-ONE?
WHERE'S GARO-NEWT?
CRUSS!
WHERE'S CRUSS?

READ THIS WAY

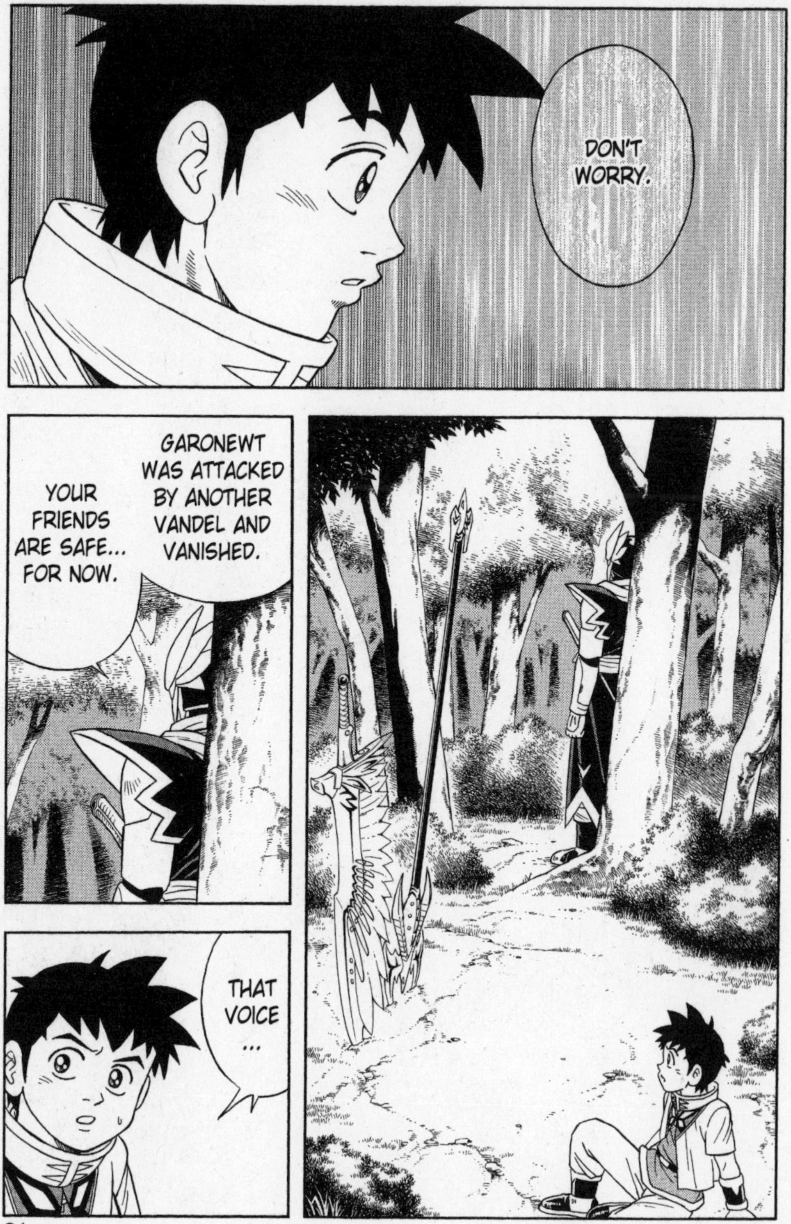
DON'T WORRY.
GARONEWT WAS ATTACKED BY ANOTHER VANDEL AND VANISHED.
YOUR FRIENDS ARE SAFE... FOR NOW.
THAT VOICE ...

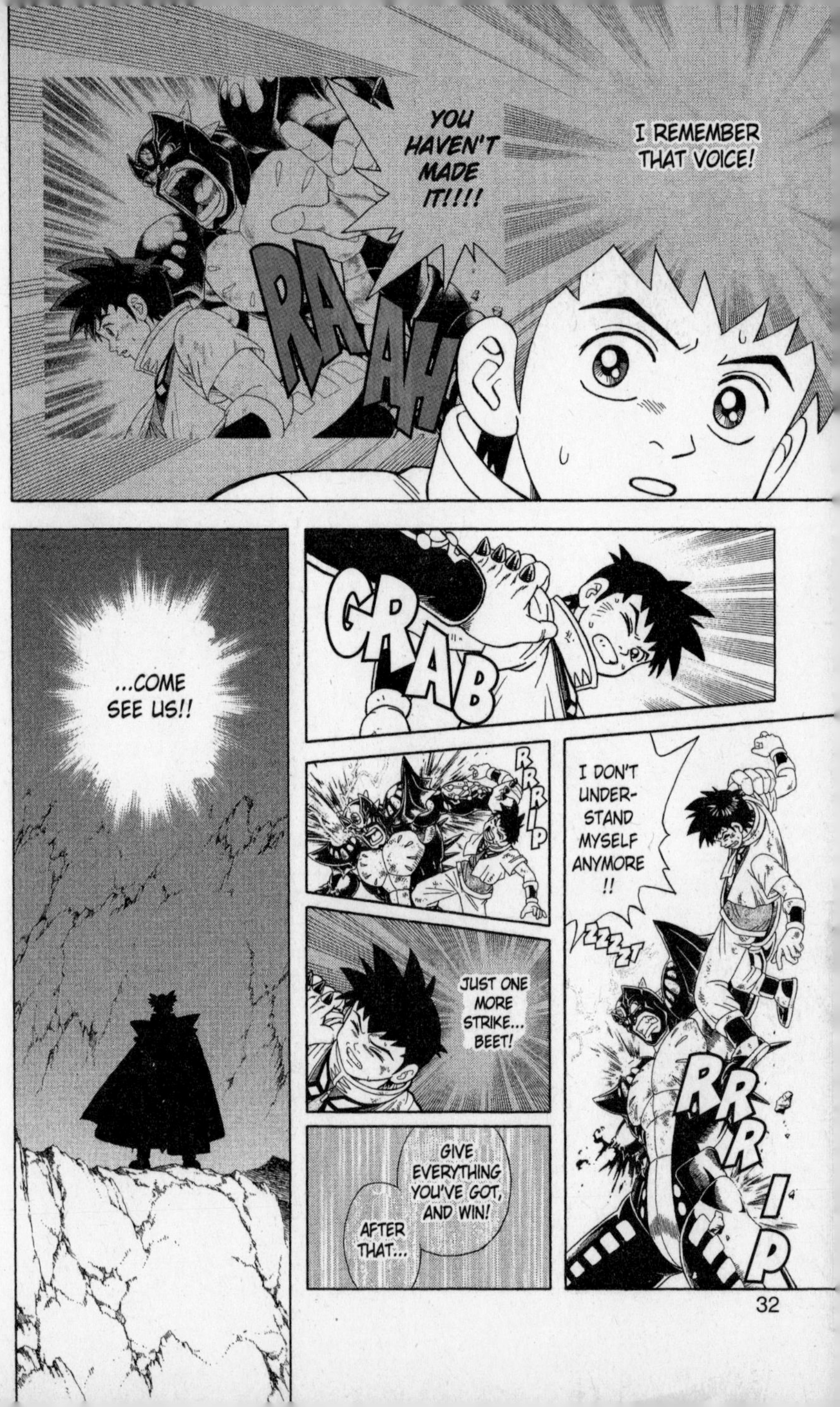
I REMEMBER THAT VOICE!
YOU HAVEN'T MADE IT!!!!
RAAAH
GRAB
I DON'T UNDERSTAND MYSELF ANYMORE!!
ZZZZT
RRRIP
RRRIP
JUST ONE MORE STRIKE... BEET!
GIVE EVERYTHING YOU'VE GOT, AND WIN!
AFTER THAT...
...COME SEE US!!

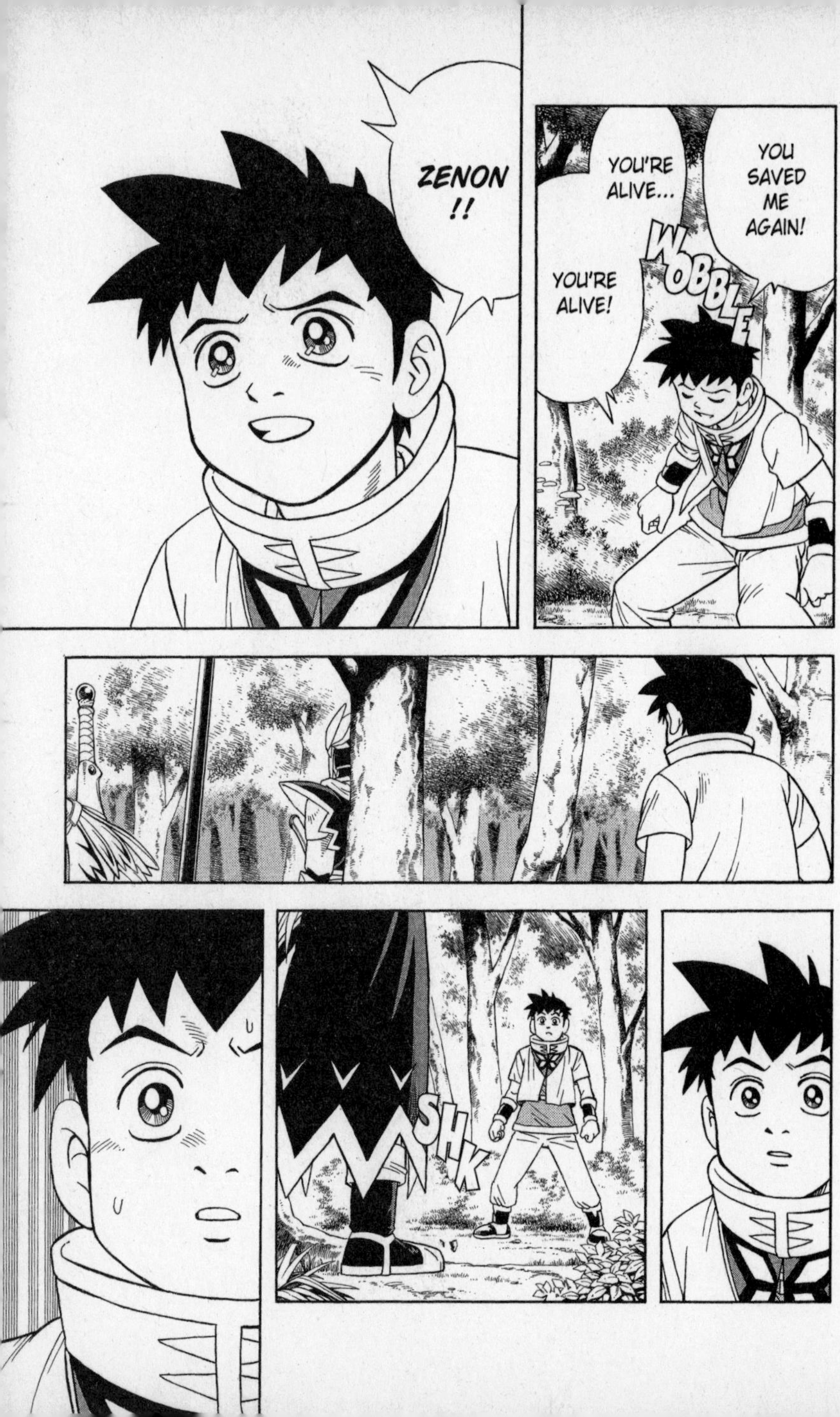
YOU SAVED ME AGAIN!
YOU'RE ALIVE...
WOBBLE
YOU'RE ALIVE!
ZENON!!
SHK

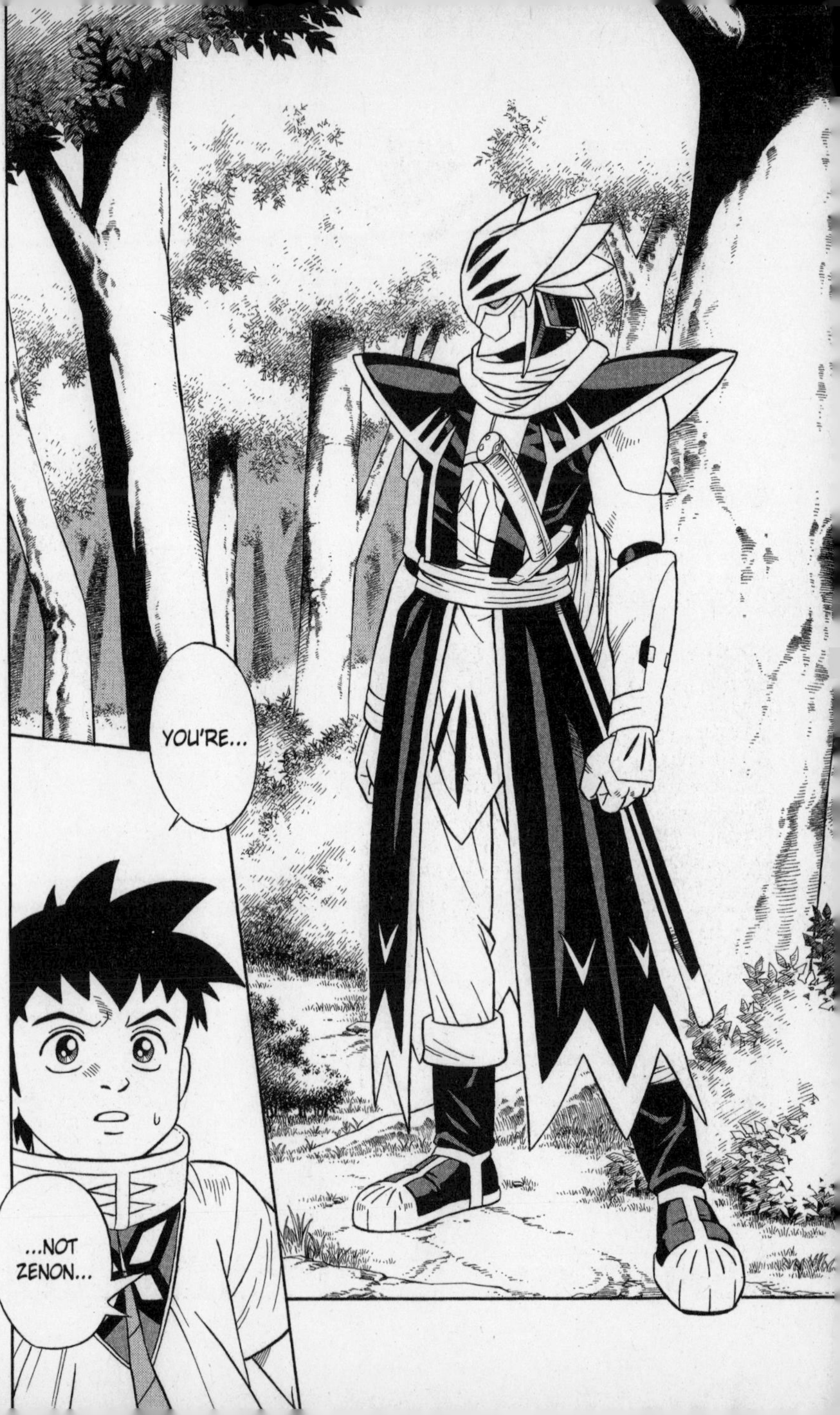
YOU'RE...
...NOT ZENON...

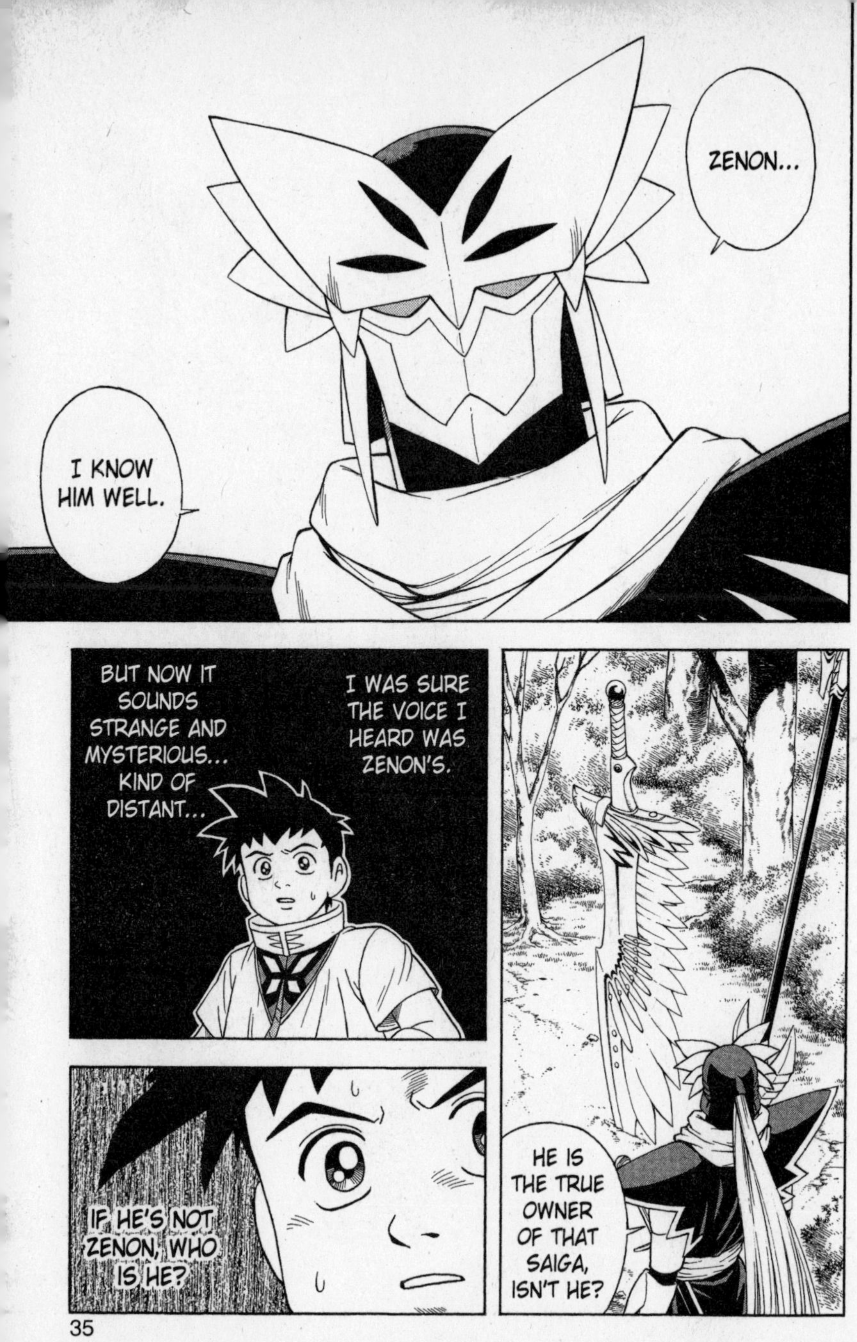
ZENON...
I KNOW HIM WELL.
HE IS THE TRUE OWNER OF THAT SAIGA, ISN'T HE?
I WAS SURE THE VOICE I HEARD WAS ZENON'S.
BUT NOW IT SOUNDS STRANGE AND MYSTERIOUS... KIND OF DISTANT...
IF HE'S NOT ZENON, WHO IS HE?

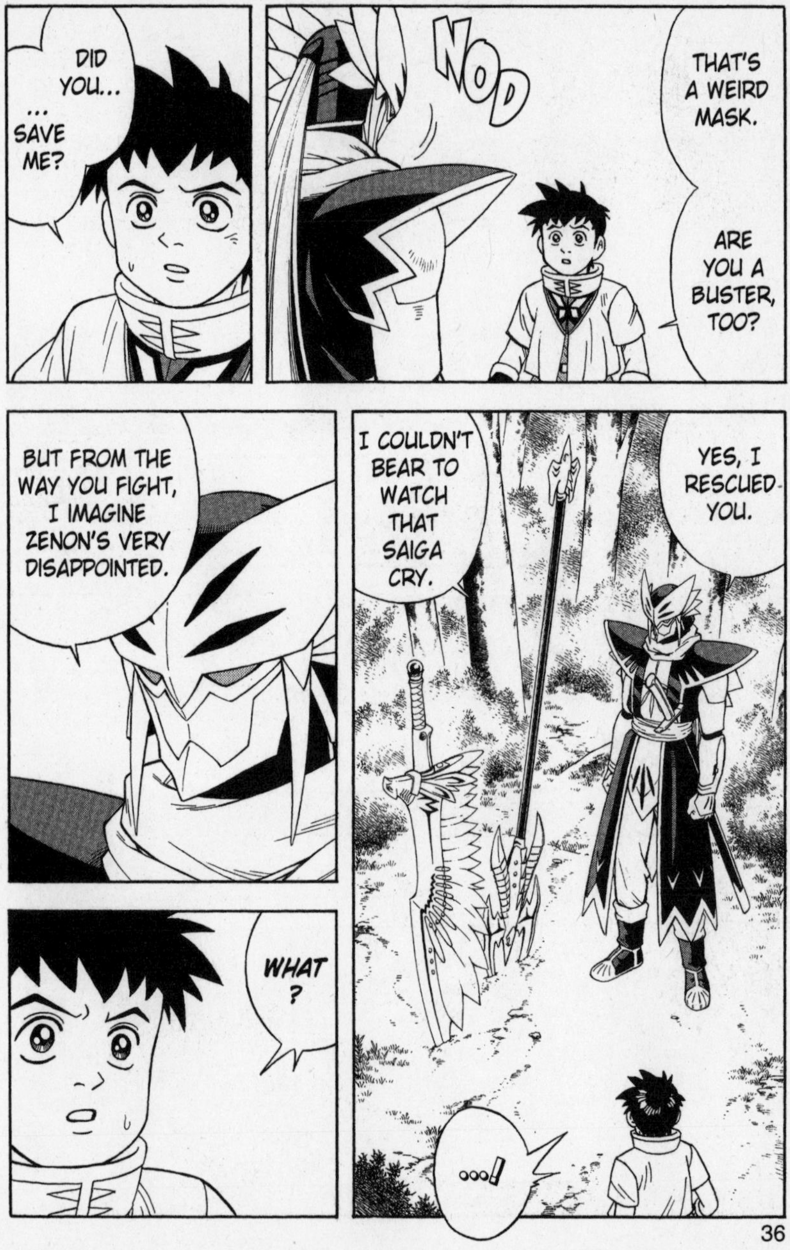
THAT'S A WEIRD MASK.
ARE YOU A BUSTER, TOO?
NOD
DID YOU...
... SAVE ME?
YES, I RESCUED YOU.
I COULDN'T BEAR TO WATCH THAT SAIGA CRY.
...!
BUT FROM THE WAY YOU FIGHT, I IMAGINE ZENON'S VERY DISAPPOINTED.
WHAT?

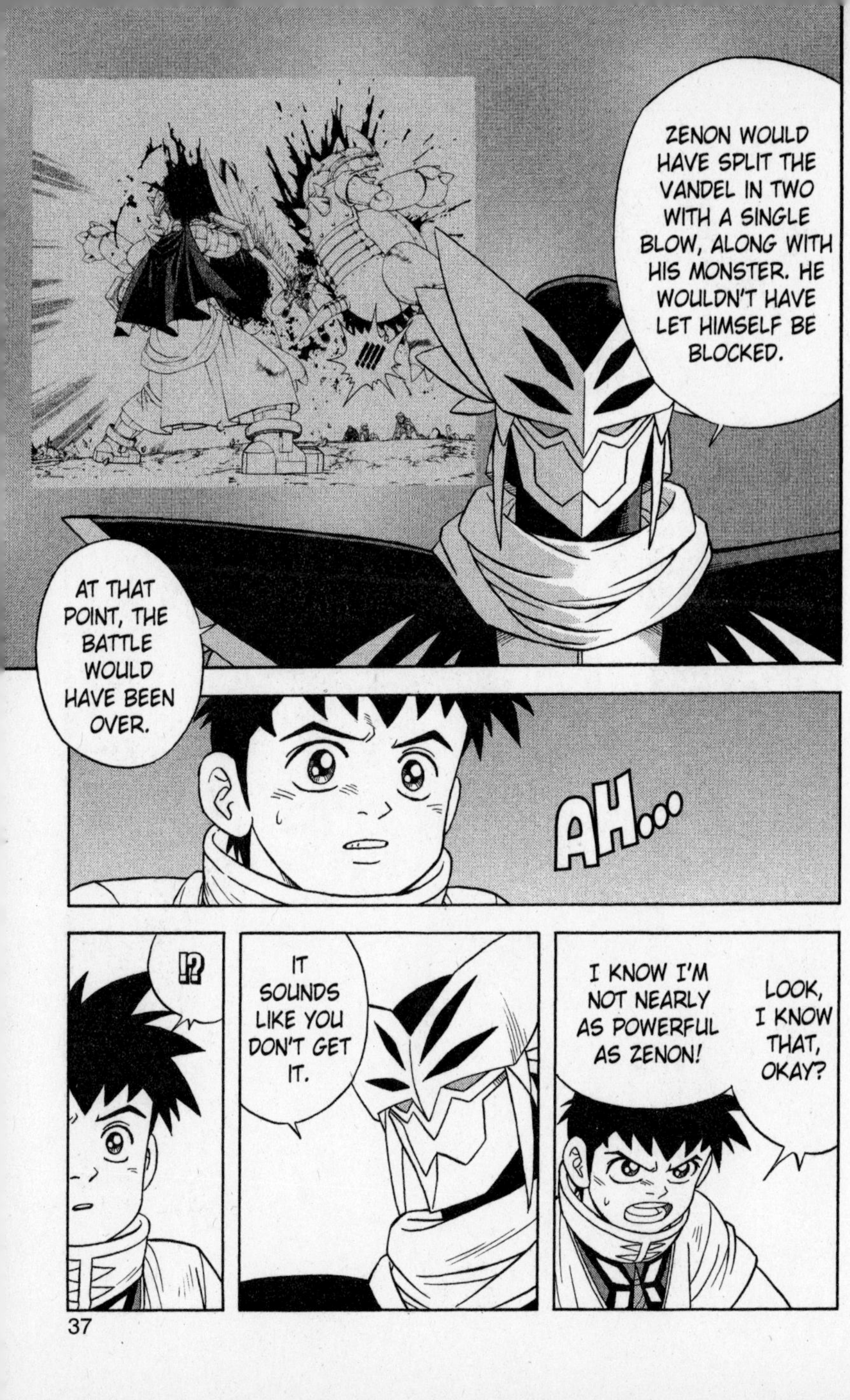
ZENON WOULD HAVE SPLIT THE VANDEL IN TWO WITH A SINGLE BLOW, ALONG WITH HIS MONSTER. HE WOULDN'T HAVE LET HIMSELF BE BLOCKED.
AT THAT POINT, THE BATTLE WOULD HAVE BEEN OVER.
AH...
LOOK, I KNOW THAT, OKAY?
I KNOW I'M NOT NEARLY AS POWERFUL AS ZENON!
IT SOUNDS LIKE YOU DON'T GET IT.
!?

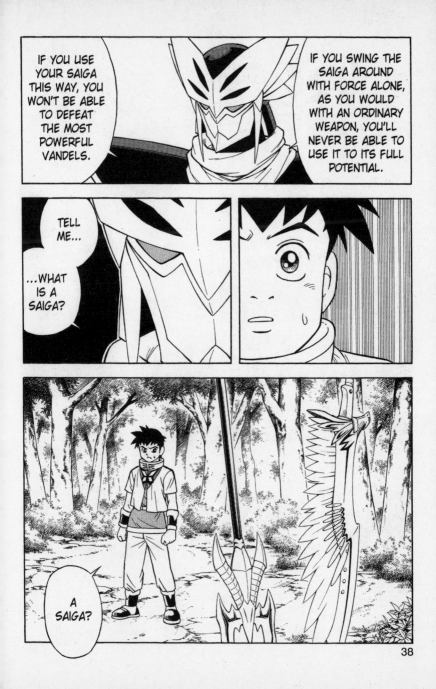

IF YOU SWING THE SAIGA AROUND WITH FORCE ALONE, AS YOU WOULD WITH AN ORDINARY WEAPON, YOU'LL NEVER BE ABLE TO USE IT TO ITS FULL POTENTIAL.
IF YOU USE YOUR SAIGA THIS WAY, YOU WON'T BE ABLE TO DEFEAT THE MOST POWERFUL VANDELS.
TELL ME...
...WHAT IS A SAIGA?
A SAIGA?

READ THIS WAY

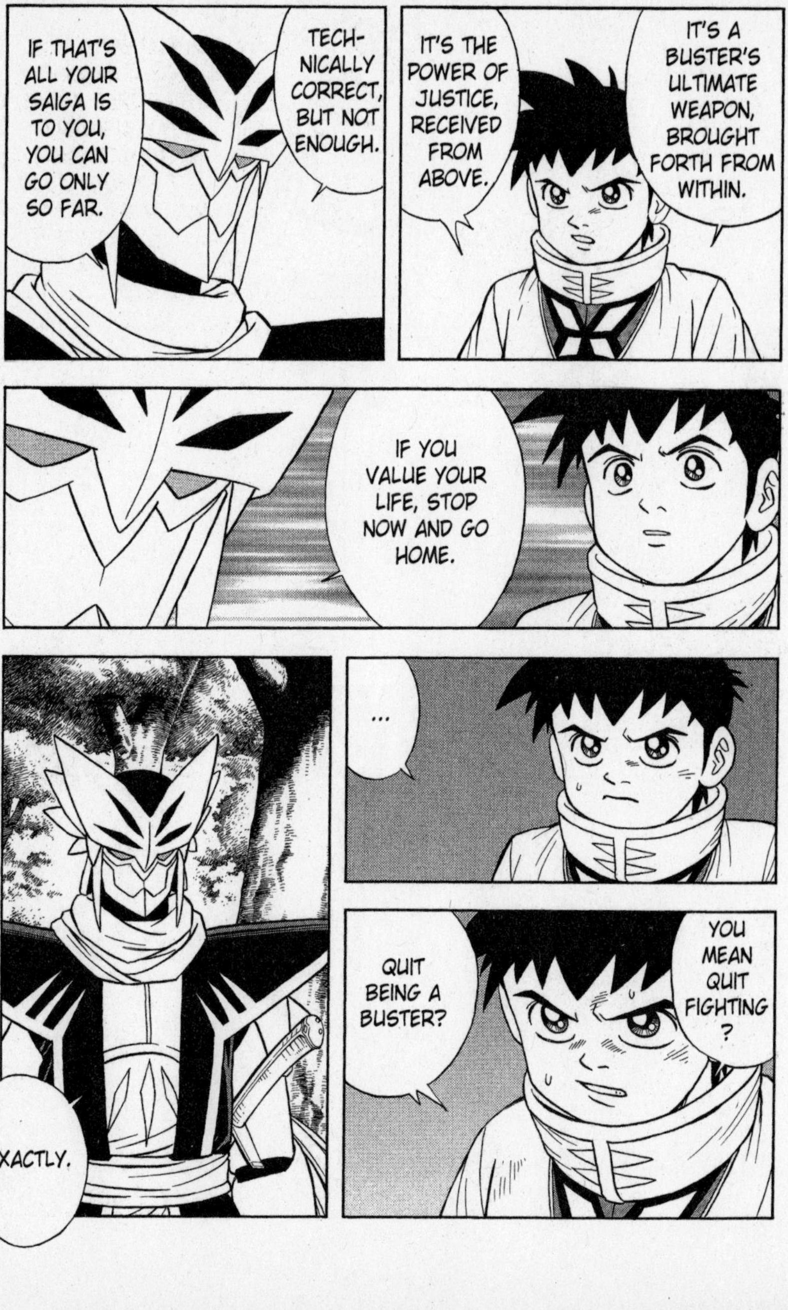
IT'S A BUSTER'S ULTIMATE WEAPON, BROUGHT FORTH FROM WITHIN.
IT'S THE POWER OF JUSTICE, RECEIVED FROM ABOVE.
TECH-NICALLY CORRECT, BUT NOT ENOUGH.
IF THAT'S ALL YOUR SAIGA IS TO YOU, YOU CAN GO ONLY SO FAR.
IF YOU VALUE YOUR LIFE, STOP NOW AND GO HOME.
...
YOU MEAN QUIT FIGHTING?
QUIT BEING A BUSTER?
EXACTLY.

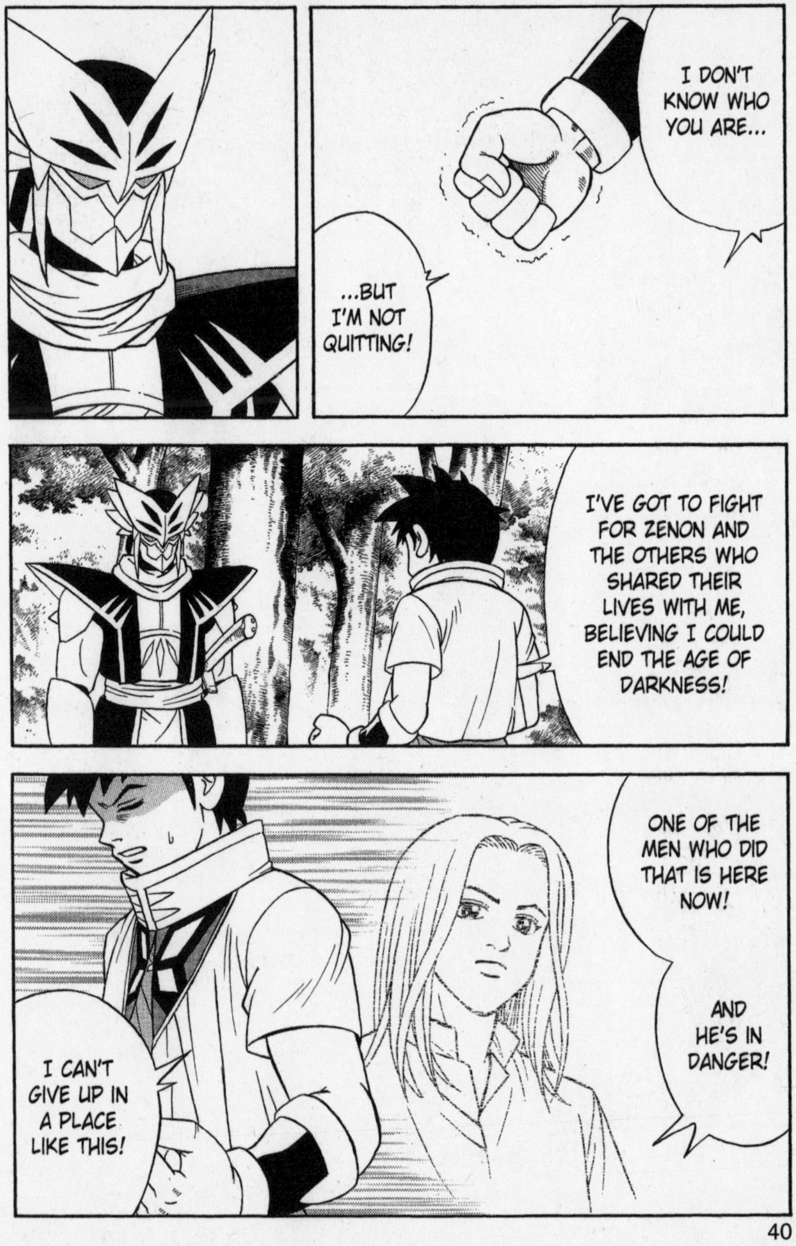
I DON'T KNOW WHO YOU ARE...
...BUT I'M NOT QUITTING!
I'VE GOT TO FIGHT FOR ZENON AND THE OTHERS WHO SHARED THEIR LIVES WITH ME, BELIEVING I COULD END THE AGE OF DARKNESS!
ONE OF THE MEN WHO DID THAT IS HERE NOW!
AND HE'S IN DANGER!
I CAN'T GIVE UP IN A PLACE LIKE THIS!

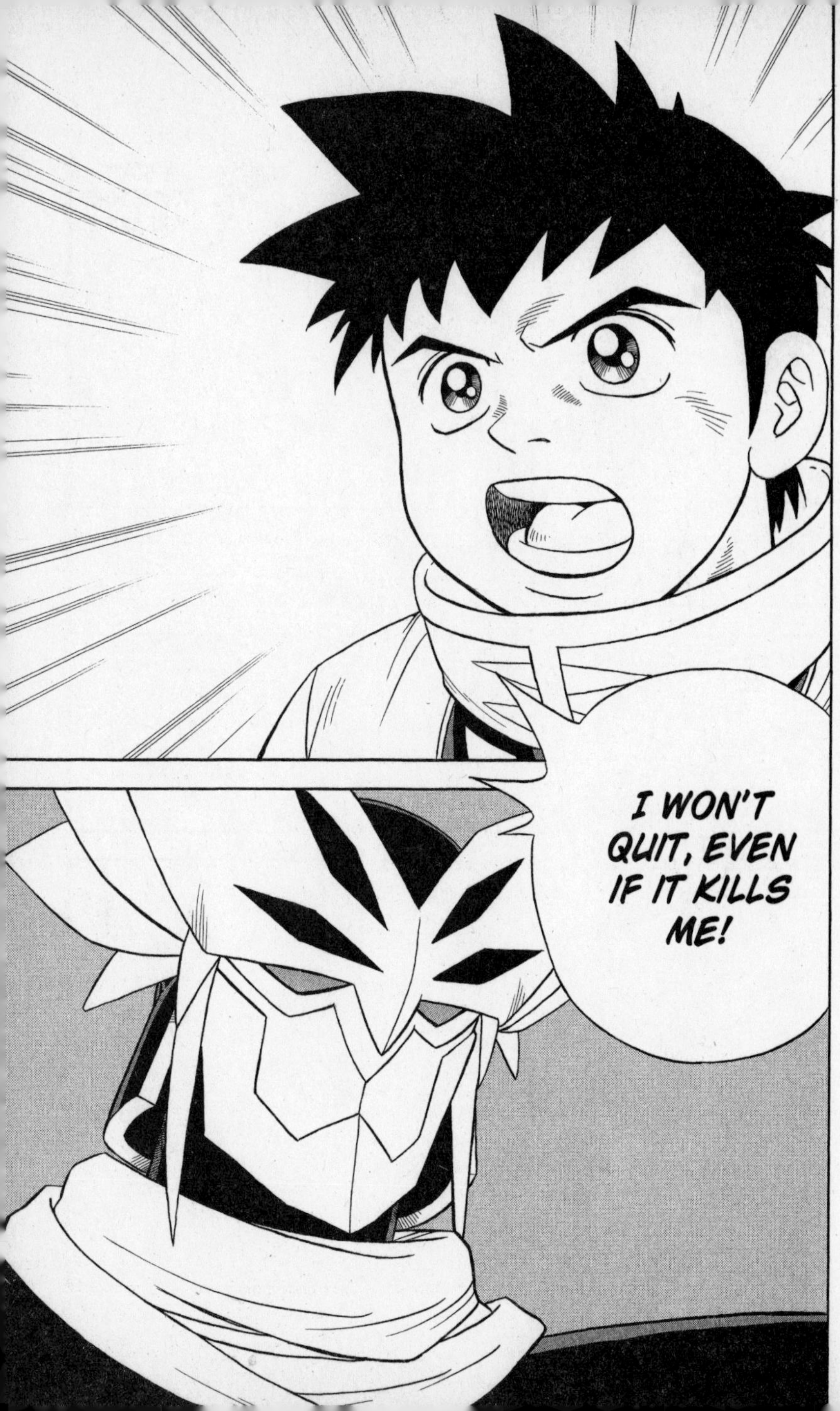
I WON'T QUIT, EVEN IF IT KILLS ME!

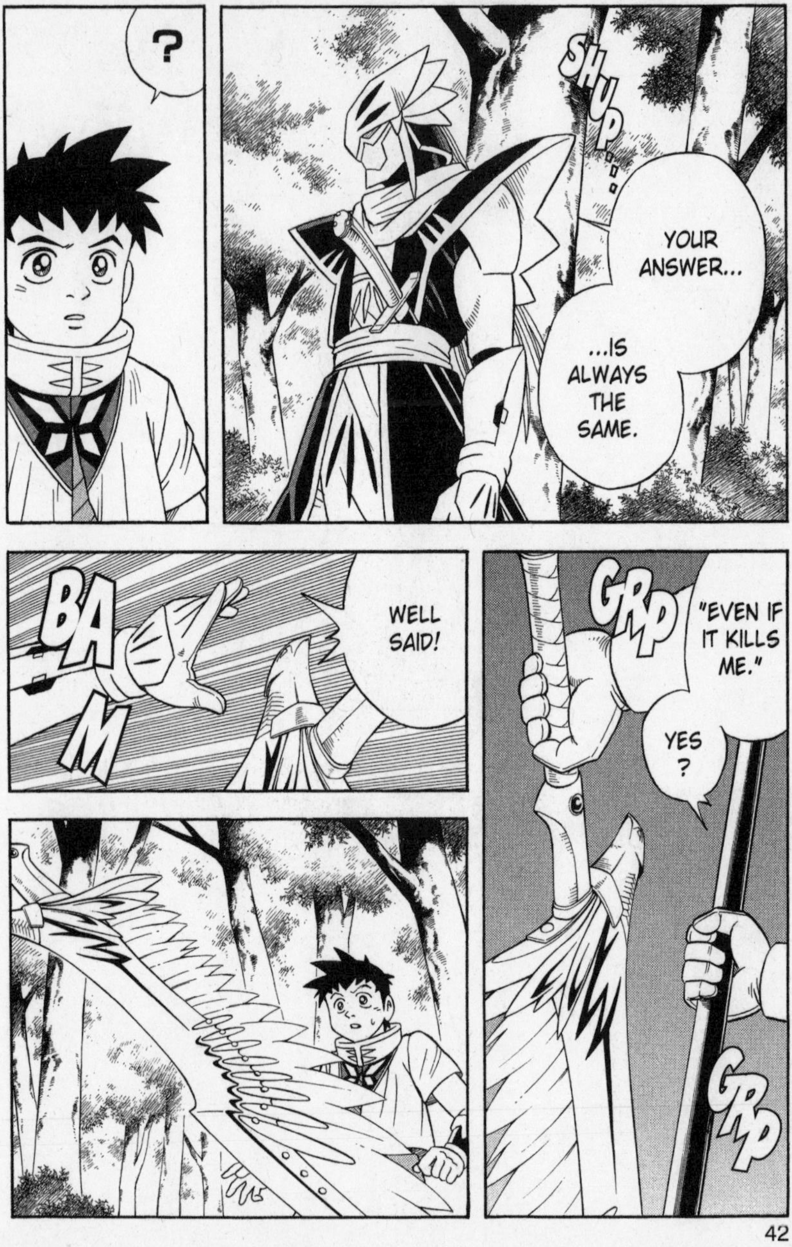
SHUP...
YOUR ANSWER...
...IS ALWAYS THE SAME.
?
GRP
"EVEN IF IT KILLS ME."
YES?
GRP
BAM
WELL SAID!

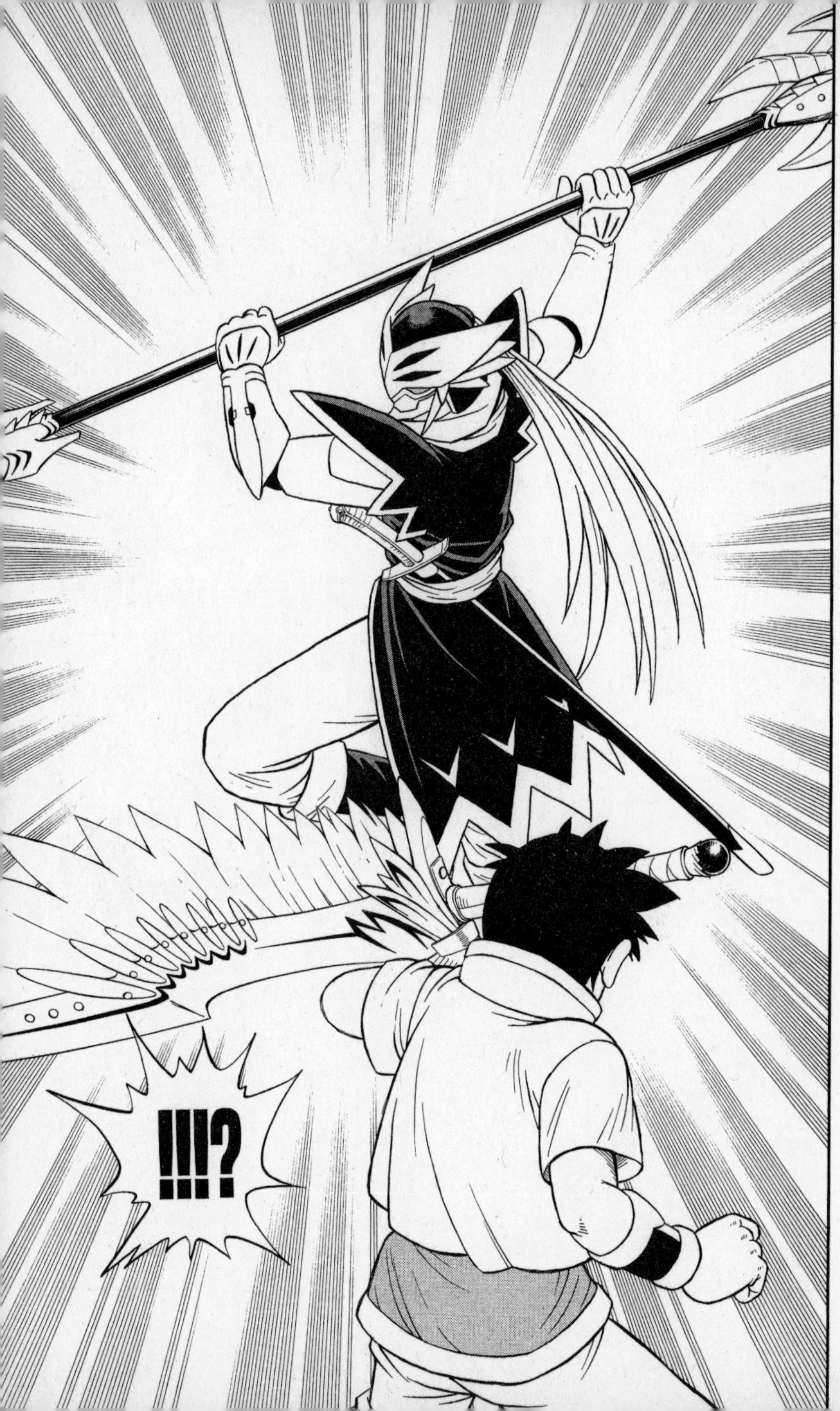
!!!?

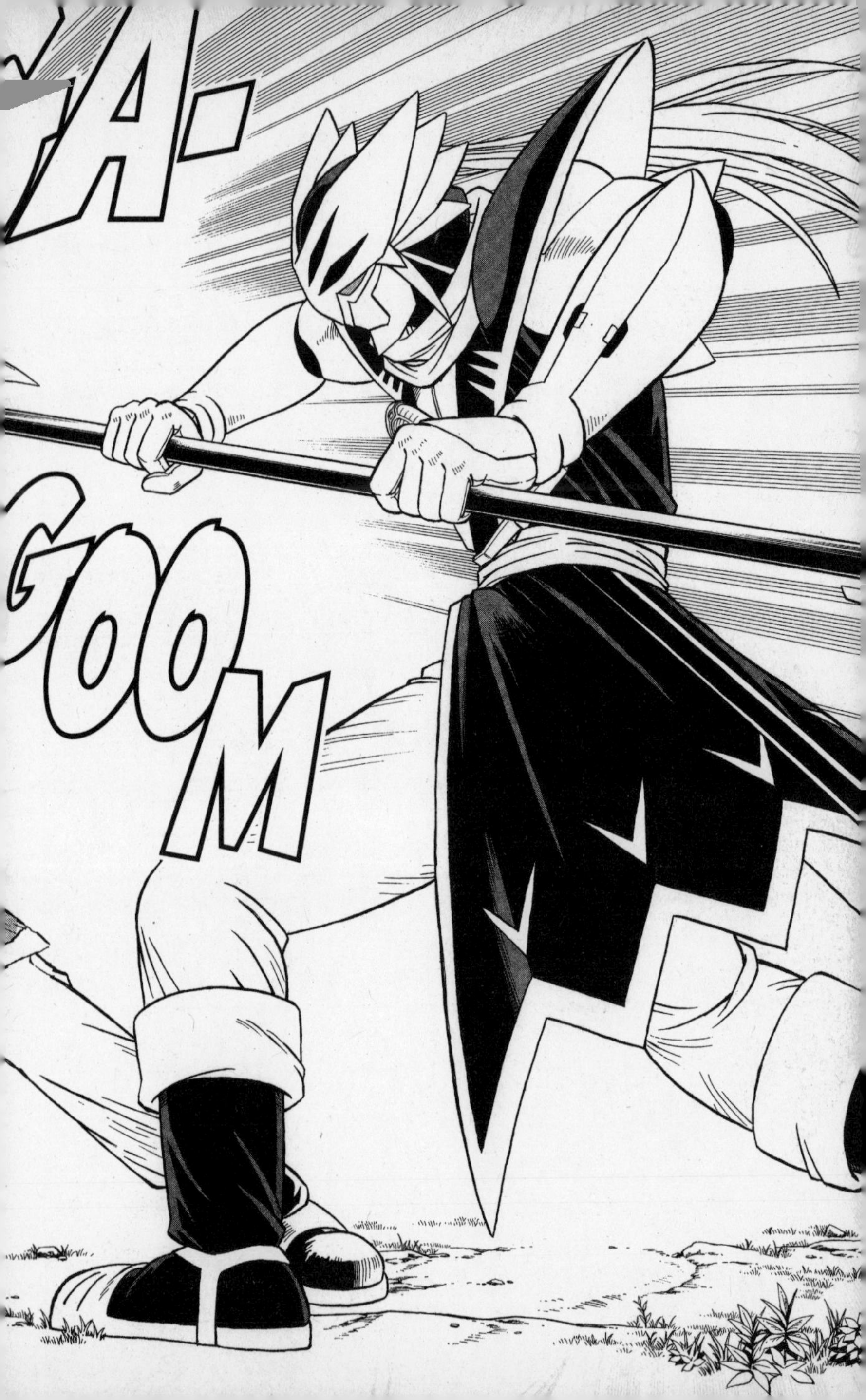
A-
GOOM

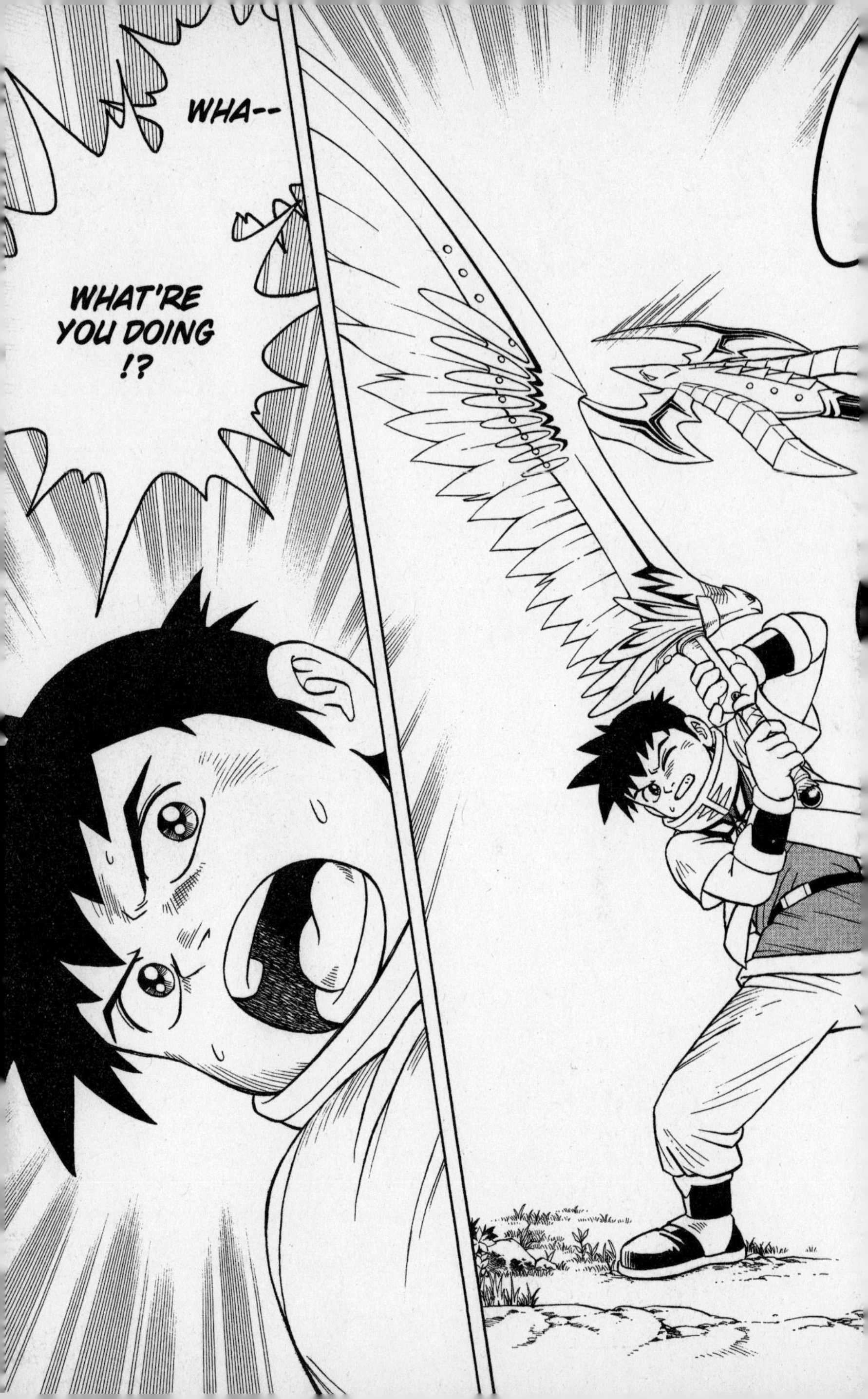
WHA--
WHAT'RE YOU DOING !?

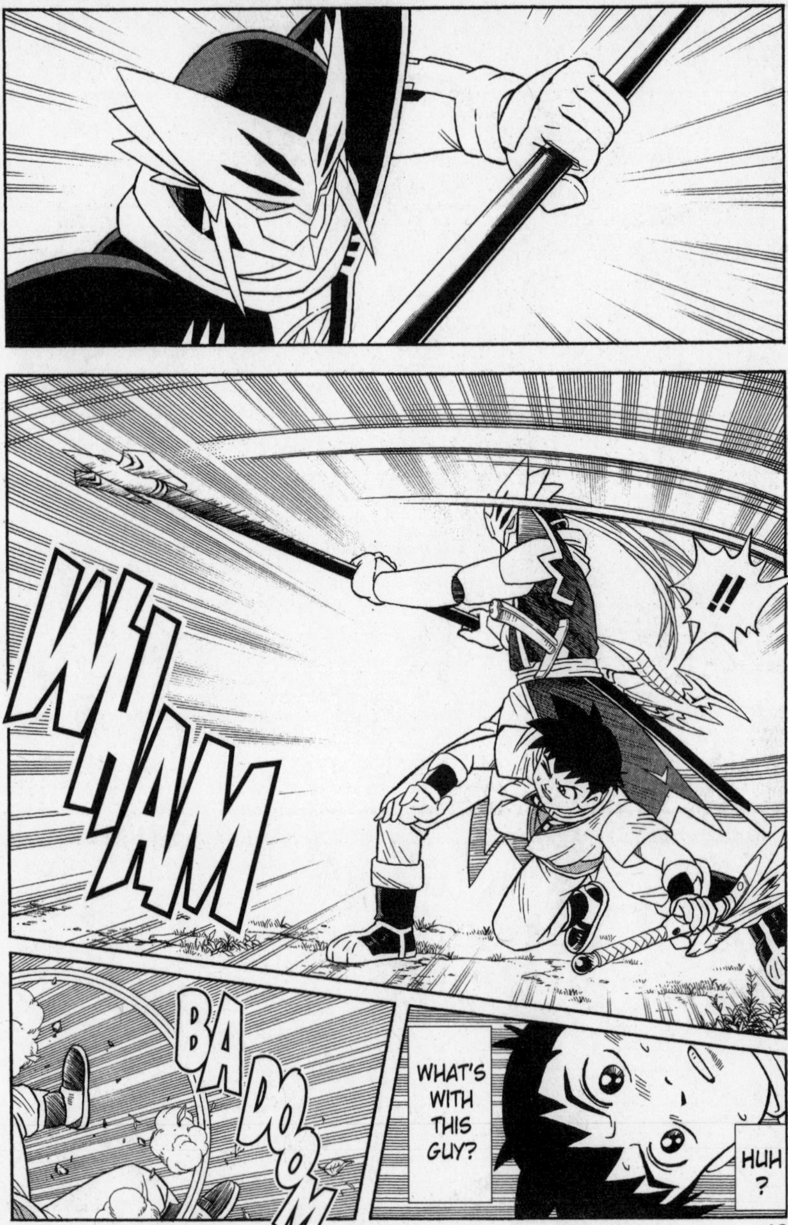
!!
WHAM
HUH?
WHAT'S WITH THIS GUY?
BADOOM

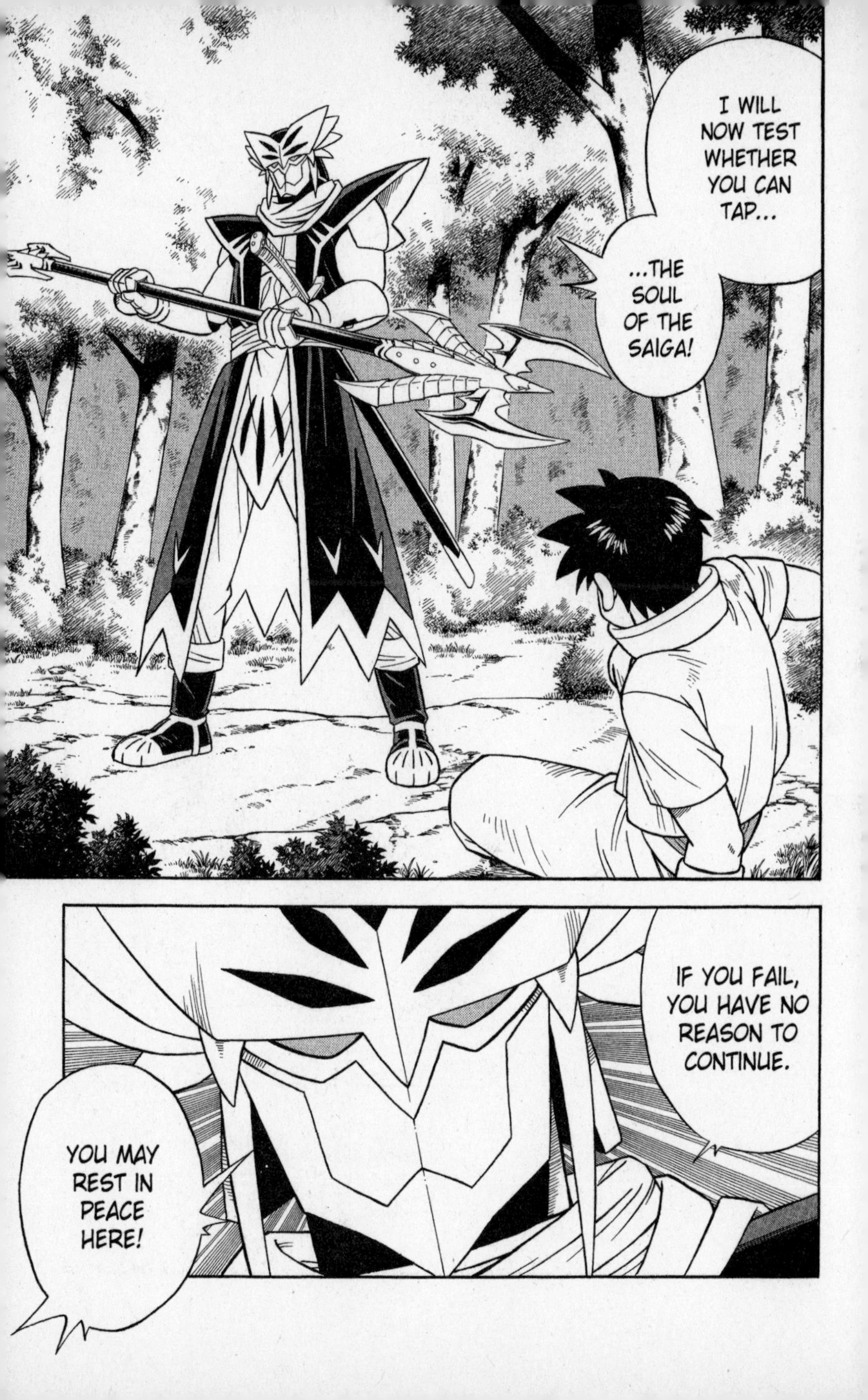
I WILL NOW TEST WHETHER YOU CAN TAP...
...THE SOUL OF THE SAIGA!
IF YOU FAIL, YOU HAVE NO REASON TO CONTINUE.
YOU MAY REST IN PEACE HERE!

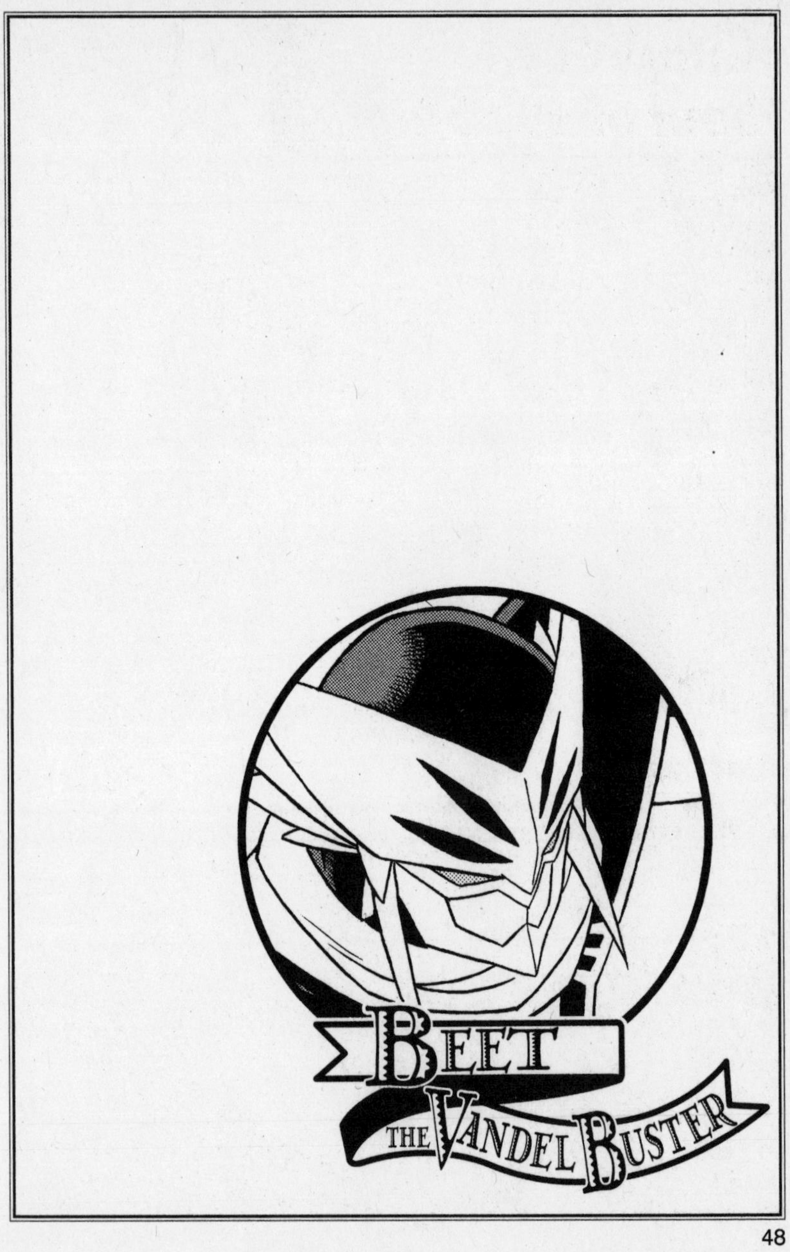
BEET
THE VANDEL BUSTER

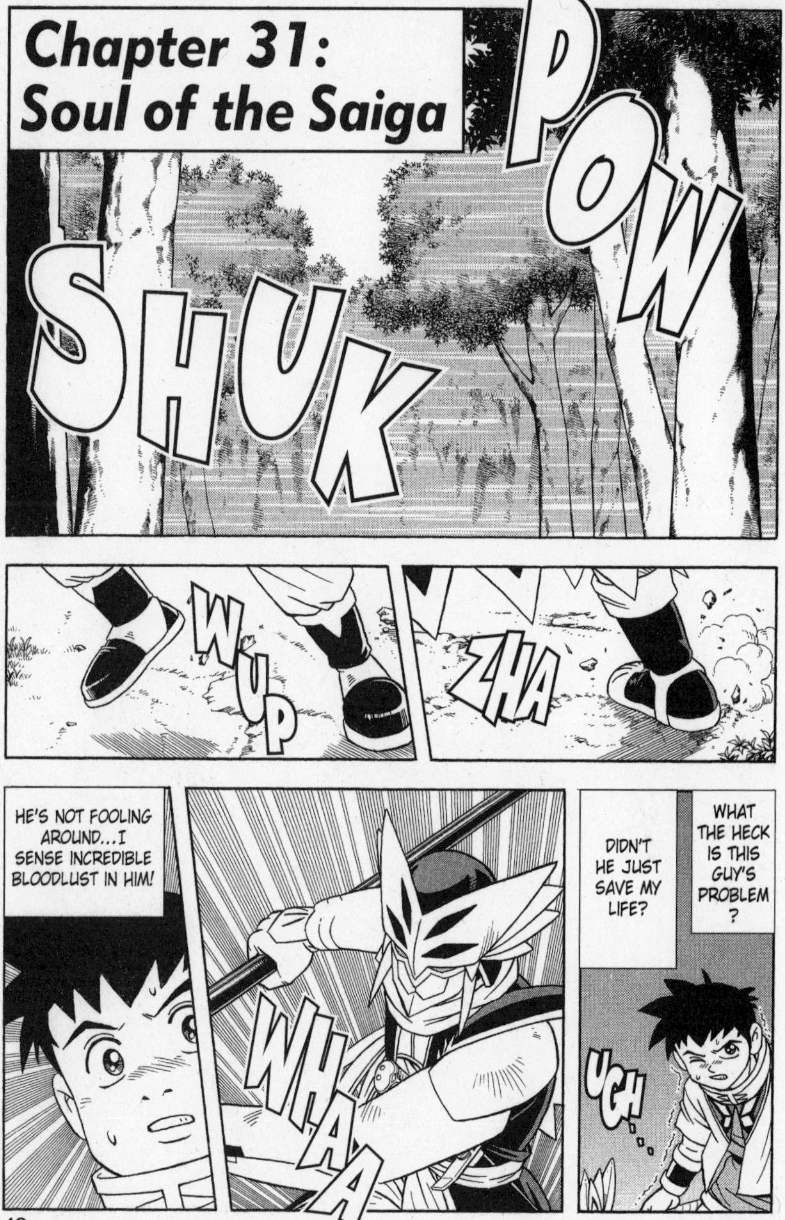
POW
Chapter 31: Soul of the Saiga
SHUK
ZHA
WUP
WHAT THE HECK IS THIS GUY'S PROBLEM?
DIDN'T HE JUST SAVE MY LIFE?
UGH
WHAAA
HE'S NOT FOOLING AROUND...I SENSE INCREDIBLE BLOODLUST IN HIM!

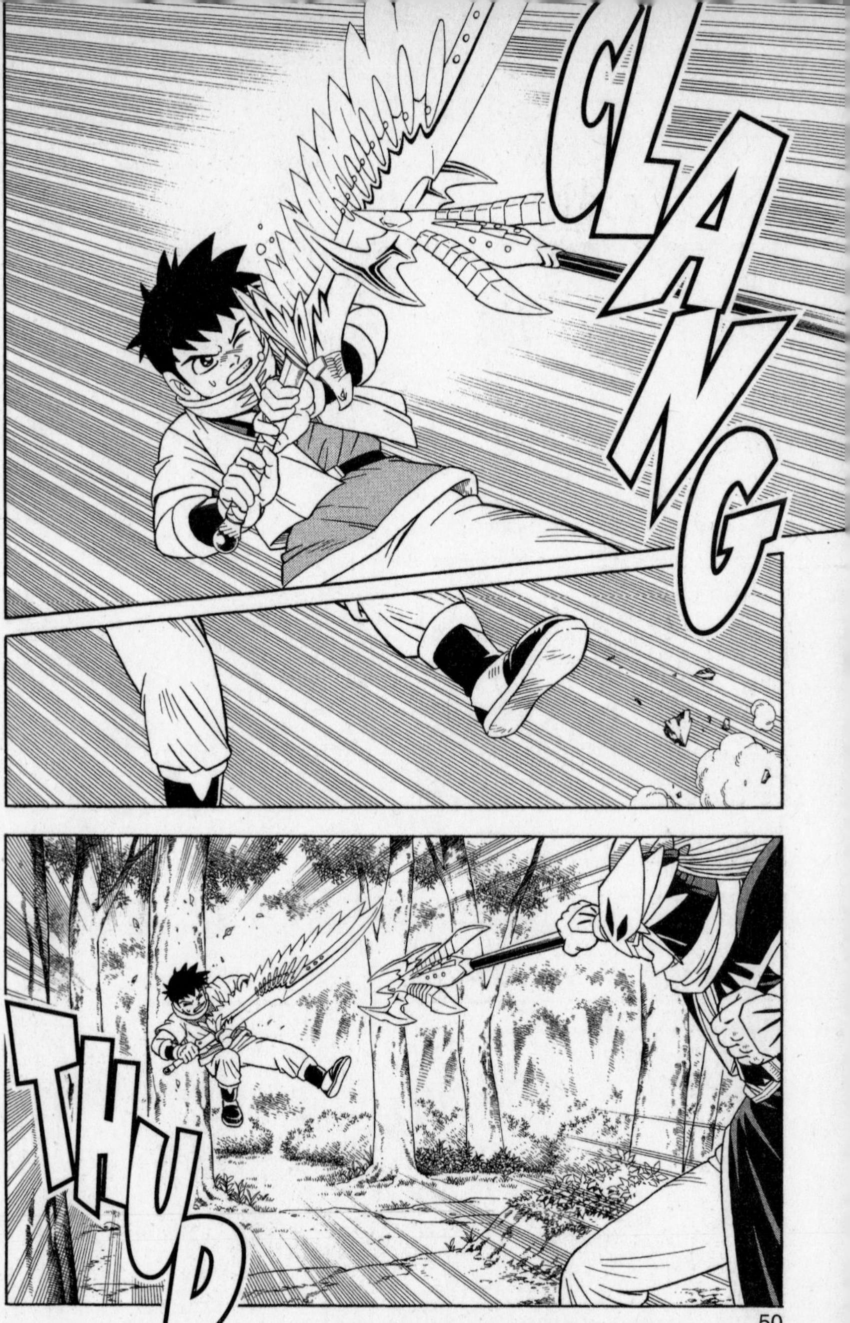
CLANG
THUD

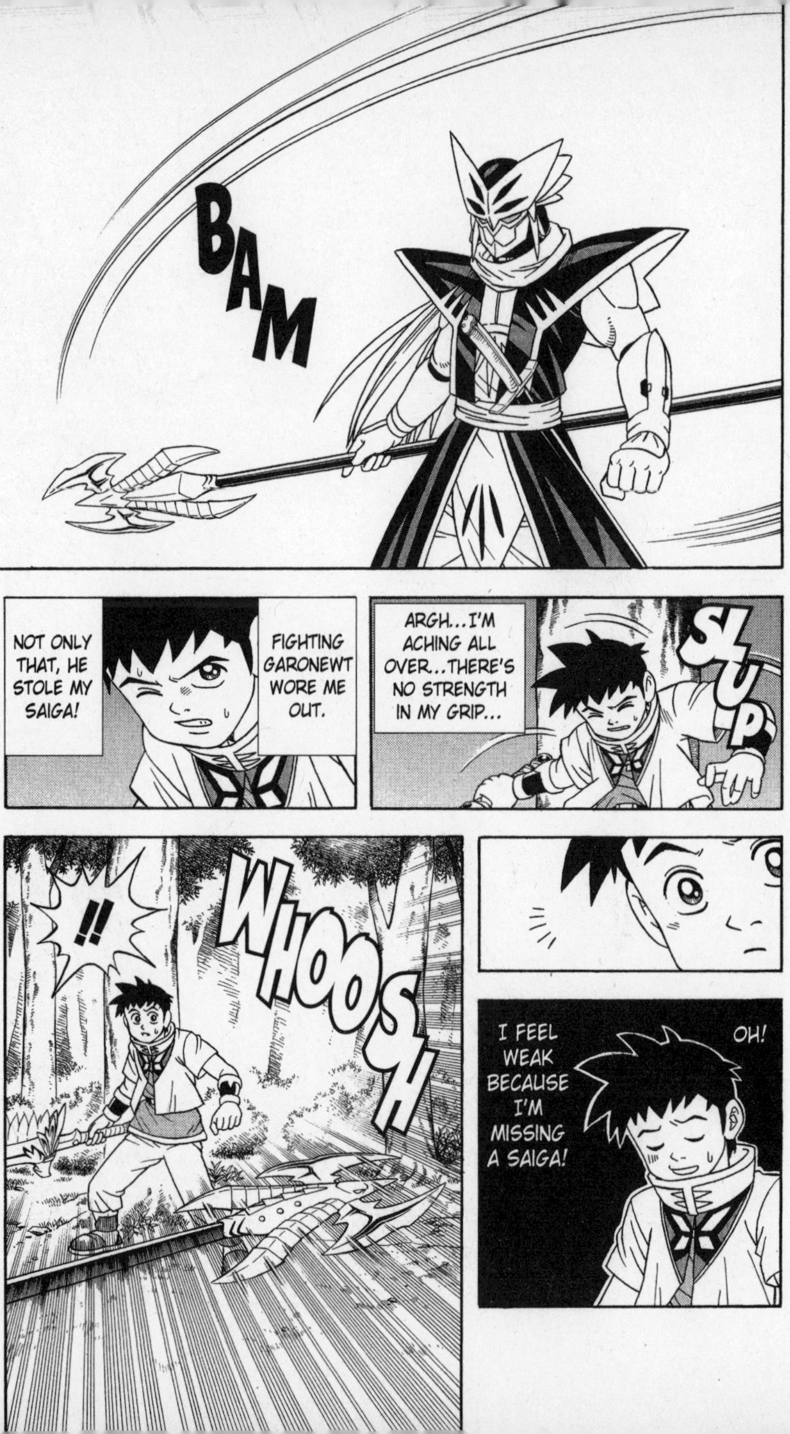
BAM
ARGH...I'M ACHING ALL OVER...THERE'S NO STRENGTH IN MY GRIP...
SLUP
FIGHTING GARONEWT WORE ME OUT.
NOT ONLY THAT, HE STOLE MY SAIGA!
OH!
I FEEL WEAK BECAUSE I'M MISSING A SAIGA!
WHOOSH
!!

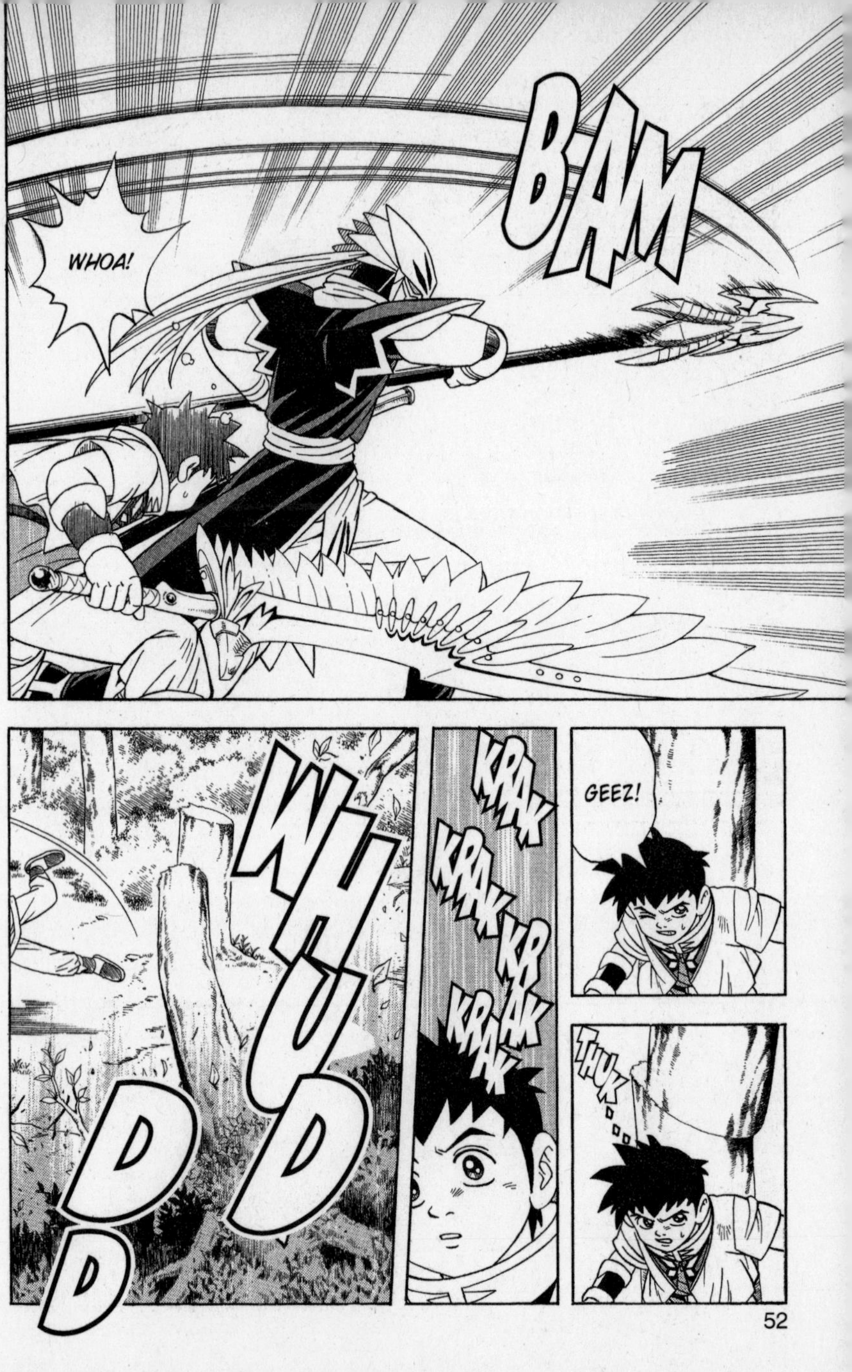

BAM
WHOA!
GEEZ!
THUK
D D D
KRAK KRAK KR AK KRAK
WHUD D D D

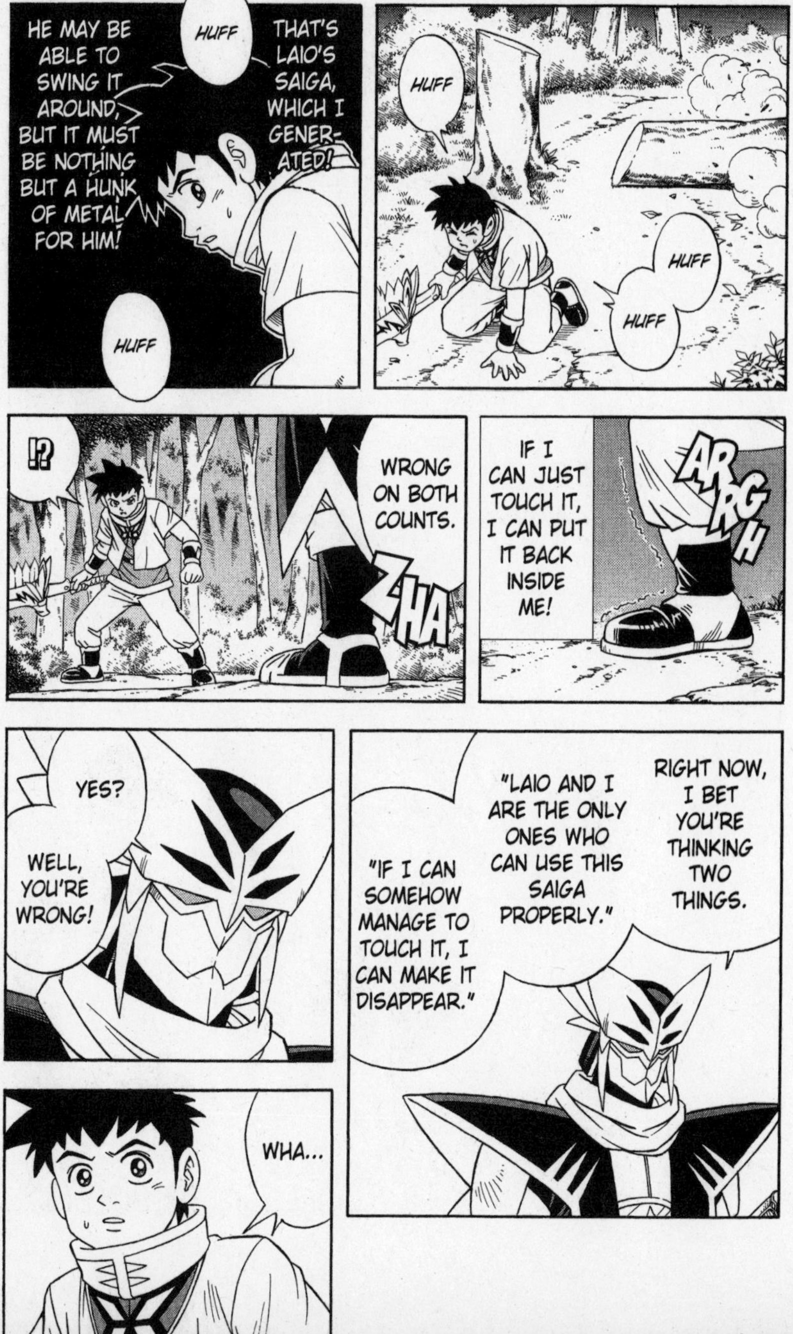
HUFF
HUFF
HUFF
THAT'S LAIO'S SAIGA, WHICH I GENERATED!
HUFF
HE MAY BE ABLE TO SWING IT AROUND, BUT IT MUST BE NOTHING BUT A HUNK OF METAL FOR HIM!
HUFF
IF I CAN JUST TOUCH IT, I CAN PUT IT BACK INSIDE ME!
ARGH
WRONG ON BOTH COUNTS.
ZHA
!?
RIGHT NOW, I BET YOU'RE THINKING TWO THINGS.
"LAIO AND I ARE THE ONLY ONES WHO CAN USE THIS SAIGA PROPERLY."
"IF I CAN SOMEHOW MANAGE TO TOUCH IT, I CAN MAKE IT DISAPPEAR."
YES?
WELL, YOU'RE WRONG!
WHA...

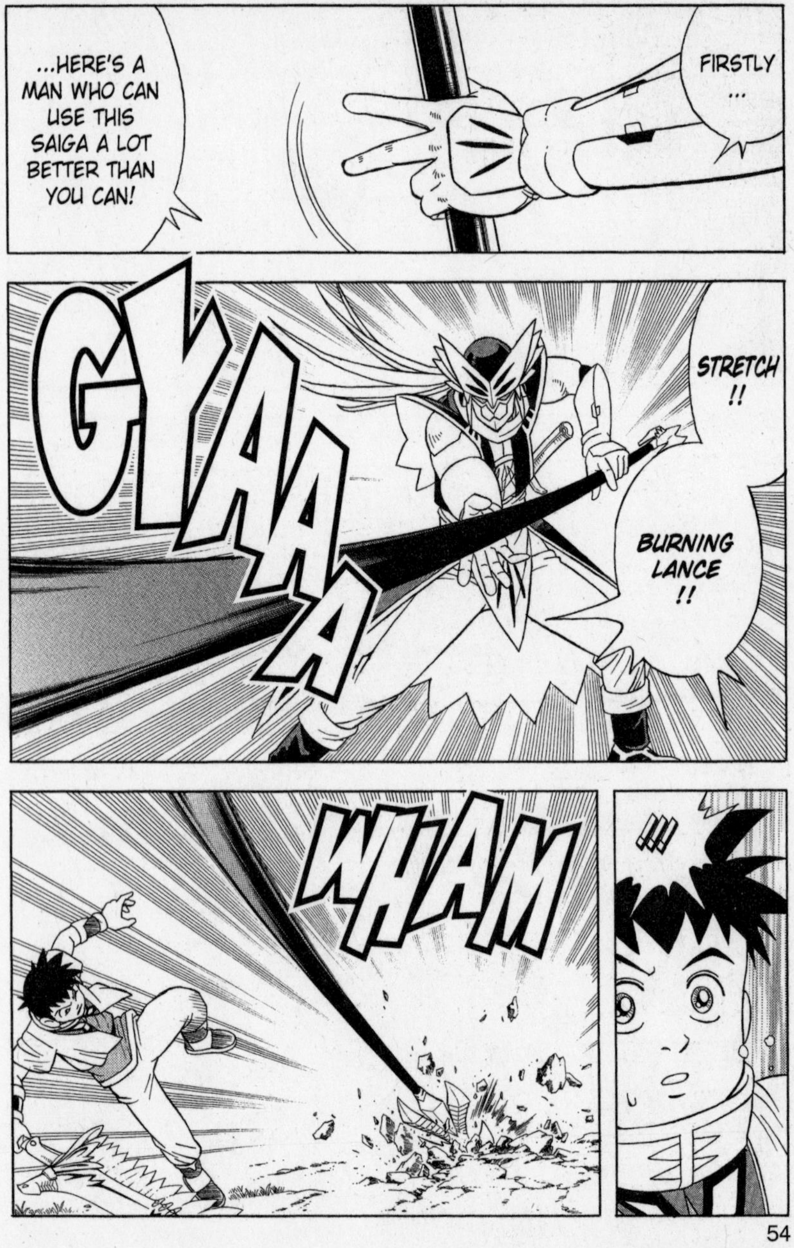
FIRSTLY ...
...HERE'S A MAN WHO CAN USE THIS SAIGA A LOT BETTER THAN YOU CAN!
STRETCH !!
BURNING LANCE !!
GYAAAA
!!!
WHAM

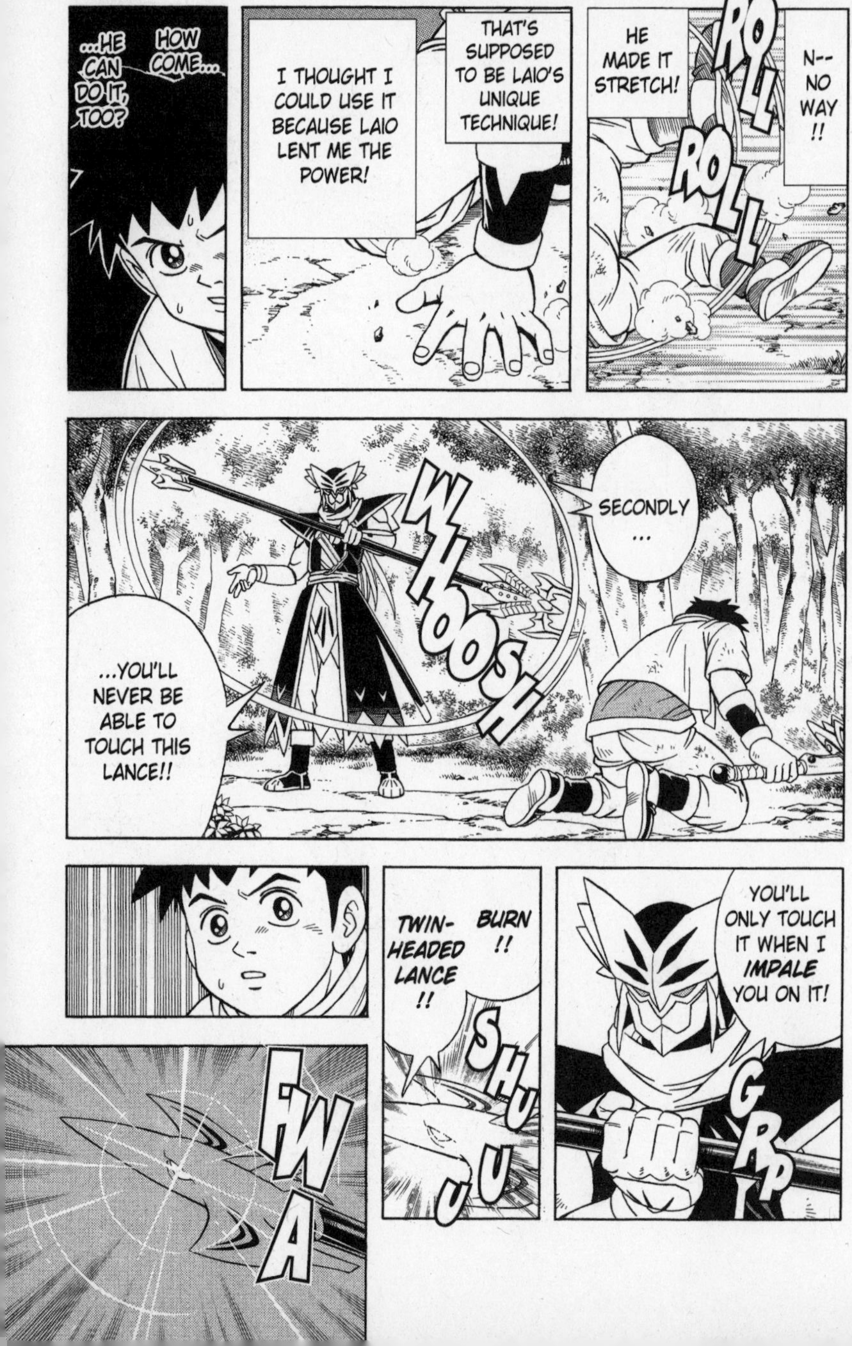
READ THIS WAY
N-- NO WAY !!
ROLL ROLL
HE MADE IT STRETCH!
THAT'S SUPPOSED TO BE LAIO'S UNIQUE TECHNIQUE!
I THOUGHT I COULD USE IT BECAUSE LAIO LENT ME THE POWER!
HOW COME...
...HE CAN DO IT, TOO?
SECONDLY ...
WHOOSH
...YOU'LL NEVER BE ABLE TO TOUCH THIS LANCE!!
YOU'LL ONLY TOUCH IT WHEN I IMPALE YOU ON IT!
GRP
BURN !!
TWIN-HEADED LANCE !!
SHUUU
FWA

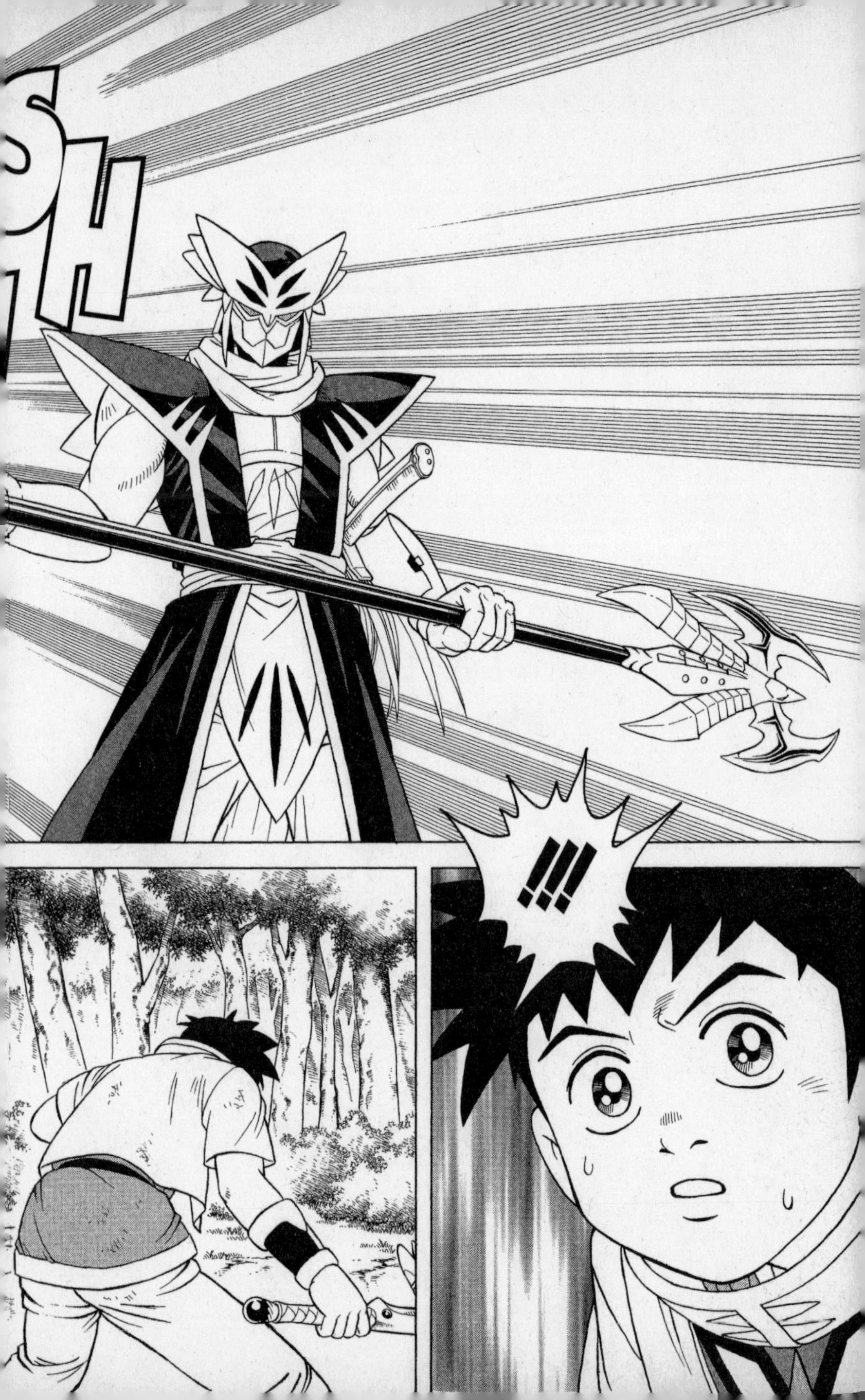
SH
!!!!

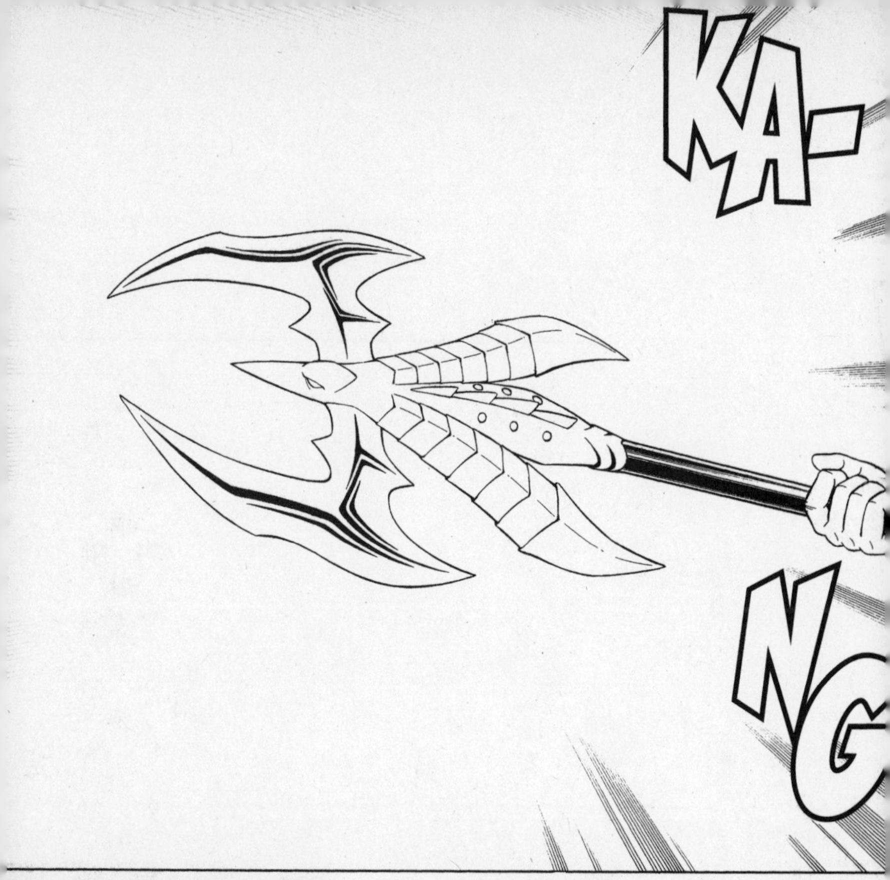
KA-
NG
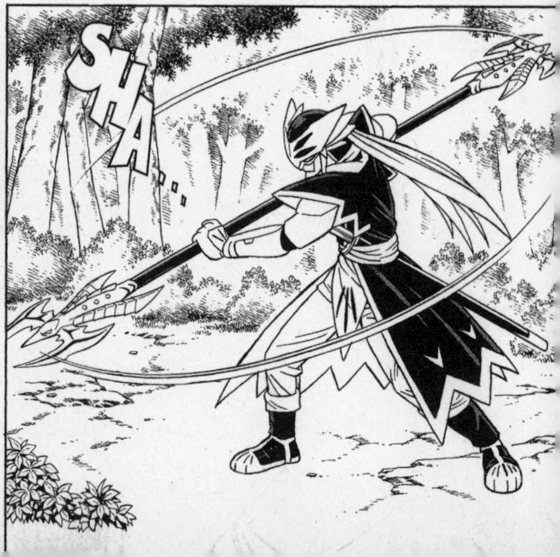
SHA...
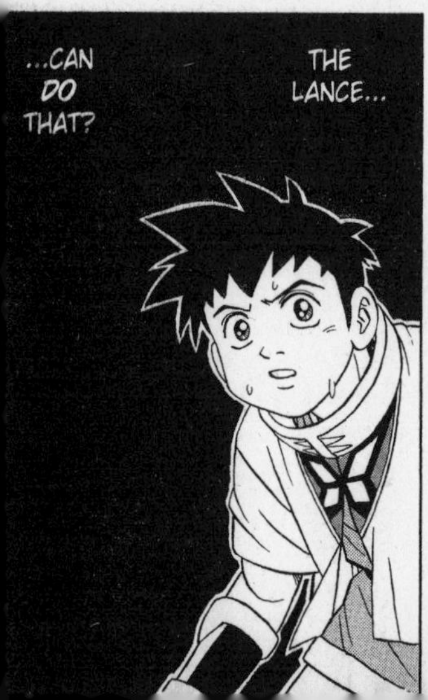
THE LANCE...
...CAN DO THAT?

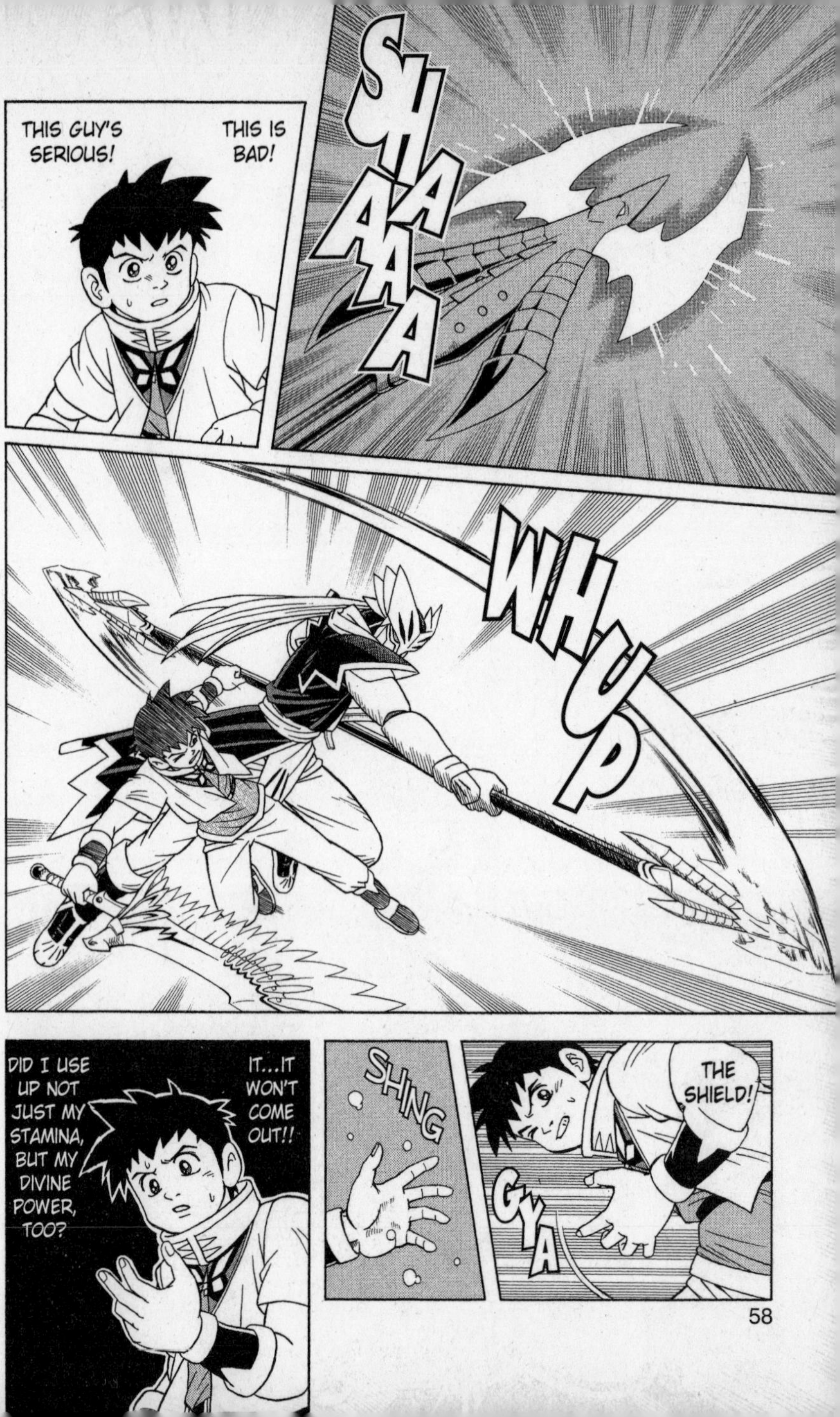
SHAAAAA
THIS IS BAD!
THIS GUY'S SERIOUS!
WHUP
THE SHIELD!
GYA
SHING
IT...IT WON'T COME OUT!!
DID I USE UP NOT JUST MY STAMINA, BUT MY DIVINE POWER, TOO?

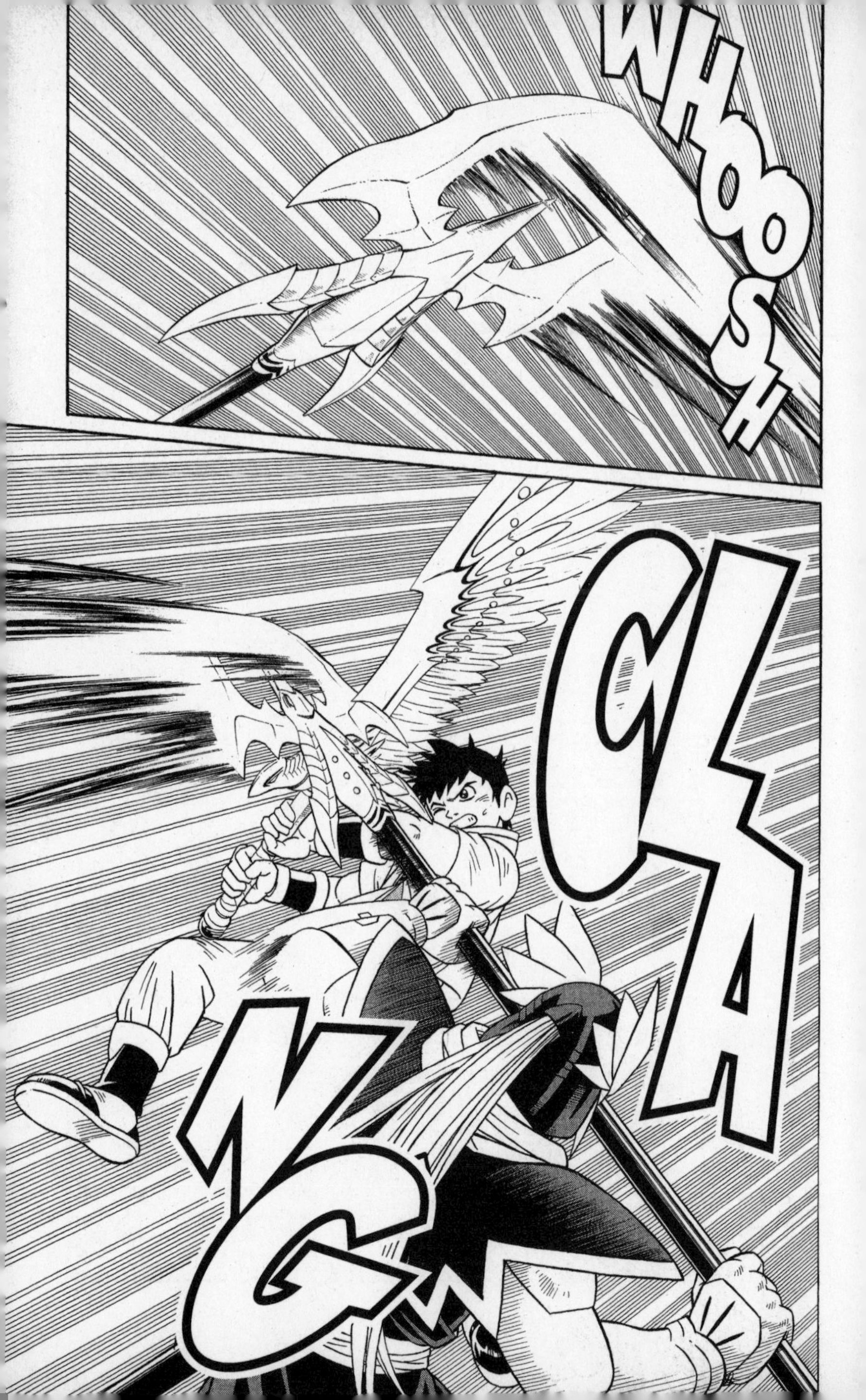
WHOOSH
CLANG

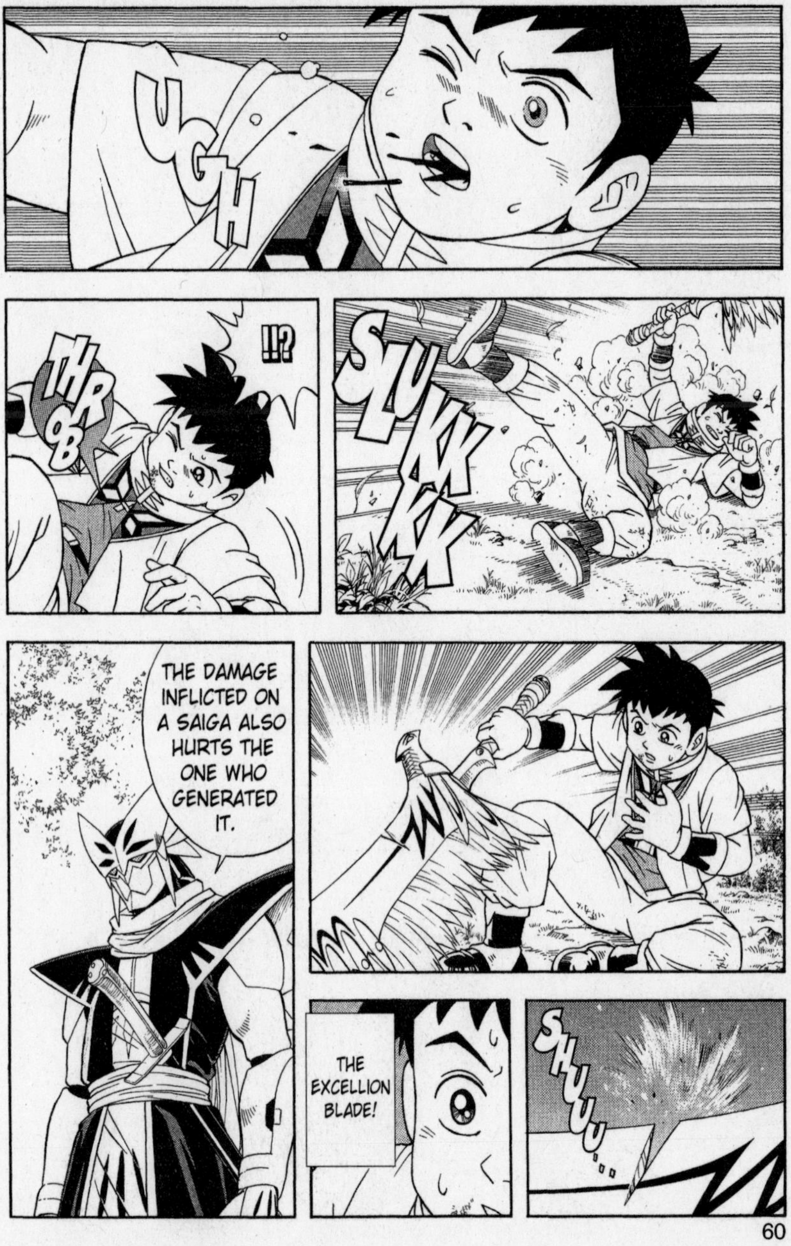
UGH
SLUKKKK
THROB
!!?
SHUUU...
THE EXCELLION BLADE!
THE DAMAGE INFLICTED ON A SAIGA ALSO HURTS THE ONE WHO GENERATED IT.

READ THIS WAY

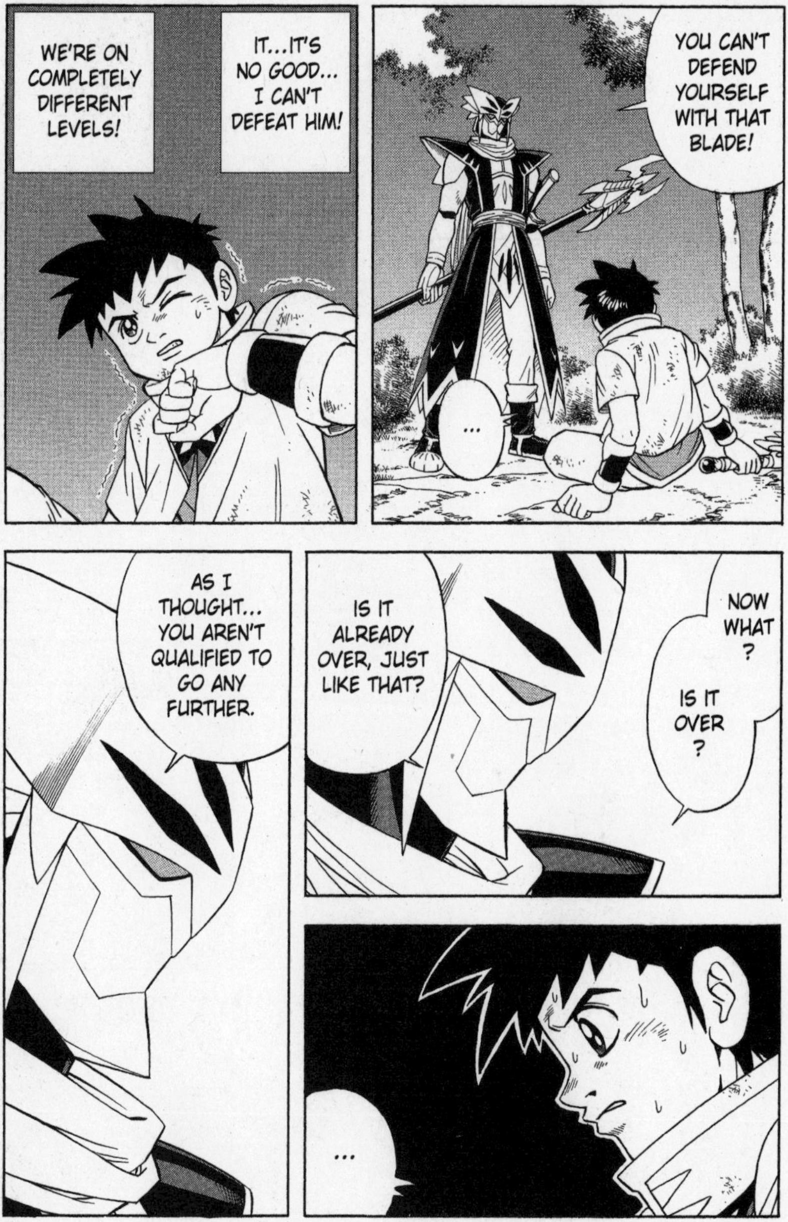

YOU CAN'T DEFEND YOURSELF WITH THAT BLADE!
...
IT...IT'S NO GOOD... I CAN'T DEFEAT HIM!
WE'RE ON COMPLETELY DIFFERENT LEVELS!
NOW WHAT?
IS IT OVER?
IS IT ALREADY OVER, JUST LIKE THAT?
...
AS I THOUGHT... YOU AREN'T QUALIFIED TO GO ANY FURTHER.

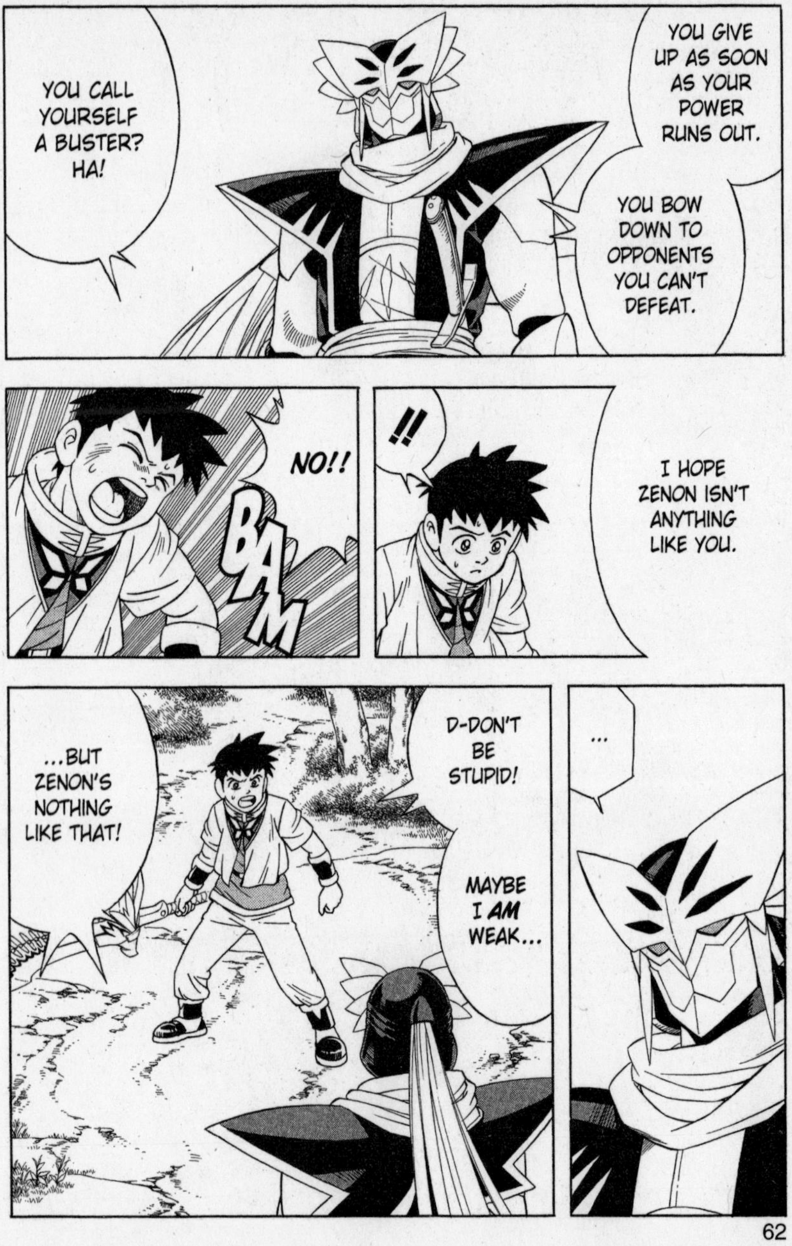
YOU GIVE UP AS SOON AS YOUR POWER RUNS OUT.
YOU BOW DOWN TO OPPONENTS YOU CAN'T DEFEAT.
YOU CALL YOURSELF A BUSTER? HA!
I HOPE ZENON ISN'T ANYTHING LIKE YOU.
!!
NO!!
BAM
...
D-DON'T BE STUPID!
MAYBE I *AM* WEAK...
...BUT ZENON'S NOTHING LIKE THAT!

READ THIS WAY

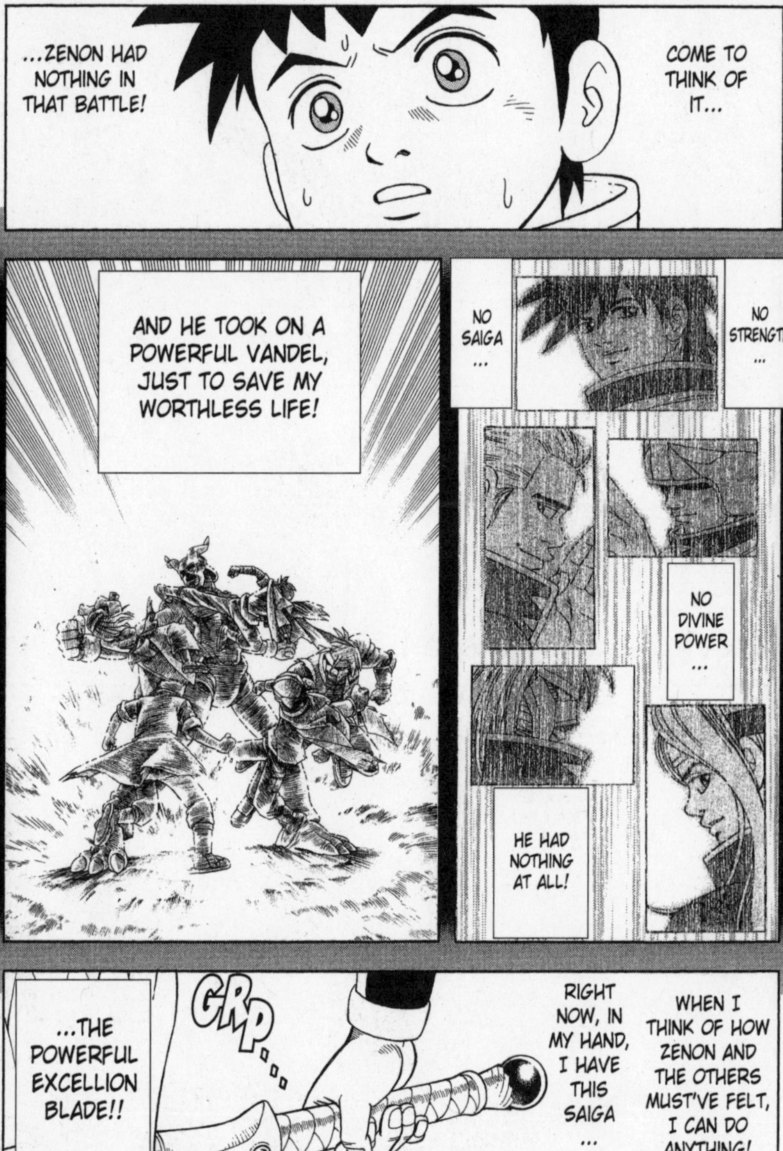
COME TO THINK OF IT...
...ZENON HAD NOTHING IN THAT BATTLE!
NO STRENGTH...
NO SAIGA...
NO DIVINE POWER...
HE HAD NOTHING AT ALL!
AND HE TOOK ON A POWERFUL VANDEL, JUST TO SAVE MY WORTHLESS LIFE!
WHEN I THINK OF HOW ZENON AND THE OTHERS MUST'VE FELT, I CAN DO ANYTHING!
RIGHT NOW, IN MY HAND, I HAVE THIS SAIGA...
GRP...
...THE POWERFUL EXCELLION BLADE!!

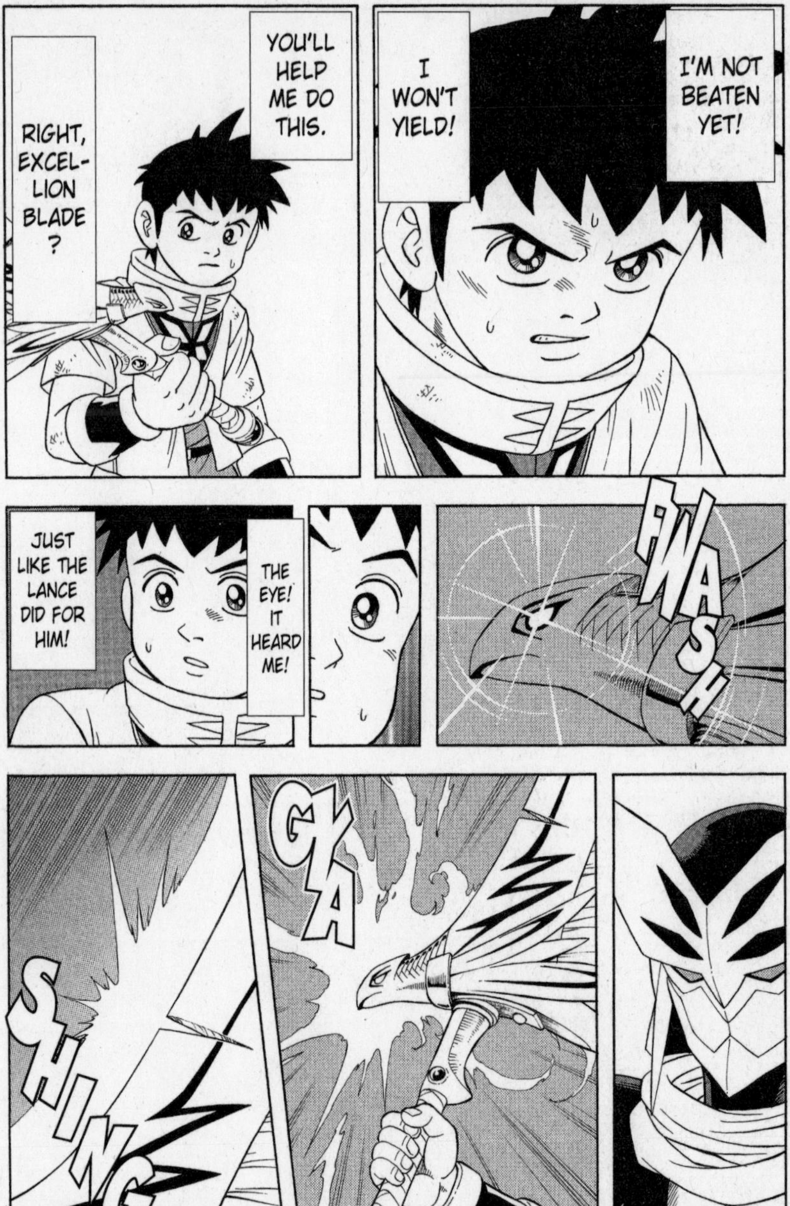
I'M NOT BEATEN YET!
I WON'T YIELD!
YOU'LL HELP ME DO THIS.
RIGHT, EXCEL-LION BLADE?
FWASH
THE EYE! IT HEARD ME!
JUST LIKE THE LANCE DID FOR HIM!
GYA
SHING

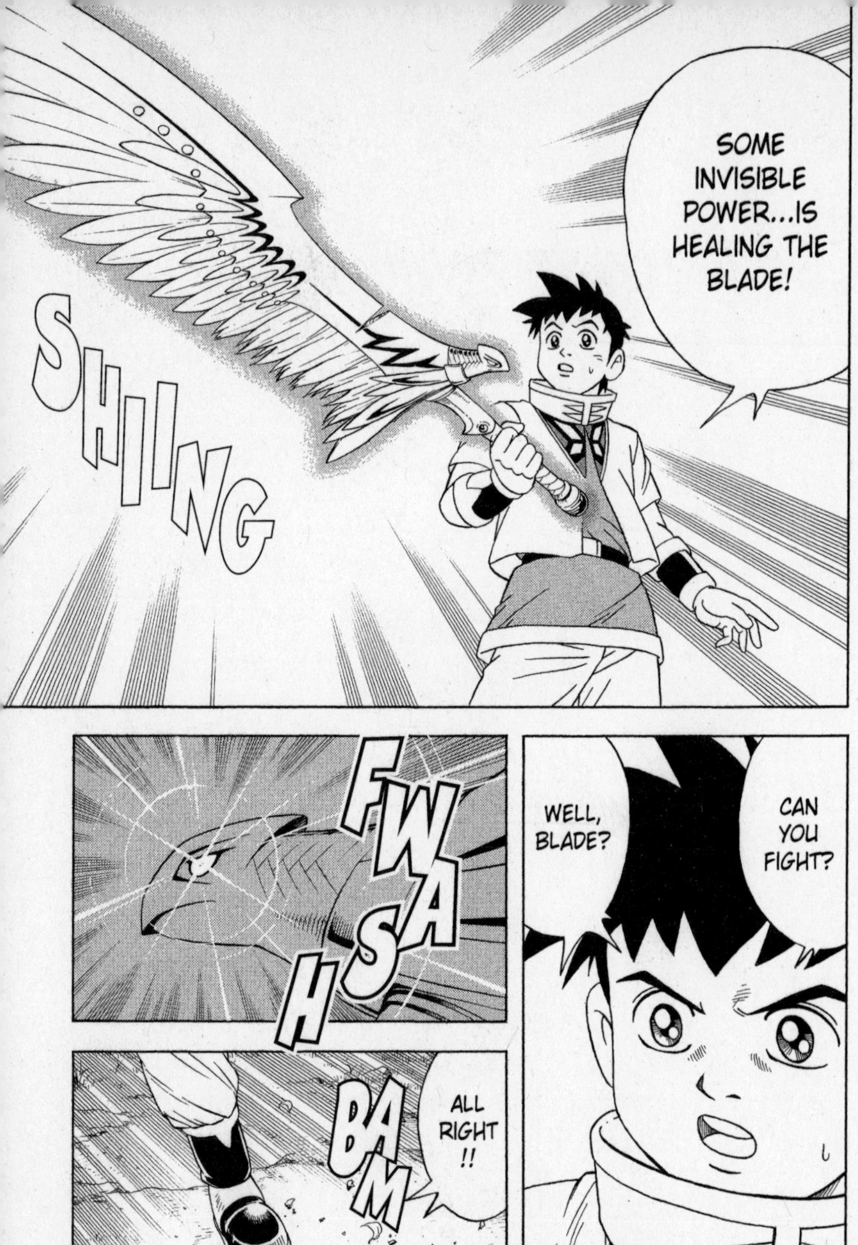
SOME INVISIBLE POWER...IS HEALING THE BLADE!
SHIING
CAN YOU FIGHT?
WELL, BLADE?
FWASH
ALL RIGHT !!
BAM

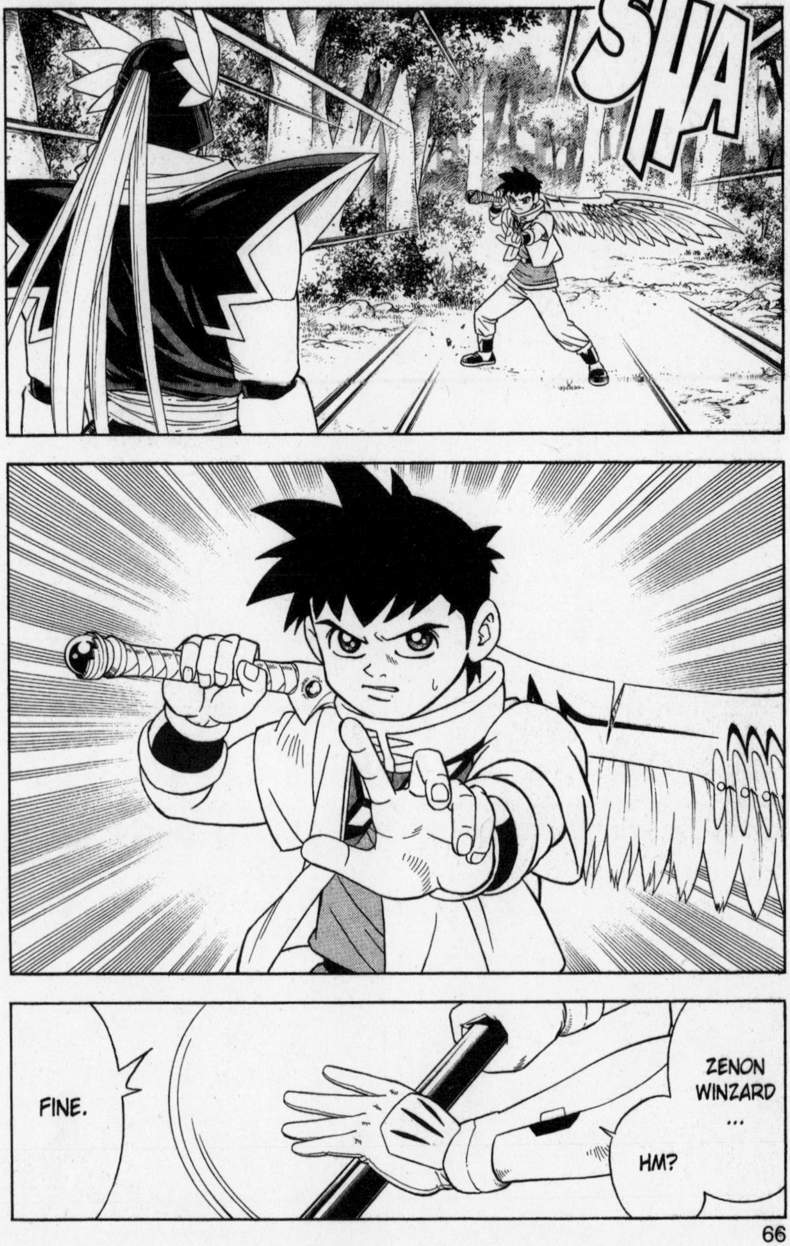
SHA
ZENON WINZARD ...
HM?
FINE.

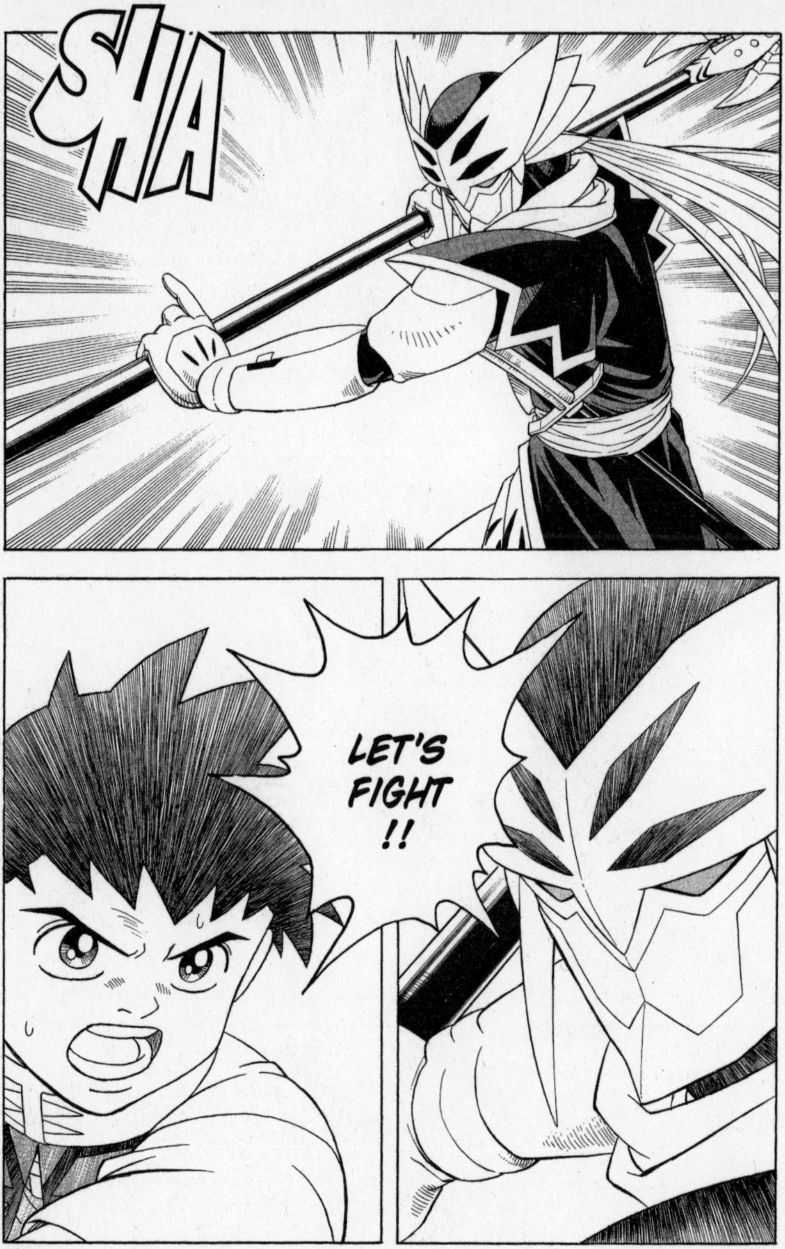
SHA
LET'S FIGHT !!

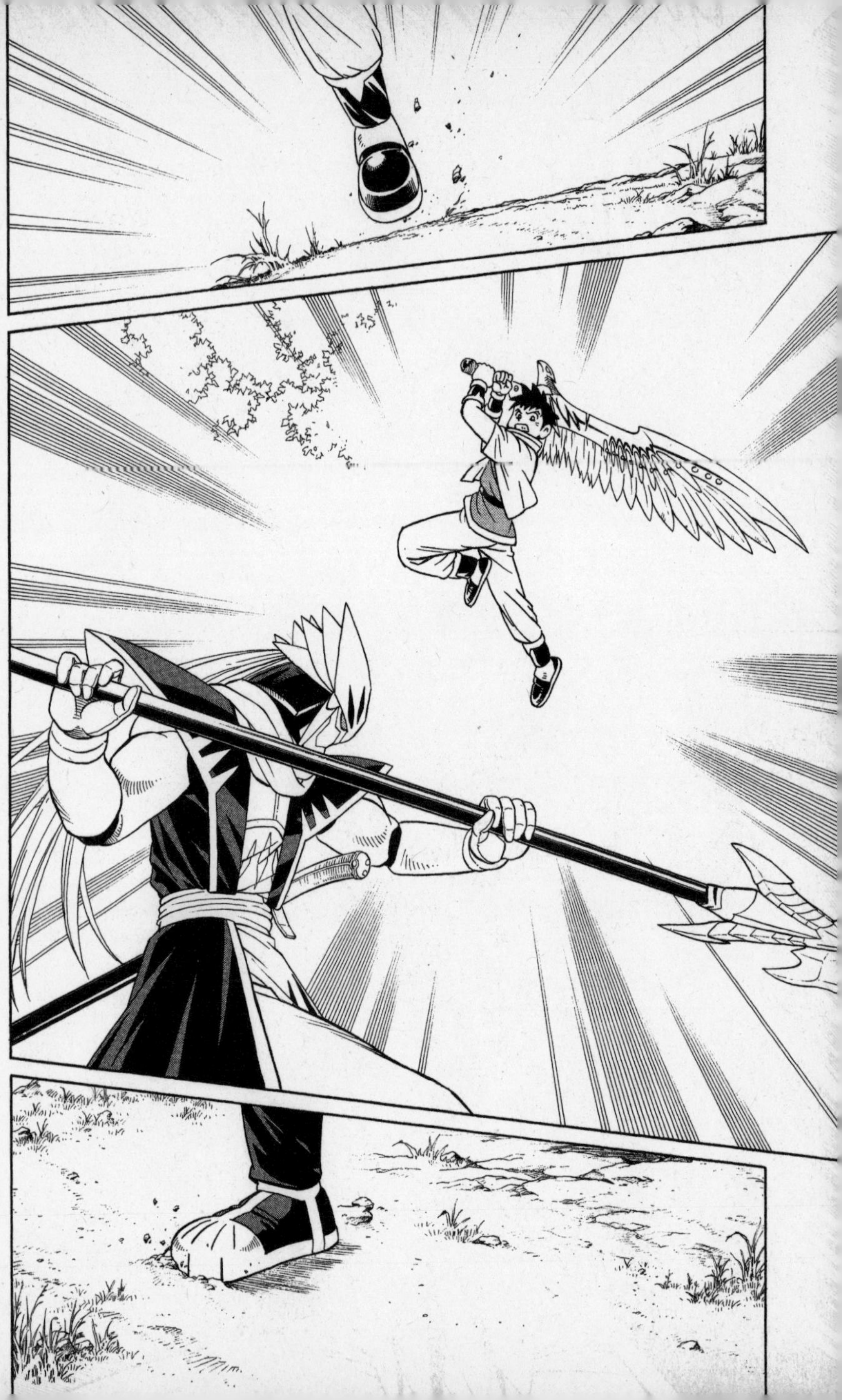

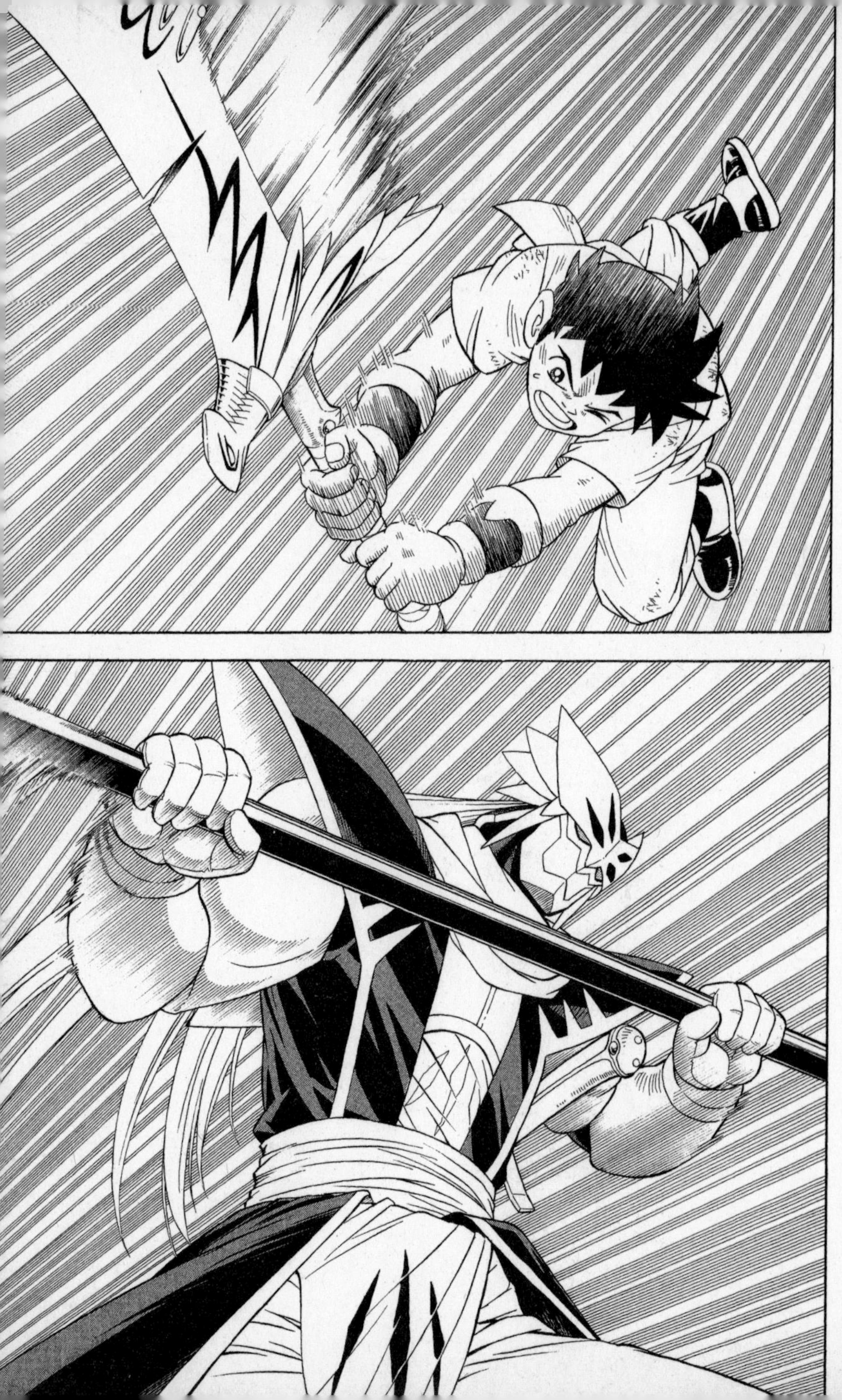

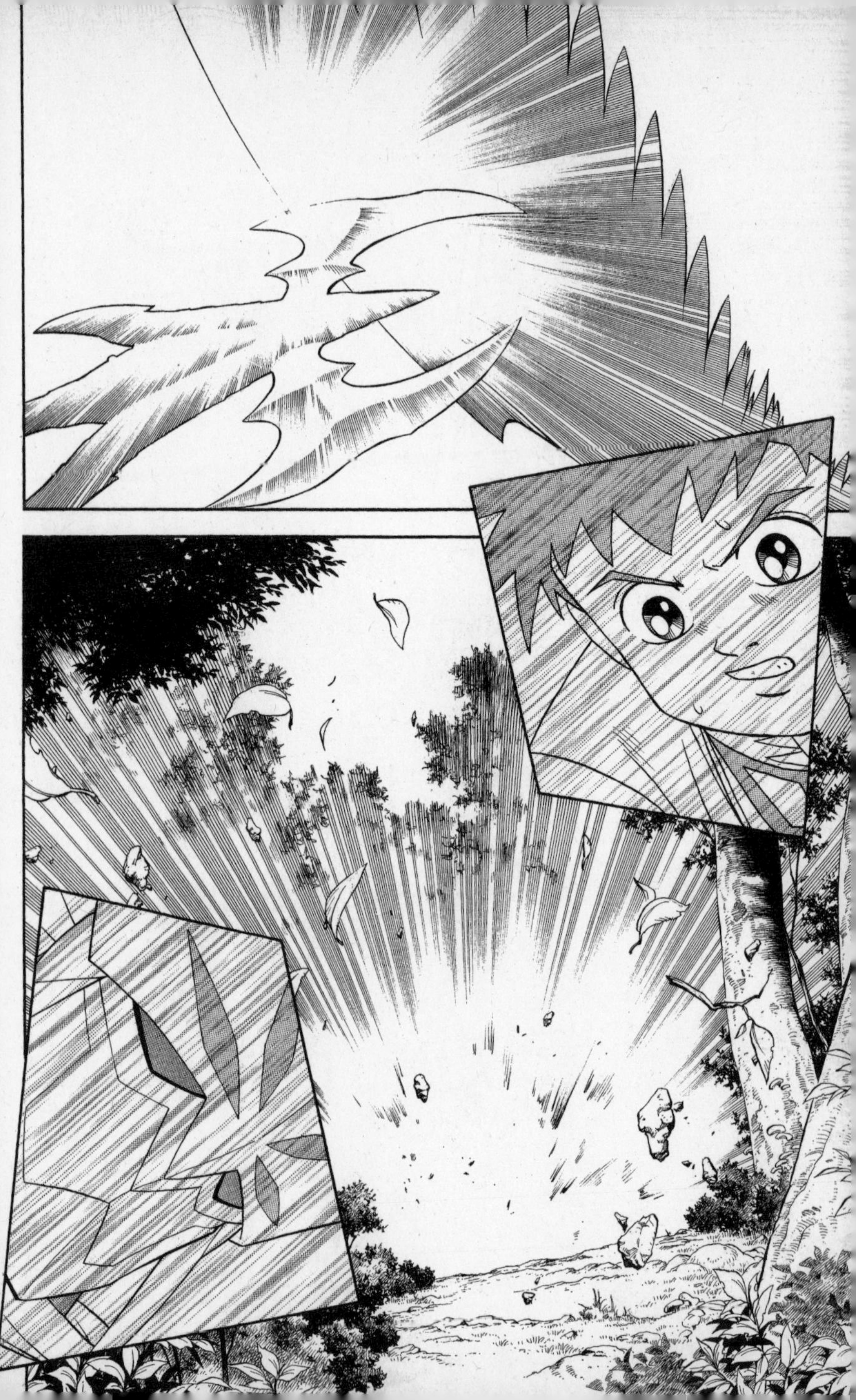

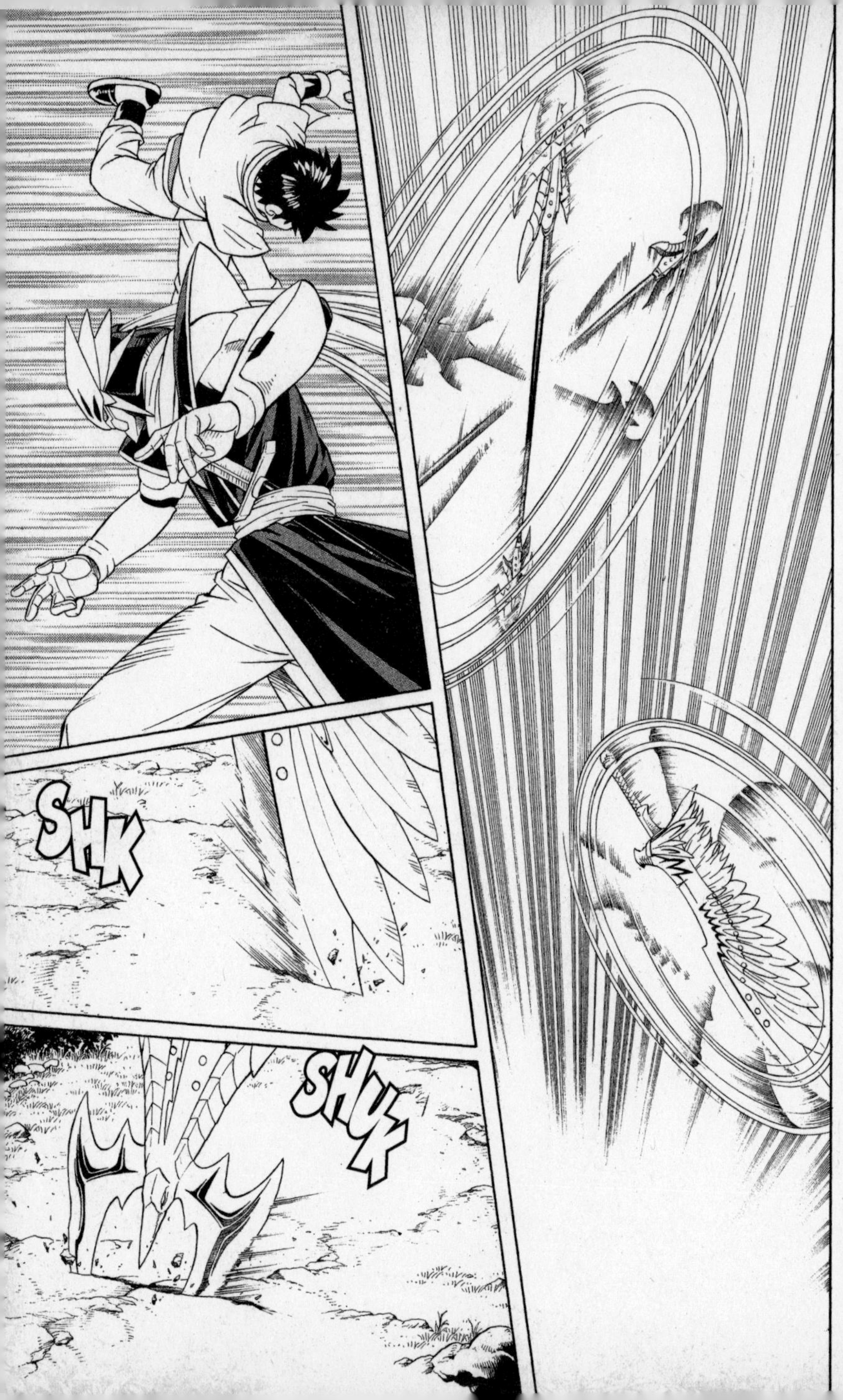
SHK
SHUK

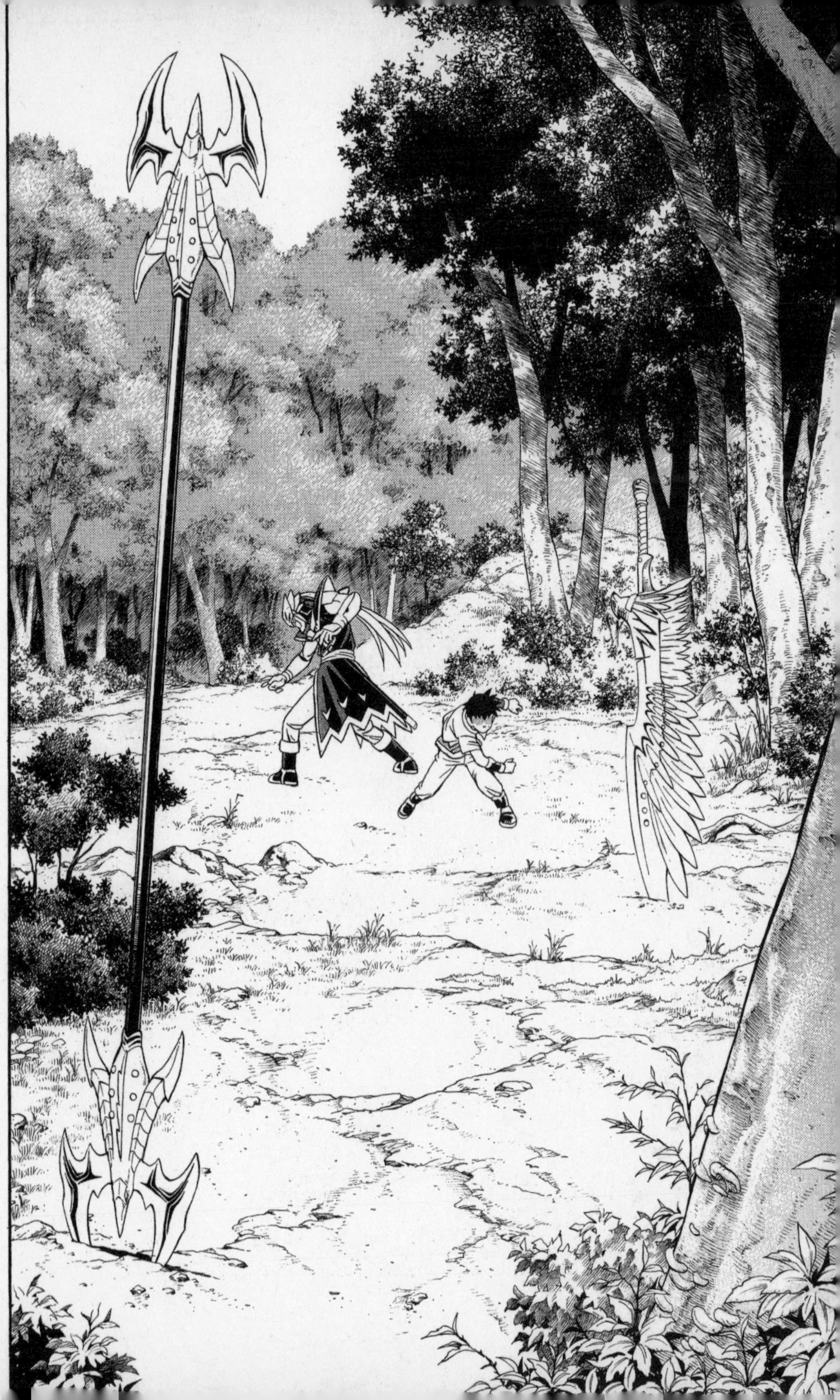

READ THIS WAY

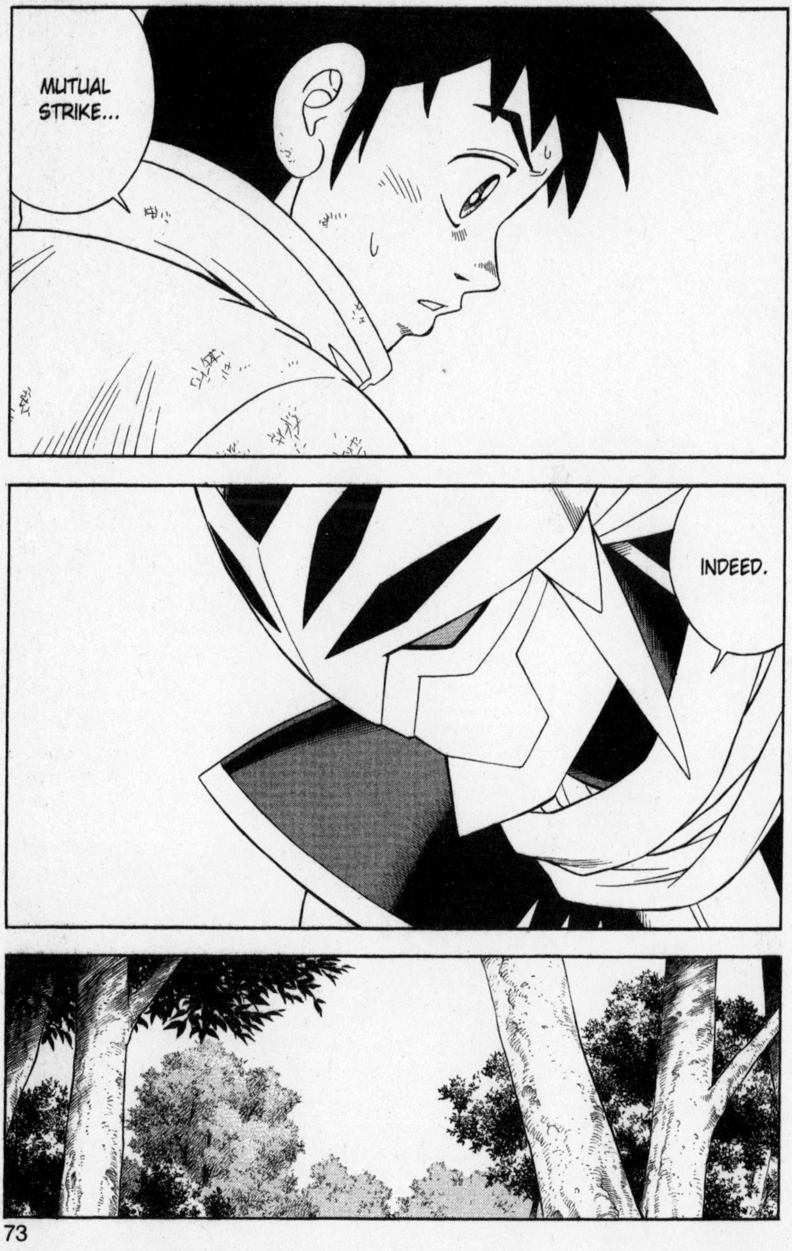
MUTUAL STRIKE...
INDEED.

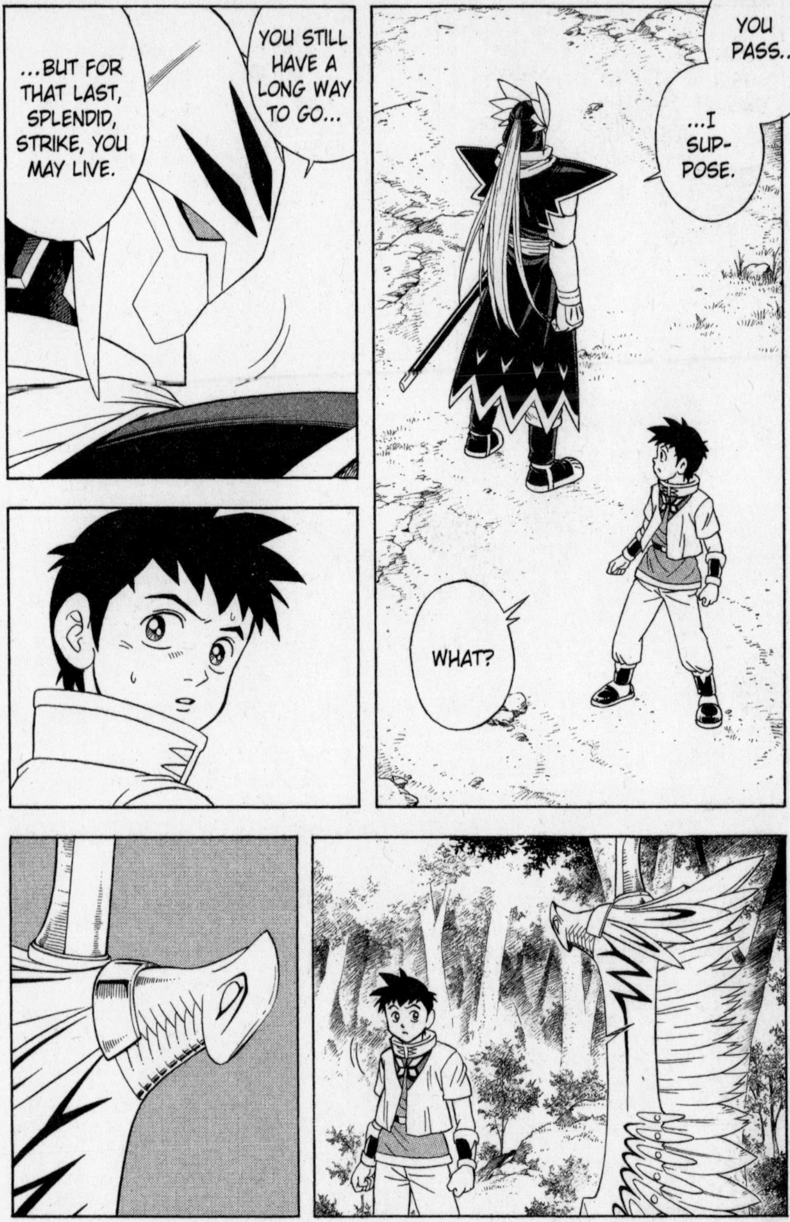
YOU PASS...
...I SUPPOSE.
WHAT?
YOU STILL HAVE A LONG WAY TO GO...
...BUT FOR THAT LAST, SPLENDID, STRIKE, YOU MAY LIVE.

READ THIS WAY

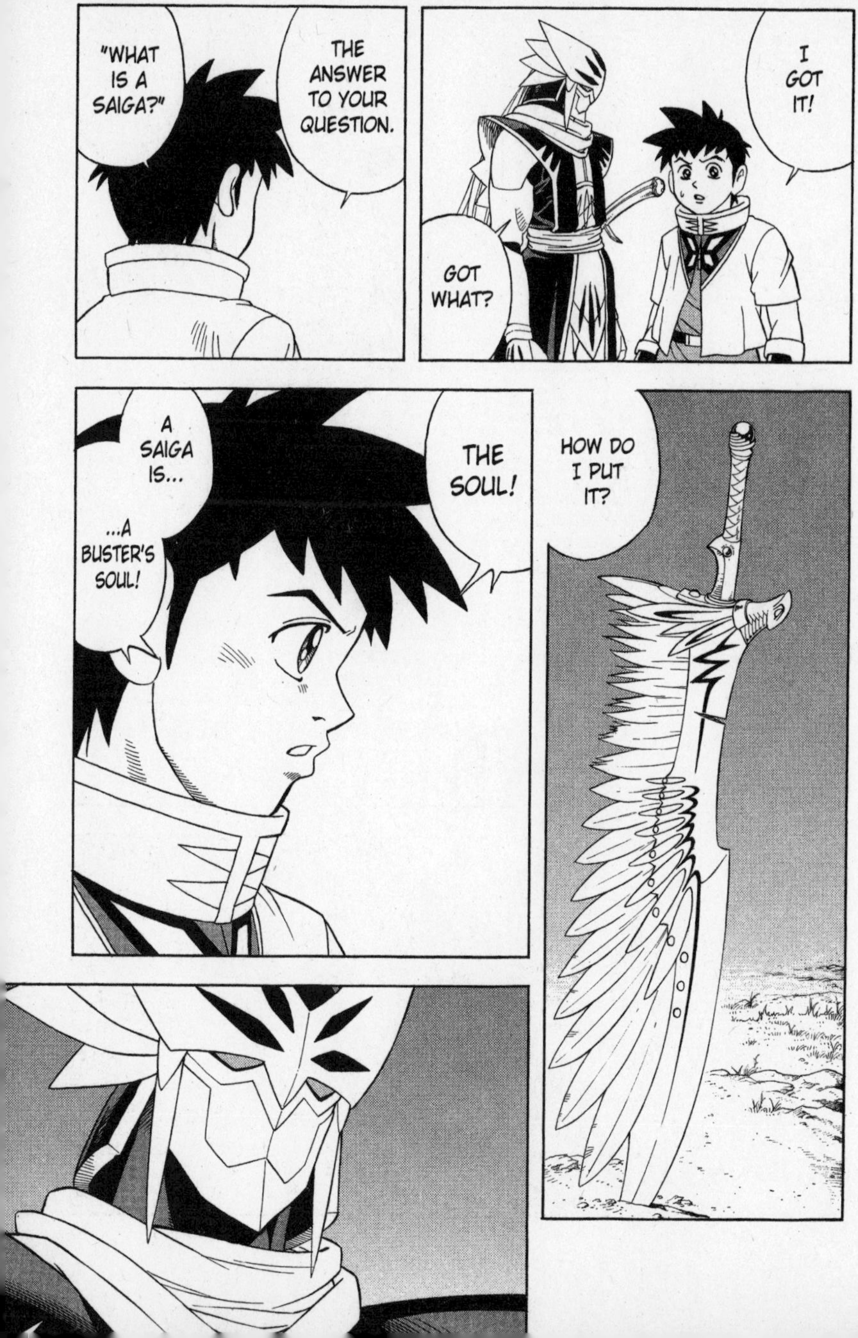
I GOT IT!
GOT WHAT?
THE ANSWER TO YOUR QUESTION.
"WHAT IS A SAIGA?"
HOW DO I PUT IT?
THE SOUL!
A SAIGA IS...
...A BUSTER'S SOUL!

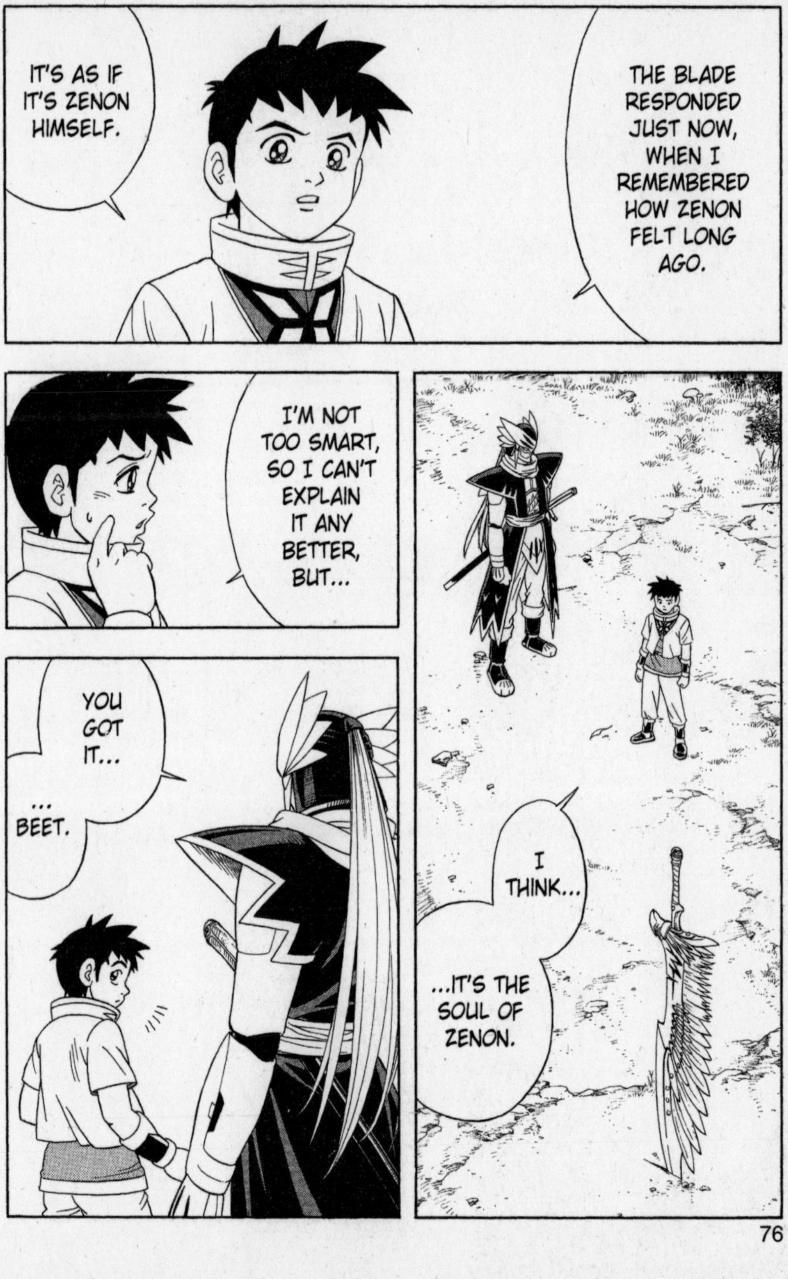
THE BLADE RESPONDED JUST NOW, WHEN I REMEMBERED HOW ZENON FELT LONG AGO.
IT'S AS IF IT'S ZENON HIMSELF.
I THINK...
...IT'S THE SOUL OF ZENON.
I'M NOT TOO SMART, SO I CAN'T EXPLAIN IT ANY BETTER, BUT...
YOU GOT IT...
...BEET.

READ THIS WAY

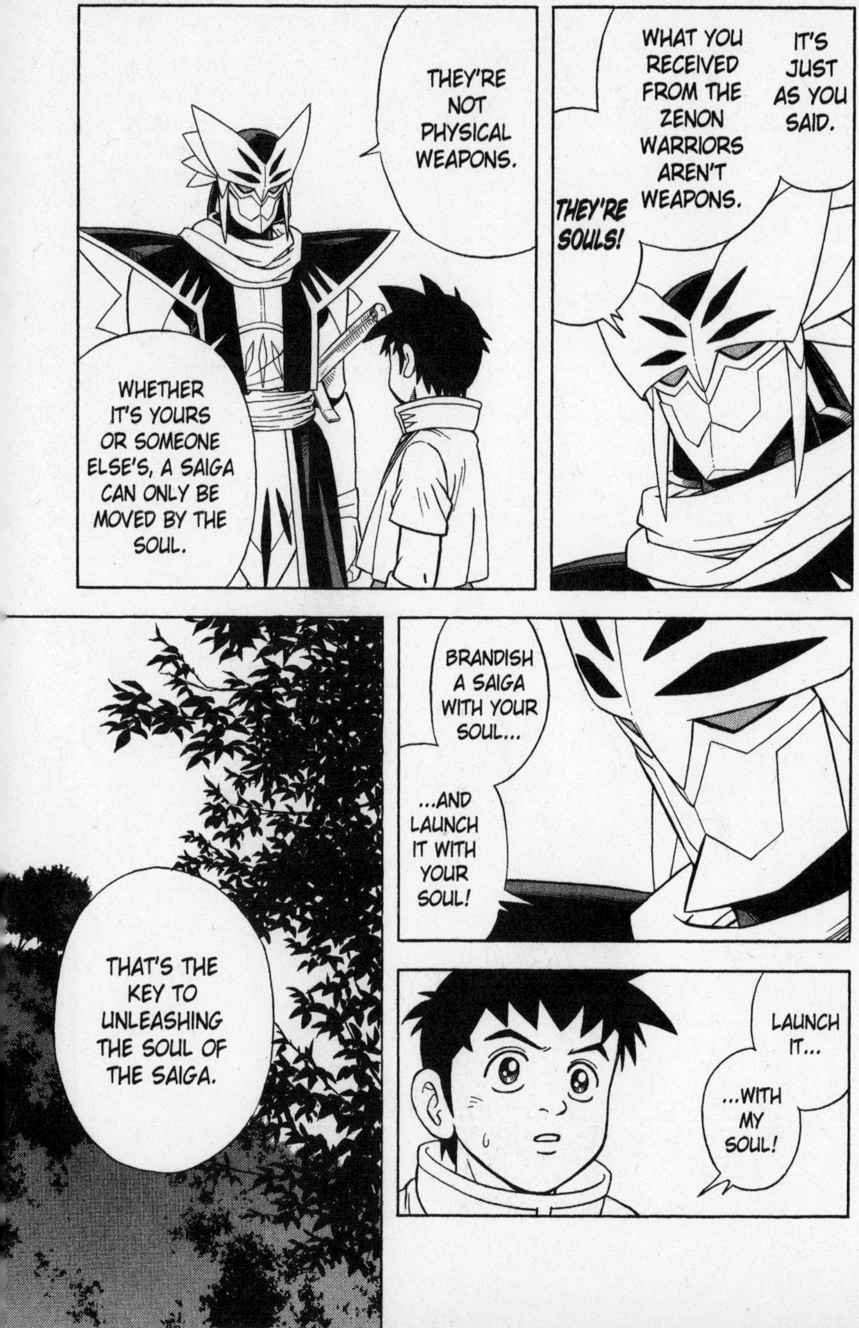
IT'S JUST AS YOU SAID.
WHAT YOU RECEIVED FROM THE ZENON WARRIORS AREN'T WEAPONS.
THEY'RE SOULS!
THEY'RE NOT PHYSICAL WEAPONS.
WHETHER IT'S YOURS OR SOMEONE ELSE'S, A SAIGA CAN ONLY BE MOVED BY THE SOUL.
BRANDISH A SAIGA WITH YOUR SOUL...
...AND LAUNCH IT WITH YOUR SOUL!
LAUNCH IT...
...WITH MY SOUL!
THAT'S THE KEY TO UNLEASHING THE SOUL OF THE SAIGA.

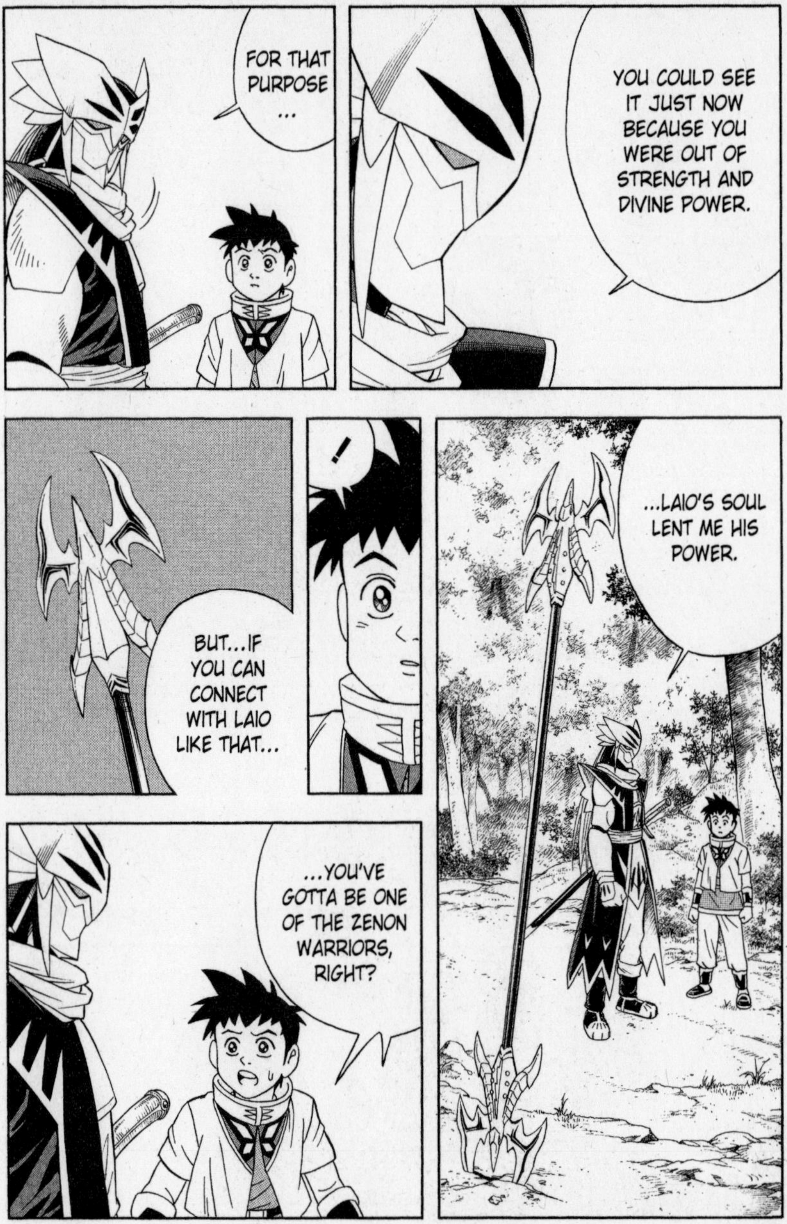
YOU COULD SEE IT JUST NOW BECAUSE YOU WERE OUT OF STRENGTH AND DIVINE POWER.
FOR THAT PURPOSE ...
...LAIO'S SOUL LENT ME HIS POWER.
!
BUT...IF YOU CAN CONNECT WITH LAIO LIKE THAT...
...YOU'VE GOTTA BE ONE OF THE ZENON WARRIORS, RIGHT?

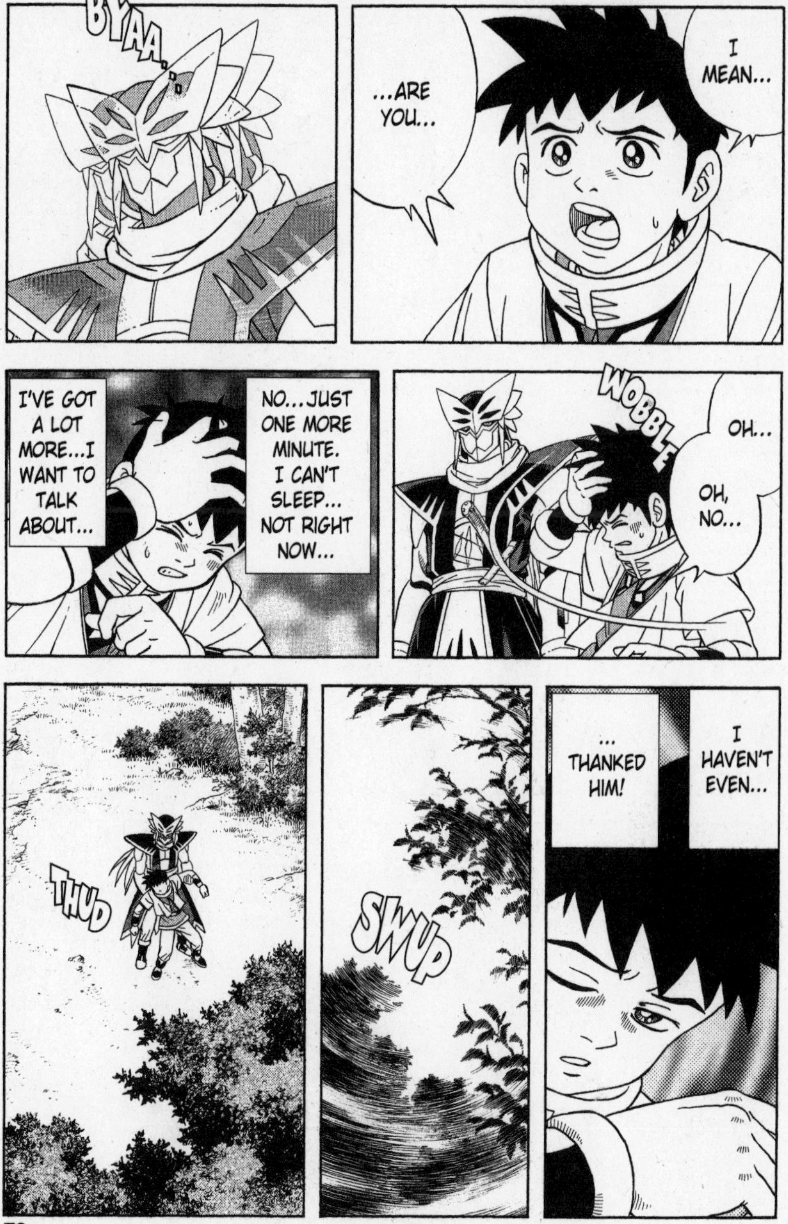
I MEAN...
...ARE YOU...
BYAA...
WOBBLE
OH...
OH, NO...
NO...JUST ONE MORE MINUTE. I CAN'T SLEEP... NOT RIGHT NOW...
I'VE GOT A LOT MORE...I WANT TO TALK ABOUT...
I HAVEN'T EVEN...
...THANKED HIM!
SWUP
THUD

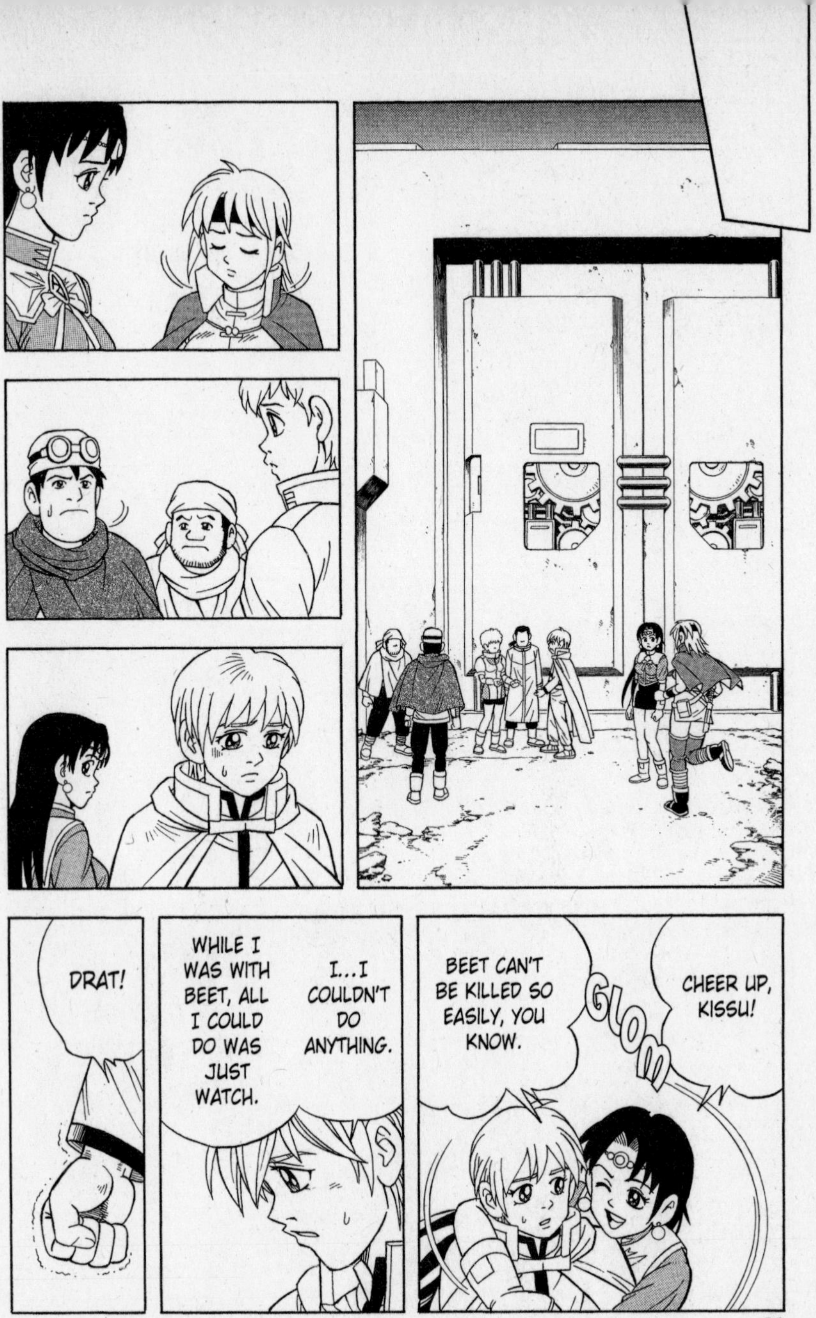
CHEER UP, KISSU!
GLOM
BEET CAN'T BE KILLED SO EASILY, YOU KNOW.
I...I COULDN'T DO ANYTHING.
WHILE I WAS WITH BEET, ALL I COULD DO WAS JUST WATCH.
DRAT!

READ THIS WAY

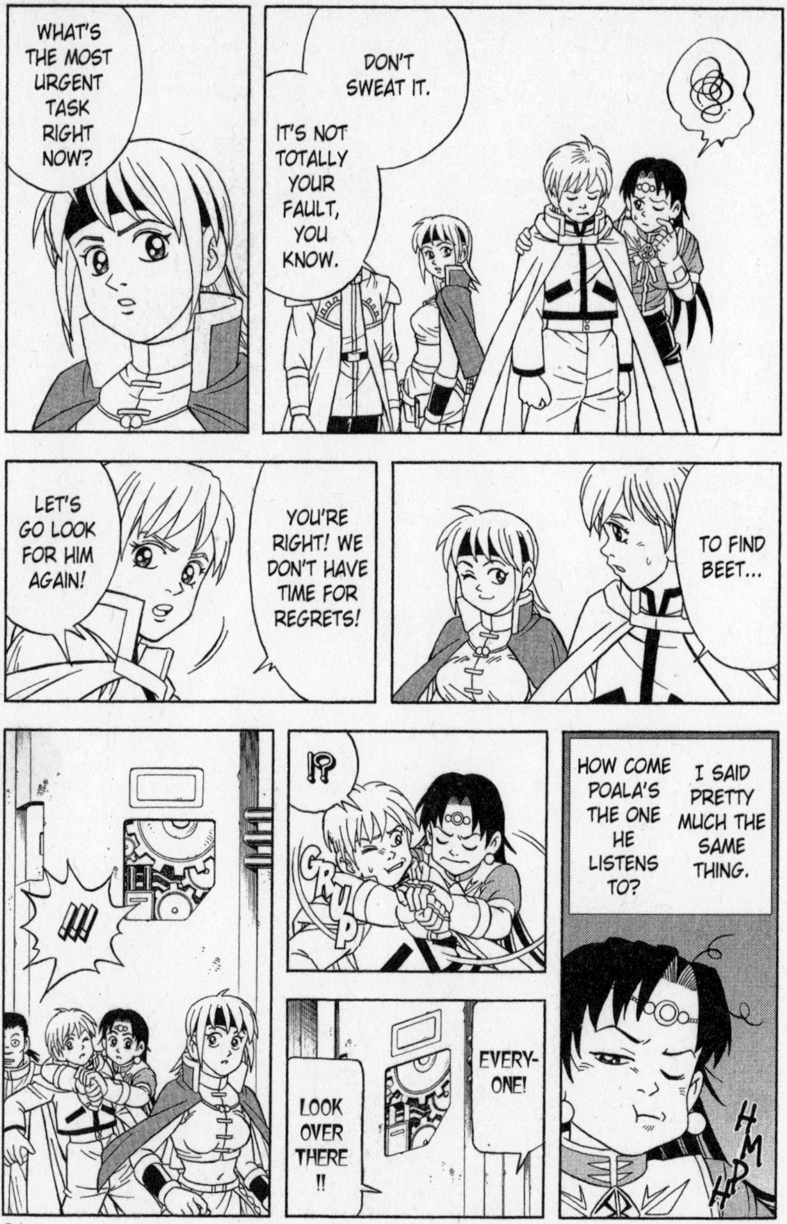
DON'T SWEAT IT.
IT'S NOT TOTALLY YOUR FAULT, YOU KNOW.
WHAT'S THE MOST URGENT TASK RIGHT NOW?
TO FIND BEET...
YOU'RE RIGHT! WE DON'T HAVE TIME FOR REGRETS!
LET'S GO LOOK FOR HIM AGAIN!
I SAID PRETTY MUCH THE SAME THING.
HOW COME POALA'S THE ONE HE LISTENS TO?
HMPH
!?
GRUP
EVERY-ONE!
LOOK OVER THERE!!
!!!

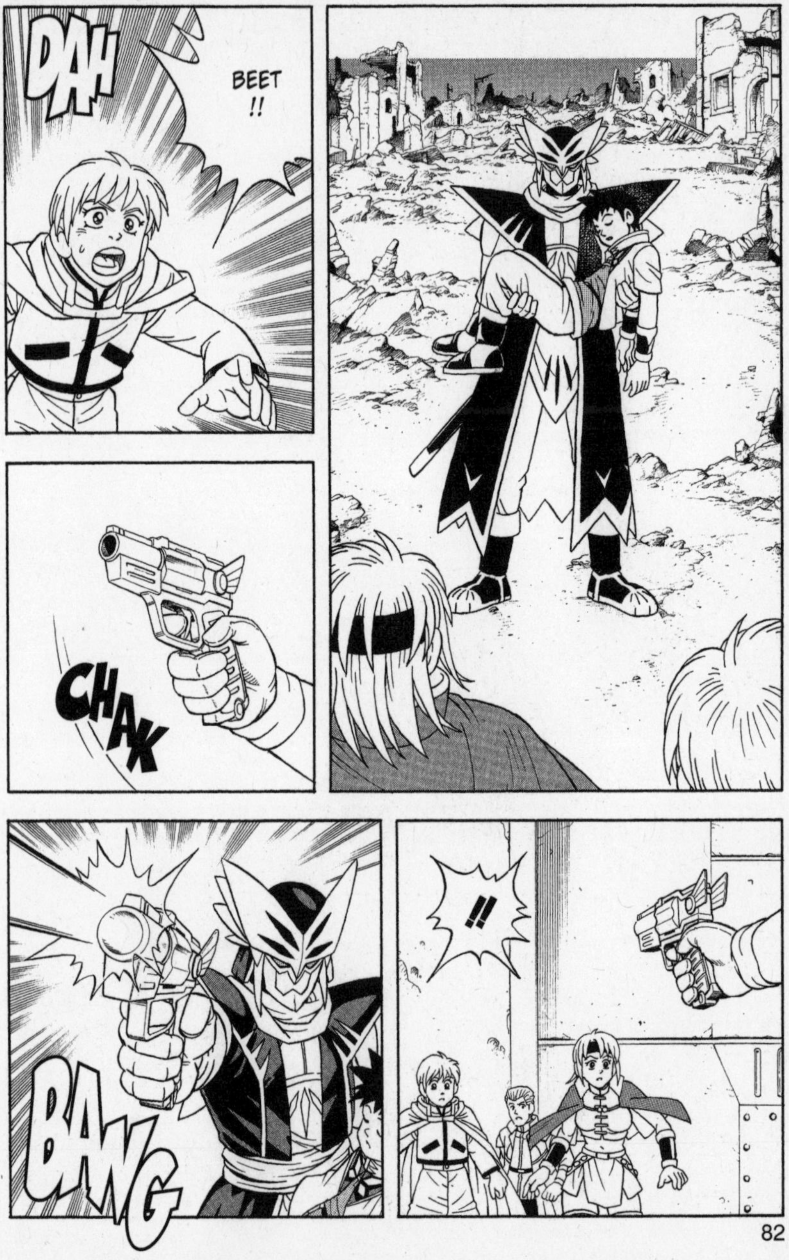
DAH
BEET !!
CHAK
!!
BANG

READ THIS WAY

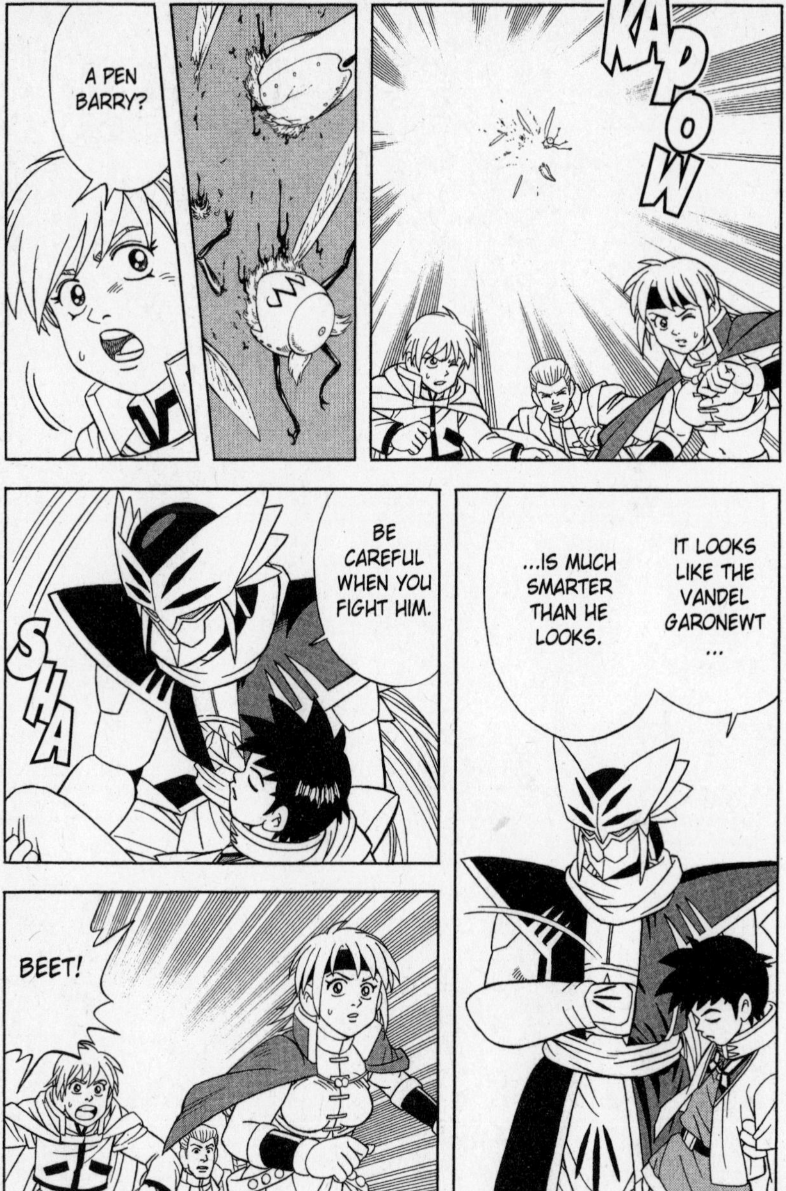
KAPOW
A PEN BARRY?
IT LOOKS LIKE THE VANDEL GARONEWT ...
...IS MUCH SMARTER THAN HE LOOKS.
BE CAREFUL WHEN YOU FIGHT HIM.
SHA
BEET!

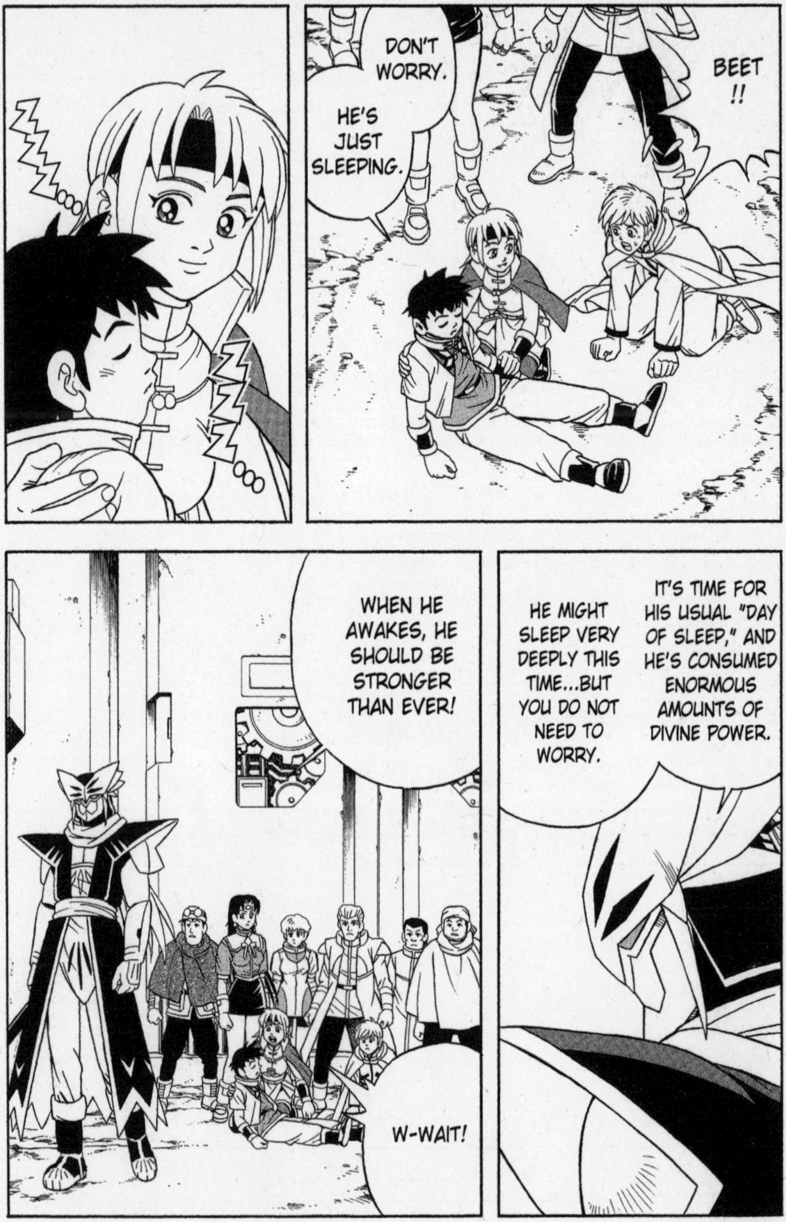
BEET !!
DON'T WORRY.
HE'S JUST SLEEPING.
IT'S TIME FOR HIS USUAL "DAY OF SLEEP," AND HE'S CONSUMED ENORMOUS AMOUNTS OF DIVINE POWER.
HE MIGHT SLEEP VERY DEEPLY THIS TIME...BUT YOU DO NOT NEED TO WORRY.
WHEN HE AWAKES, HE SHOULD BE STRONGER THAN EVER!
W-WAIT!

READ THIS WAY

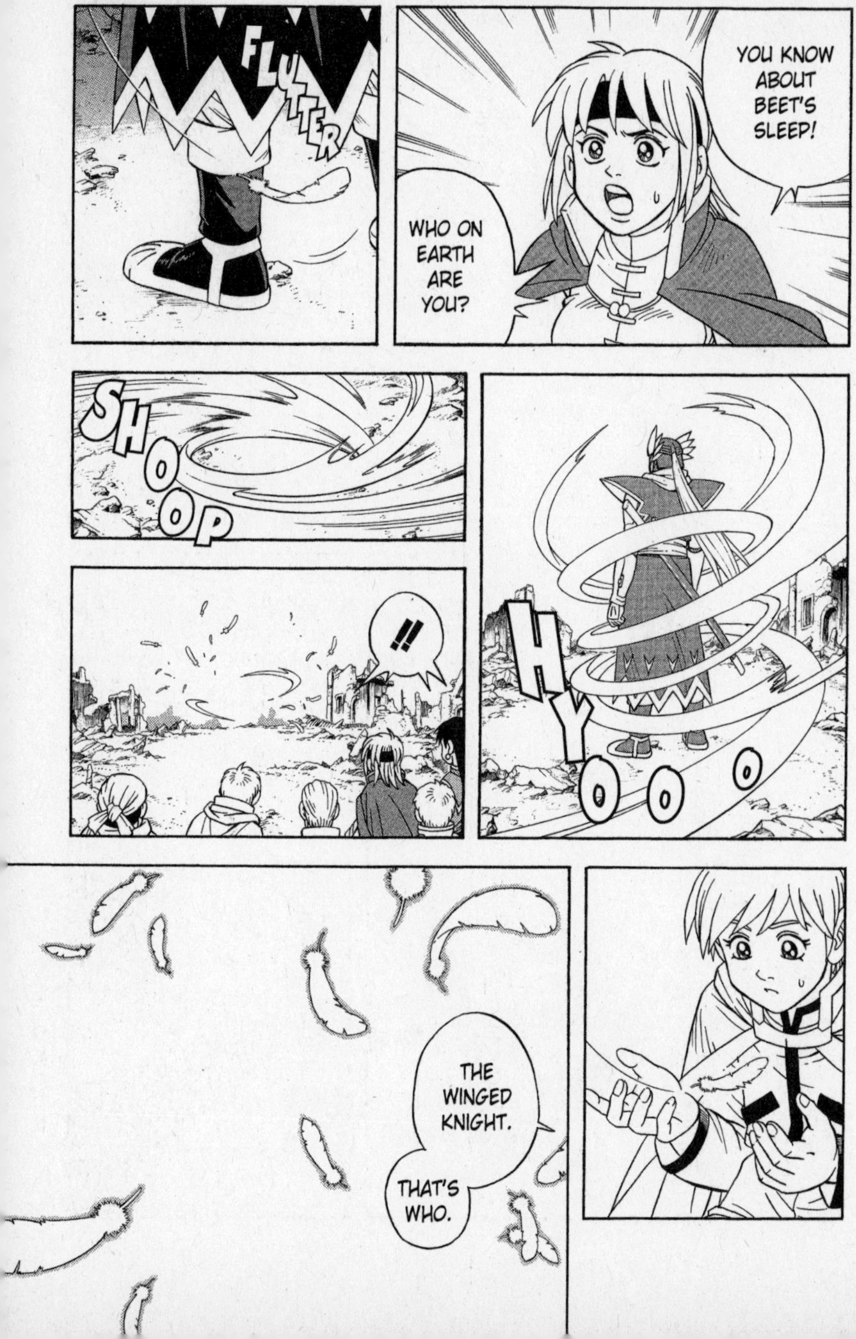
YOU KNOW ABOUT BEET'S SLEEP!
WHO ON EARTH ARE YOU?
FLUTTER
HYOOOO
SHOOOP
!!
THE WINGED KNIGHT.
THAT'S WHO.

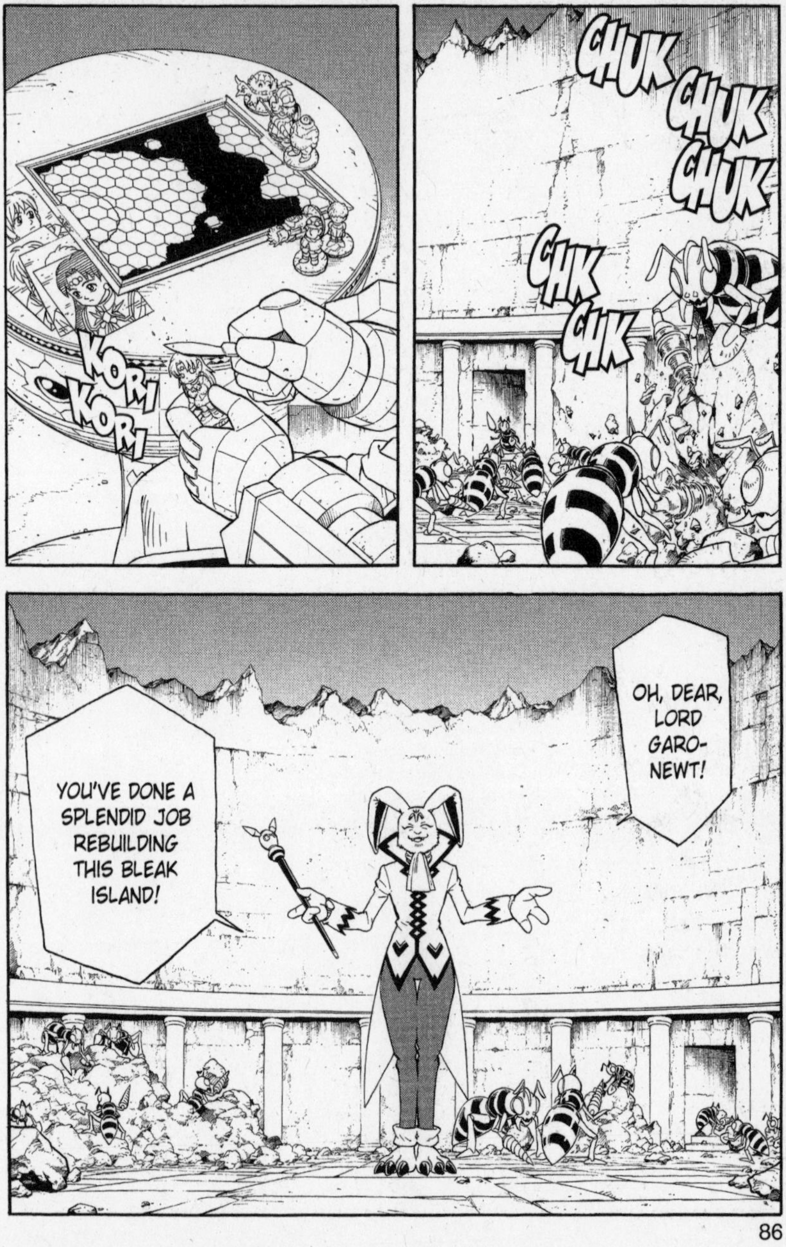
CHUK CHUK CHUK
CHK CHK
KORI KORI
OH, DEAR, LORD GARO-NEWT!
YOU'VE DONE A SPLENDID JOB REBUILDING THIS BLEAK ISLAND!

READ THIS WAY

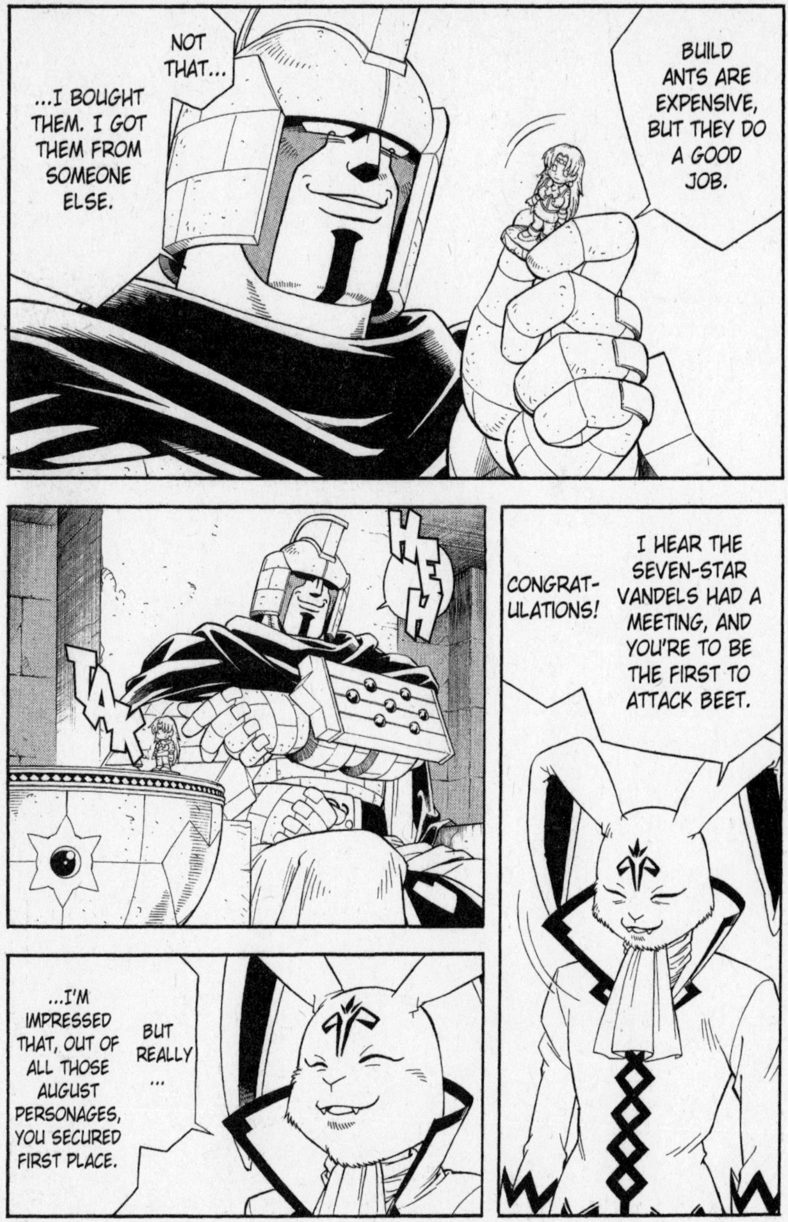
BUILD ANTS ARE EXPENSIVE, BUT THEY DO A GOOD JOB.
NOT THAT...
...I BOUGHT THEM. I GOT THEM FROM SOMEONE ELSE.
I HEAR THE SEVEN-STAR VANDELS HAD A MEETING, AND YOU'RE TO BE THE FIRST TO ATTACK BEET.
CONGRAT-ULATIONS!
HEH
TAK
BUT REALLY...
...I'M IMPRESSED THAT, OUT OF ALL THOSE AUGUST PERSONAGES, YOU SECURED FIRST PLACE.

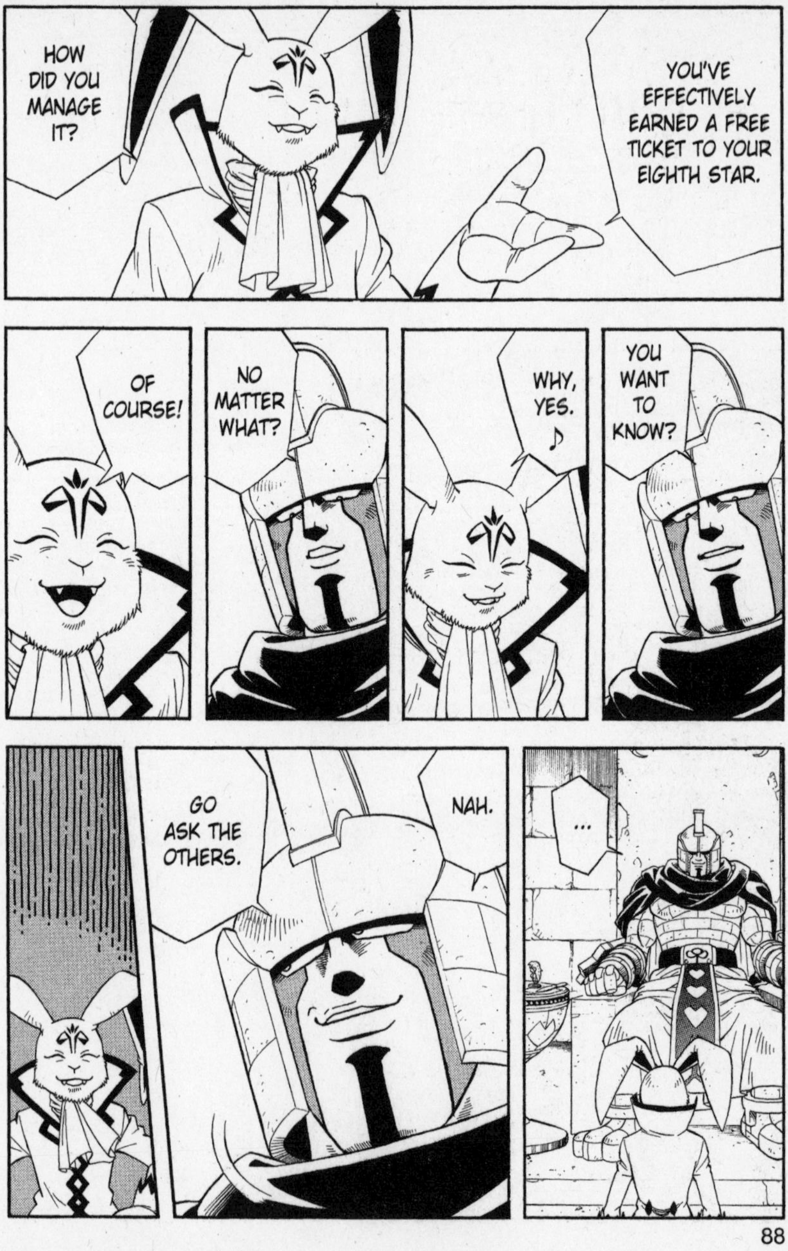
YOU'VE EFFECTIVELY EARNED A FREE TICKET TO YOUR EIGHTH STAR.
HOW DID YOU MANAGE IT?
YOU WANT TO KNOW?
WHY, YES. ♪
NO MATTER WHAT?
OF COURSE!
...
NAH.
GO ASK THE OTHERS.

READ THIS WAY

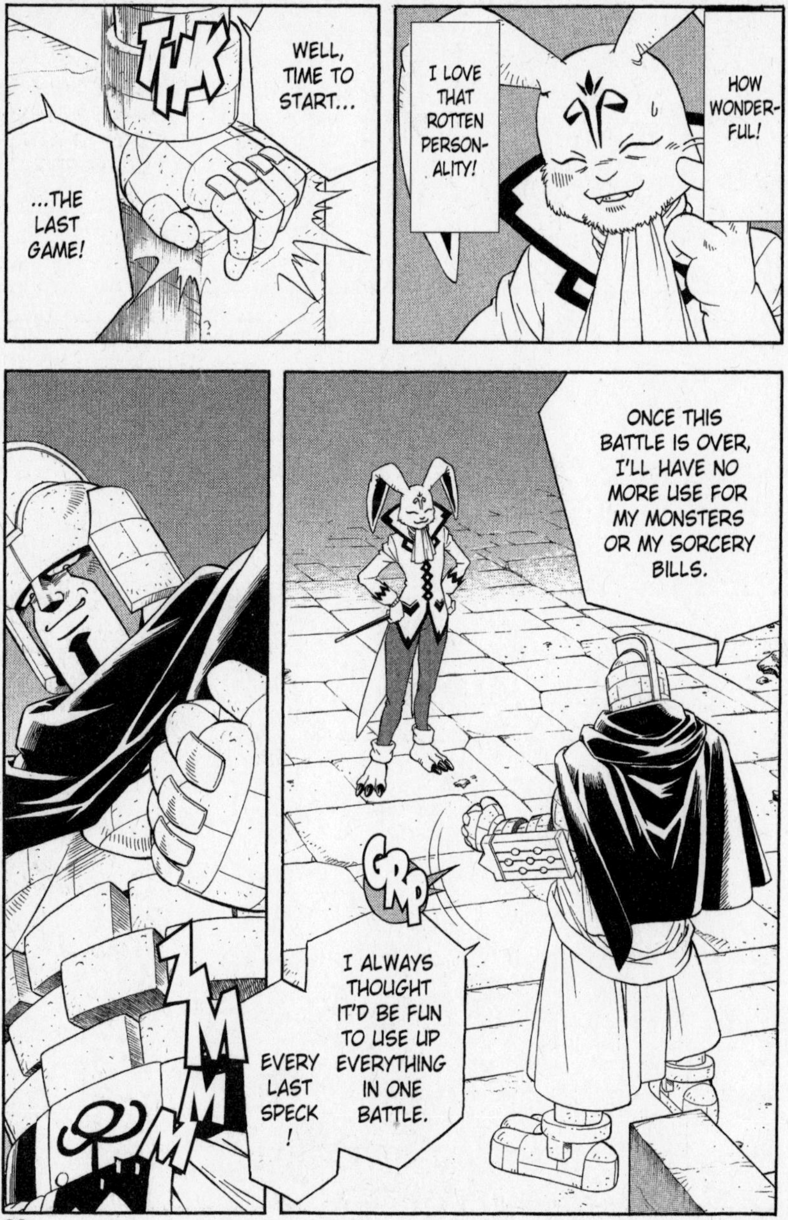
HOW WONDERFUL!
I LOVE THAT ROTTEN PERSONALITY!
WELL, TIME TO START...
THK
...THE LAST GAME!
ONCE THIS BATTLE IS OVER, I'LL HAVE NO MORE USE FOR MY MONSTERS OR MY SORCERY BILLS.
GRP
I ALWAYS THOUGHT IT'D BE FUN TO USE UP EVERYTHING IN ONE BATTLE.
EVERY LAST SPECK!
ZMMM

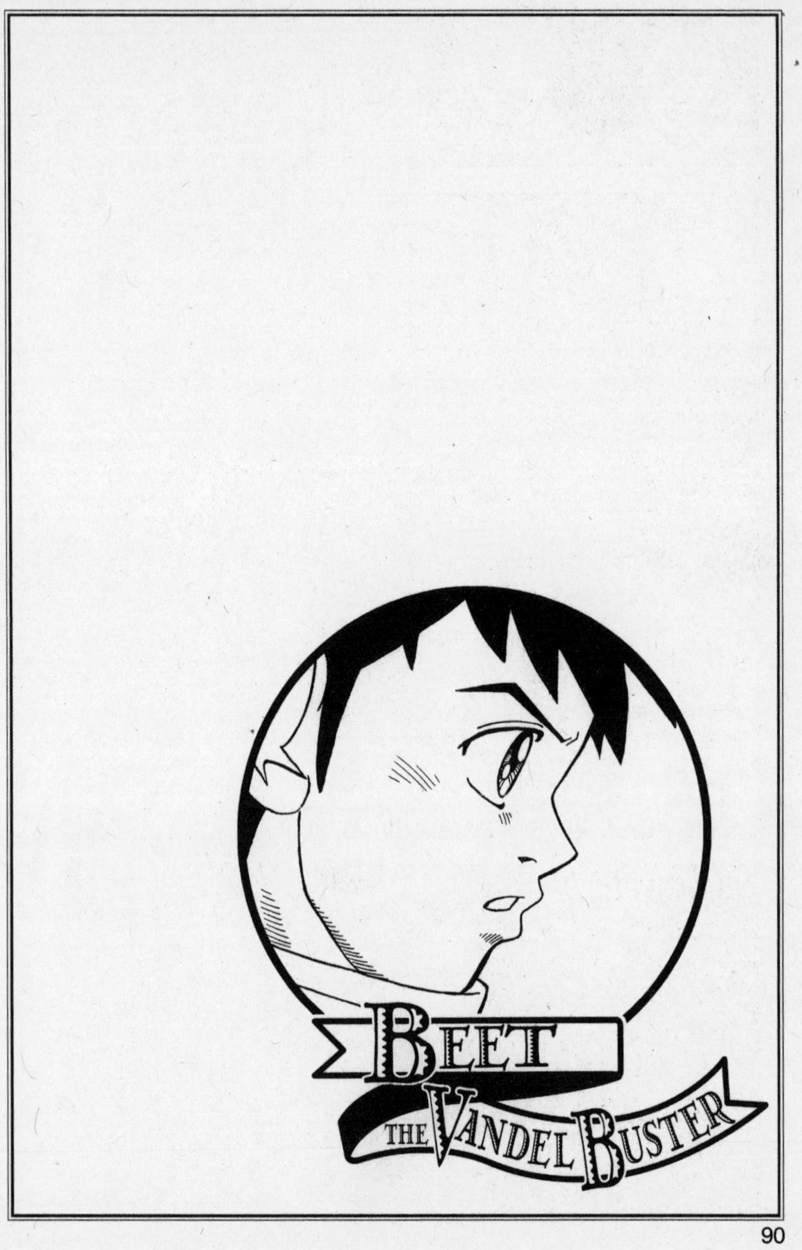
BEET
THE VANDEL BUSTER

Chapter 32: Cain's True Identity

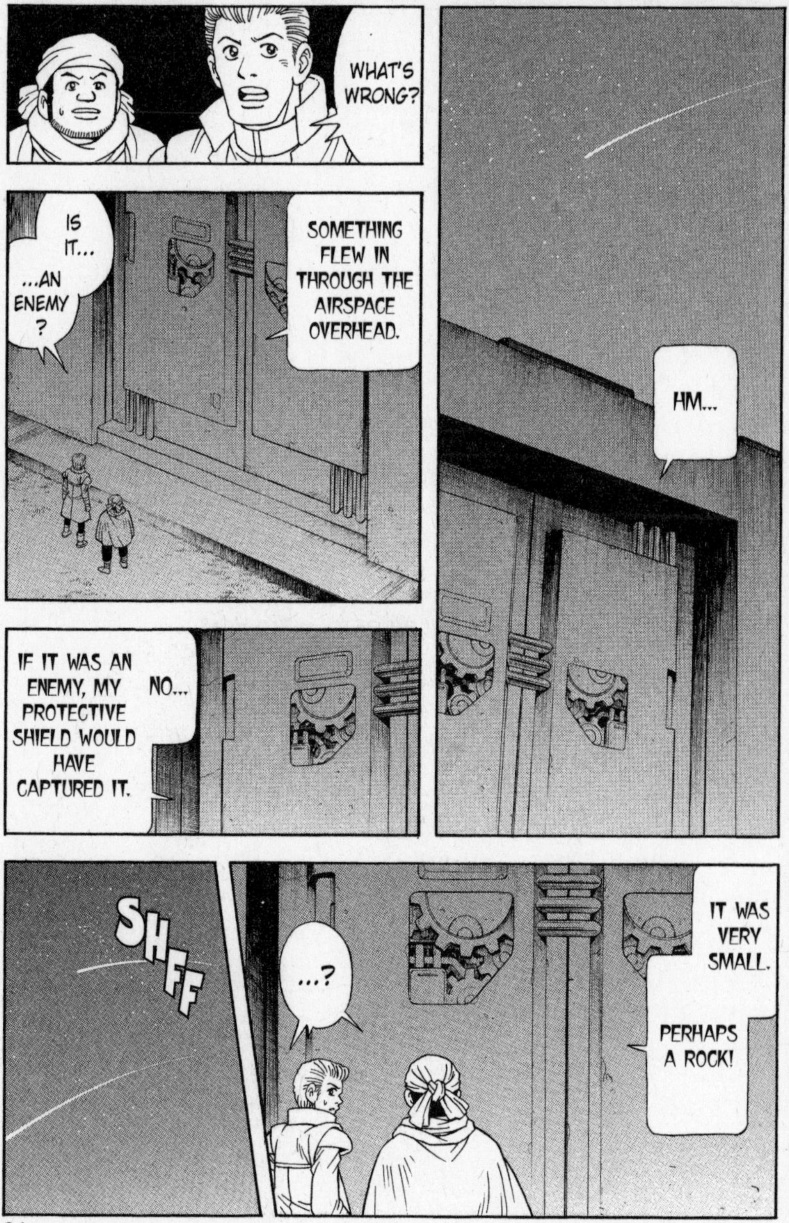
HM...
WHAT'S WRONG?
SOMETHING FLEW IN THROUGH THE AIRSPACE OVERHEAD.
IS IT...
...AN ENEMY?
NO...
IF IT WAS AN ENEMY, MY PROTECTIVE SHIELD WOULD HAVE CAPTURED IT.
IT WAS VERY SMALL.
PERHAPS A ROCK!
...?
SHFF

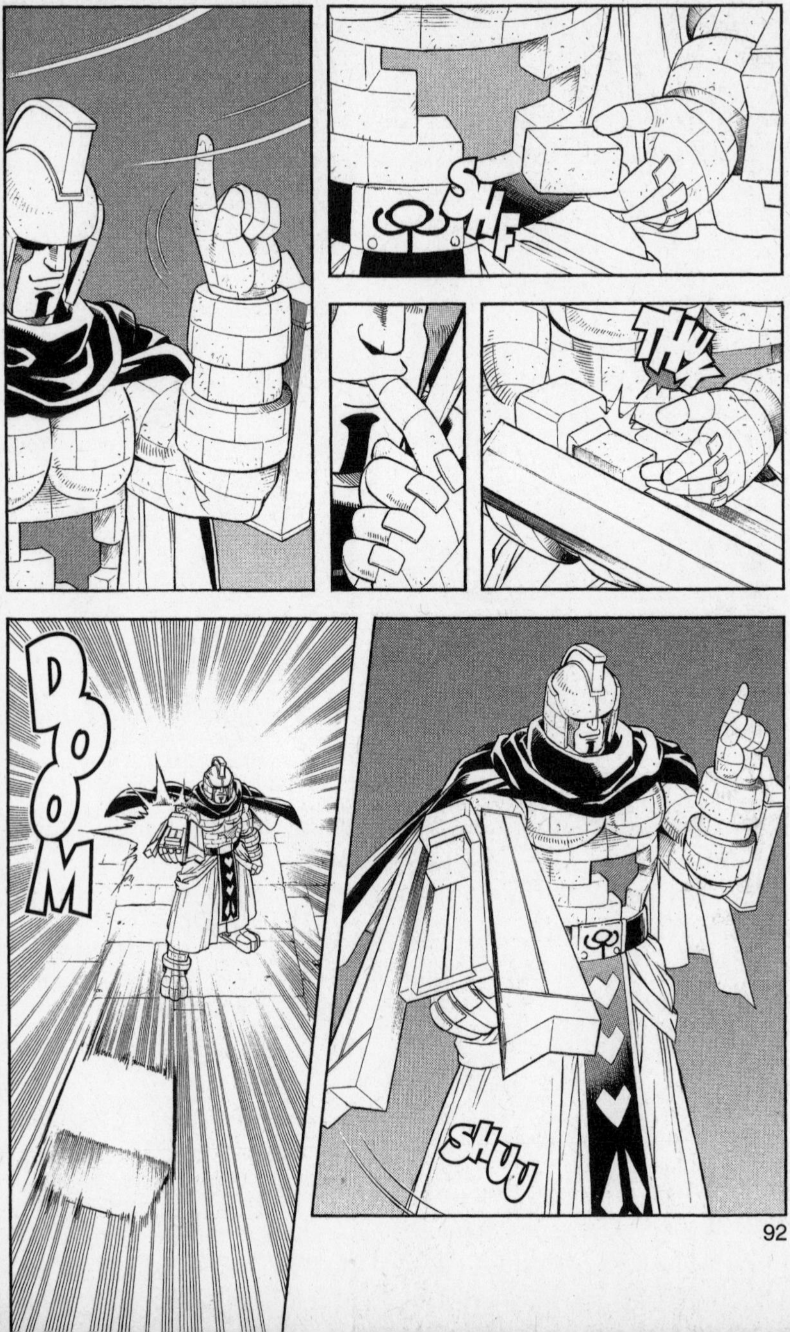
SHF
THUK
SHUU
DOOM

READ THIS WAY

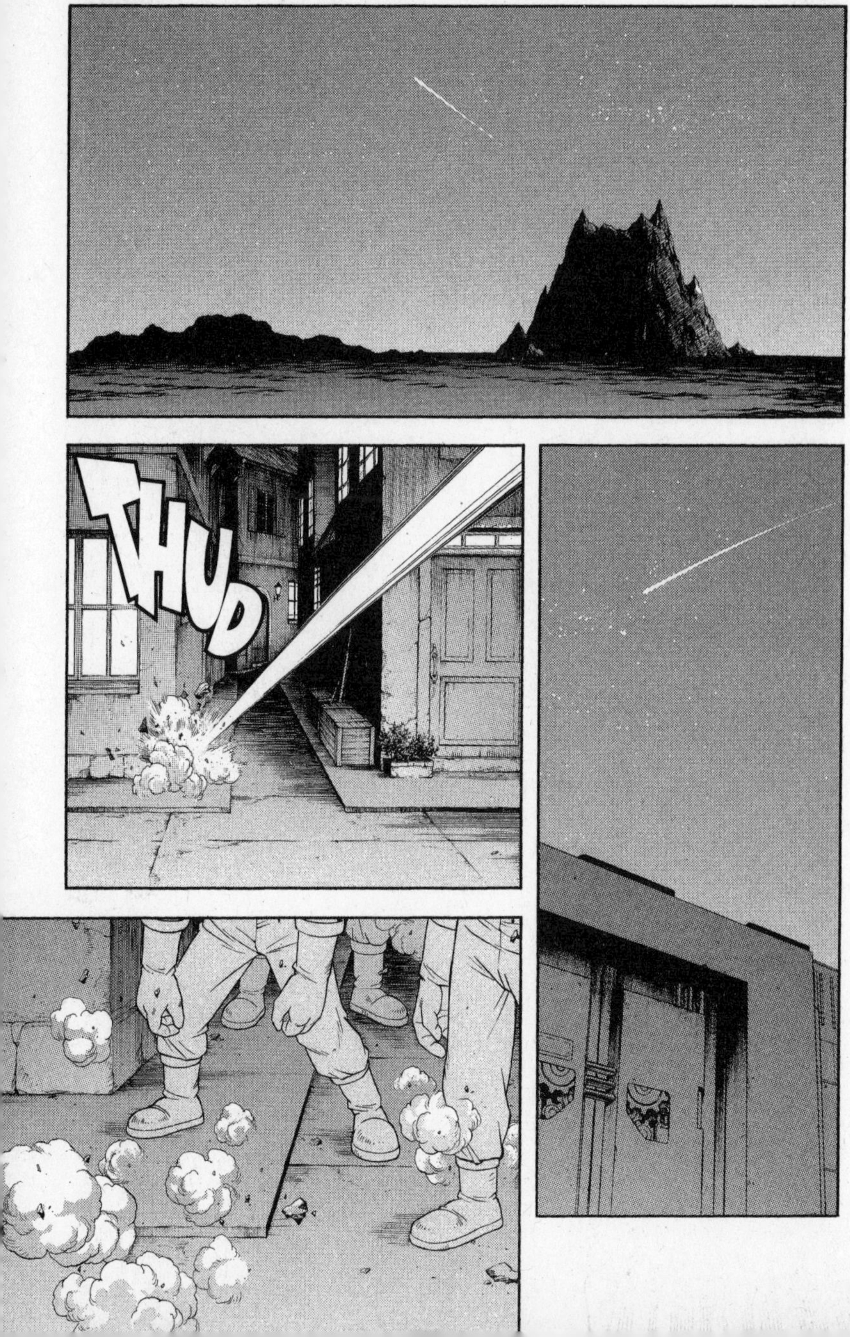
THUD

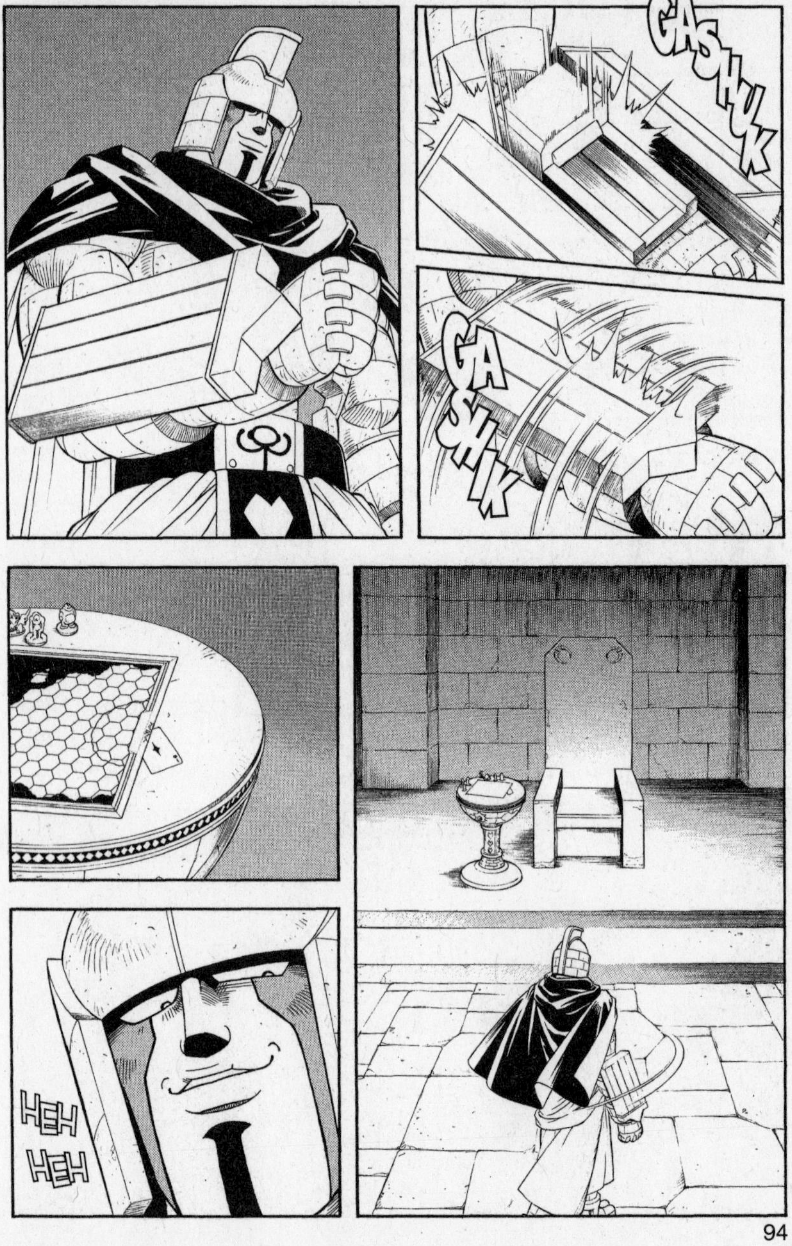
GASHUK
GA SHIK
HEH HEH

READ THIS WAY

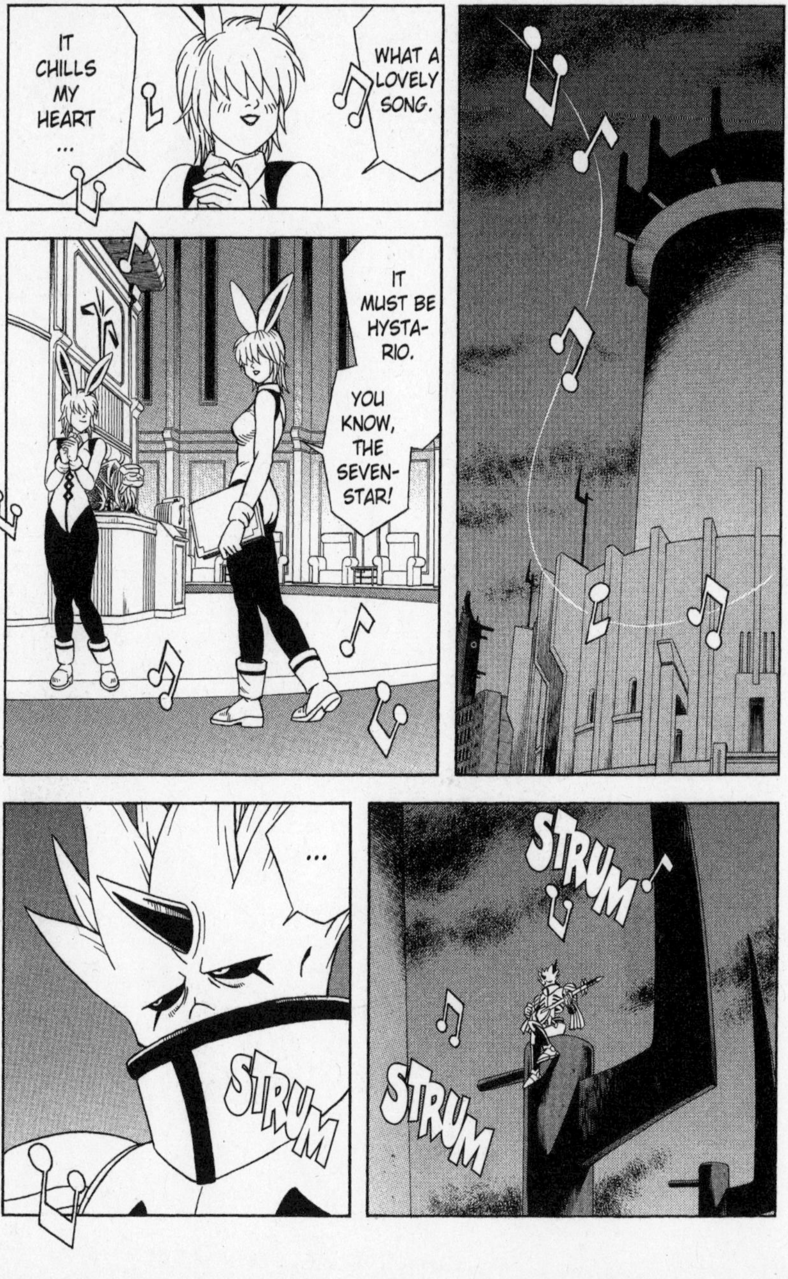
WHAT A LOVELY SONG.
IT CHILLS MY HEART...
IT MUST BE HYSTARIO.
YOU KNOW, THE SEVEN-STAR!
STRUM
STRUM
...
STRUM

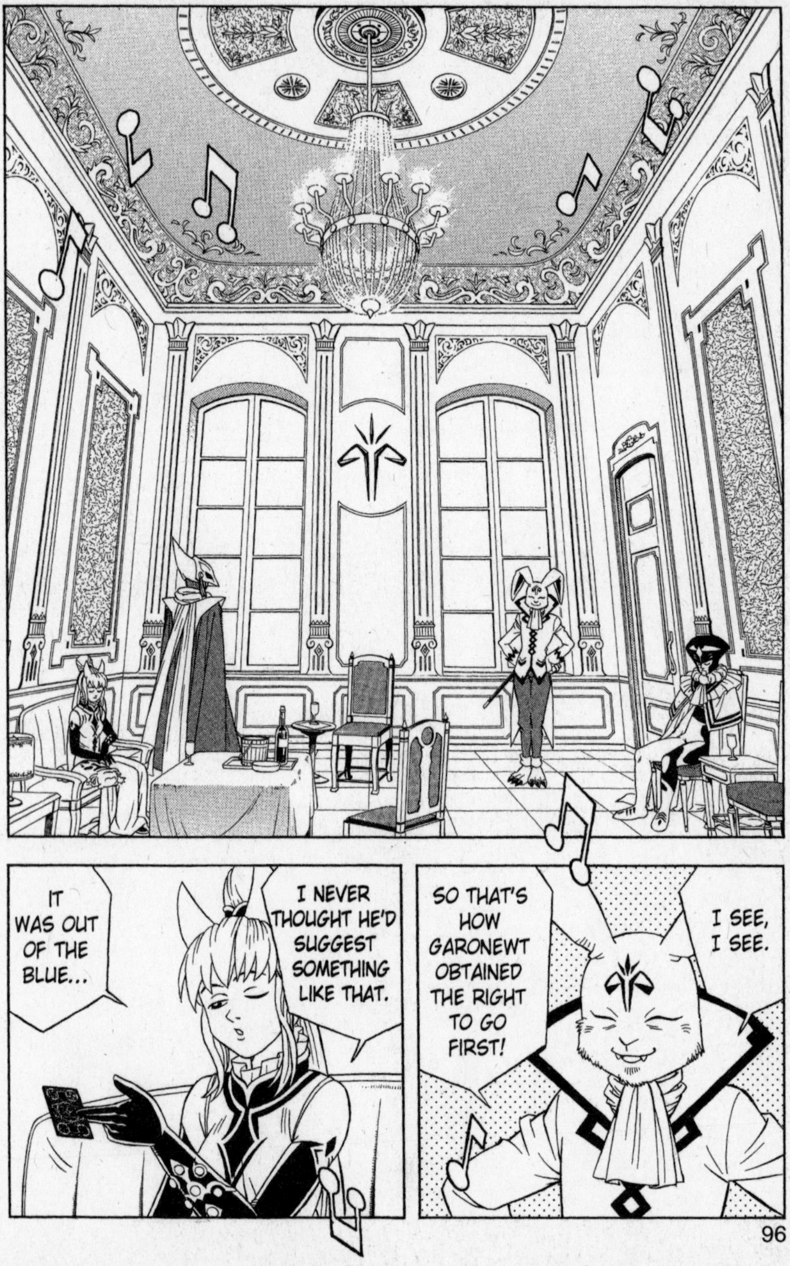
I SEE, I SEE.
SO THAT'S HOW GARONEWT OBTAINED THE RIGHT TO GO FIRST!
I NEVER THOUGHT HE'D SUGGEST SOMETHING LIKE THAT.
IT WAS OUT OF THE BLUE...

READ THIS WAY

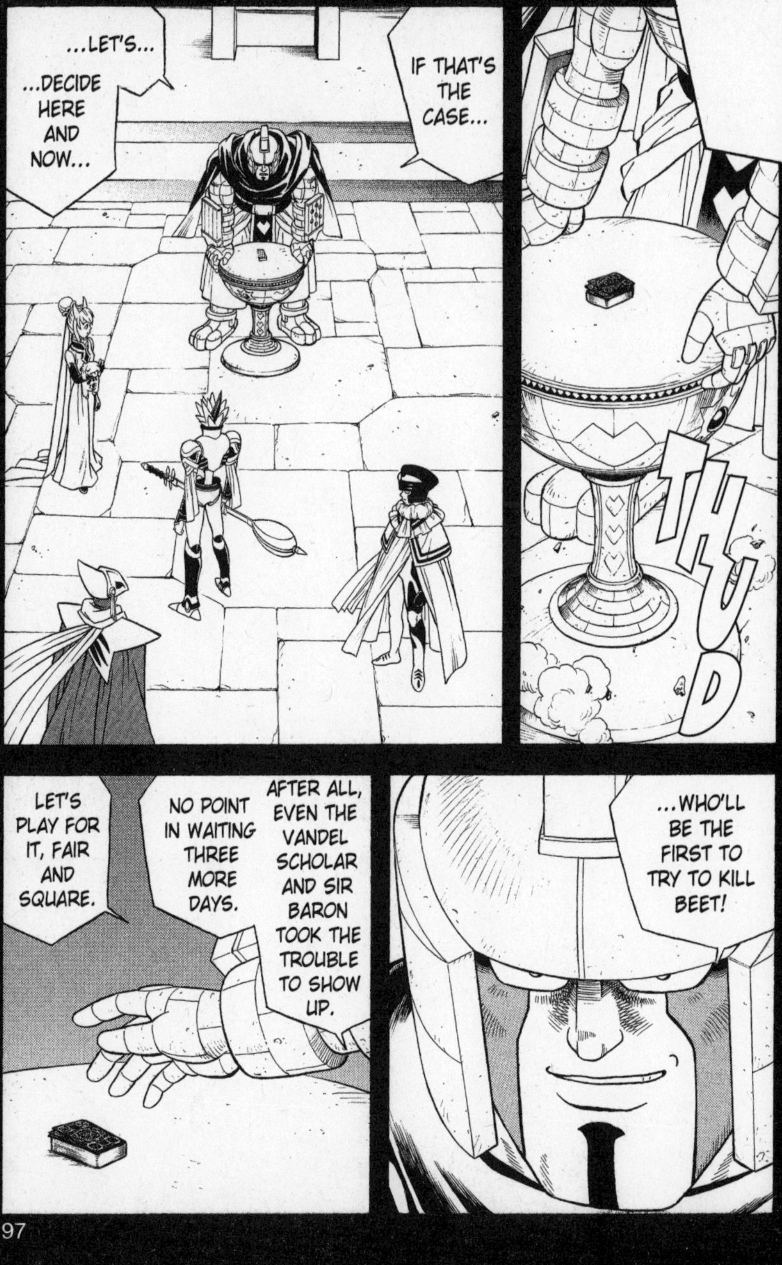
THUD
IF THAT'S THE CASE...
...LET'S...
...DECIDE HERE AND NOW...
...WHO'LL BE THE FIRST TO TRY TO KILL BEET!
AFTER ALL, EVEN THE VANDEL SCHOLAR AND SIR BARON TOOK THE TROUBLE TO SHOW UP.
NO POINT IN WAITING THREE MORE DAYS.
LET'S PLAY FOR IT, FAIR AND SQUARE.

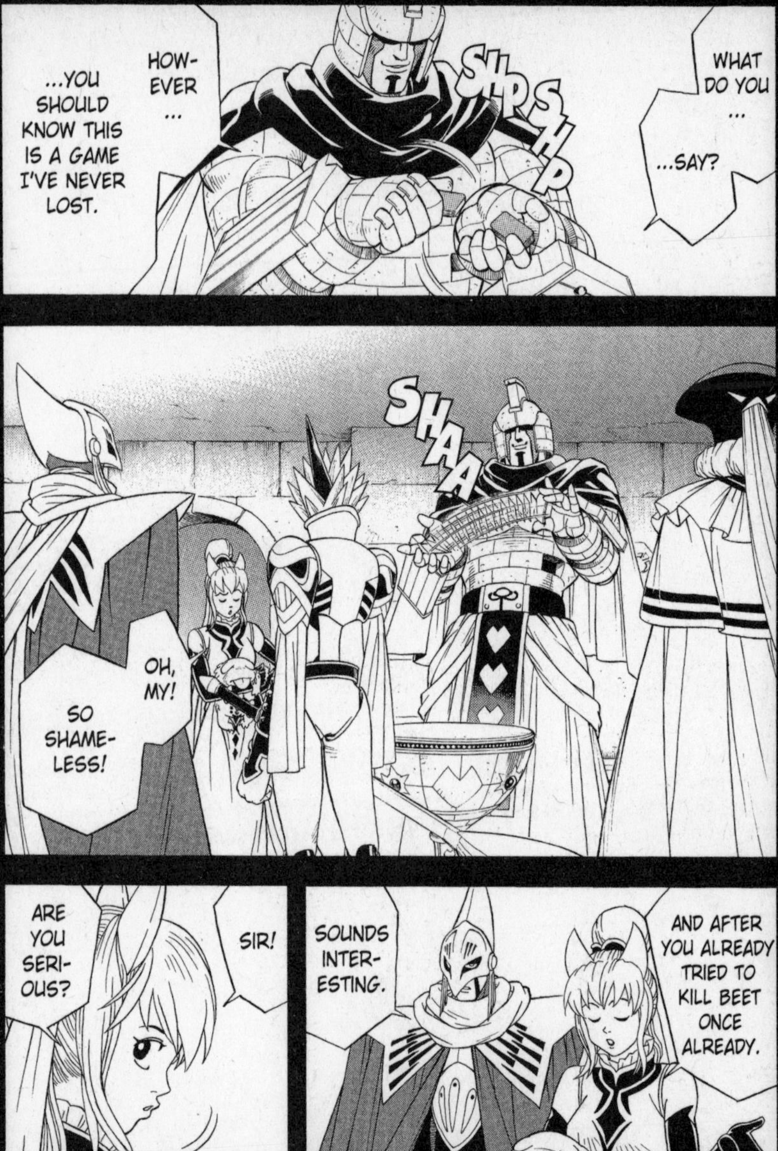
WHAT DO YOU ... ...SAY?
SHP SHP
HOW-EVER ...
...YOU SHOULD KNOW THIS IS A GAME I'VE NEVER LOST.
SHAAA
OH, MY!
SO SHAME-LESS!
AND AFTER YOU ALREADY TRIED TO KILL BEET ONCE ALREADY.
SOUNDS INTER-ESTING.
SIR!
ARE YOU SERI-OUS?

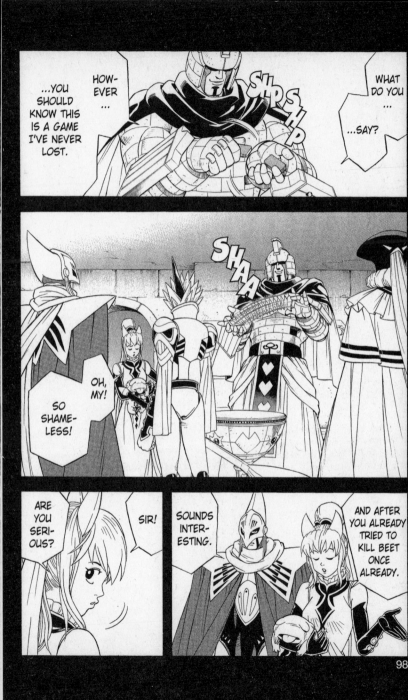

READ THIS WAY

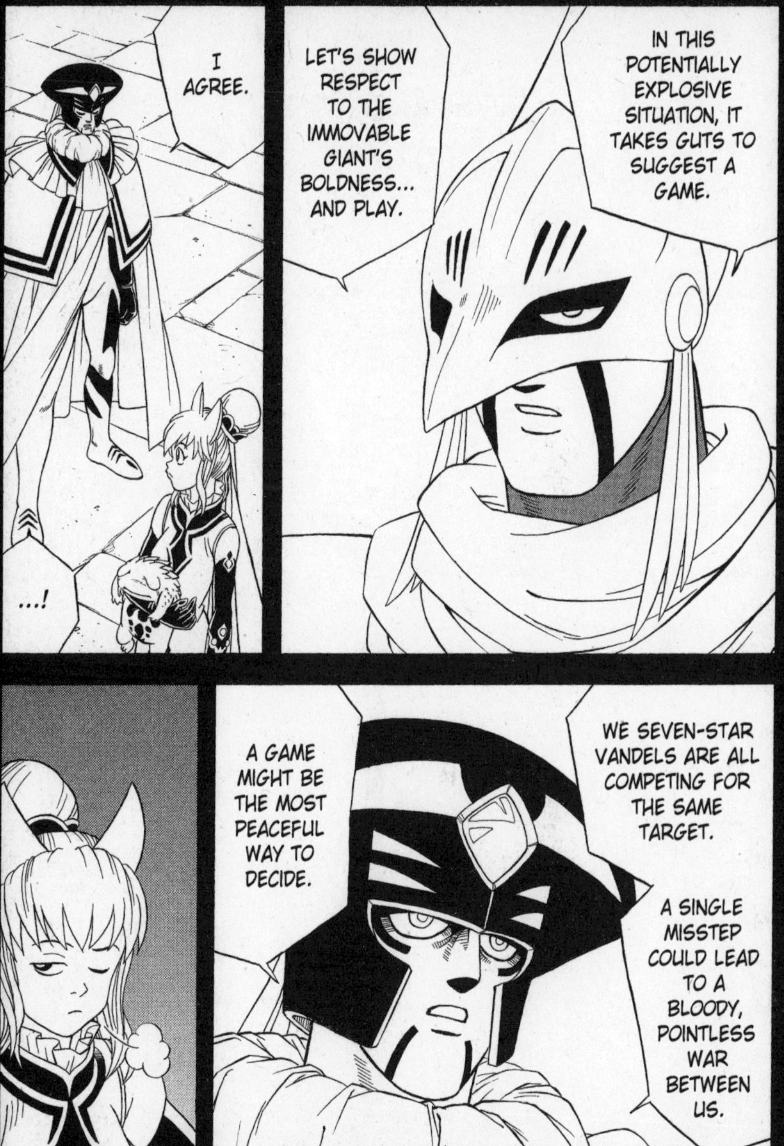

IN THIS POTENTIALLY EXPLOSIVE SITUATION, IT TAKES GUTS TO SUGGEST A GAME.
LET'S SHOW RESPECT TO THE IMMOVABLE GIANT'S BOLDNESS... AND PLAY.
I AGREE.
...!
WE SEVEN-STAR VANDELS ARE ALL COMPETING FOR THE SAME TARGET.
A SINGLE MISSTEP COULD LEAD TO A BLOODY, POINTLESS WAR BETWEEN US.
A GAME MIGHT BE THE MOST PEACEFUL WAY TO DECIDE.

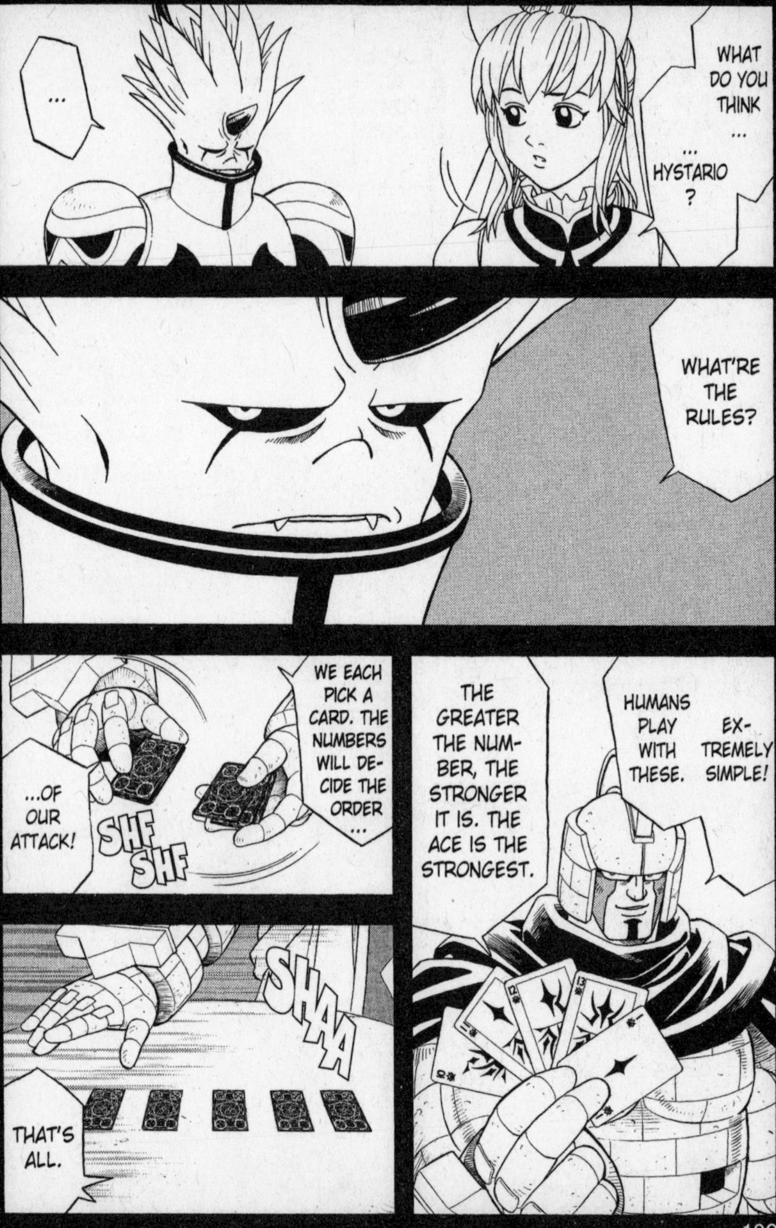
WHAT DO YOU THINK ... ... HYSTARIO ?
...
WHAT'RE THE RULES?
EX-TREMELY SIMPLE!
HUMANS PLAY WITH THESE.
THE GREATER THE NUM-BER, THE STRONGER IT IS. THE ACE IS THE STRONGEST.
WE EACH PICK A CARD. THE NUMBERS WILL DE-CIDE THE ORDER ...
...OF OUR ATTACK!
SHF SHF
SHAA
THAT'S ALL.

READ THIS WAY

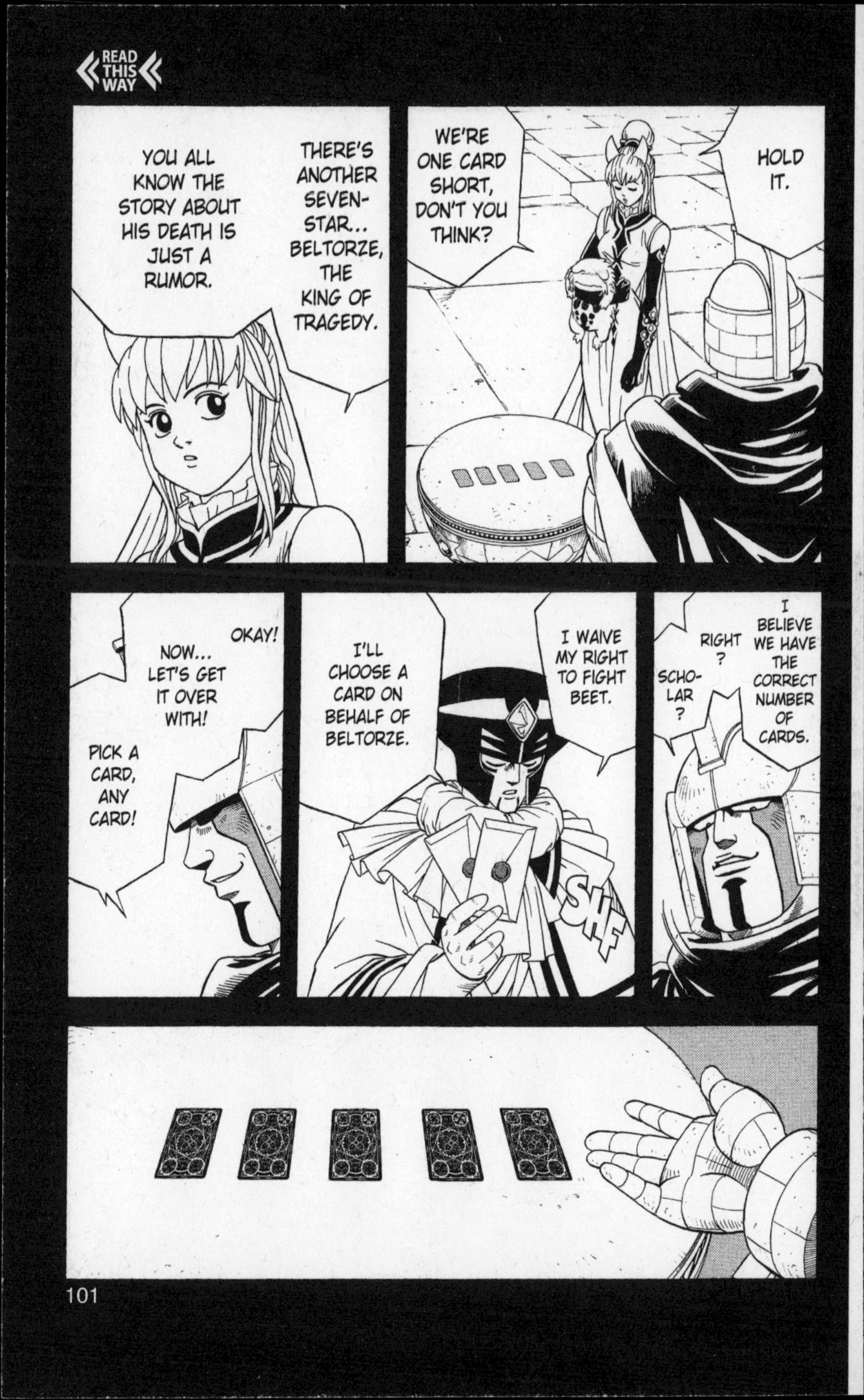
HOLD IT.
WE'RE ONE CARD SHORT, DON'T YOU THINK?
THERE'S ANOTHER SEVEN-STAR... BELTORZE, THE KING OF TRAGEDY.
YOU ALL KNOW THE STORY ABOUT HIS DEATH IS JUST A RUMOR.
I BELIEVE WE HAVE THE CORRECT NUMBER OF CARDS.
RIGHT?
SCHOLAR?
I WAIVE MY RIGHT TO FIGHT BEET.
I'LL CHOOSE A CARD ON BEHALF OF BELTORZE.
SHF
OKAY!
NOW... LET'S GET IT OVER WITH!
PICK A CARD, ANY CARD!

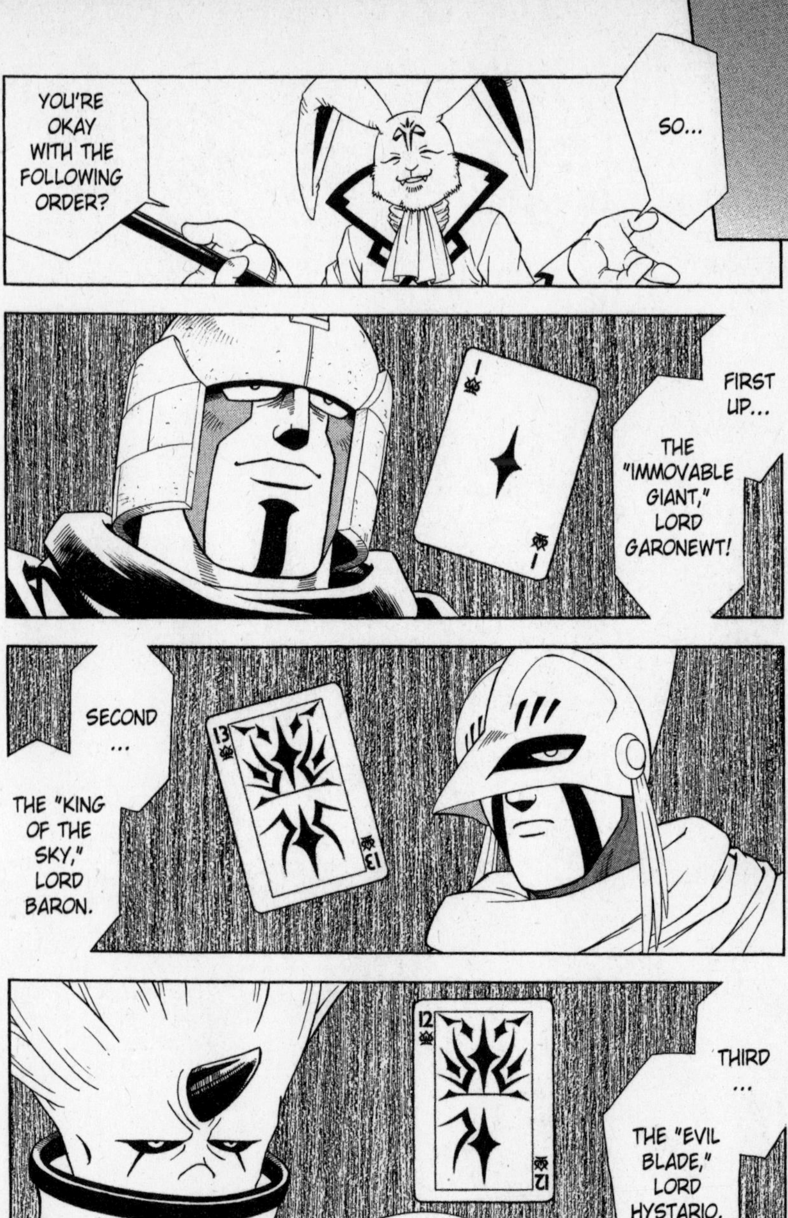
SO...
YOU'RE OKAY WITH THE FOLLOWING ORDER?
FIRST UP...
THE "IMMOVABLE GIANT," LORD GARONEWT!
SECOND ...
THE "KING OF THE SKY," LORD BARON.
THIRD ...
THE "EVIL BLADE," LORD HYSTARIO.

READ THIS WAY

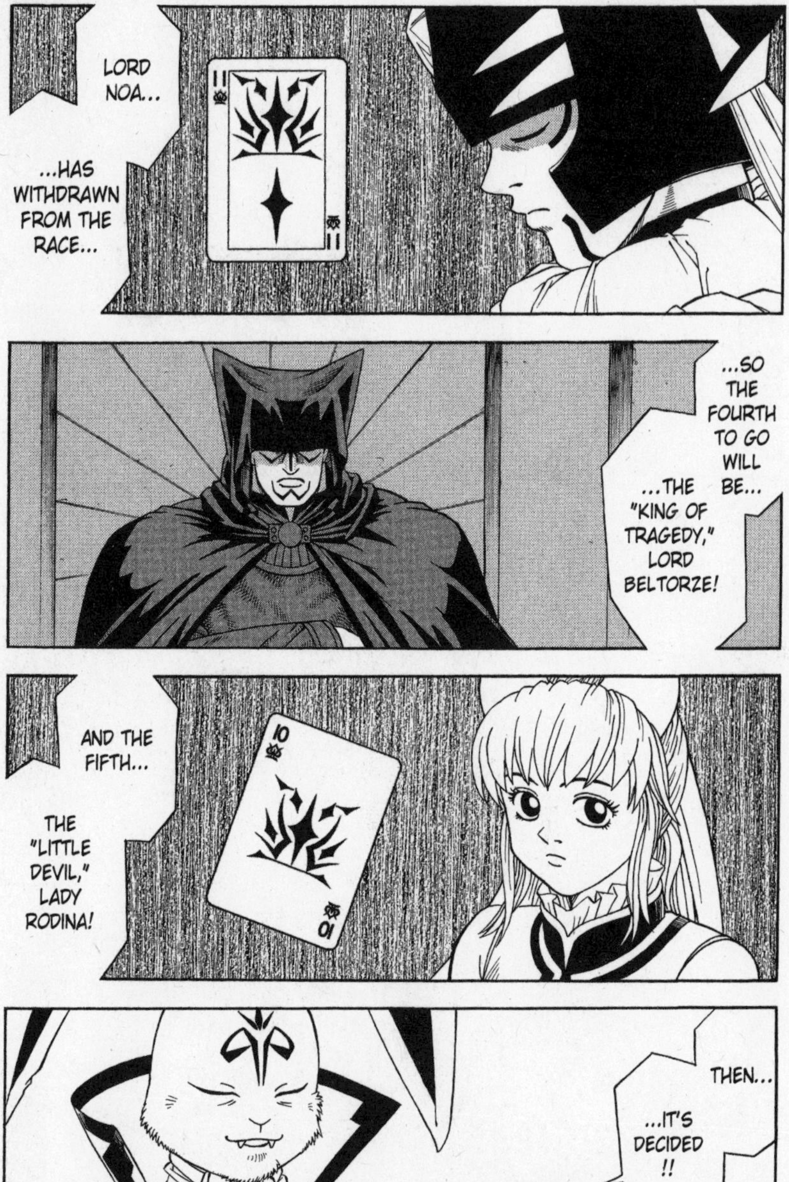
LORD NOA...
...HAS WITHDRAWN FROM THE RACE...
...SO THE FOURTH TO GO WILL BE...
...THE "KING OF TRAGEDY," LORD BELTORZE!
AND THE FIFTH...
THE "LITTLE DEVIL," LADY RODINA!
THEN...
...IT'S DECIDED !!

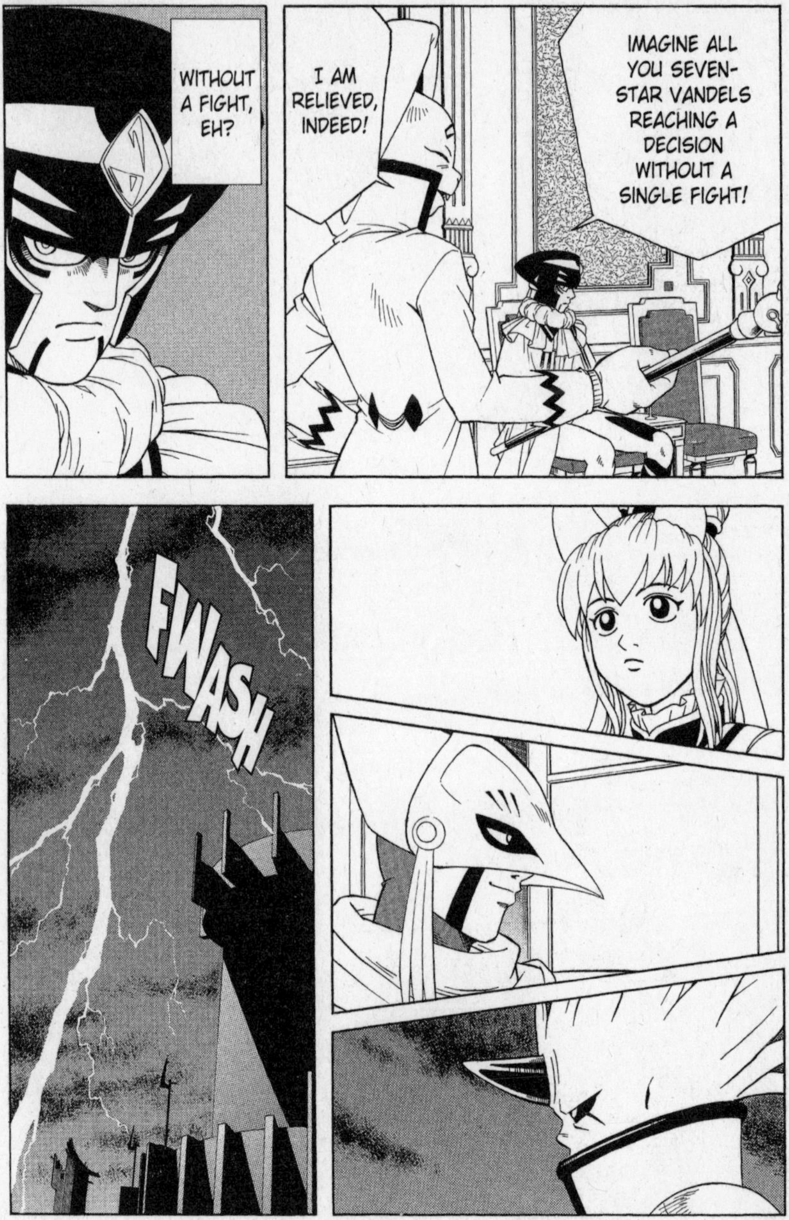
IMAGINE ALL YOU SEVEN-STAR VANDELS REACHING A DECISION WITHOUT A SINGLE FIGHT!
I AM RELIEVED, INDEED!
WITHOUT A FIGHT, EH?
FWASH

READ THIS WAY

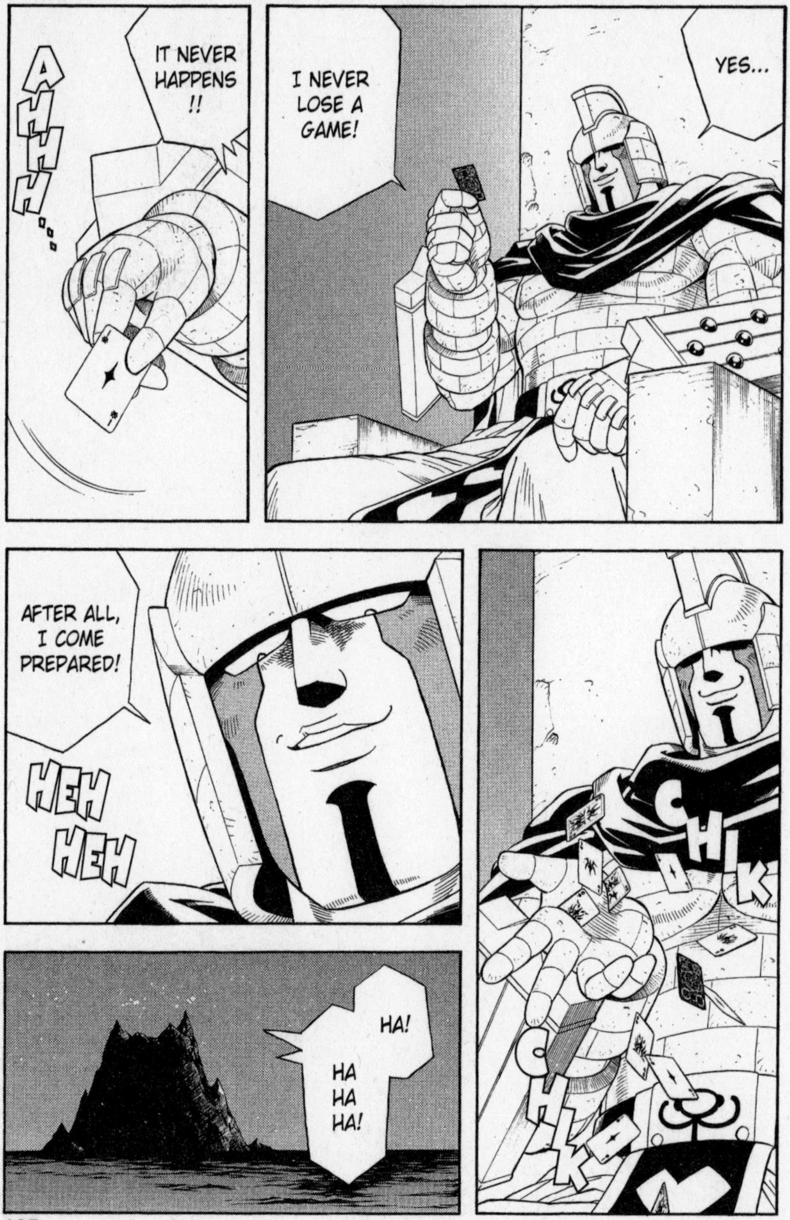

YES...
I NEVER LOSE A GAME!
IT NEVER HAPPENS!!
AHHHH...
CHIK
CHIK
AFTER ALL, I COME PREPARED!
HEH HEH
HA!
HA HA HA!

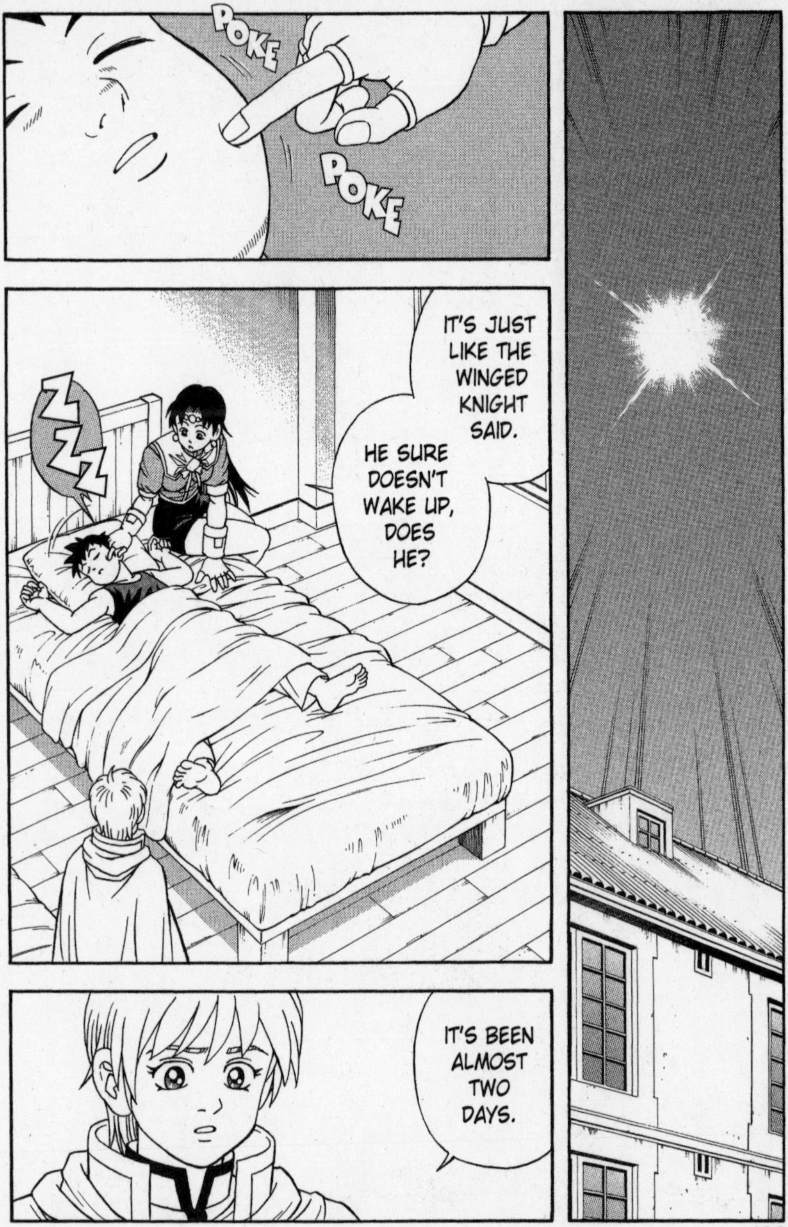
POKE
POKE
IT'S JUST LIKE THE WINGED KNIGHT SAID.
HE SURE DOESN'T WAKE UP, DOES HE?
ZZZ
IT'S BEEN ALMOST TWO DAYS.

READ THIS WAY

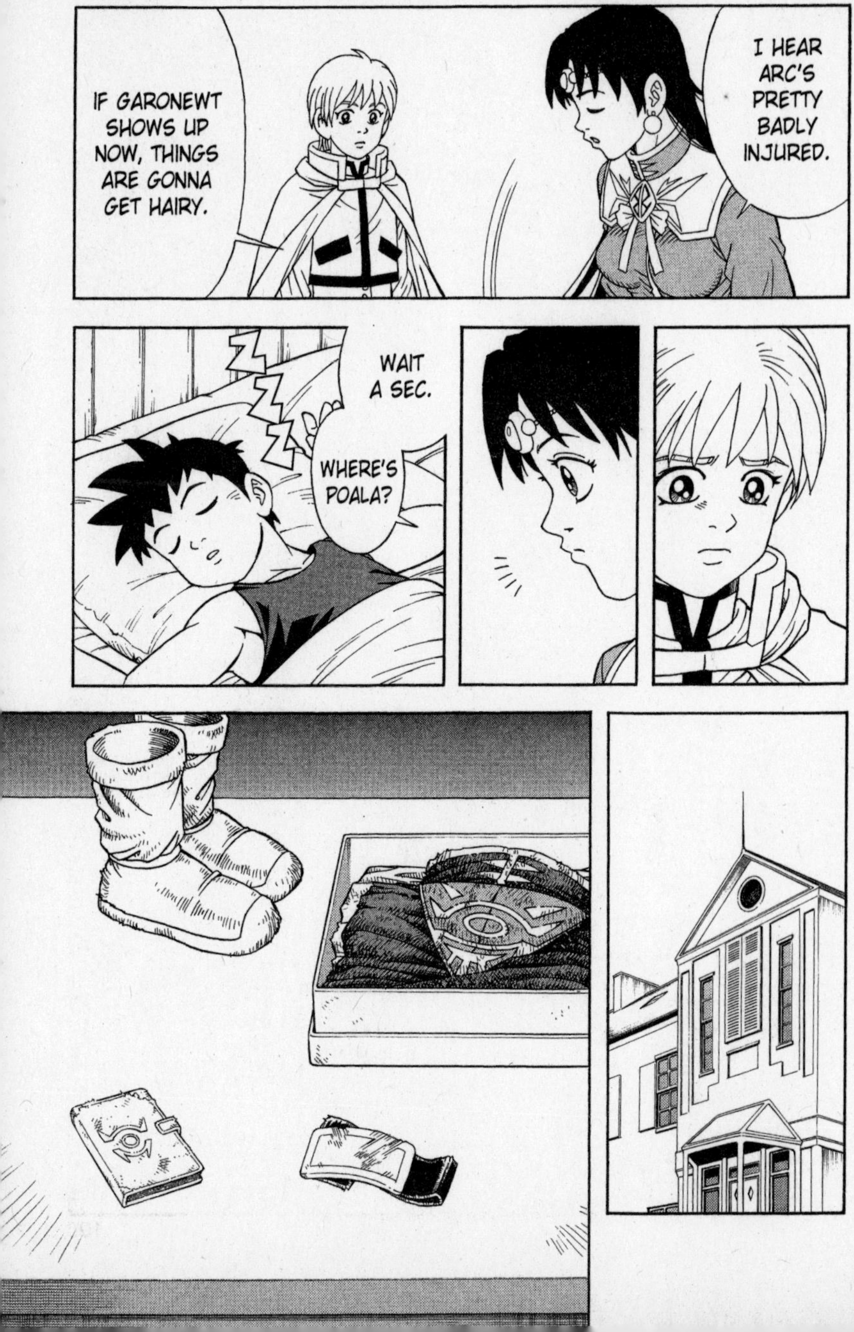
I HEAR ARC'S PRETTY BADLY INJURED.
IF GARONEWT SHOWS UP NOW, THINGS ARE GONNA GET HAIRY.
WAIT A SEC.
WHERE'S POALA?

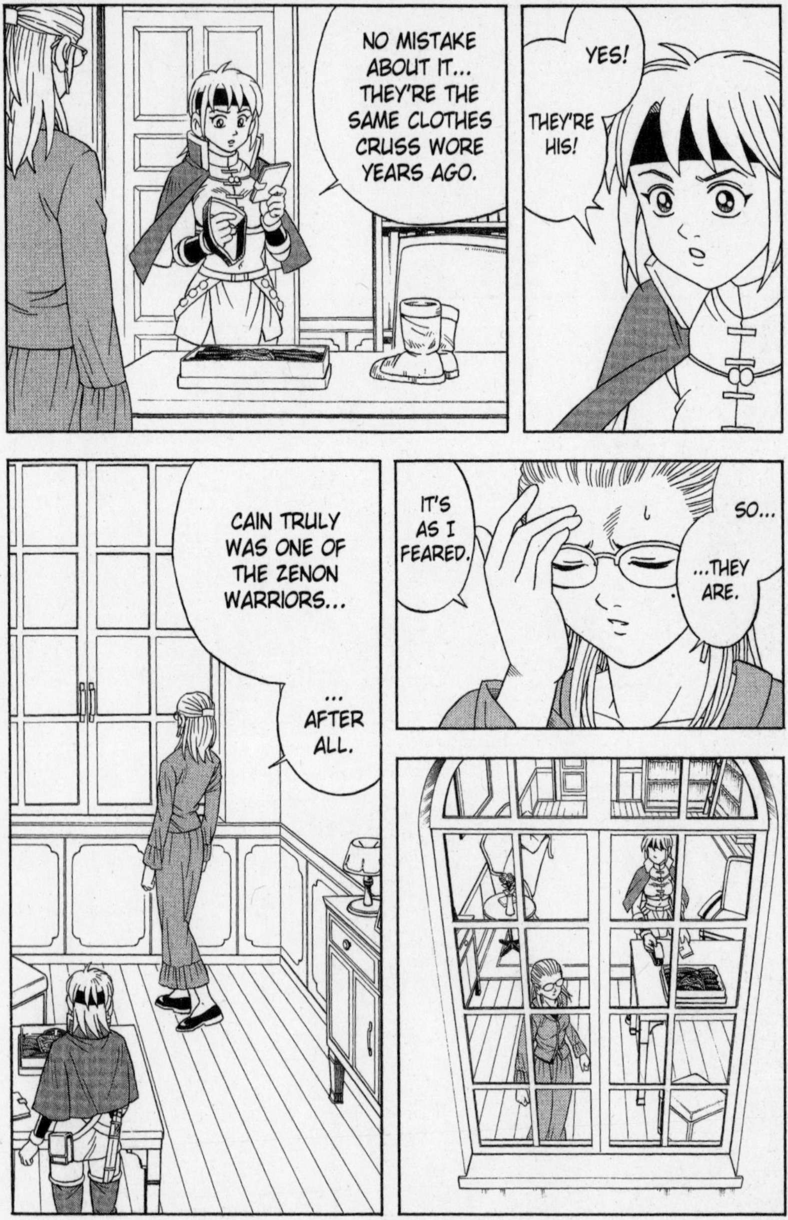
YES!
THEY'RE HIS!
NO MISTAKE ABOUT IT... THEY'RE THE SAME CLOTHES CRUSS WORE YEARS AGO.
SO...
...THEY ARE.
IT'S AS I FEARED.
CAIN TRULY WAS ONE OF THE ZENON WARRIORS...
... AFTER ALL.

READ THIS WAY

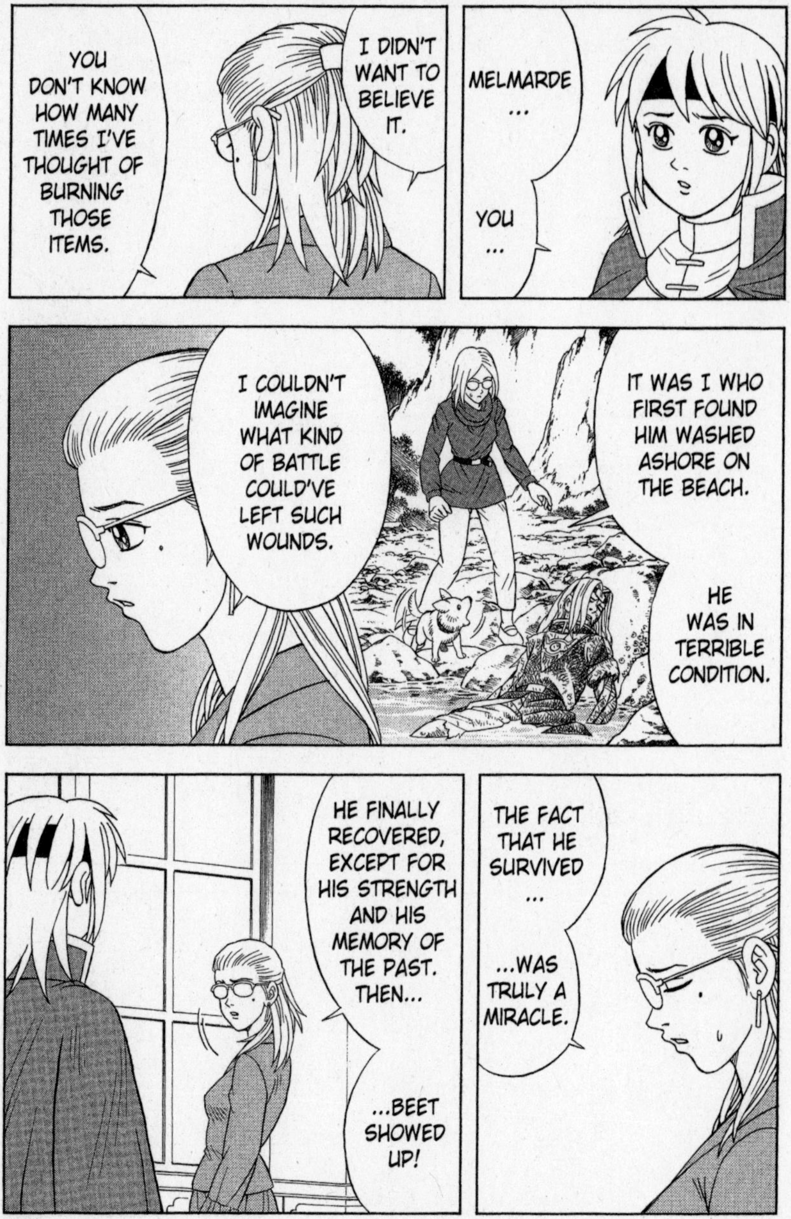

MELMARDE ...
YOU ...
I DIDN'T WANT TO BELIEVE IT.
YOU DON'T KNOW HOW MANY TIMES I'VE THOUGHT OF BURNING THOSE ITEMS.
IT WAS I WHO FIRST FOUND HIM WASHED ASHORE ON THE BEACH.
HE WAS IN TERRIBLE CONDITION.
I COULDN'T IMAGINE WHAT KIND OF BATTLE COULD'VE LEFT SUCH WOUNDS.
THE FACT THAT HE SURVIVED ...
...WAS TRULY A MIRACLE.
HE FINALLY RECOVERED, EXCEPT FOR HIS STRENGTH AND HIS MEMORY OF THE PAST. THEN...
...BEET SHOWED UP!

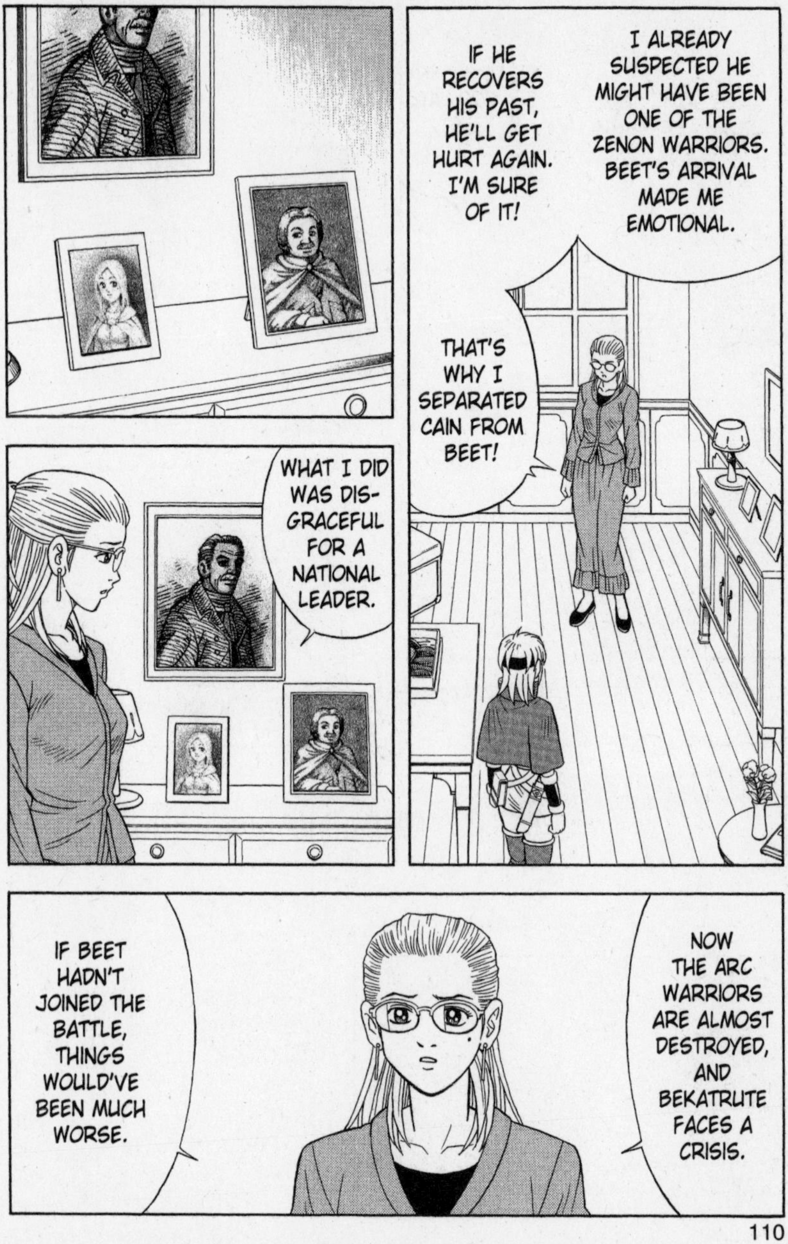
I ALREADY SUSPECTED HE MIGHT HAVE BEEN ONE OF THE ZENON WARRIORS. BEET'S ARRIVAL MADE ME EMOTIONAL.
IF HE RECOVERS HIS PAST, HE'LL GET HURT AGAIN. I'M SURE OF IT!
THAT'S WHY I SEPARATED CAIN FROM BEET!
WHAT I DID WAS DIS-GRACEFUL FOR A NATIONAL LEADER.
NOW THE ARC WARRIORS ARE ALMOST DESTROYED, AND BEKATRUTE FACES A CRISIS.
IF BEET HADN'T JOINED THE BATTLE, THINGS WOULD'VE BEEN MUCH WORSE.

READ THIS WAY

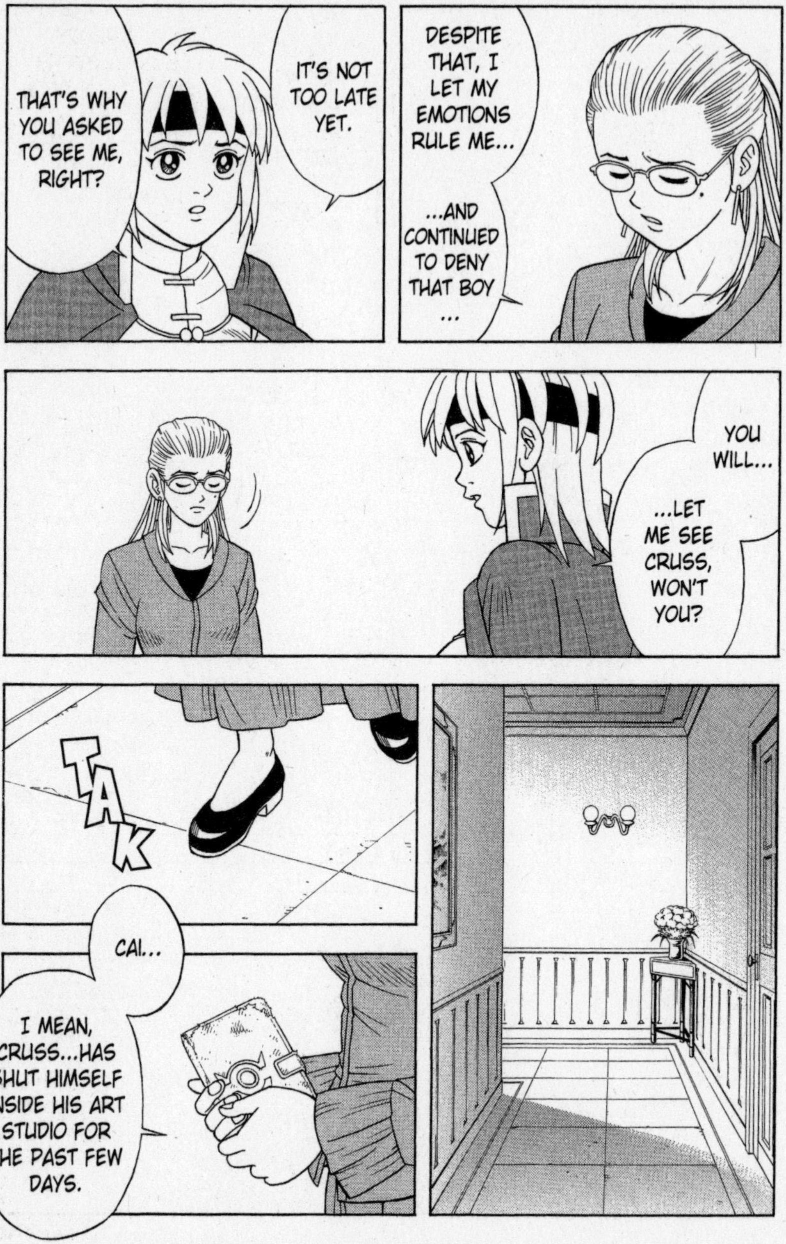

DESPITE THAT, I LET MY EMOTIONS RULE ME...
...AND CONTINUED TO DENY THAT BOY...
IT'S NOT TOO LATE YET.
THAT'S WHY YOU ASKED TO SEE ME, RIGHT?
YOU WILL...
...LET ME SEE CRUSS, WON'T YOU?
TAK
CAI...
I MEAN, CRUSS...HAS SHUT HIMSELF INSIDE HIS ART STUDIO FOR THE PAST FEW DAYS.

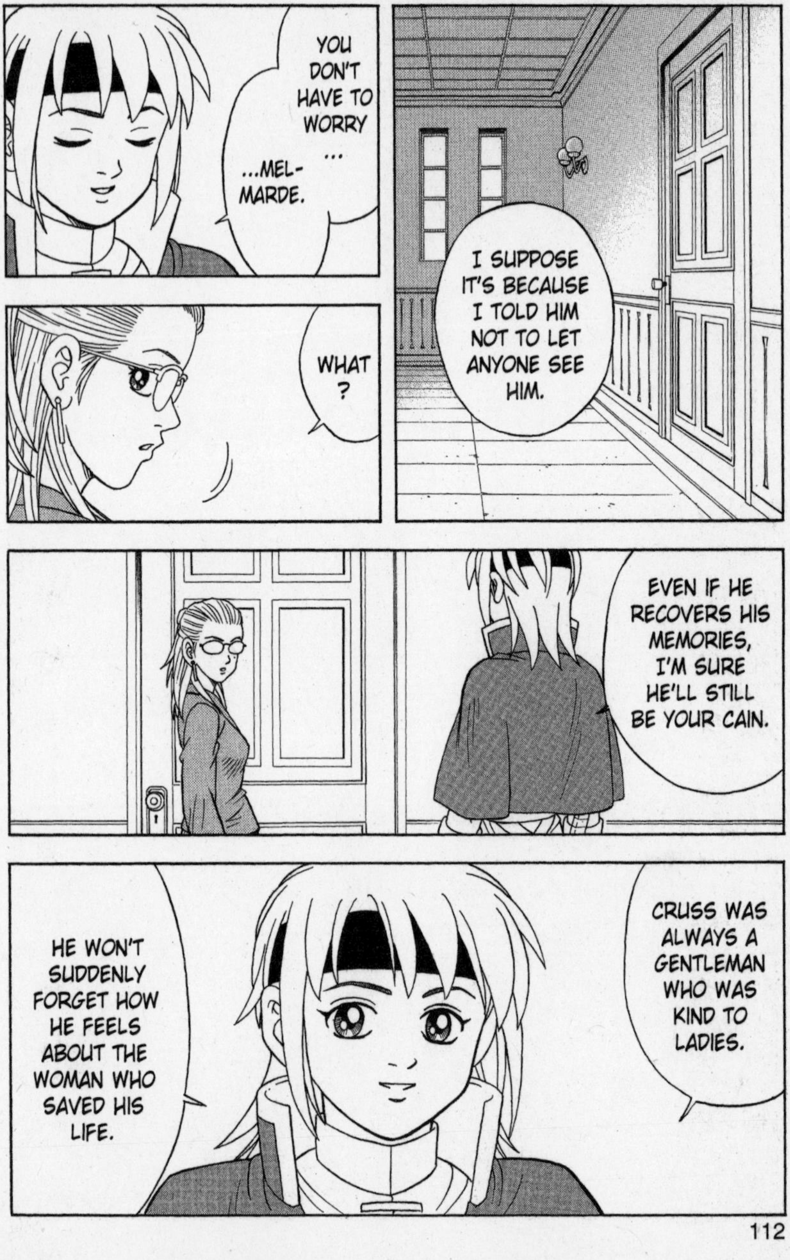
I SUPPOSE IT'S BECAUSE I TOLD HIM NOT TO LET ANYONE SEE HIM.
YOU DON'T HAVE TO WORRY ...
...MEL-MARDE.
WHAT?
EVEN IF HE RECOVERS HIS MEMORIES, I'M SURE HE'LL STILL BE YOUR CAIN.
CRUSS WAS ALWAYS A GENTLEMAN WHO WAS KIND TO LADIES.
HE WON'T SUDDENLY FORGET HOW HE FEELS ABOUT THE WOMAN WHO SAVED HIS LIFE.

READ THIS WAY

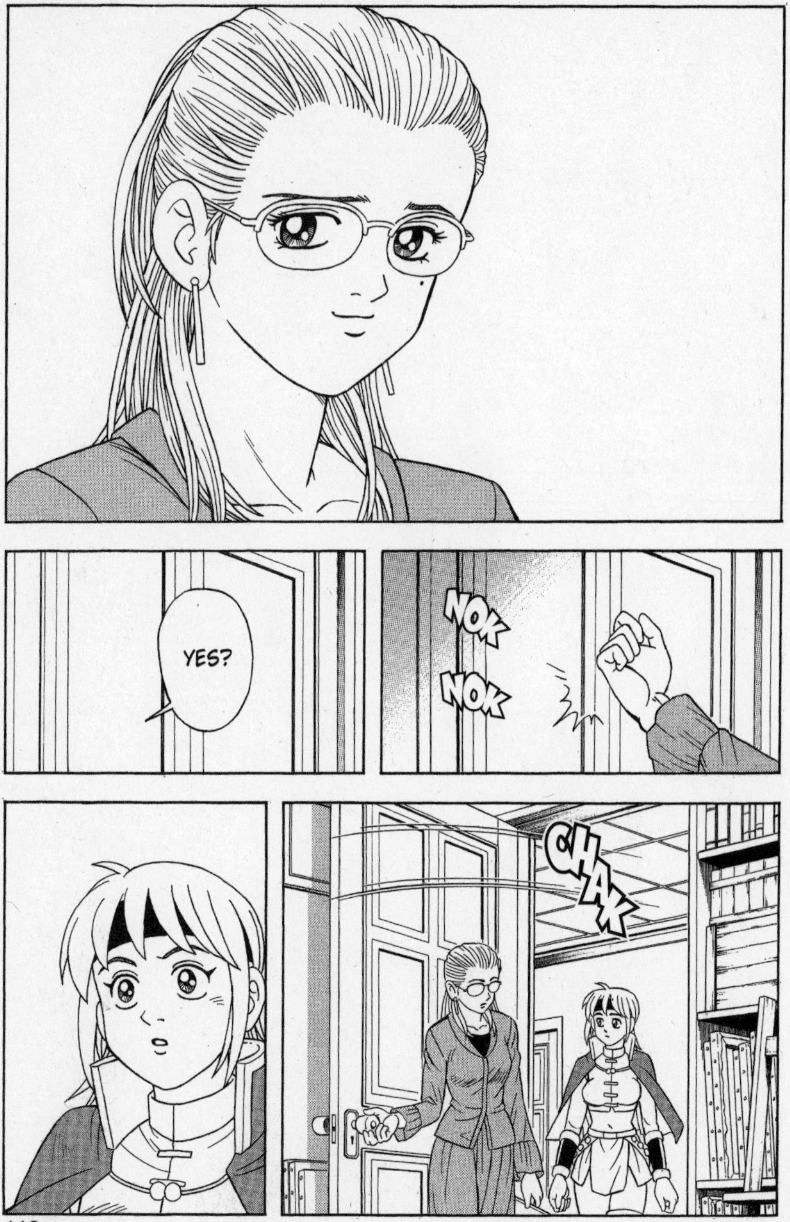
NOK
NOK
YES?
CHAK

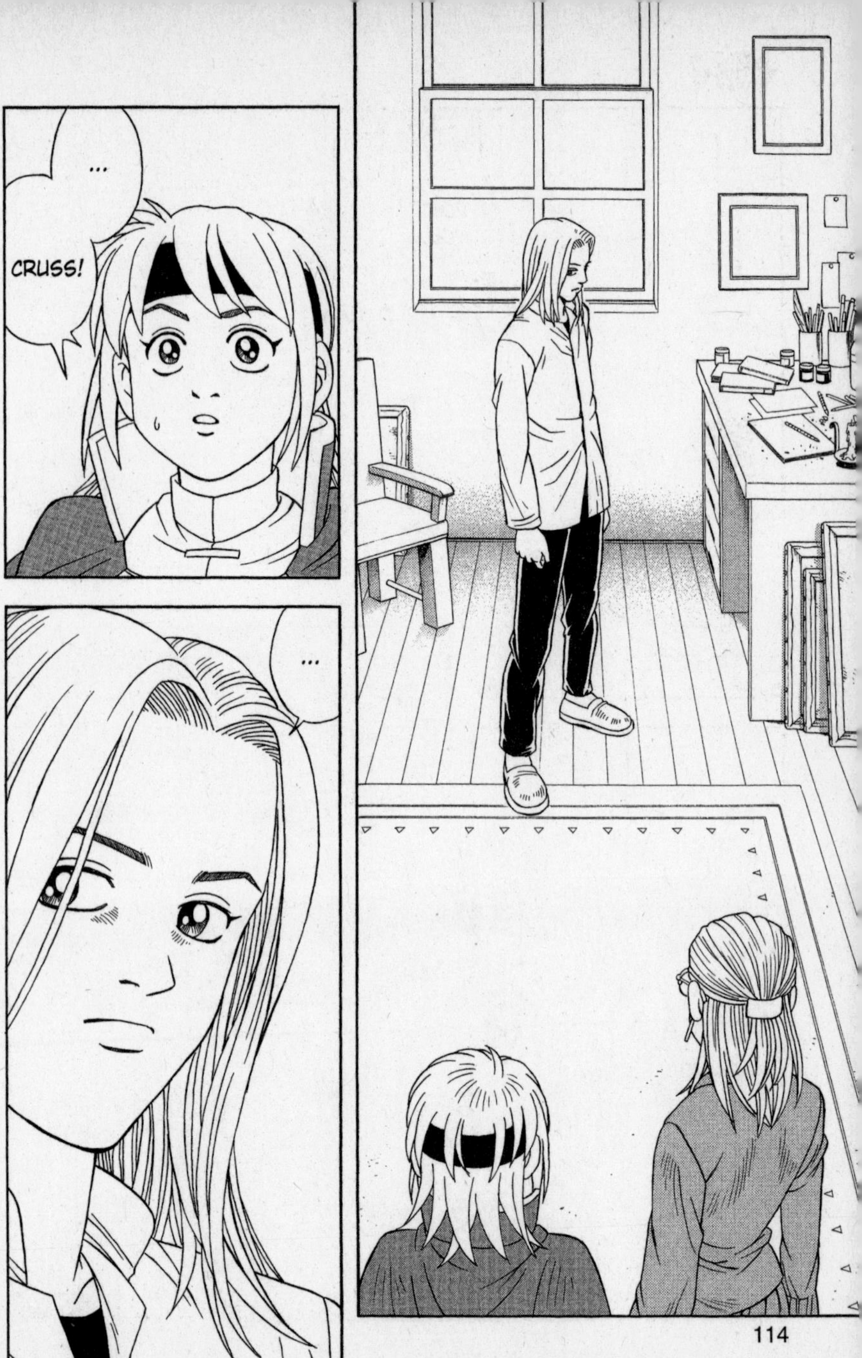
...
CRUSS!
...

READ THIS WAY

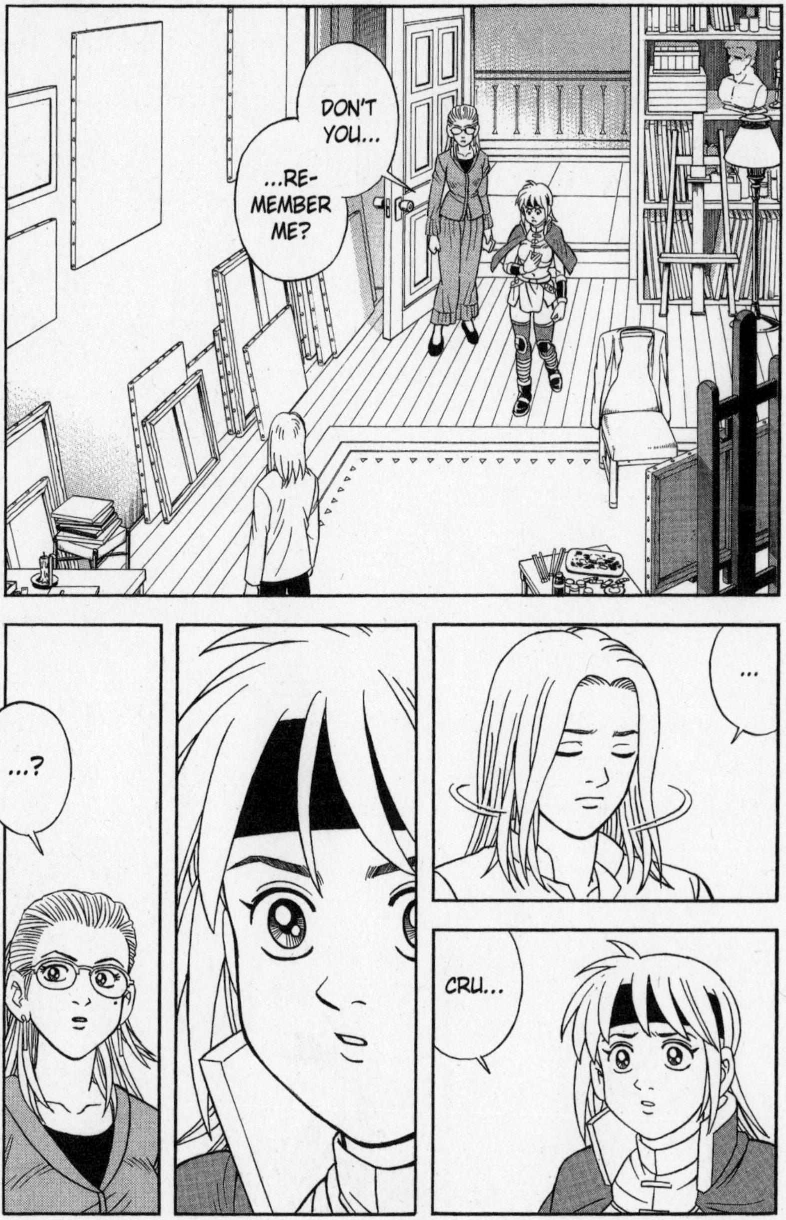
DON'T YOU...
...RE-MEMBER ME?
...
CRU...
...?

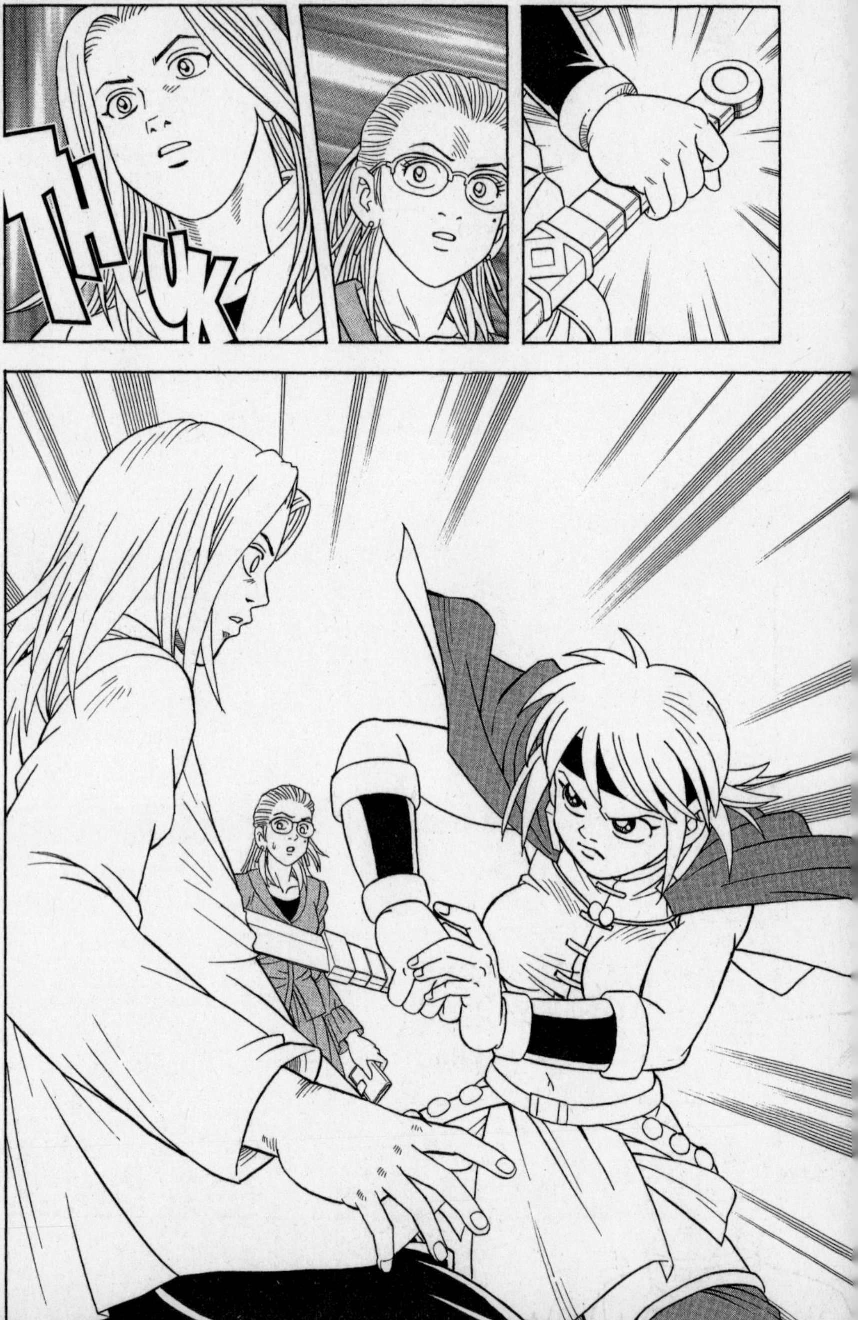
THUK

READ THIS WAY

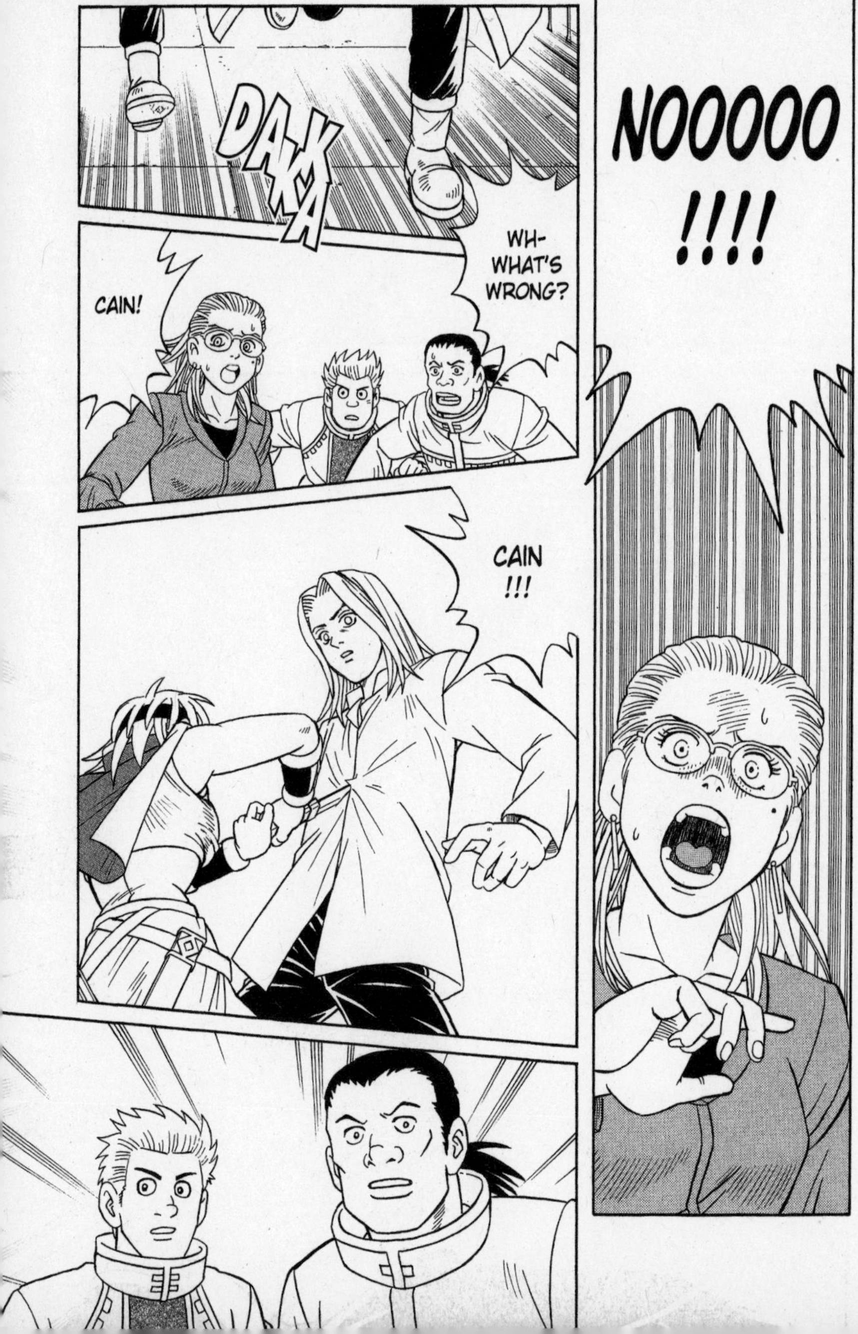
NOOOOO !!!!
DAKA
WH- WHAT'S WRONG?
CAIN!
CAIN !!!

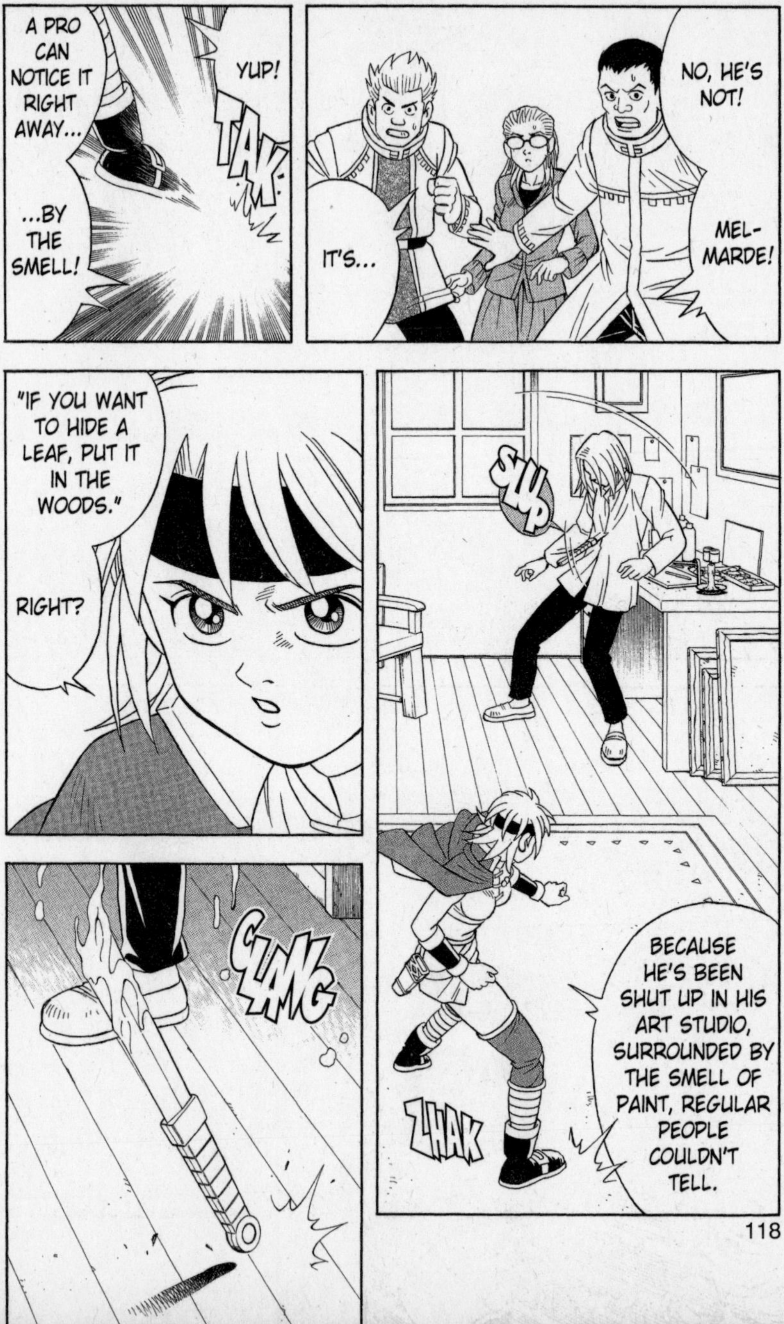
NO, HE'S NOT!
IT'S...
MEL-MARDE!
YUP!
TAK
A PRO CAN NOTICE IT RIGHT AWAY...
...BY THE SMELL!
SLIP
BECAUSE HE'S BEEN SHUT UP IN HIS ART STUDIO, SURROUNDED BY THE SMELL OF PAINT, REGULAR PEOPLE COULDN'T TELL.
ZHAK
"IF YOU WANT TO HIDE A LEAF, PUT IT IN THE WOODS."
RIGHT?
CLANG

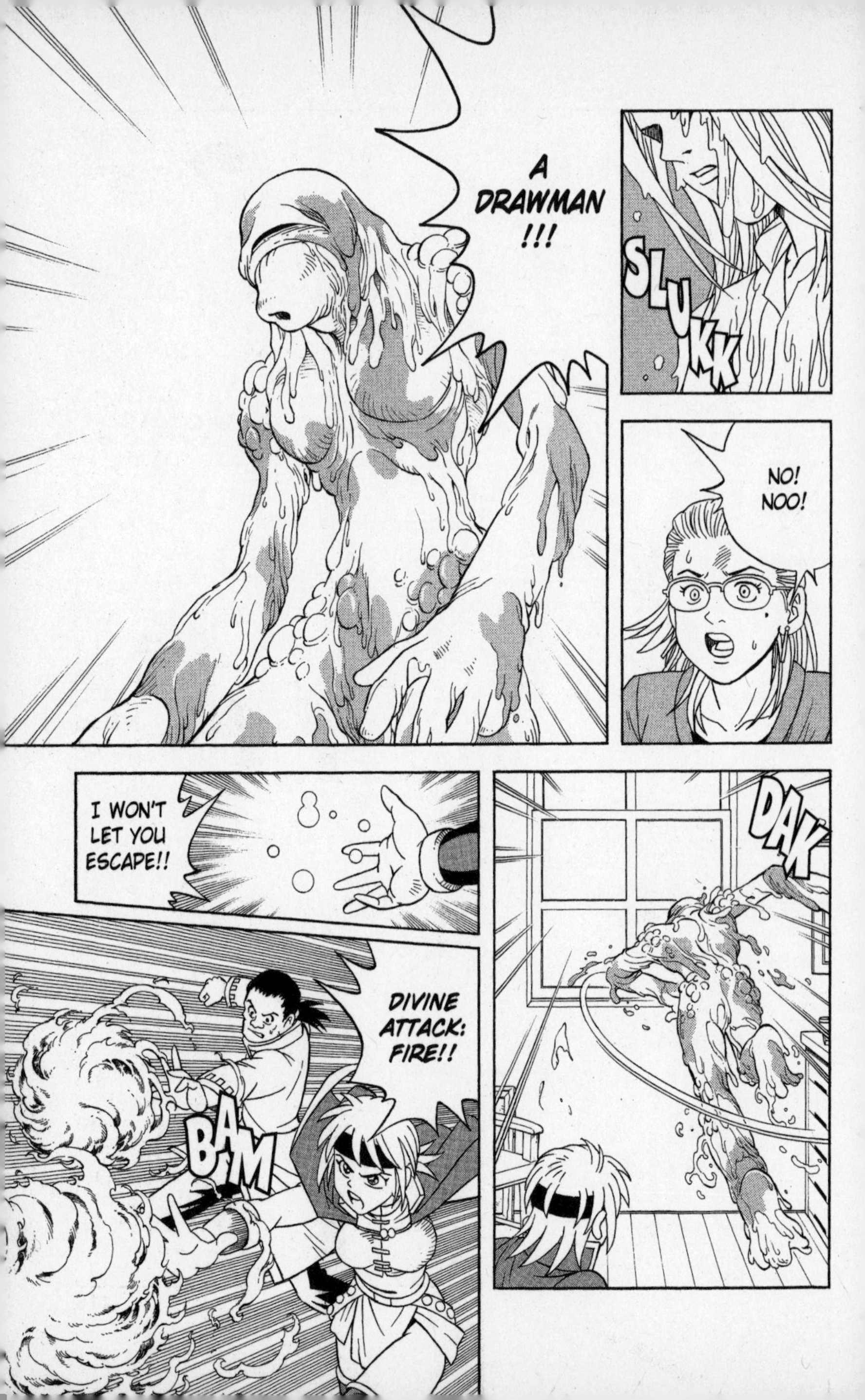
SLUKK
NO! NOO!
A DRAWMAN!!!
DAK
I WON'T LET YOU ESCAPE!!
DIVINE ATTACK: FIRE!!
BAM

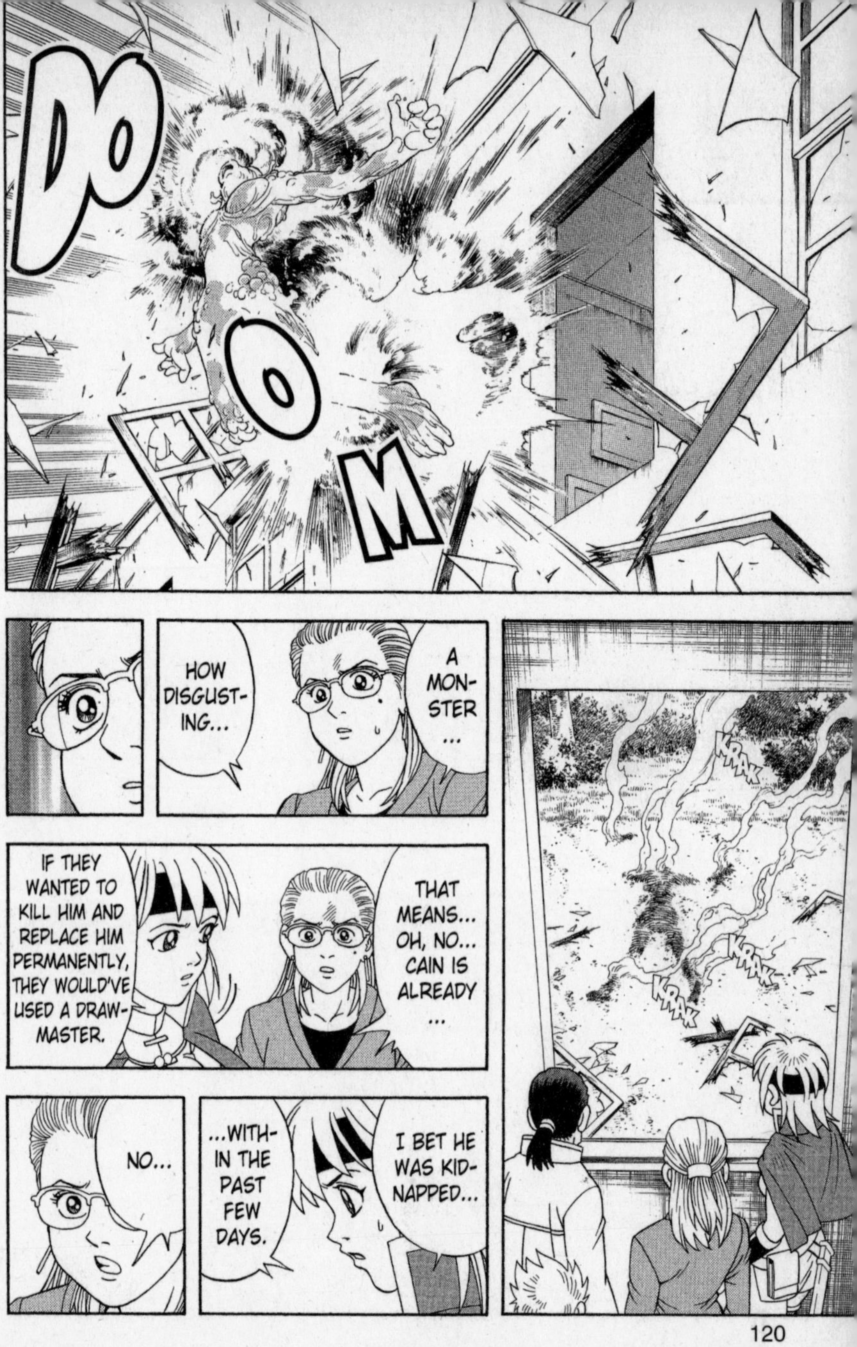
DOOM
KRAK
KRAK
KRAK
A MON-STER...
HOW DISGUST-ING...
THAT MEANS... OH, NO... CAIN IS ALREADY...
IF THEY WANTED TO KILL HIM AND REPLACE HIM PERMANENTLY, THEY WOULD'VE USED A DRAW-MASTER.
I BET HE WAS KID-NAPPED...
...WITH-IN THE PAST FEW DAYS.
NO...

READ THIS WAY

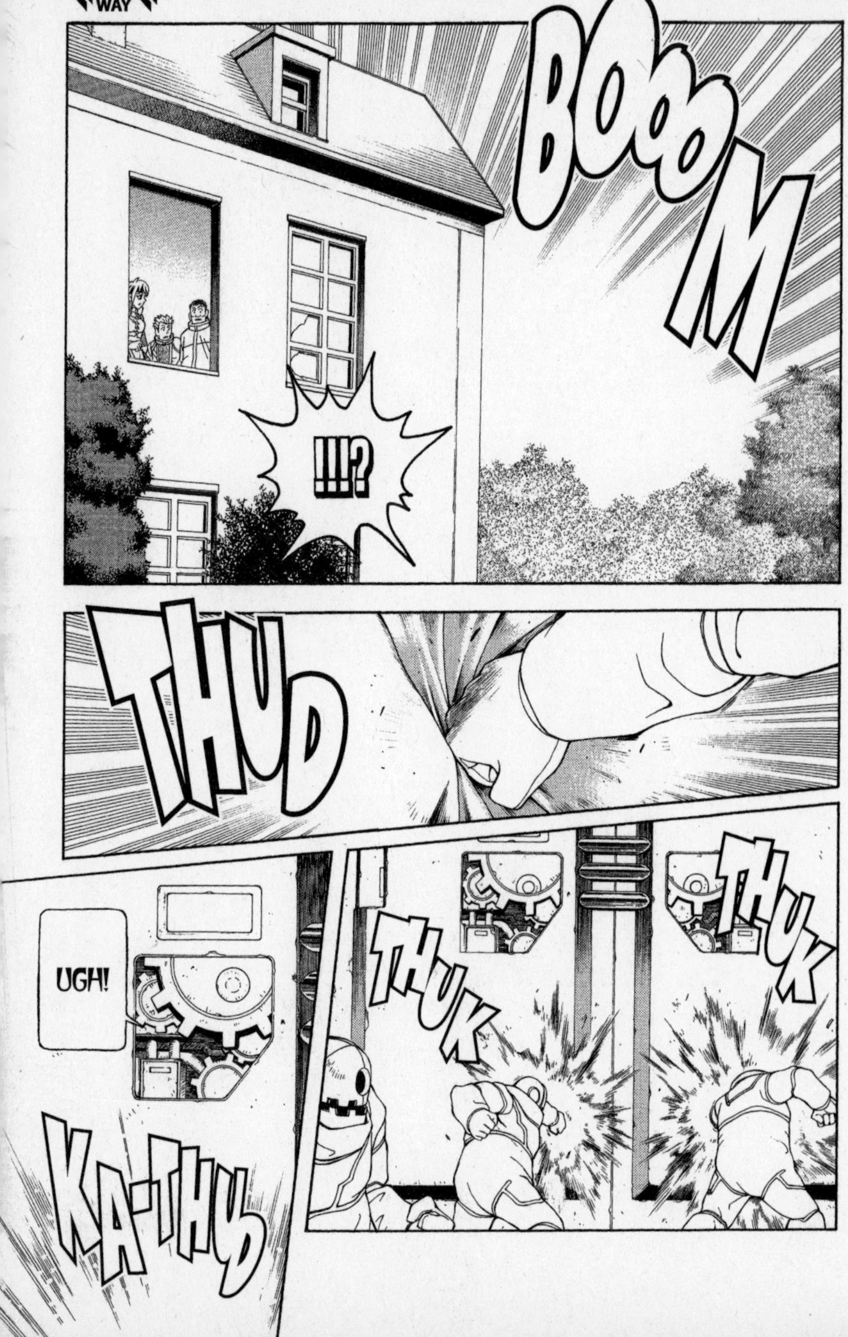
BOOOM
!!!?
THUD
THUK
THUK
UGH!
KA-THUD

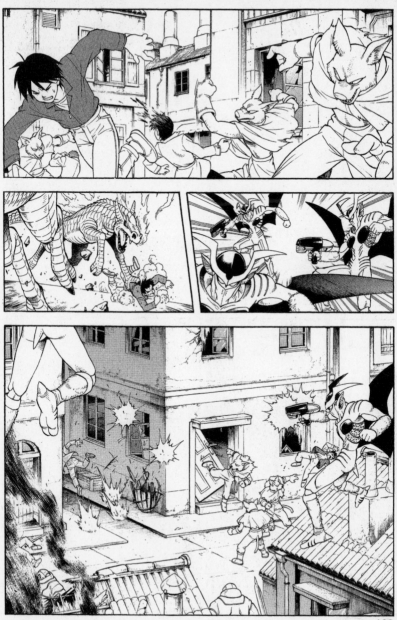

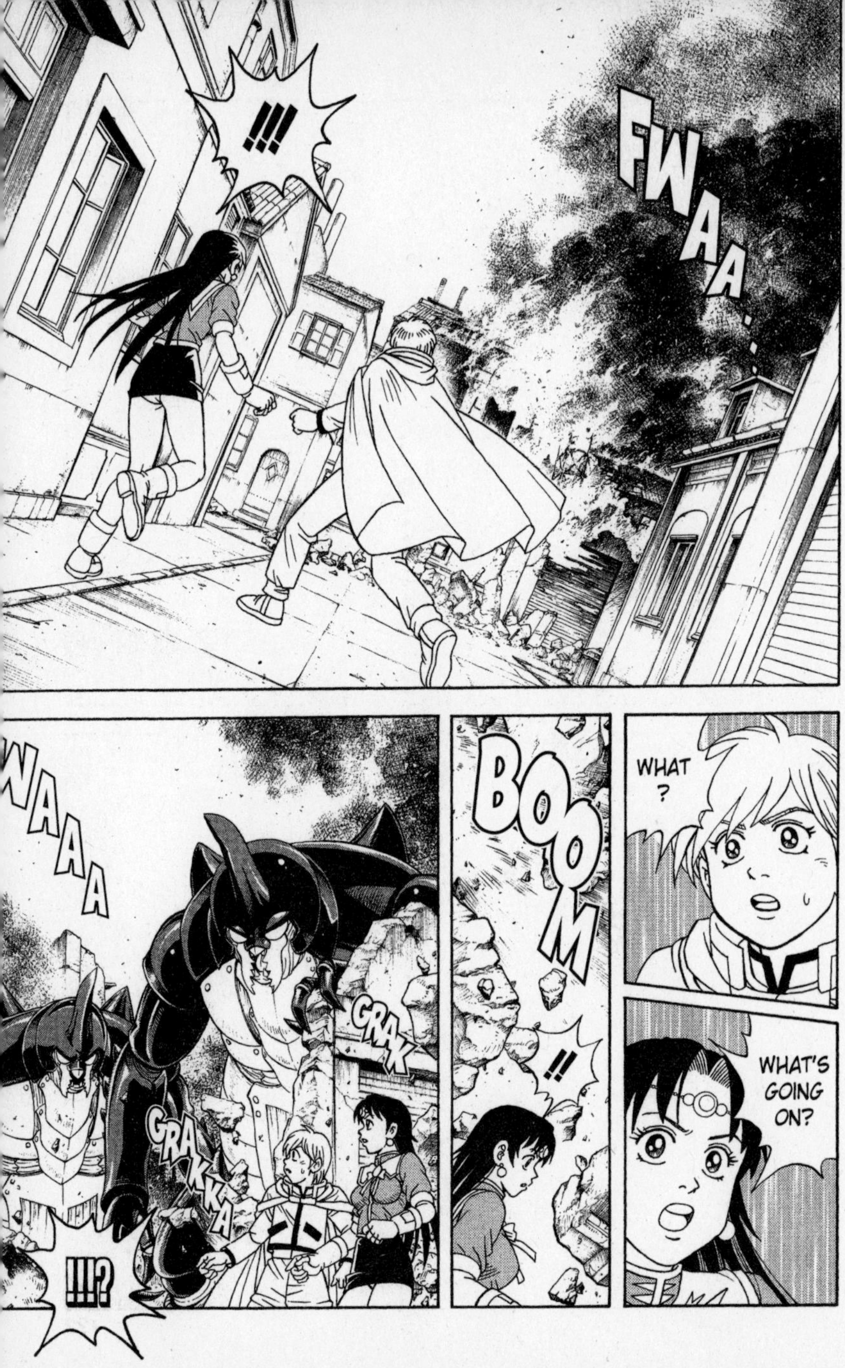
FWAA...
!!!
WHAT ?
WHAT'S GOING ON?
BOOOM
!!
WAAAA
GRAK
GRAKKA
!!!?

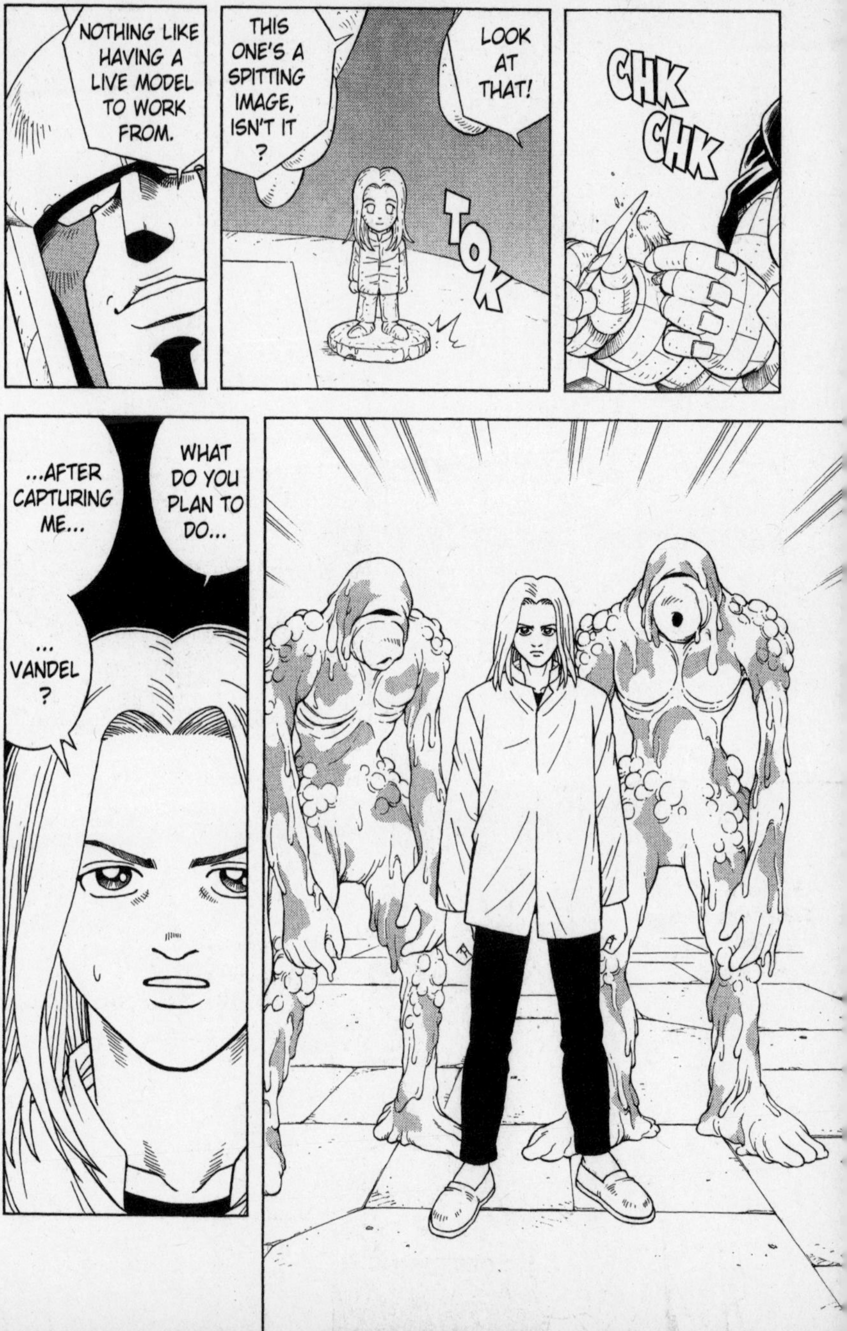
CHK CHK
LOOK AT THAT!
THIS ONE'S A SPITTING IMAGE, ISN'T IT ?
TOK
NOTHING LIKE HAVING A LIVE MODEL TO WORK FROM.
WHAT DO YOU PLAN TO DO...
...AFTER CAPTURING ME...
... VANDEL ?

READ THIS WAY

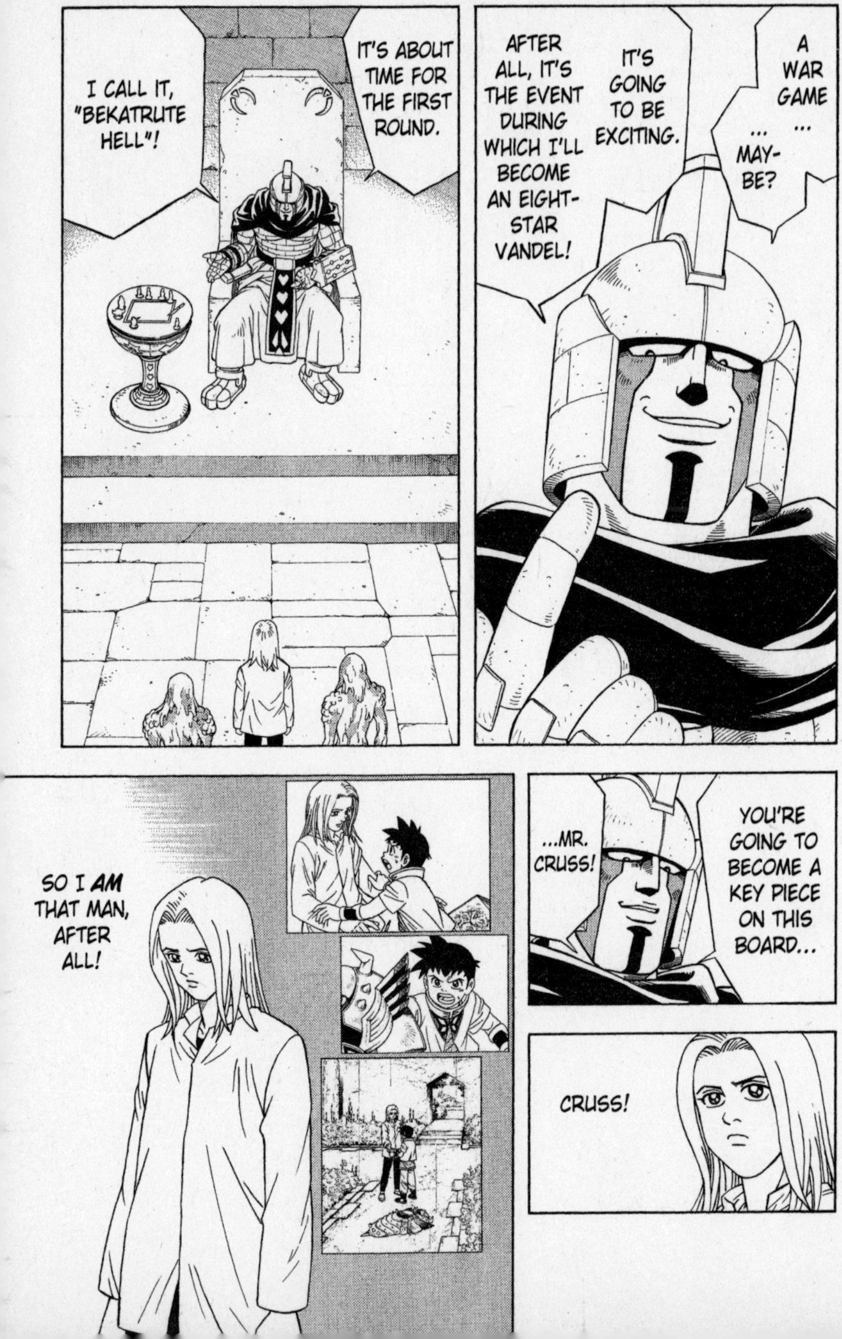
A WAR GAME... ...MAYBE?
IT'S GOING TO BE EXCITING.
AFTER ALL, IT'S THE EVENT DURING WHICH I'LL BECOME AN EIGHT-STAR VANDEL!
IT'S ABOUT TIME FOR THE FIRST ROUND.
I CALL IT, "BEKATRUTE HELL"!
YOU'RE GOING TO BECOME A KEY PIECE ON THIS BOARD...
...MR. CRUSS!
CRUSS!
SO I *AM* THAT MAN, AFTER ALL!

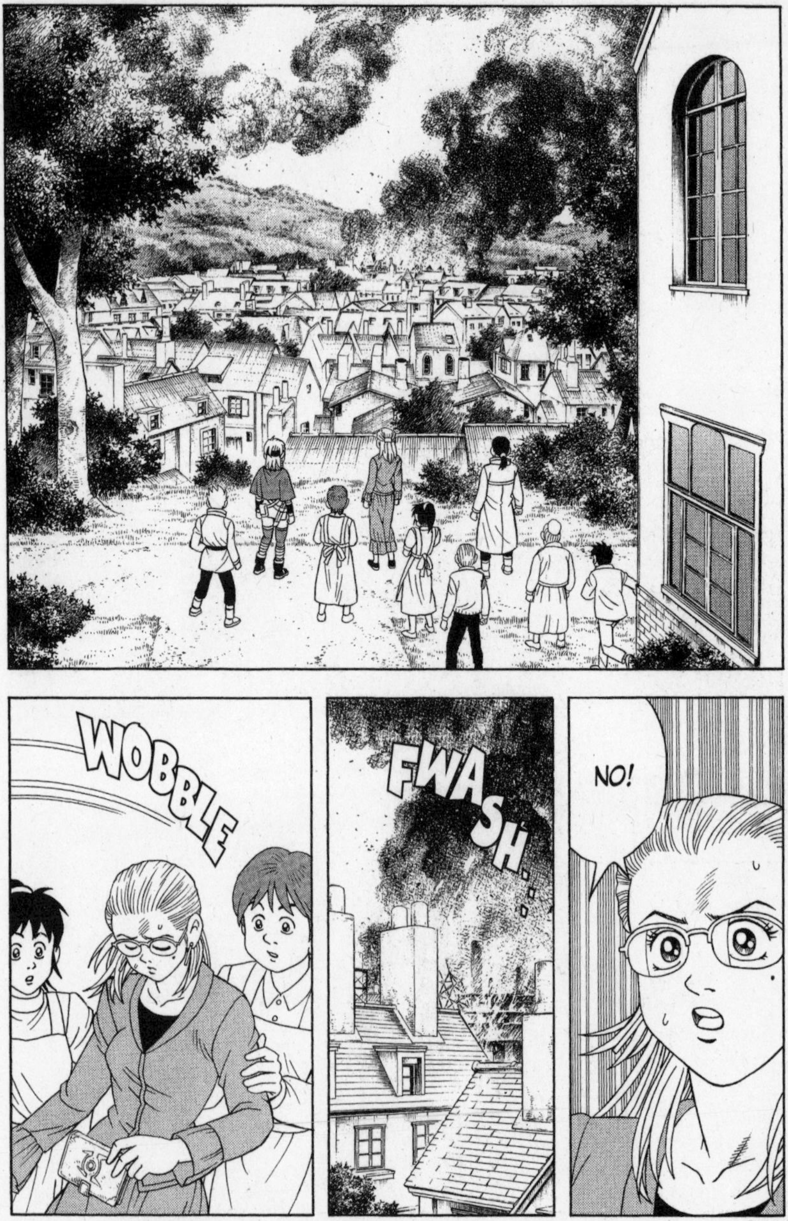
NO!
FWASH
WOBBLE

READ THIS WAY

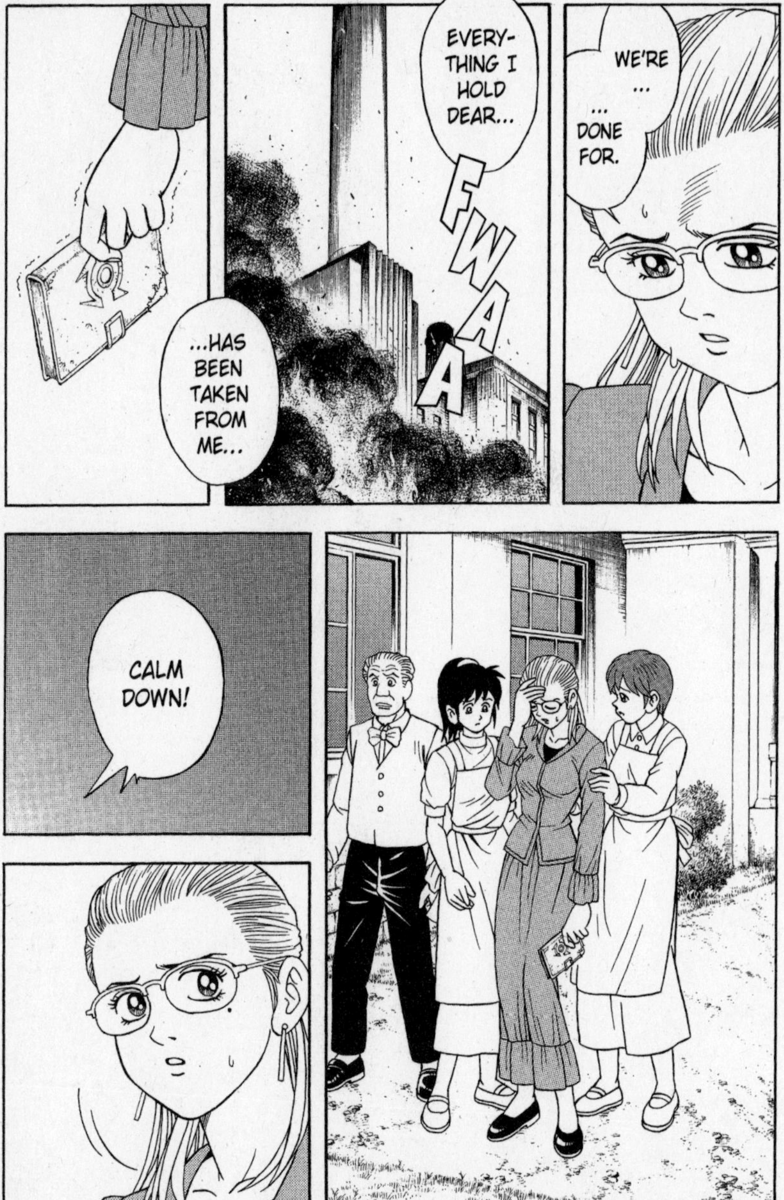
WE'RE ...
... DONE FOR.
EVERY-THING I HOLD DEAR...
FWAAA
...HAS BEEN TAKEN FROM ME...
CALM DOWN!

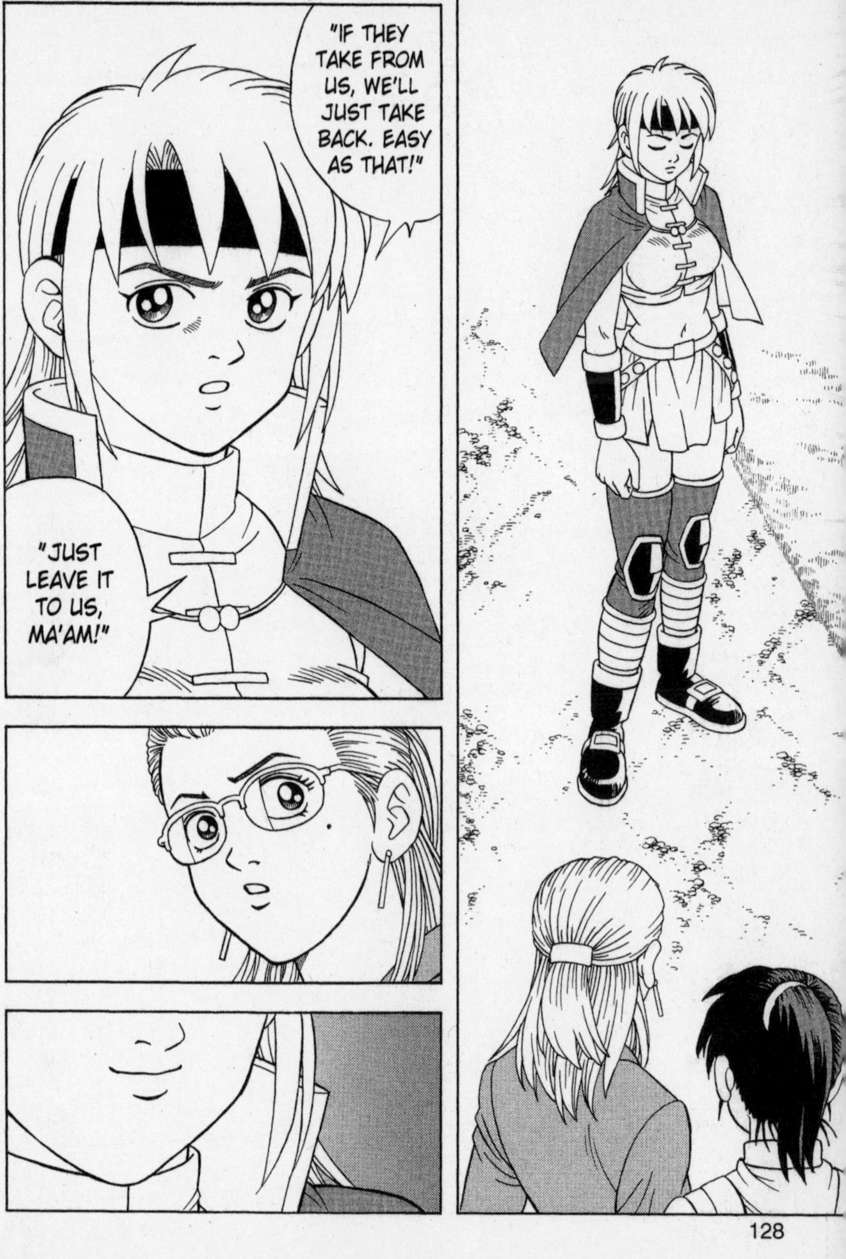
"IF THEY TAKE FROM US, WE'LL JUST TAKE BACK. EASY AS THAT!"
"JUST LEAVE IT TO US, MA'AM!"

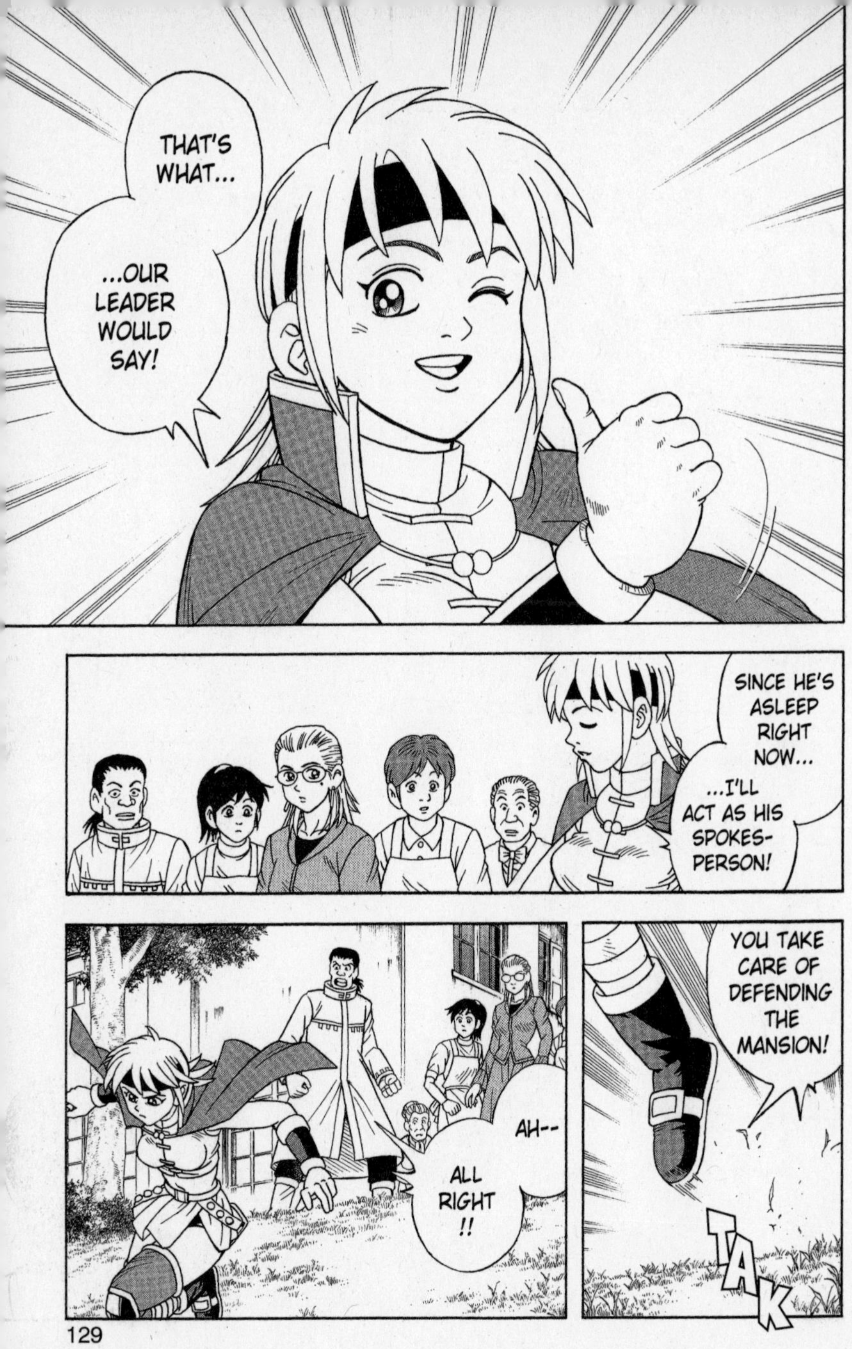

THAT'S WHAT...
...OUR LEADER WOULD SAY!
SINCE HE'S ASLEEP RIGHT NOW...
...I'LL ACT AS HIS SPOKES-PERSON!
YOU TAKE CARE OF DEFENDING THE MANSION!
TAK
AH--
ALL RIGHT !!

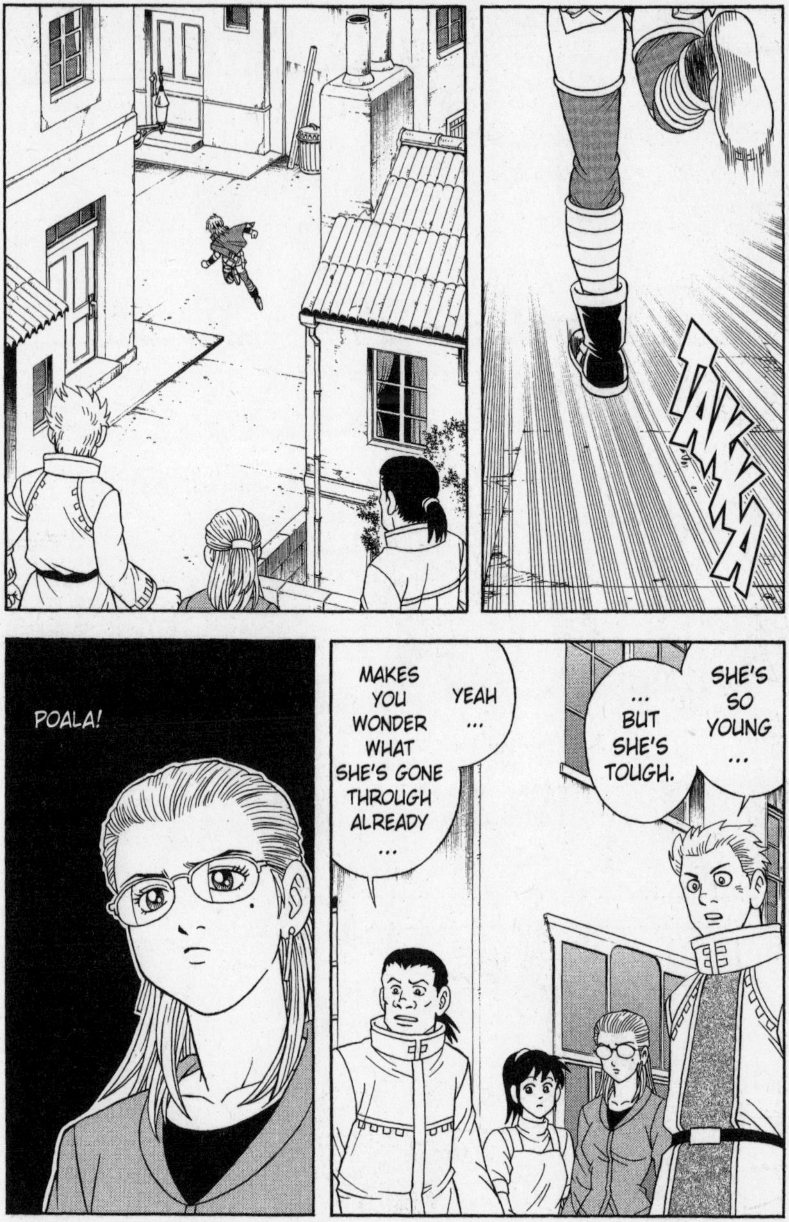
TAKKA
SHE'S SO YOUNG ...
... BUT SHE'S TOUGH.
YEAH ...
MAKES YOU WONDER WHAT SHE'S GONE THROUGH ALREADY ...
POALA!

READ THIS WAY

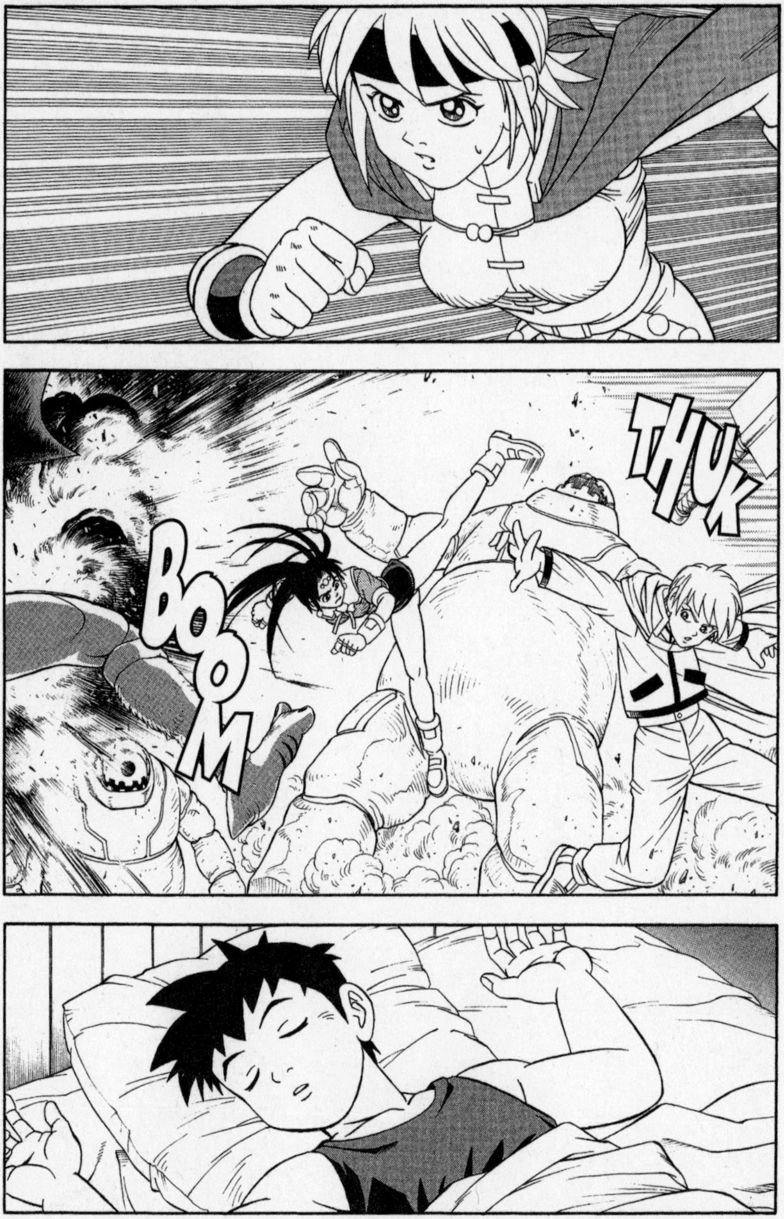
THUK
BOOM

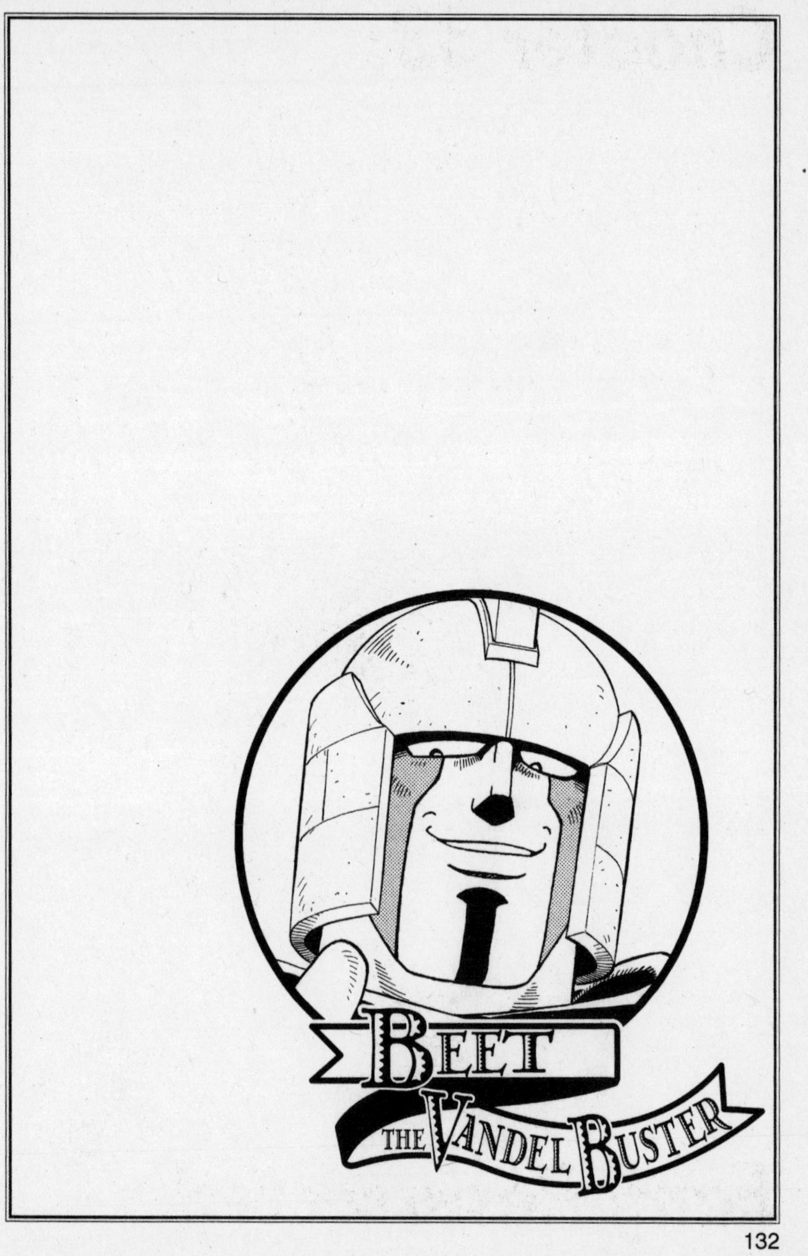
BEET
THE VANDEL BUSTER

Chapter 33:

Fang Resurrected!

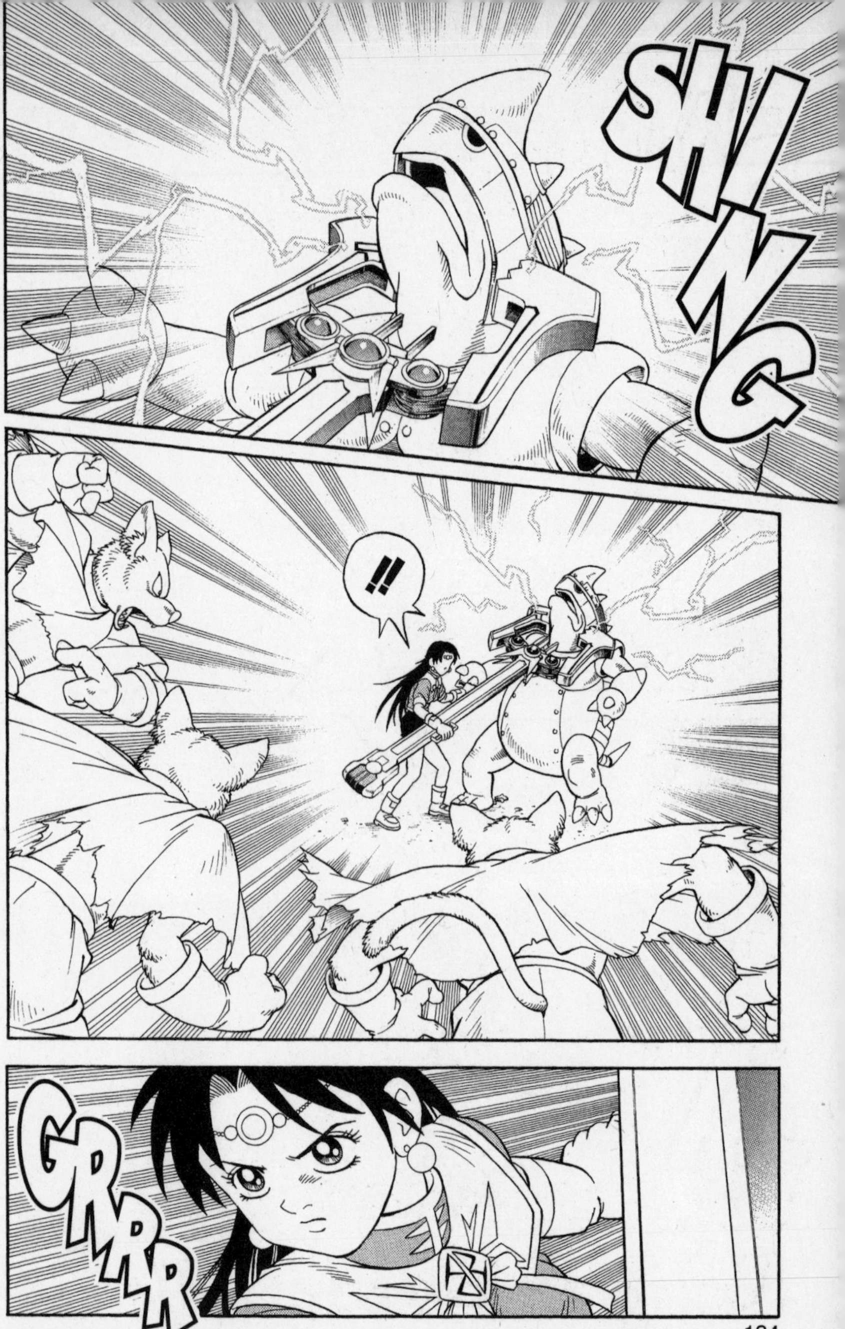
SHING
!!
GRRR

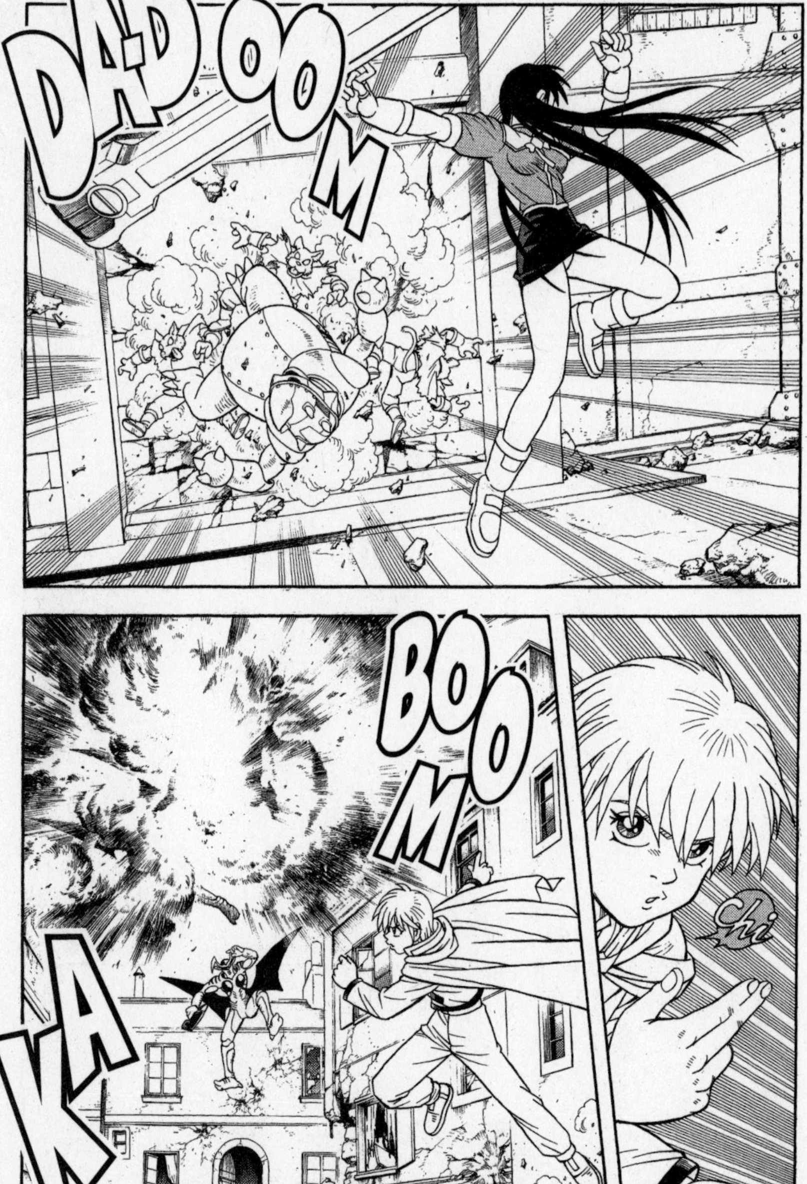
DA-DOOM
Chi
BOOOM
KA

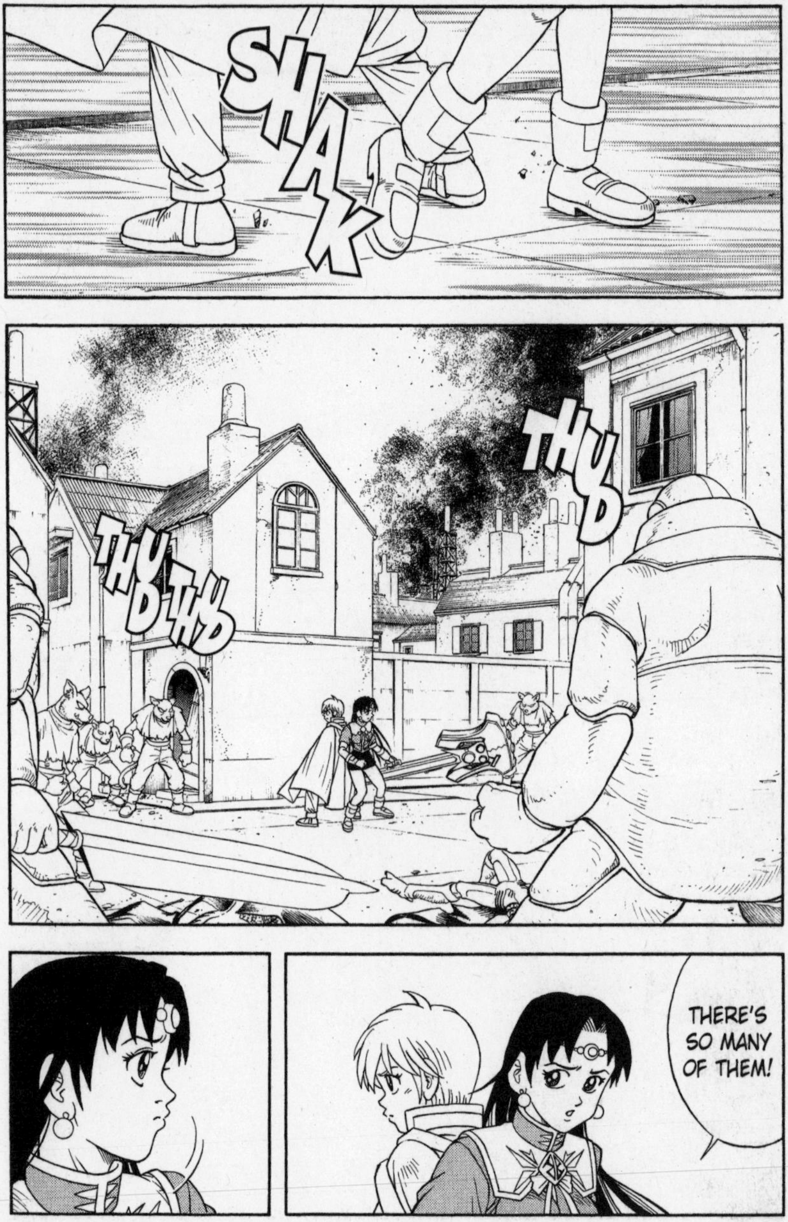
SHAK
THUD
THUD THUD
THERE'S SO MANY OF THEM!

READ THIS WAY

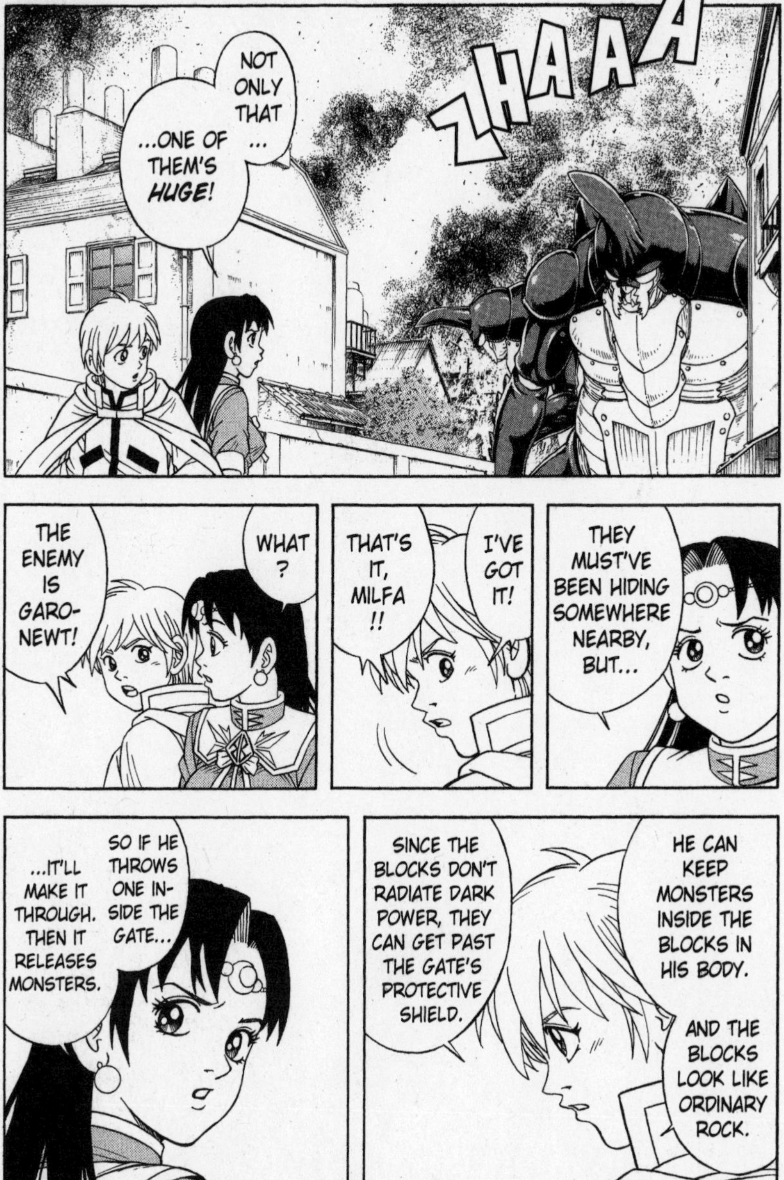

ZHAAAA
NOT ONLY THAT ...
...ONE OF THEM'S *HUGE!*
THEY MUST'VE BEEN HIDING SOMEWHERE NEARBY, BUT...
I'VE GOT IT!
THAT'S IT, MILFA!!
WHAT?
THE ENEMY IS GARO-NEWT!
HE CAN KEEP MONSTERS INSIDE THE BLOCKS IN HIS BODY.
AND THE BLOCKS LOOK LIKE ORDINARY ROCK.
SINCE THE BLOCKS DON'T RADIATE DARK POWER, THEY CAN GET PAST THE GATE'S PROTECTIVE SHIELD.
SO IF HE THROWS ONE IN-SIDE THE GATE...
...IT'LL MAKE IT THROUGH. THEN IT RELEASES MONSTERS.

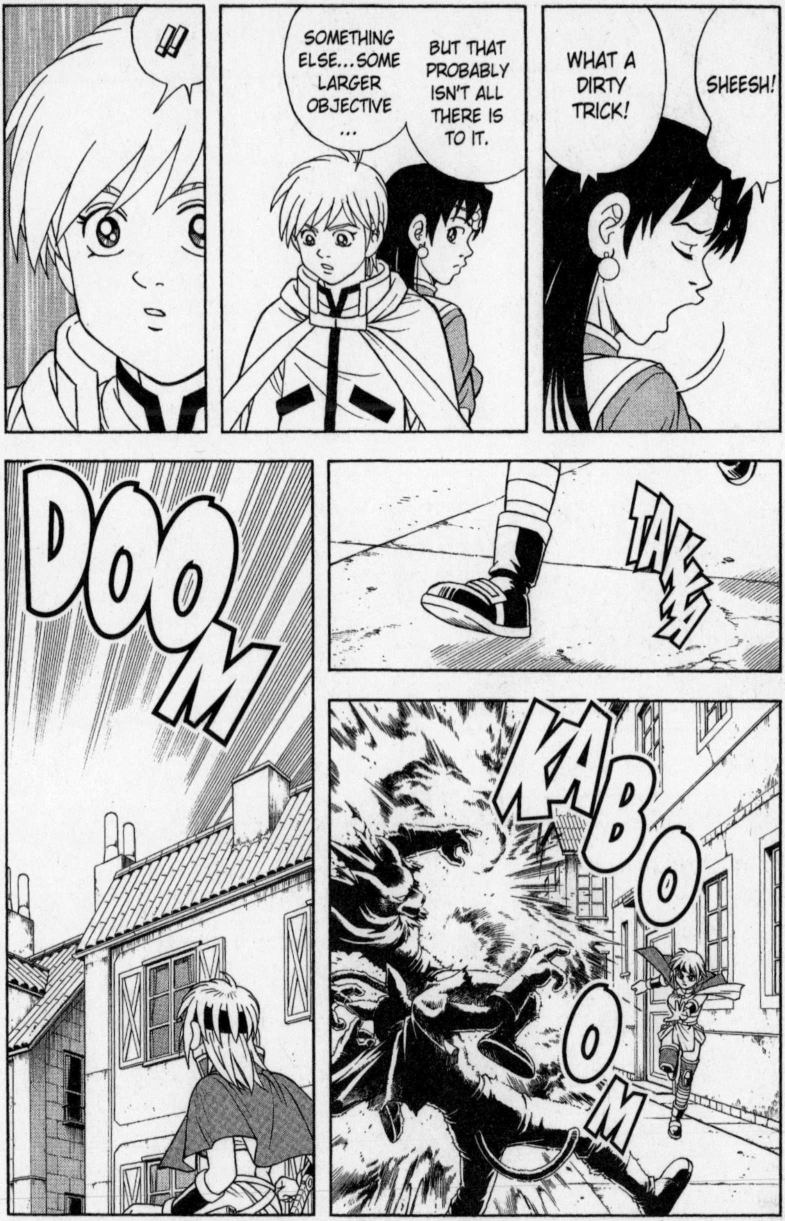
SHEESH!
WHAT A DIRTY TRICK!
BUT THAT PROBABLY ISN'T ALL THERE IS TO IT.
SOMETHING ELSE...SOME LARGER OBJECTIVE ...
!!
TAKKA
KABOOOM
DOOOM

READ THIS WAY

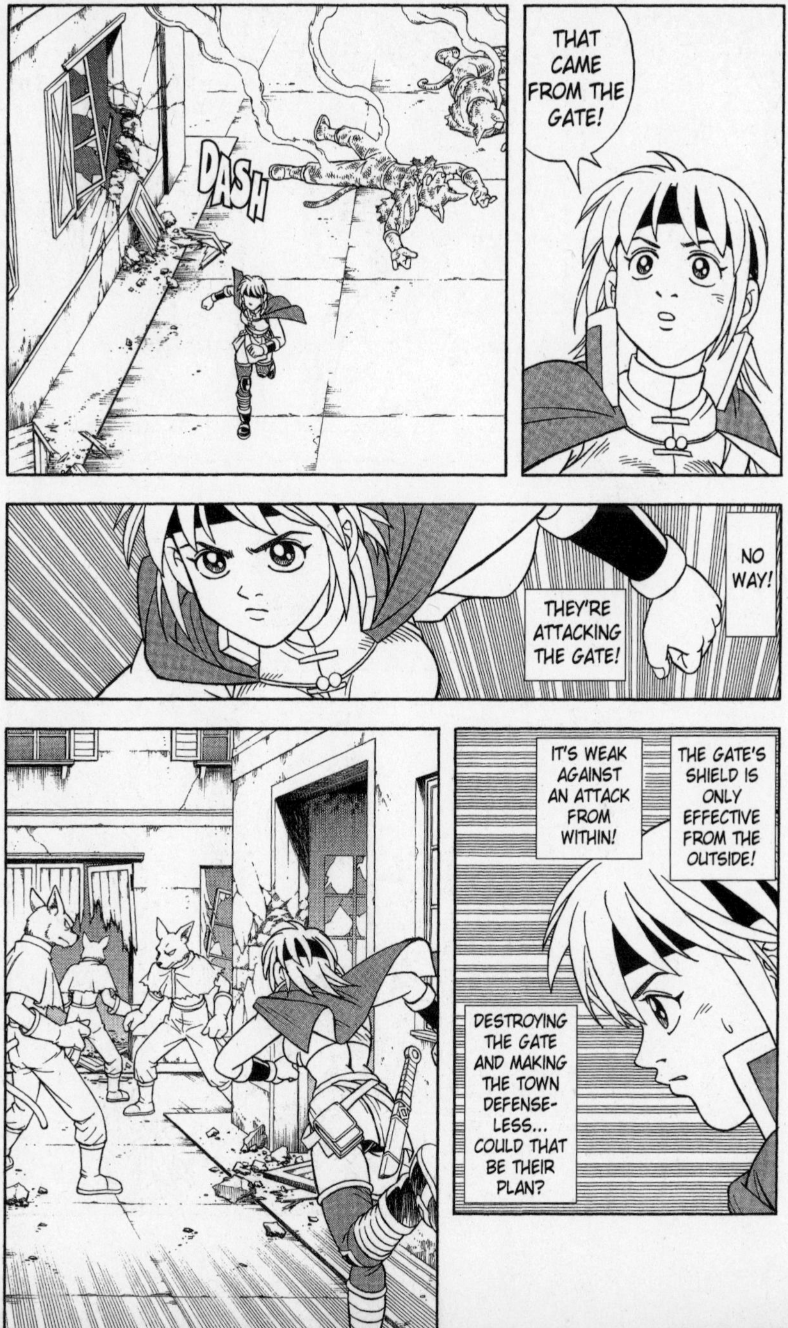
THAT CAME FROM THE GATE!
DASH
NO WAY!
THEY'RE ATTACKING THE GATE!
THE GATE'S SHIELD IS ONLY EFFECTIVE FROM THE OUTSIDE!
IT'S WEAK AGAINST AN ATTACK FROM WITHIN!
DESTROYING THE GATE AND MAKING THE TOWN DEFENSE-LESS... COULD THAT BE THEIR PLAN?

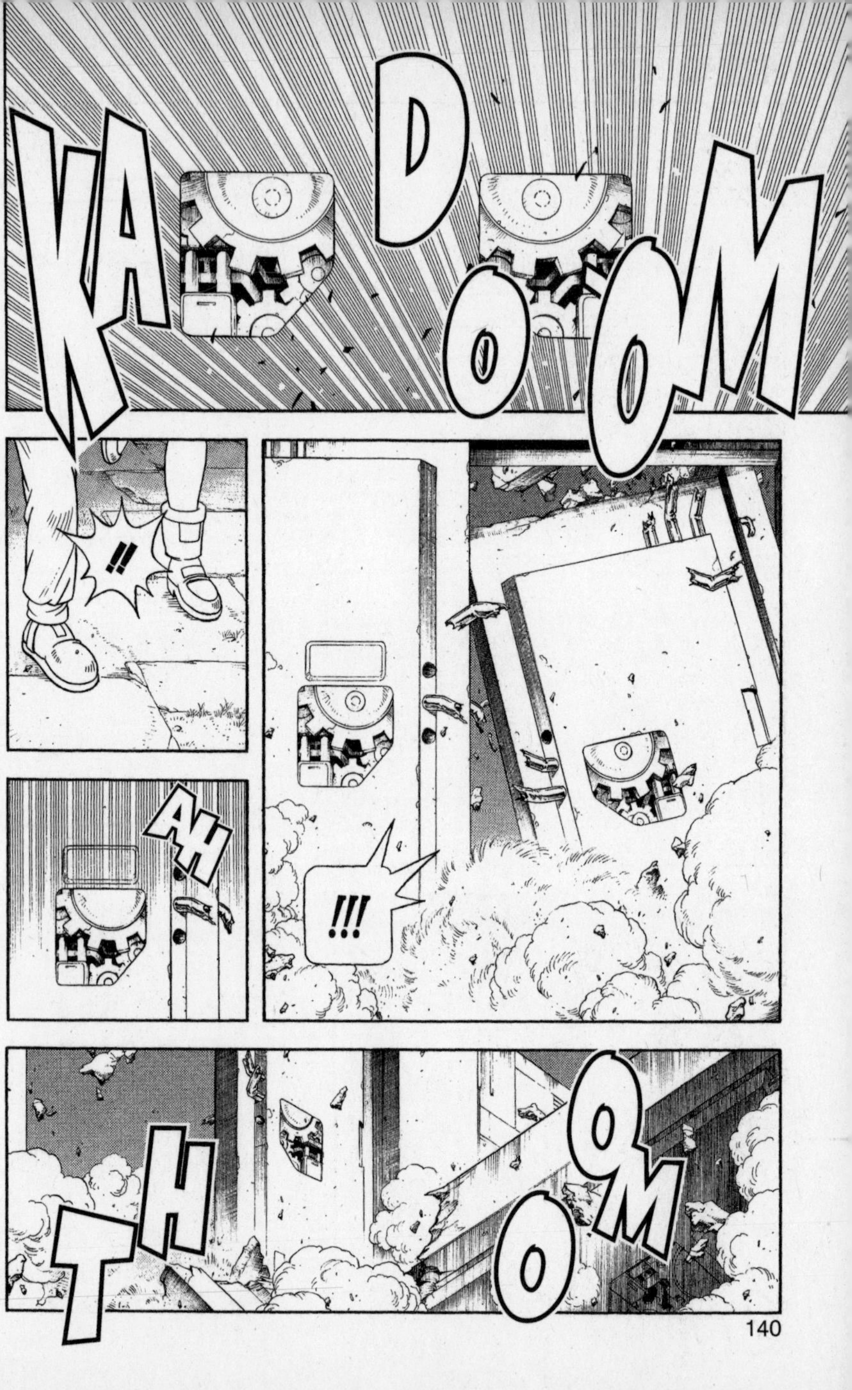
KADOOM
!!!
!!
AH
THOOM

READ THIS WAY

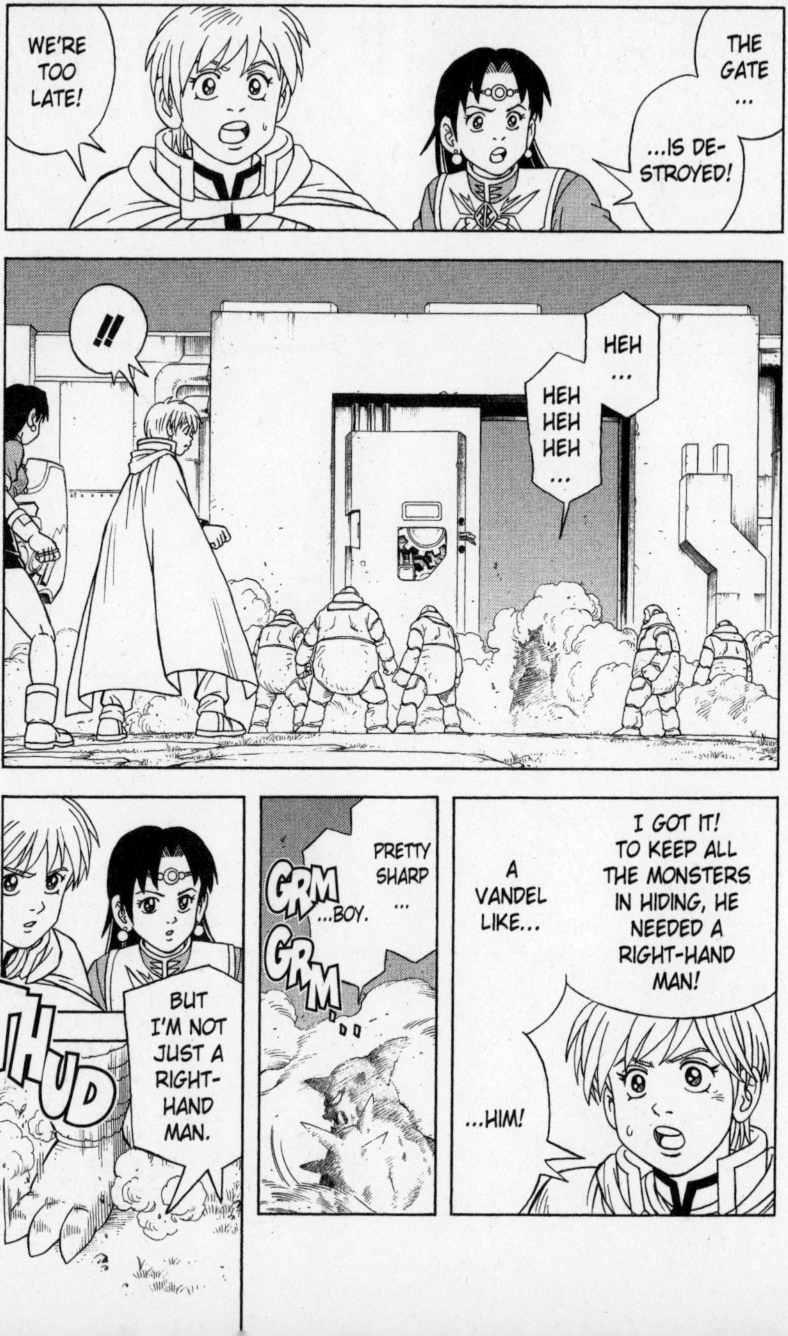
THE GATE ...
...IS DESTROYED!
WE'RE TOO LATE!
HEH ...
HEH HEH HEH ...
!!
I GOT IT! TO KEEP ALL THE MONSTERS IN HIDING, HE NEEDED A RIGHT-HAND MAN!
A VANDEL LIKE...
...HIM!
PRETTY SHARP ...
GRM
...BOY.
GRM
BUT I'M NOT JUST A RIGHT-HAND MAN.
THUD

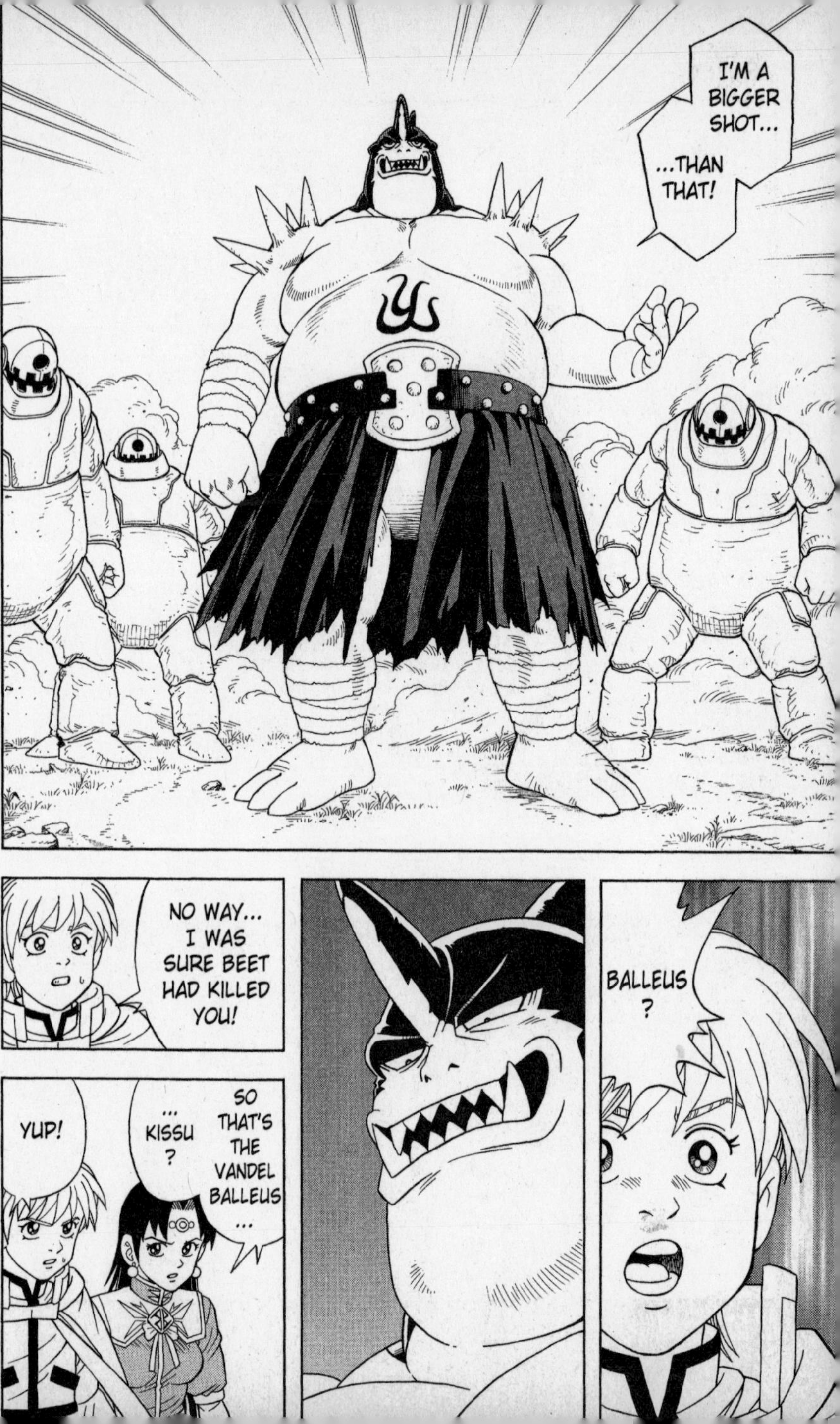
I'M A BIGGER SHOT...
...THAN THAT!
BALLEUS?
NO WAY... I WAS SURE BEET HAD KILLED YOU!
SO THAT'S THE VANDEL BALLEUS...
...KISSU?
YUP!

READ THIS WAY

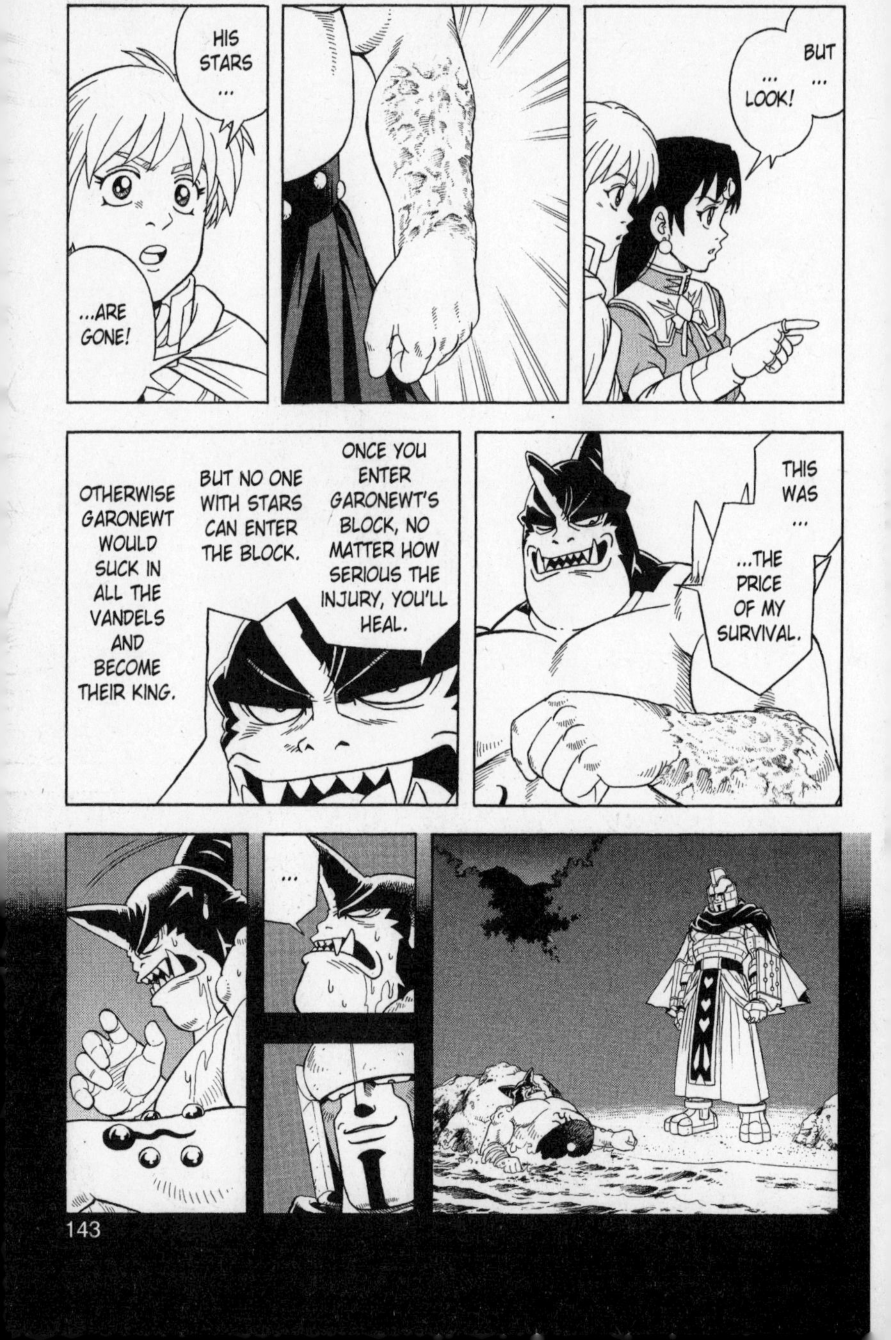
BUT ... ... LOOK!
HIS STARS ...
...ARE GONE!
THIS WAS ...
...THE PRICE OF MY SURVIVAL.
ONCE YOU ENTER GARONEWT'S BLOCK, NO MATTER HOW SERIOUS THE INJURY, YOU'LL HEAL.
BUT NO ONE WITH STARS CAN ENTER THE BLOCK.
OTHERWISE GARONEWT WOULD SUCK IN ALL THE VANDELS AND BECOME THEIR KING.
...

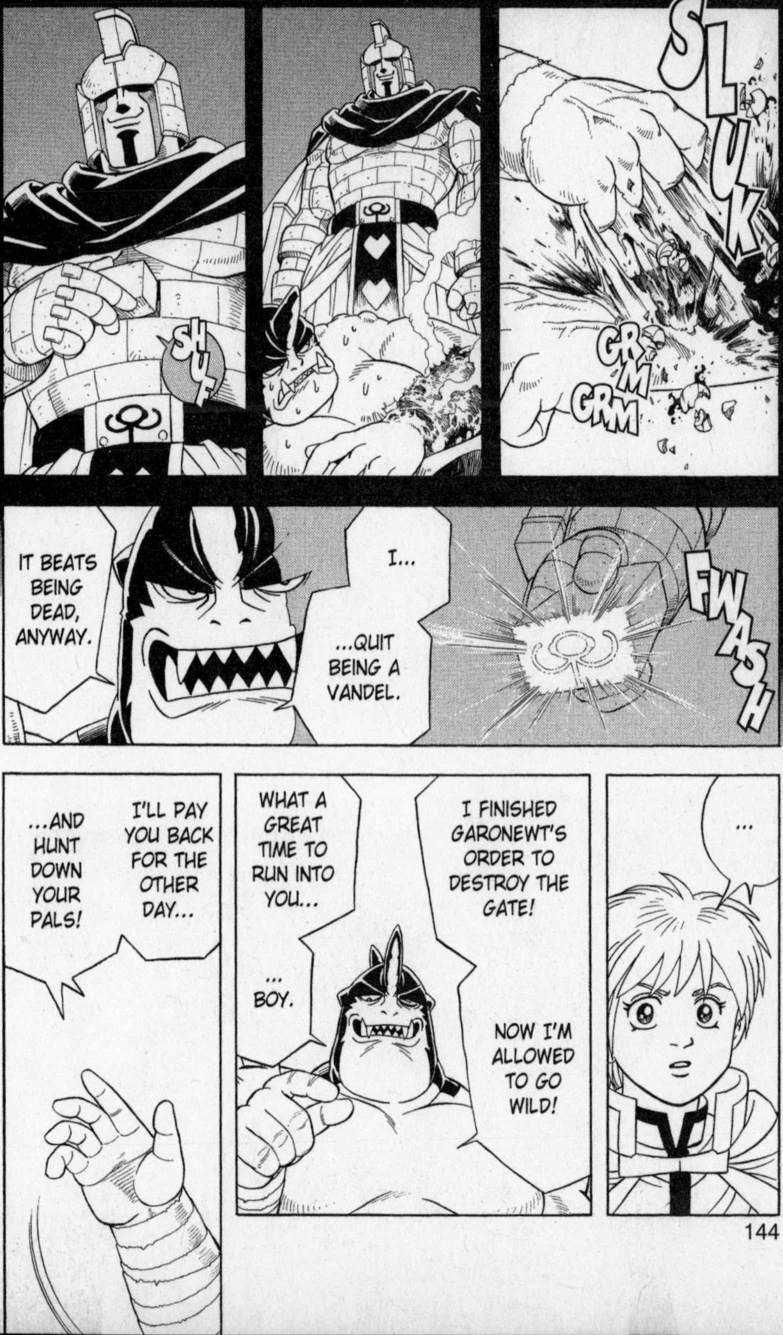
SLUK
GRM GRM
SHUF
FWASH
I...
...QUIT BEING A VANDEL.
IT BEATS BEING DEAD, ANYWAY.
...
I FINISHED GARONEWT'S ORDER TO DESTROY THE GATE!
NOW I'M ALLOWED TO GO WILD!
WHAT A GREAT TIME TO RUN INTO YOU...
... BOY.
I'LL PAY YOU BACK FOR THE OTHER DAY...
...AND HUNT DOWN YOUR PALS!

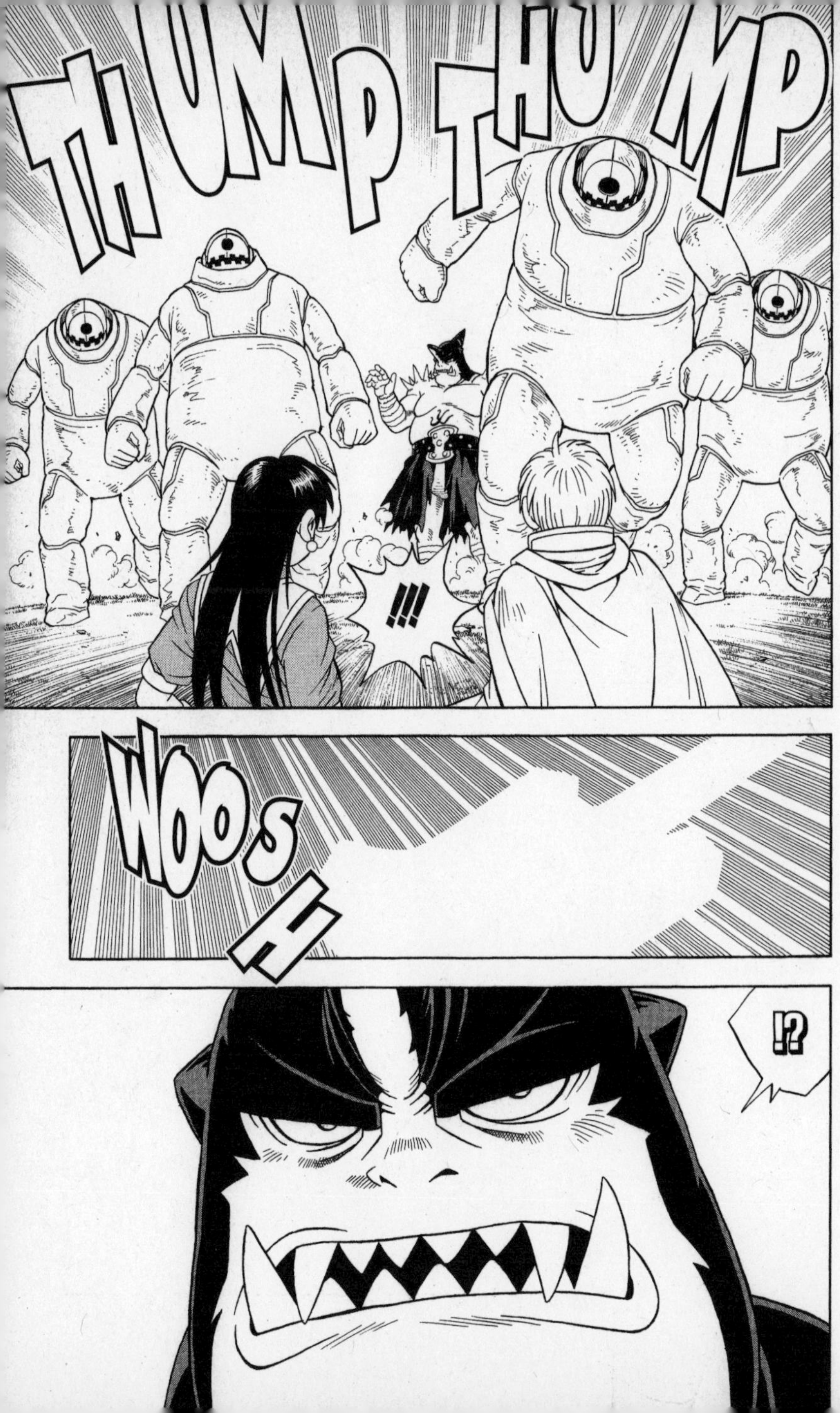
THUMP THUMP
!!!
WOOSH
!?

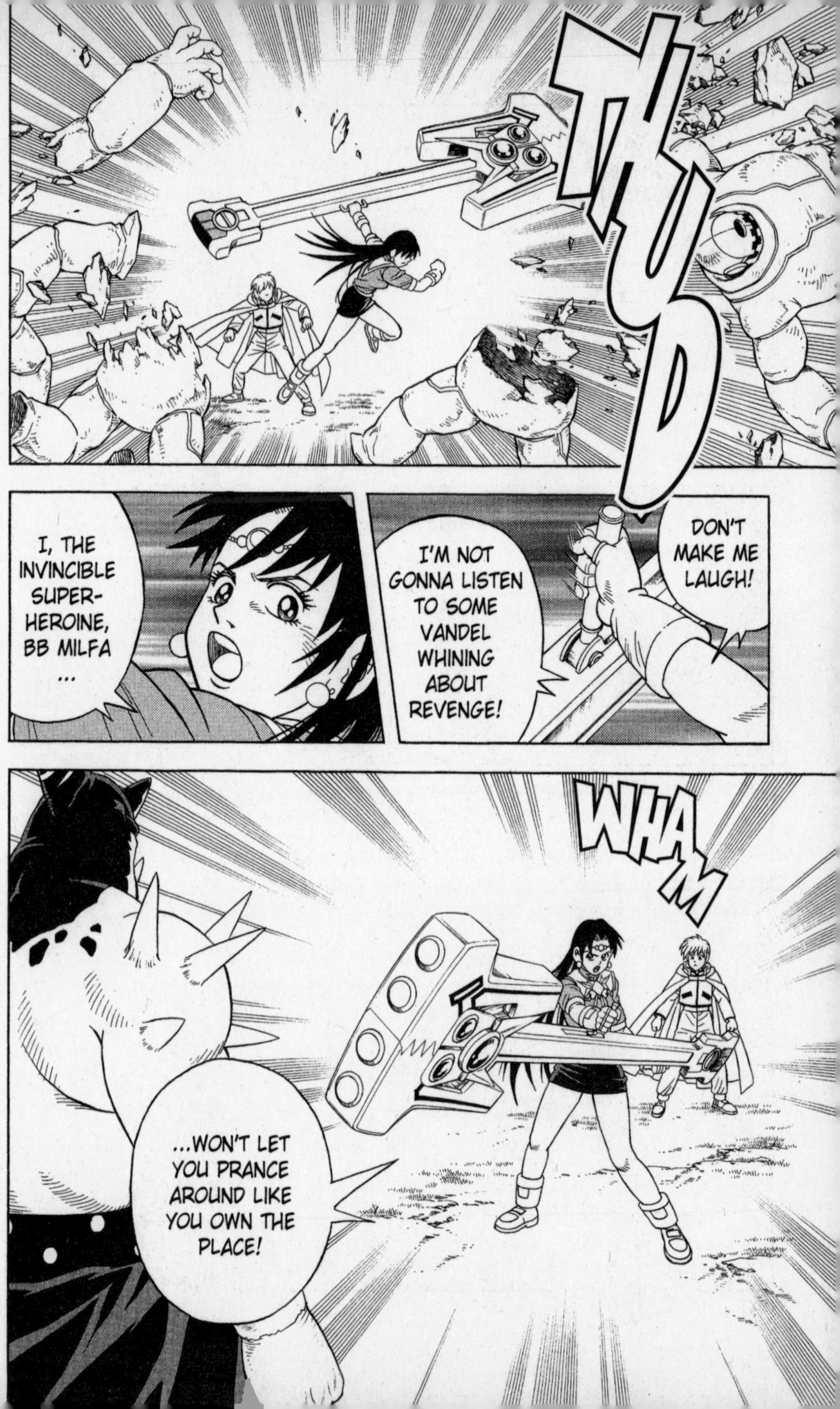
THUD
DON'T MAKE ME LAUGH!
I'M NOT GONNA LISTEN TO SOME VANDEL WHINING ABOUT REVENGE!
I, THE INVINCIBLE SUPER-HEROINE, BB MILFA ...
WHAM
...WON'T LET YOU PRANCE AROUND LIKE YOU OWN THE PLACE!

READ THIS WAY

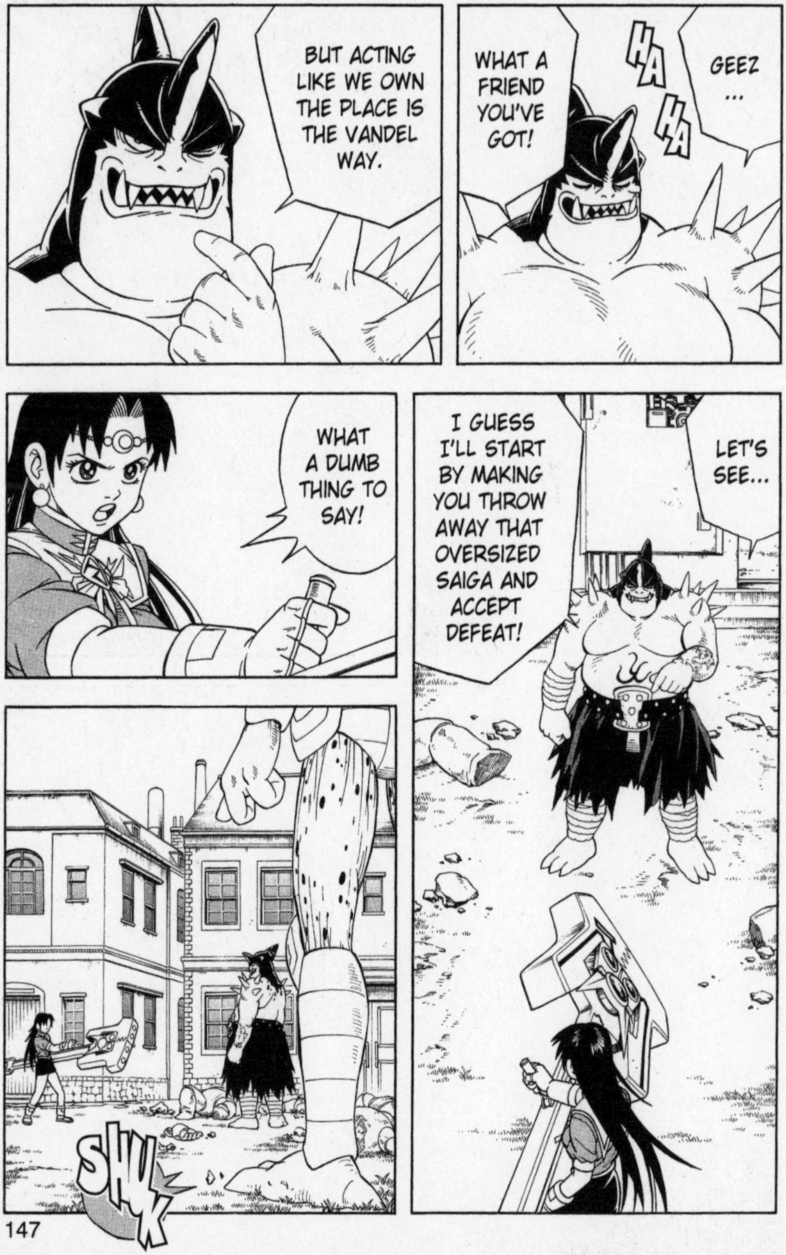
GEEZ ...
HA HA
WHAT A FRIEND YOU'VE GOT!
BUT ACTING LIKE WE OWN THE PLACE IS THE VANDEL WAY.
LET'S SEE...
I GUESS I'LL START BY MAKING YOU THROW AWAY THAT OVERSIZED SAIGA AND ACCEPT DEFEAT!
WHAT A DUMB THING TO SAY!
SHUK

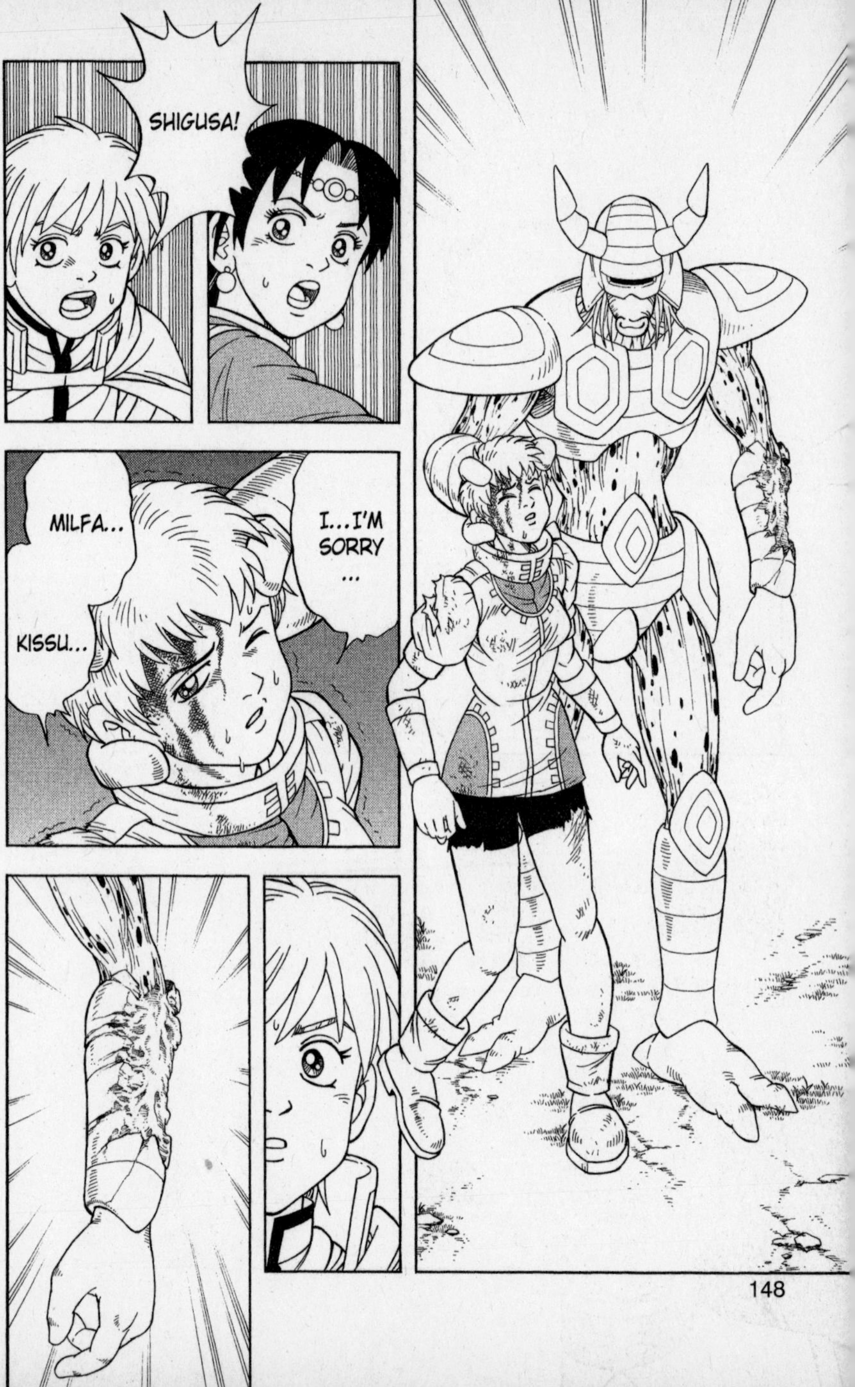
SHIGUSA!
I...I'M SORRY ...
MILFA...
KISSU...

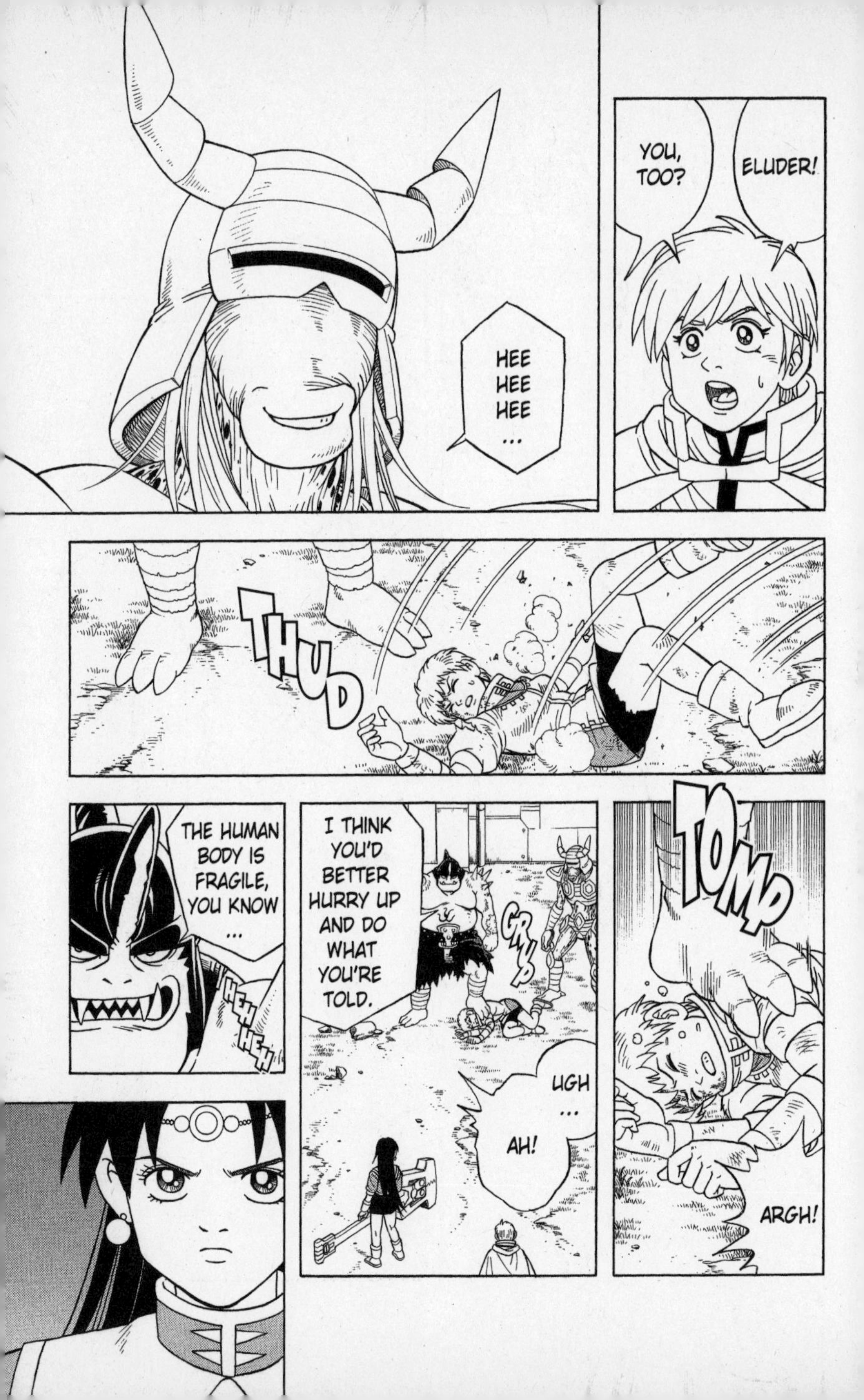
ELUDER!
YOU, TOO?
HEE HEE HEE ...
THUD
TOMP
ARGH!
I THINK YOU'D BETTER HURRY UP AND DO WHAT YOU'RE TOLD.
GRUP
UGH ...
AH!
THE HUMAN BODY IS FRAGILE, YOU KNOW ...
HEH HEH

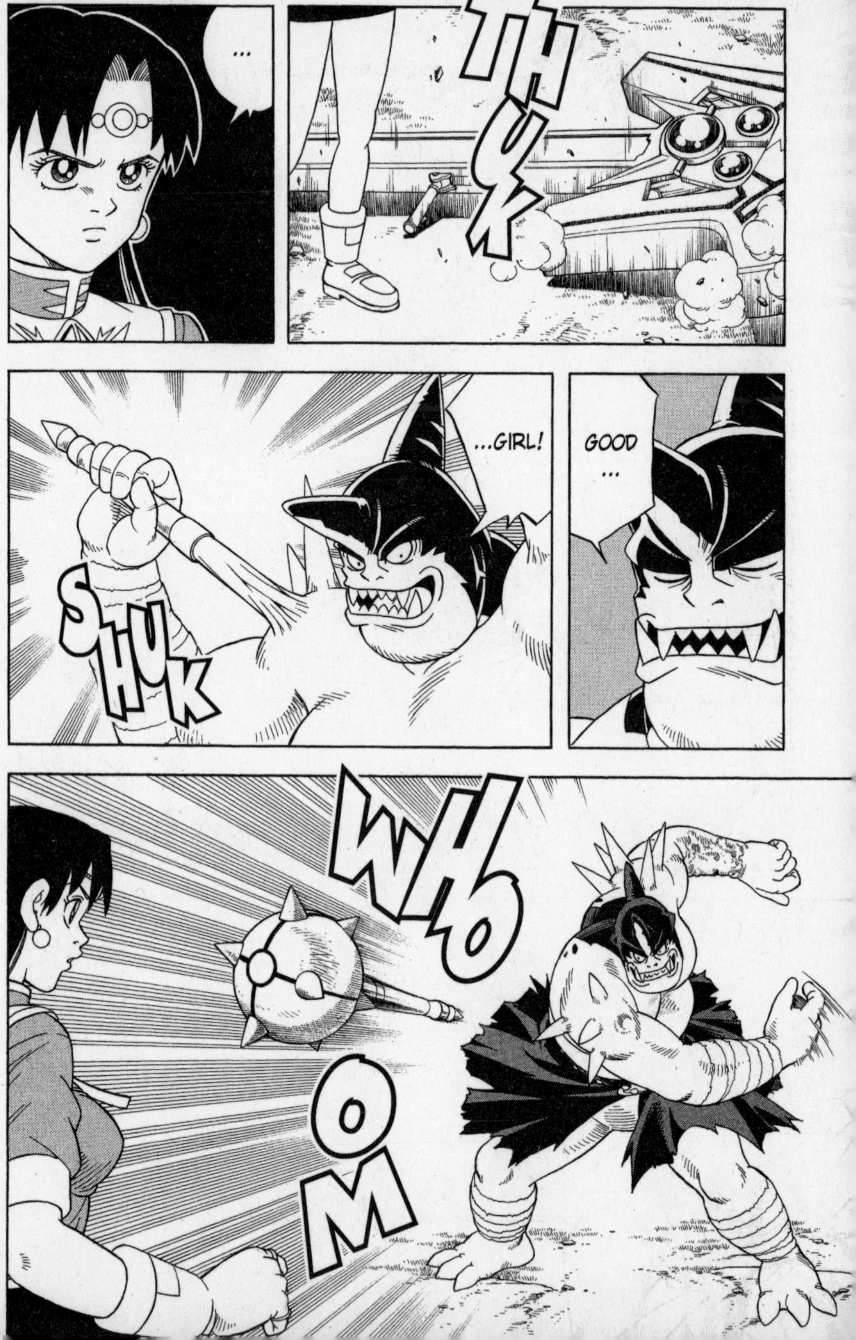
THUK
...
GOOD
...
...GIRL!
SHUK
WHOOM

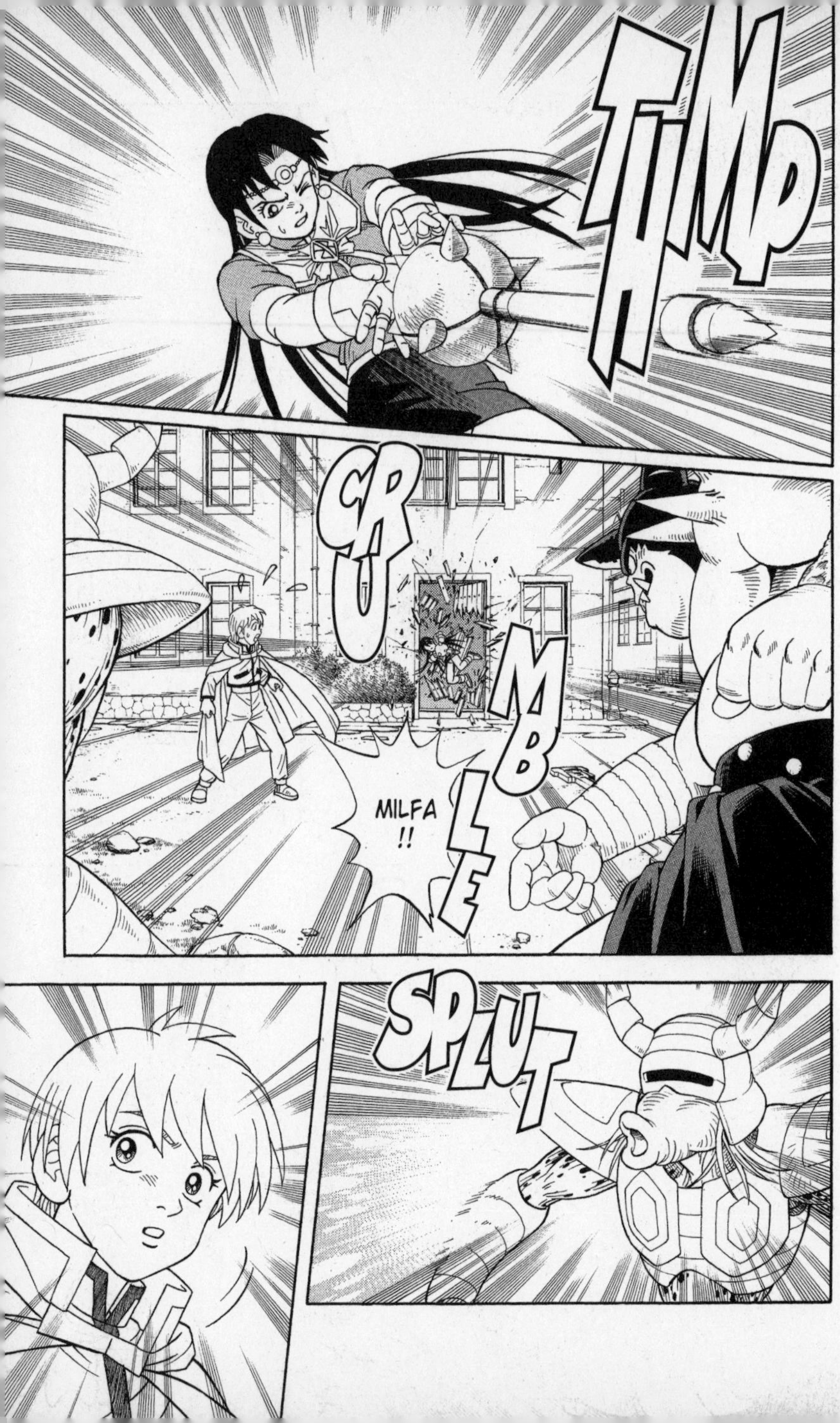
THMP
CRUMBLE
MILFA !!
SPLUT

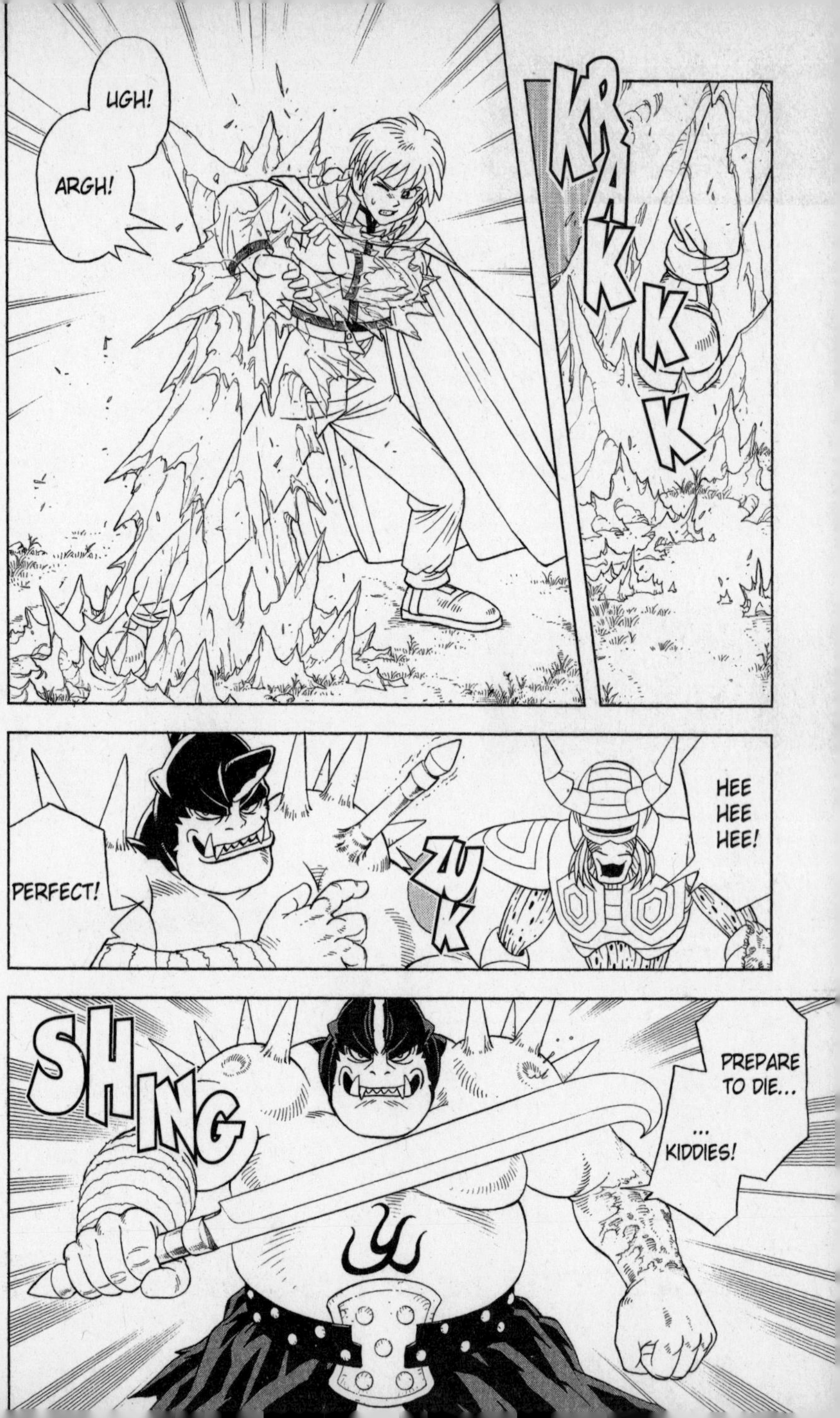
KRAKKK
UGH!
ARGH!
HEE HEE HEE!
ZUK
PERFECT!
PREPARE TO DIE...
... KIDDIES!
SHING

READ THIS WAY

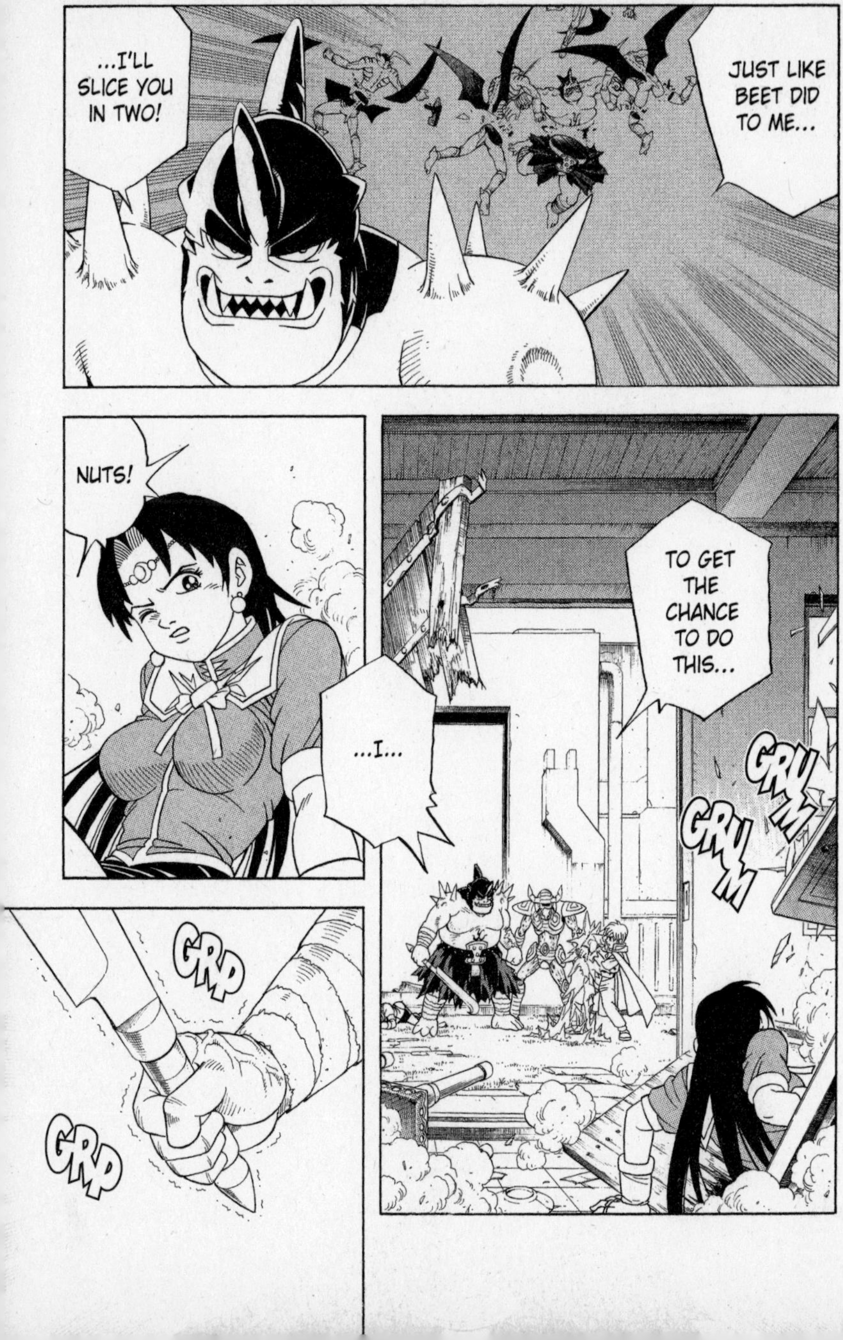
JUST LIKE BEET DID TO ME...
...I'LL SLICE YOU IN TWO!
TO GET THE CHANCE TO DO THIS...
...I...
GRUM
GRUM
NUTS!
GRP
GRP

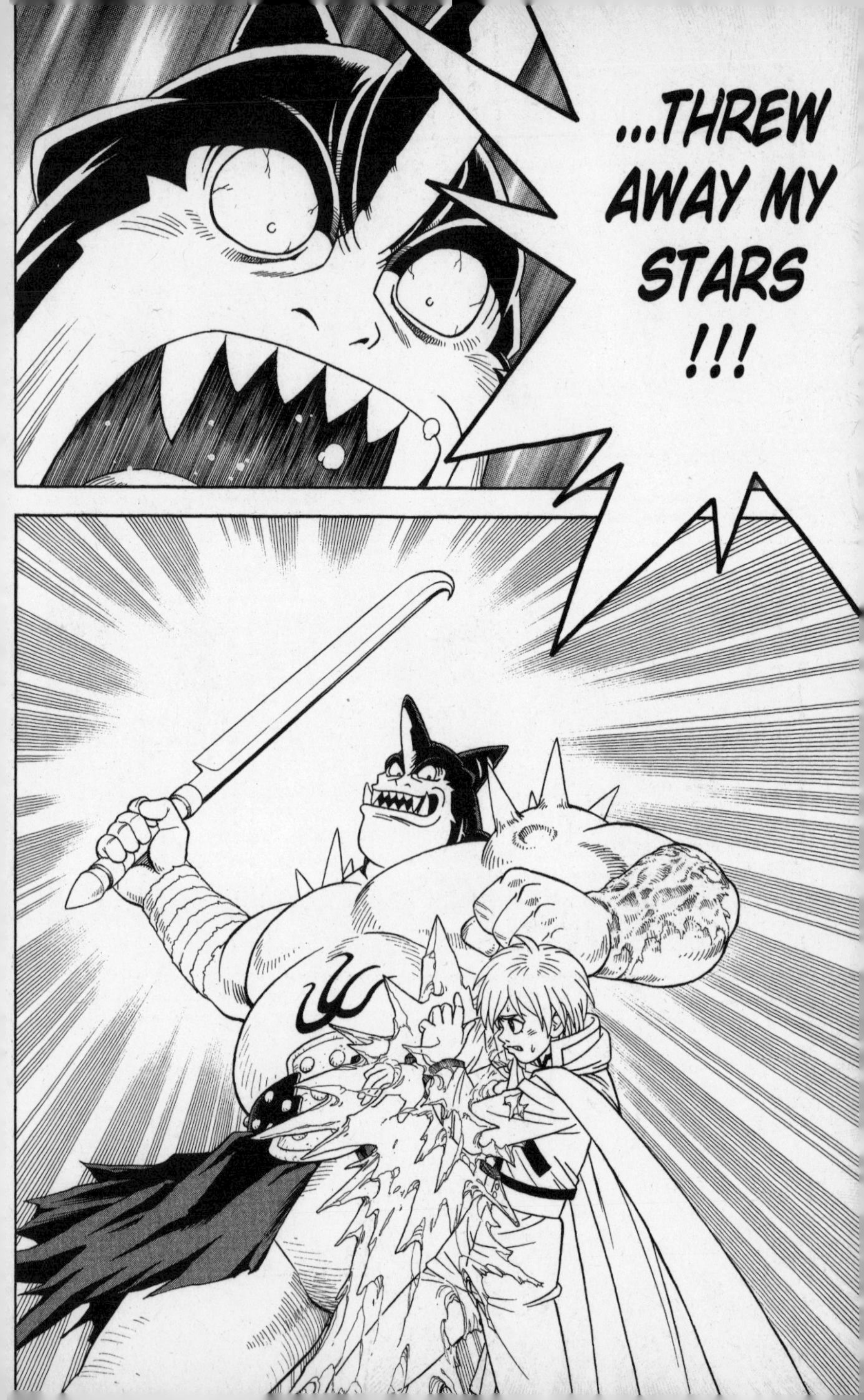
...THREW AWAY MY STARS !!!

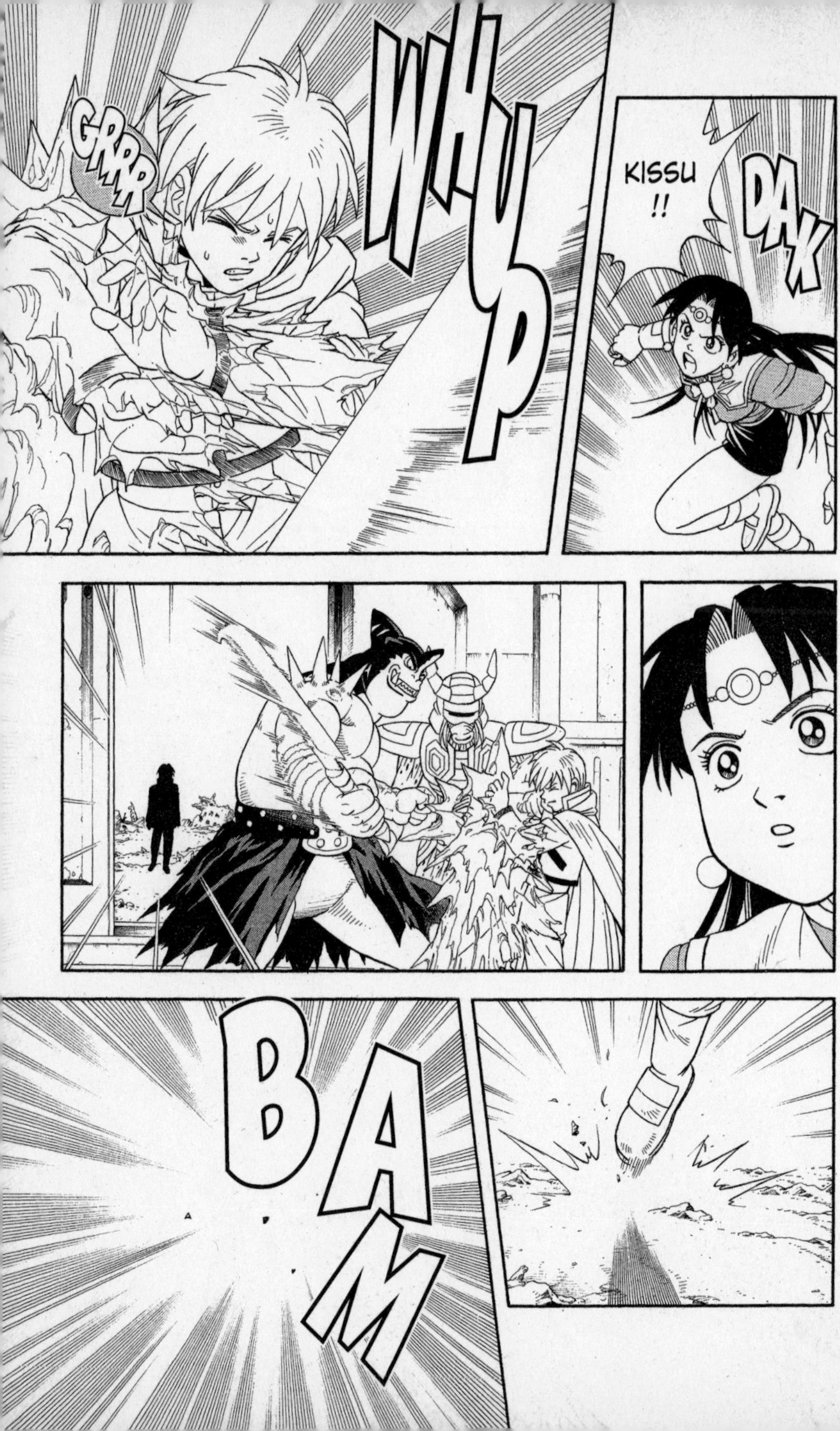
KISSU !!
DAK
WHUP
GRRR
BAM

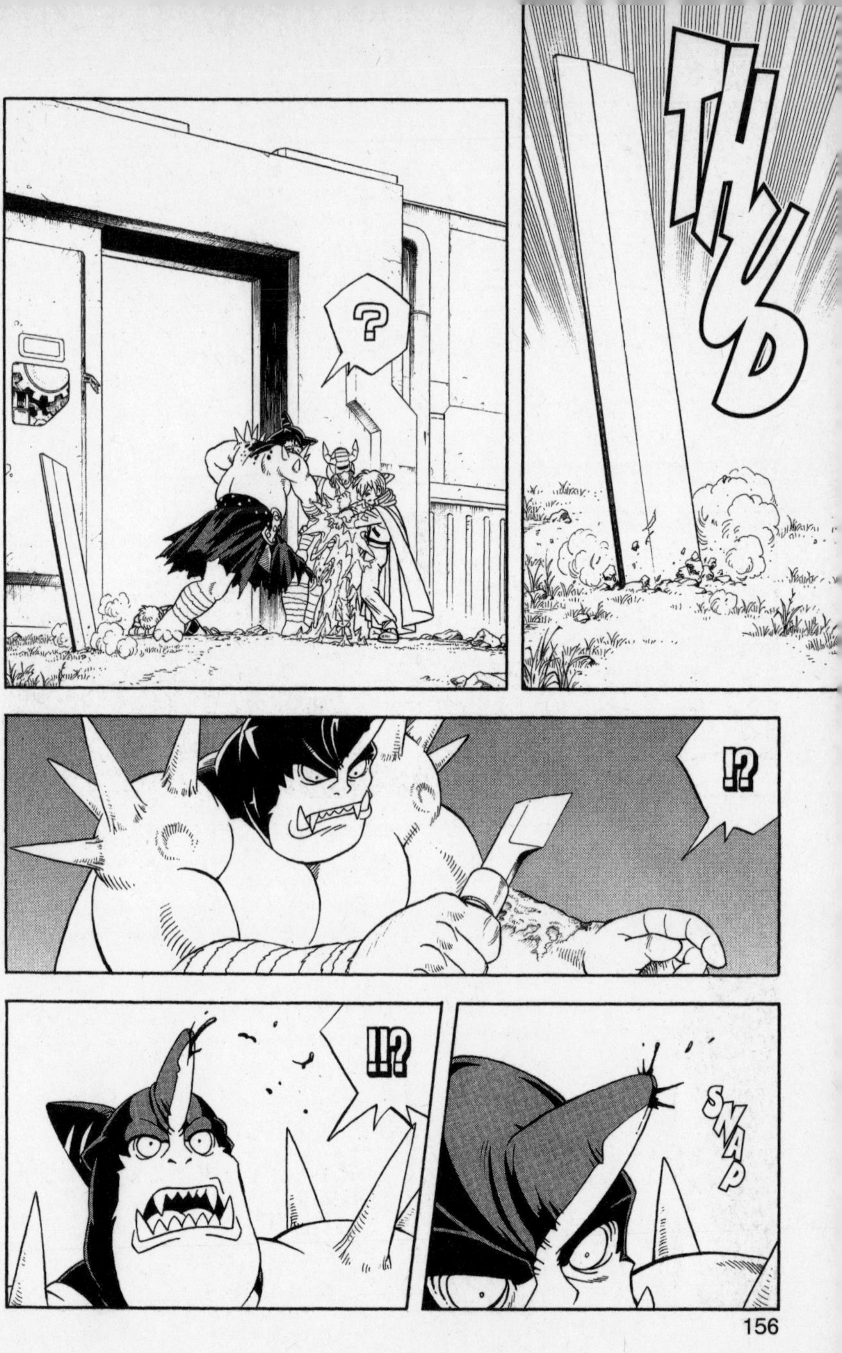
THUD
?
!?
SNAP
!!?

READ THIS WAY

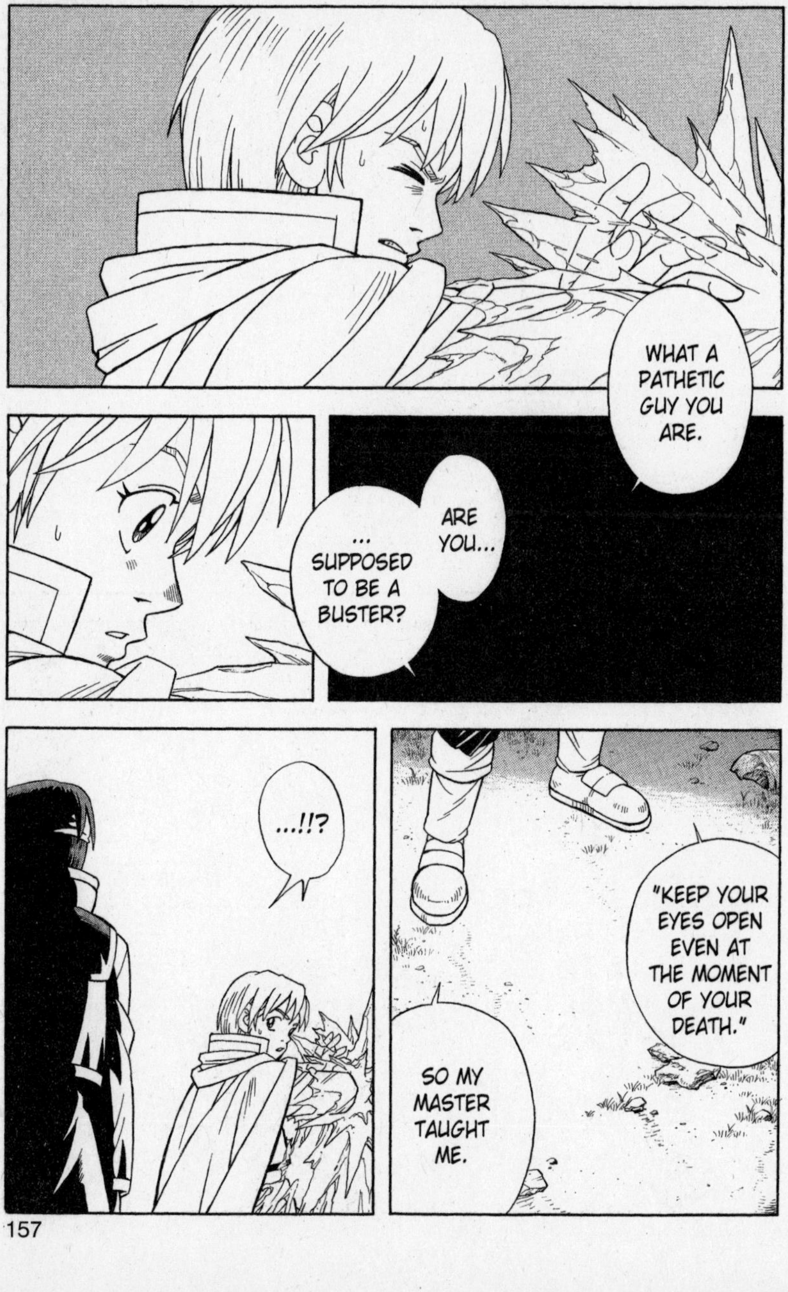
WHAT A PATHETIC GUY YOU ARE.
ARE YOU...
... SUPPOSED TO BE A BUSTER?
"KEEP YOUR EYES OPEN EVEN AT THE MOMENT OF YOUR DEATH."
SO MY MASTER TAUGHT ME.
...!!?

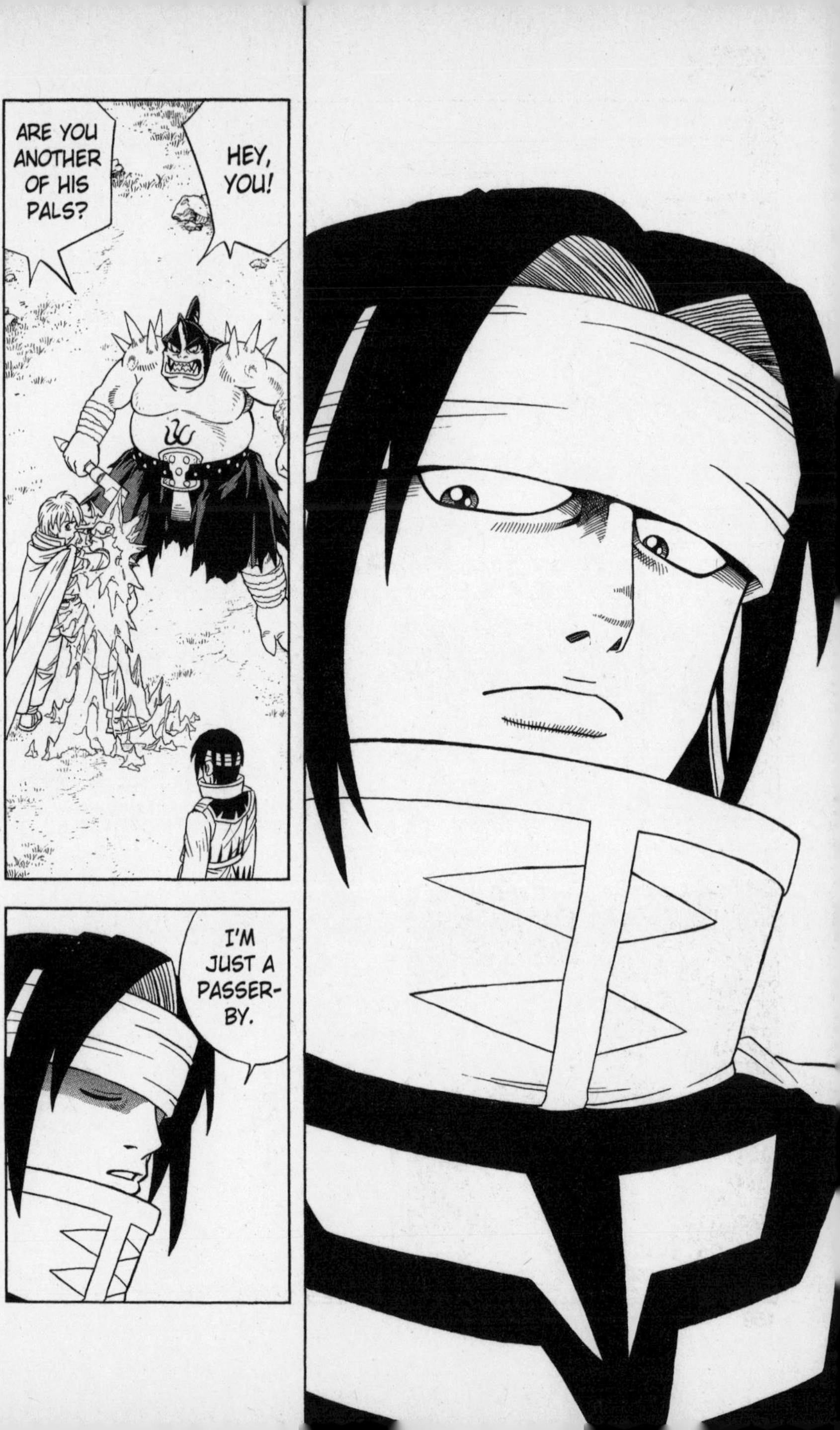
HEY, YOU!
ARE YOU ANOTHER OF HIS PALS?
I'M JUST A PASSER-BY.

READ THIS WAY

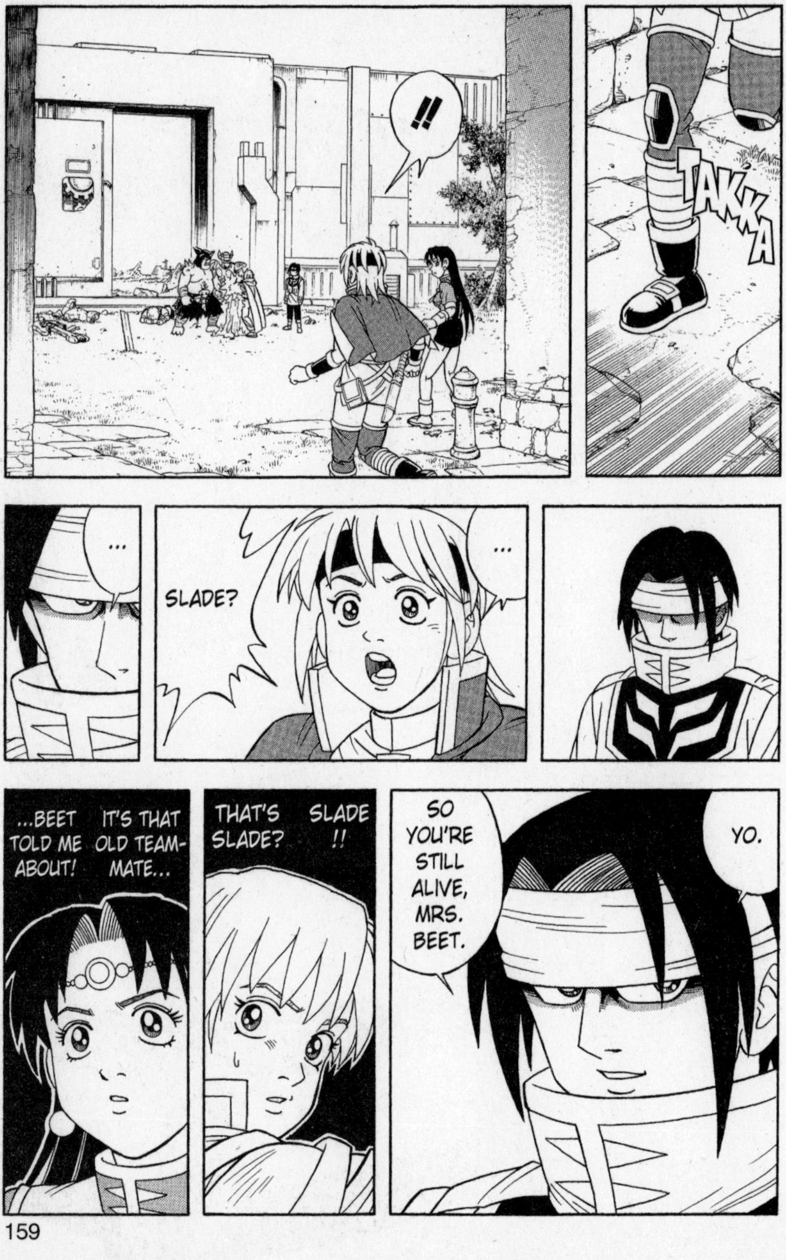
TAKKA
!!
...
SLADE?
...
YO.
SO YOU'RE STILL ALIVE, MRS. BEET.
SLADE !!
THAT'S SLADE?
IT'S THAT OLD TEAM-MATE...
...BEET TOLD ME ABOUT!

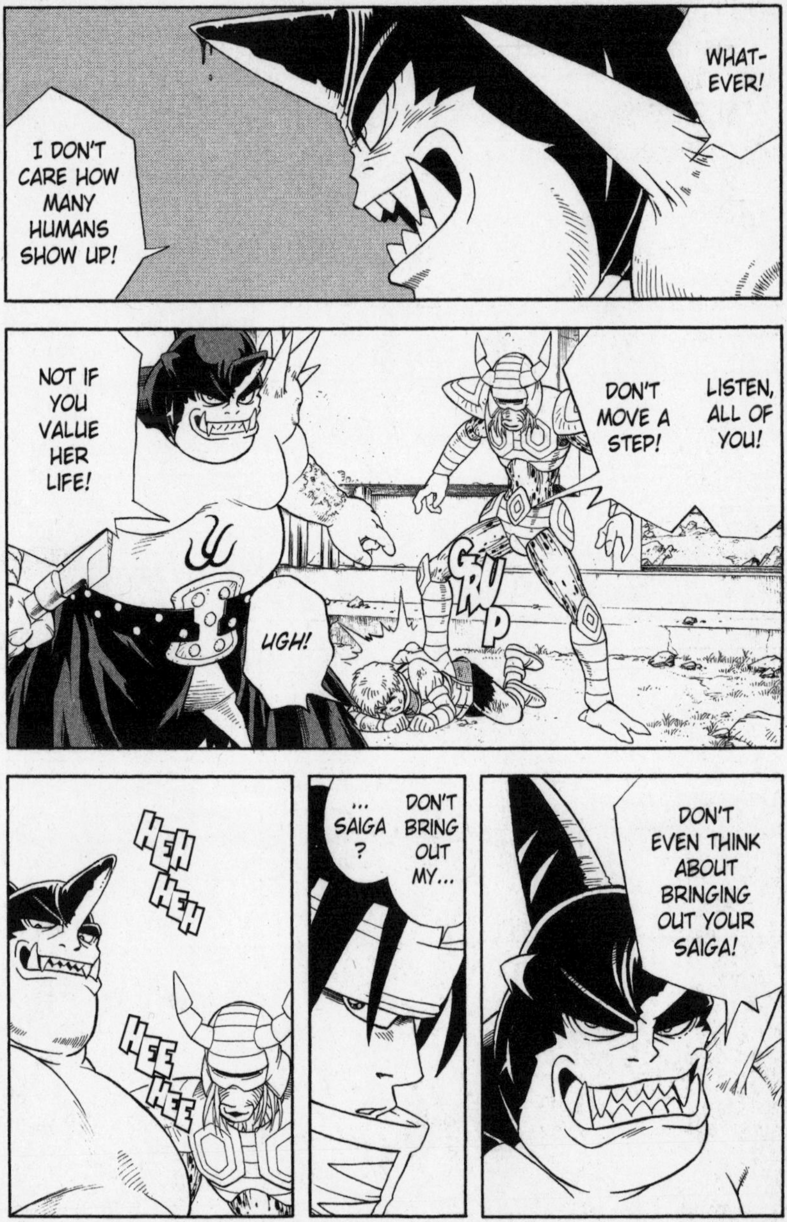
WHAT-EVER!
I DON'T CARE HOW MANY HUMANS SHOW UP!
LISTEN, ALL OF YOU!
DON'T MOVE A STEP!
NOT IF YOU VALUE HER LIFE!
GRUP
UGH!
DON'T EVEN THINK ABOUT BRINGING OUT YOUR SAIGA!
DON'T BRING OUT MY...
... SAIGA ?
HEH HEH
HEE HEE

READ THIS WAY

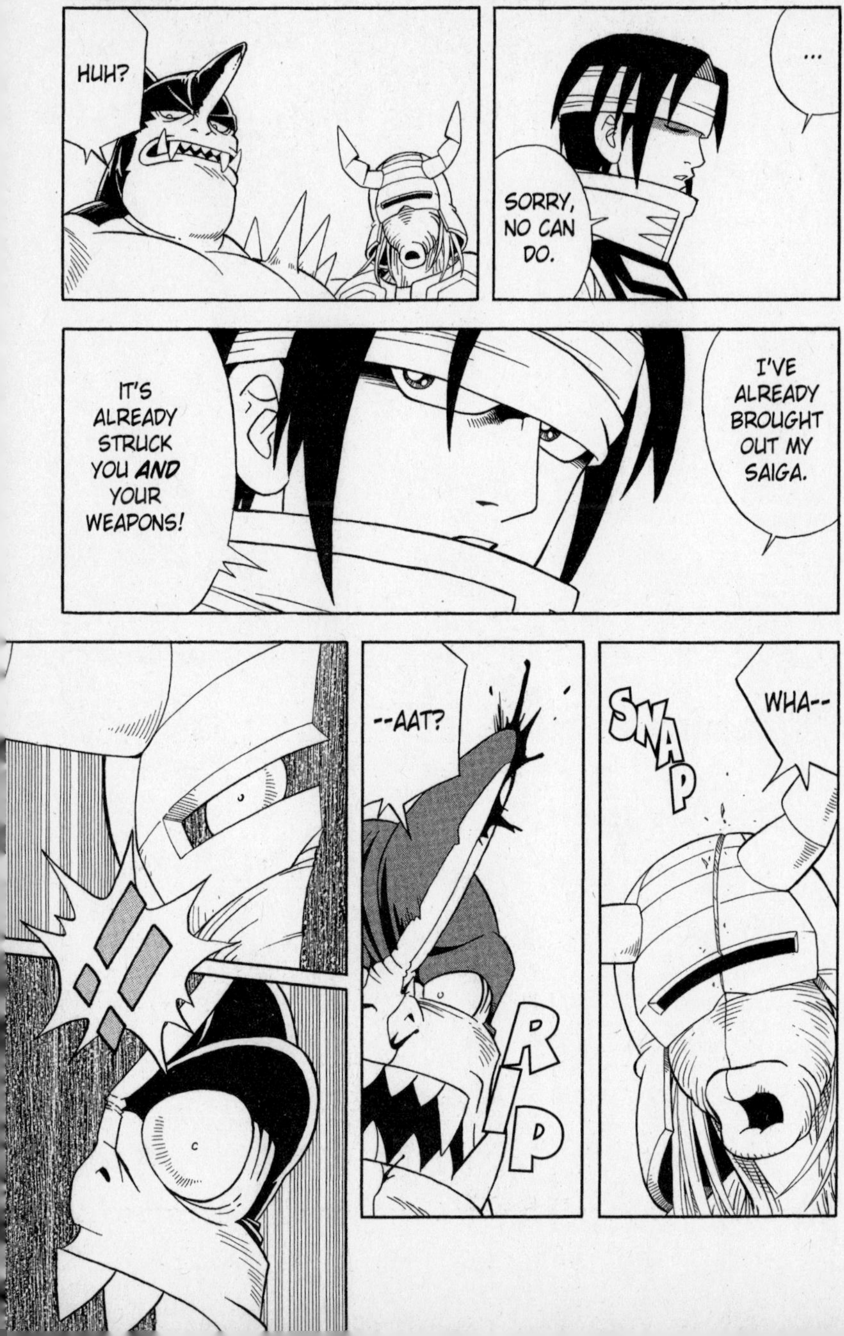
...
SORRY, NO CAN DO.
HUH?
I'VE ALREADY BROUGHT OUT MY SAIGA.
IT'S ALREADY STRUCK YOU **AND** YOUR WEAPONS!
WHA--
SNAP
--AAT?
RIP
!!

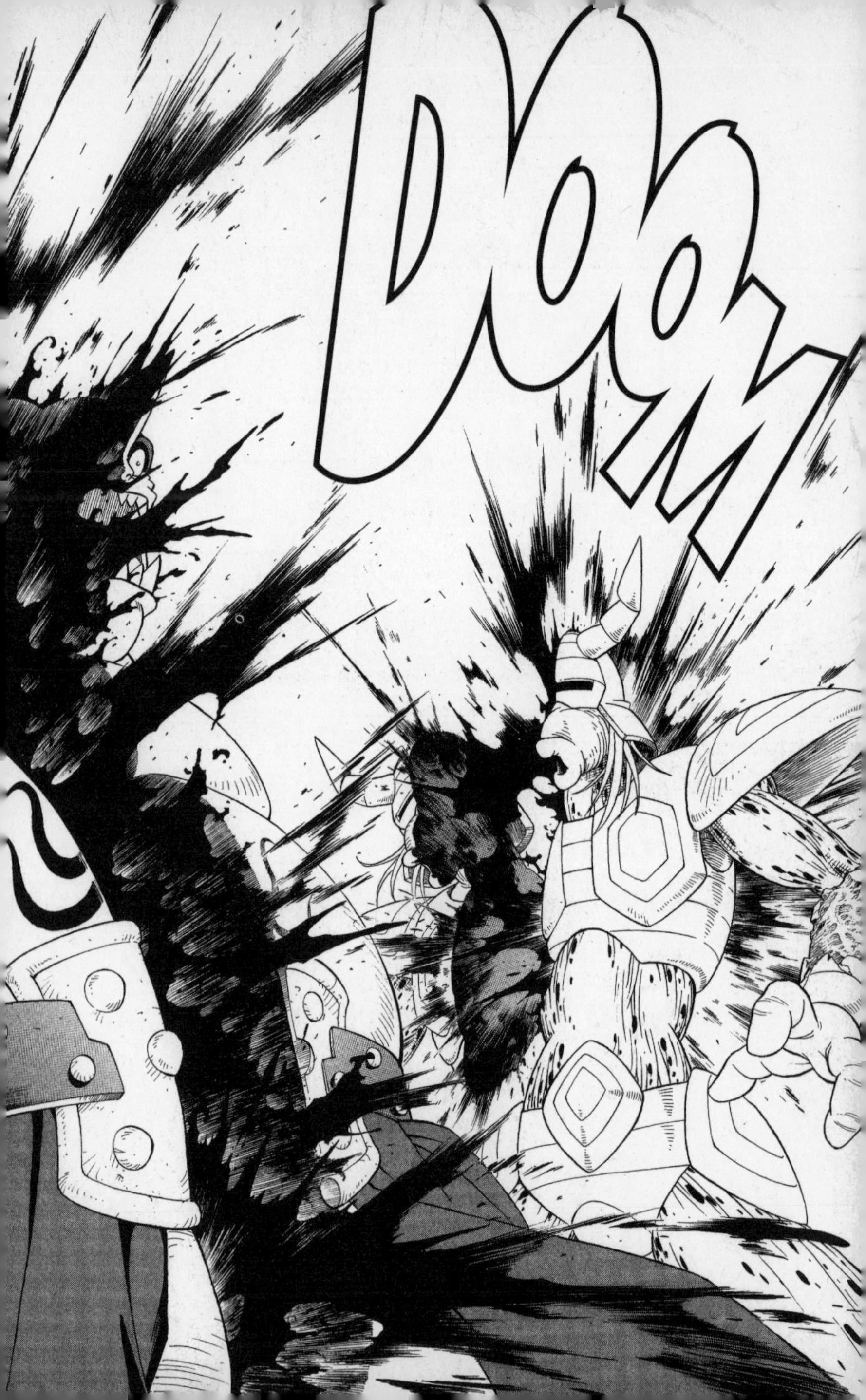
DOOM

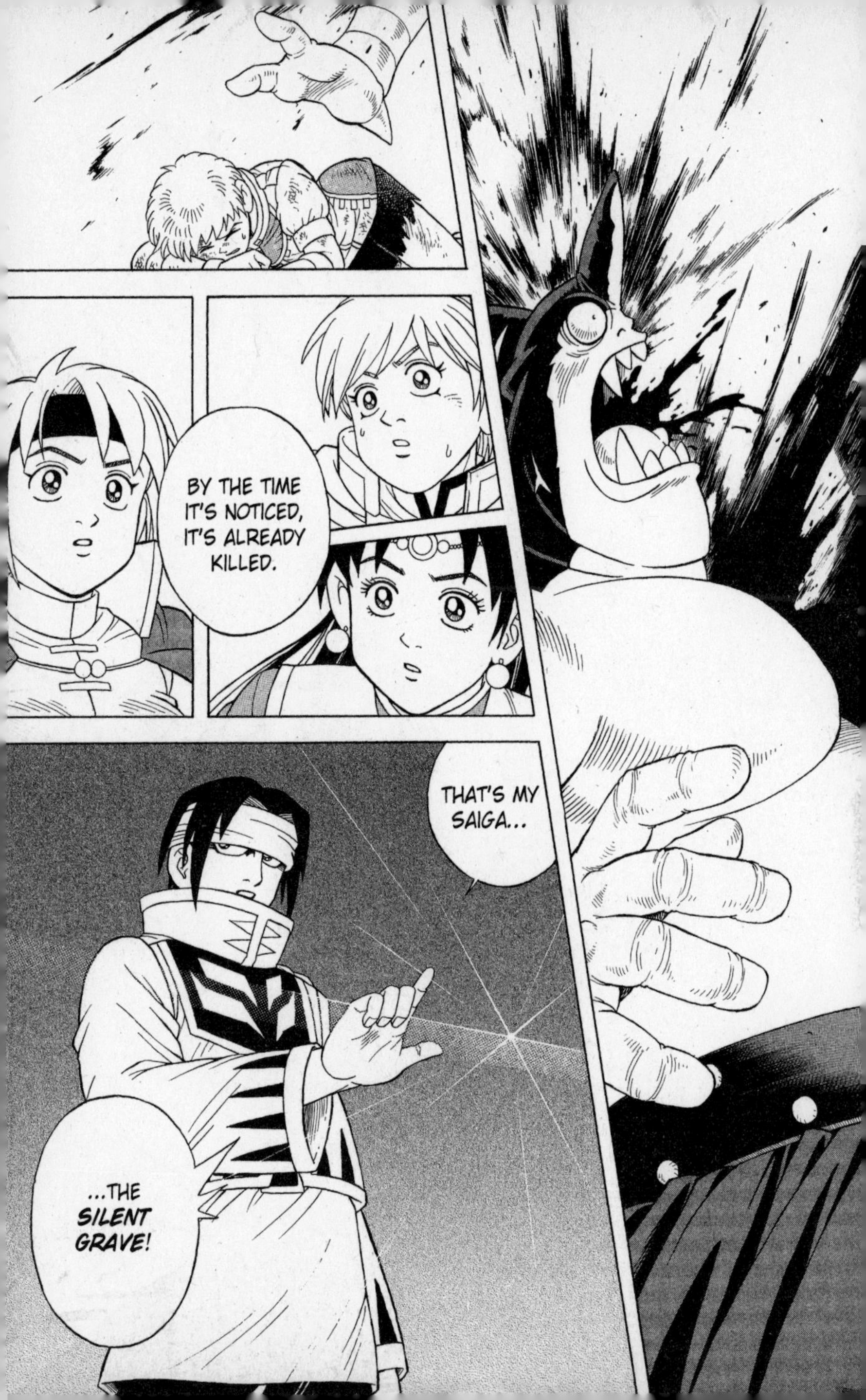
BY THE TIME IT'S NOTICED, IT'S ALREADY KILLED.
THAT'S MY SAIGA...
...THE SILENT GRAVE!

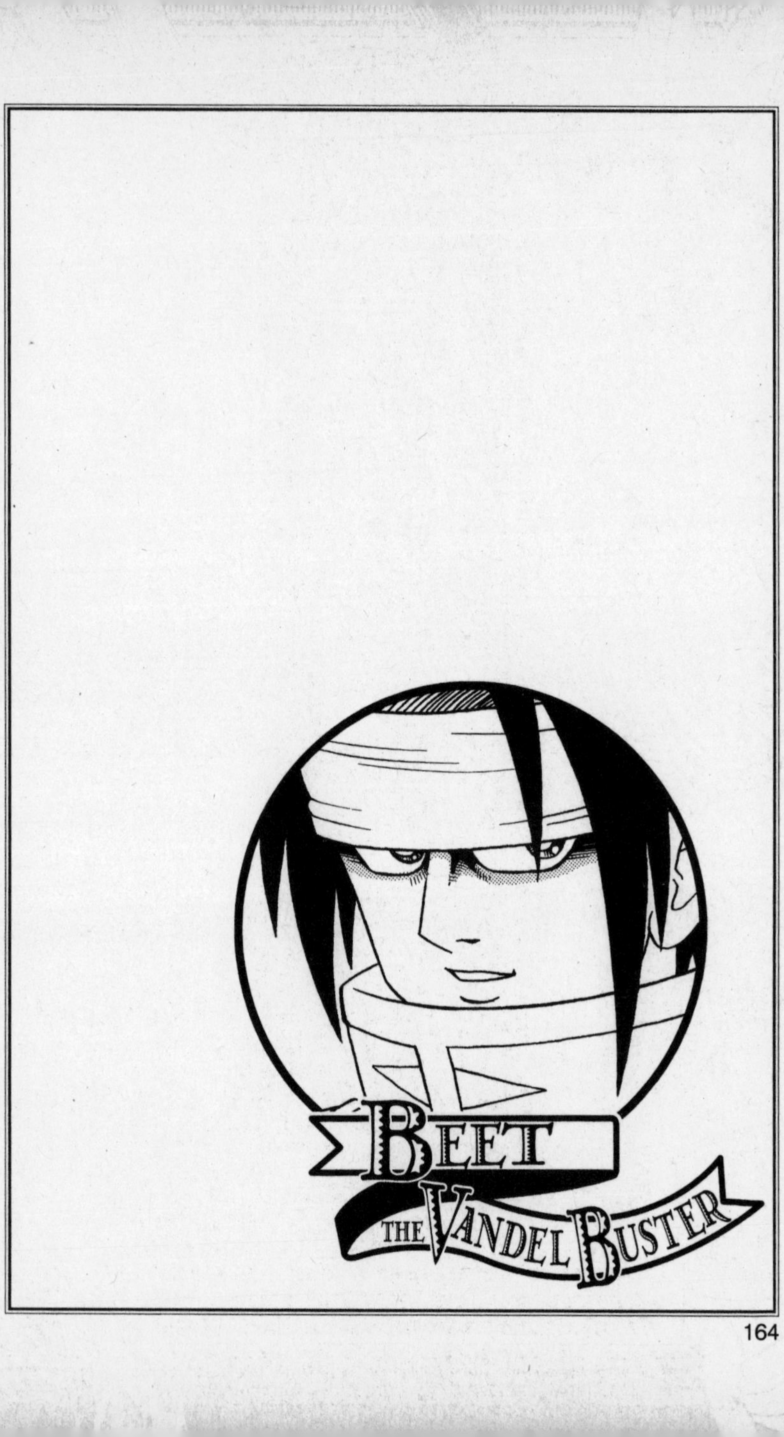
BEET
THE VANDEL BUSTER

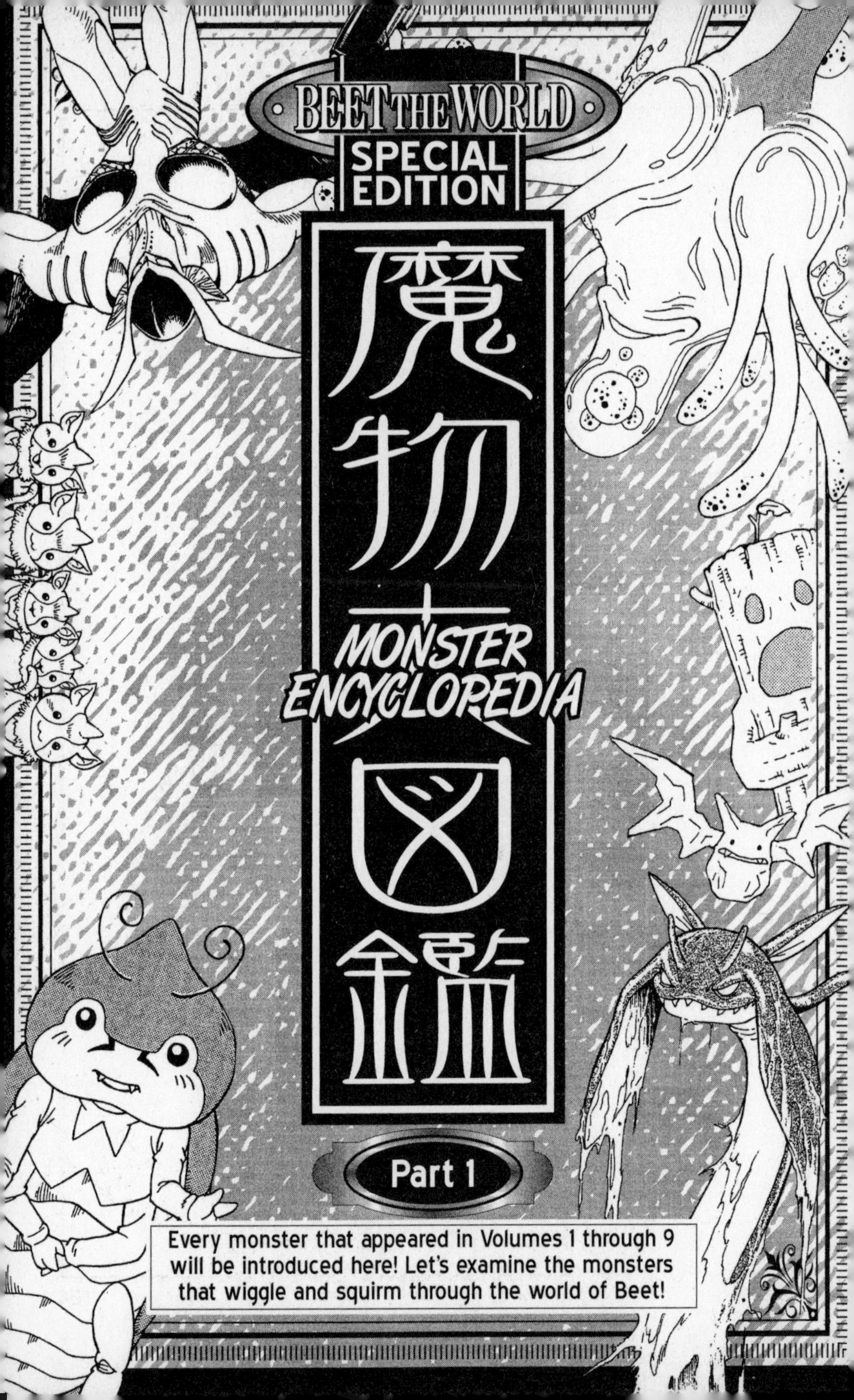
BEET THE WORLD
SPECIAL EDITION
魔物図鑑
MONSTER ENCYCLOPEDIA
Part 1
Every monster that appeared in Volumes 1 through 9 will be introduced here! Let's examine the monsters that wiggle and squirm through the world of Beet!

WHAT ARE MONSTERS?

Children of darkness that serve the Vandels--that's what the monsters of Beet's world are! Here, we'll reveal their amazing secrets!

The monsters are servants used by Vandels to inflict enormous damage on human society. They come in infinite sizes and shapes. Some are good at fighting, while others are scouts or spies. Each monster has its purpose. To obtain monsters, a Vandel must go to the Dark House of Sorcery, where Vandels gather, and buy them with Sorcery Bills. By paying an additional sum, it's possible to strengthen a monster and make it into a powerful assistant.

Monsters can be organized into 10 types by their attributes. It is said that their attributes come from the materials used by the Dark House of Sorcery to create them. Monsters have different powers and thrive in different habitats, but they're all born with ill will toward humans. They're truly humanity's natural enemies!

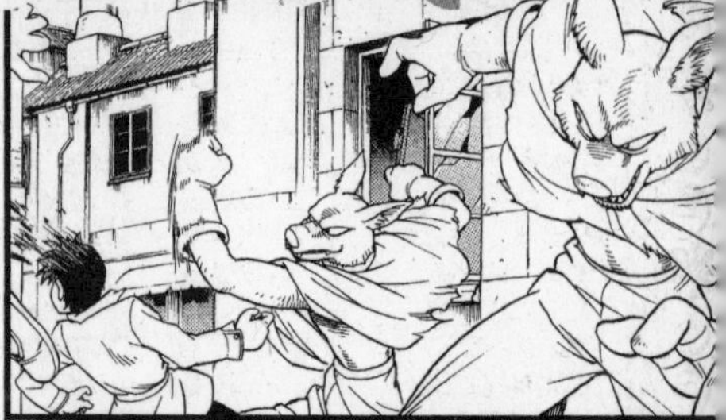

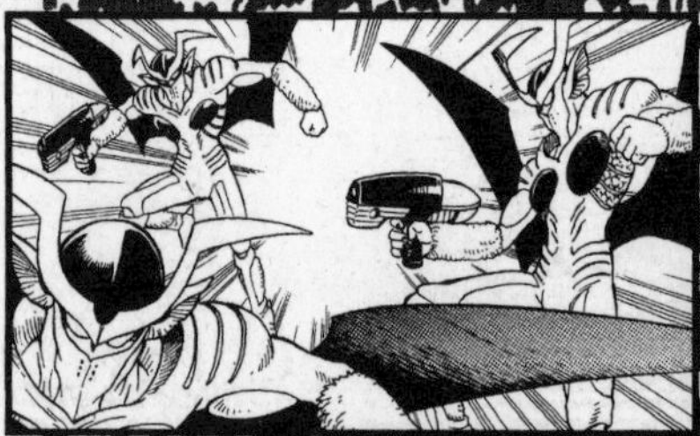

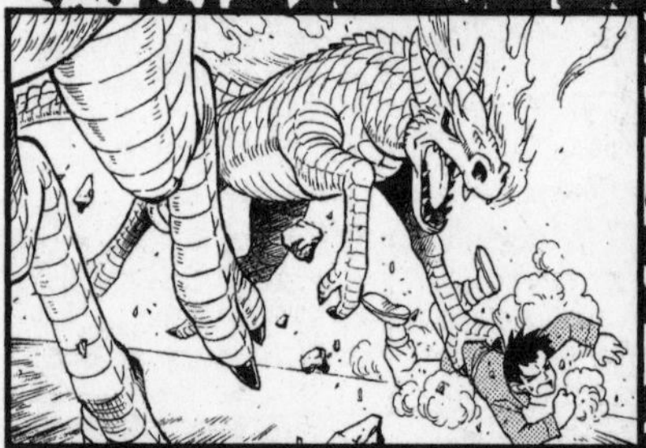

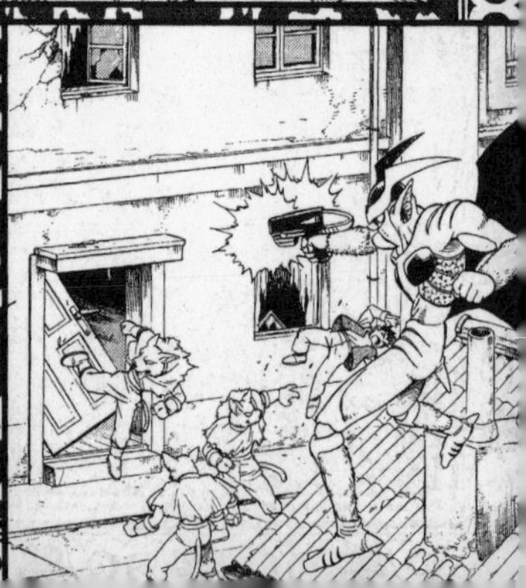

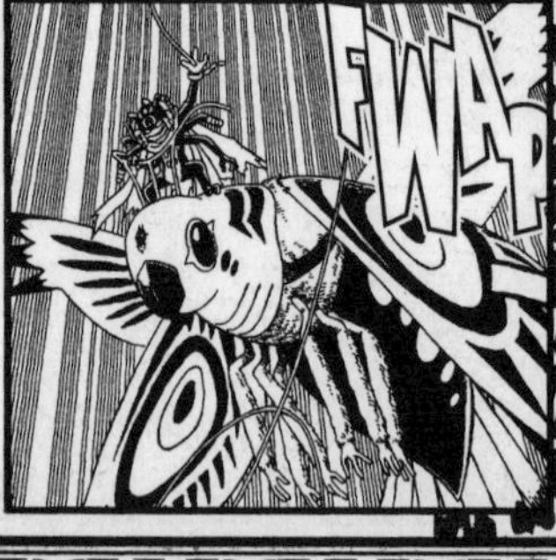
FWAP

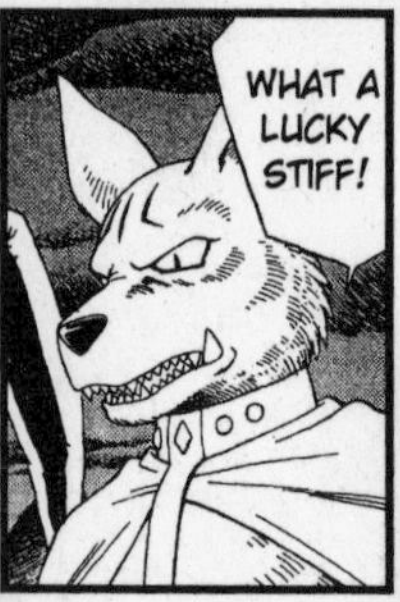
WHAT A LUCKY STIFF!

▲▶ There are many kinds--from intelligent monsters that speak human language to monsters used as long-distance transportation.

THE TEN TYPES OF MONSTERS

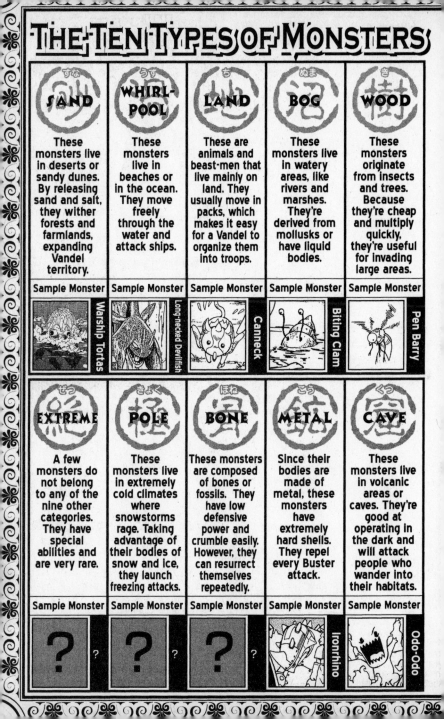

すな 砂 SAND	うず 渦 WHIRLPOOL	ち 地 LAND	ぬま 沼 BOG	き 樹 WOOD
These monsters live in deserts or sandy dunes. By releasing sand and salt, they wither forests and farmlands, expanding Vandel territory.	These monsters live in beaches or in the ocean. They move freely through the water and attack ships.	These are animals and beast-men that live mainly on land. They usually move in packs, which makes it easy for a Vandel to organize them into troops.	These monsters live in watery areas, like rivers and marshes. They're derived from mollusks or have liquid bodies.	These monsters originate from insects and trees. Because they're cheap and multiply quickly, they're useful for invading large areas.
Sample Monster	Sample Monster	Sample Monster	Sample Monster	Sample Monster
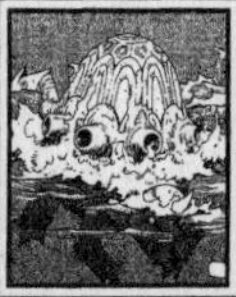 Warship Tortas	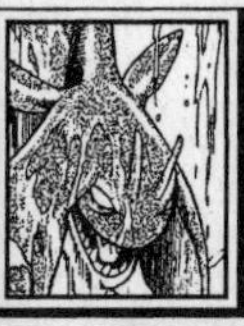 Long-necked Devilfish	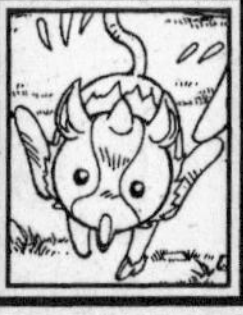 Canneck	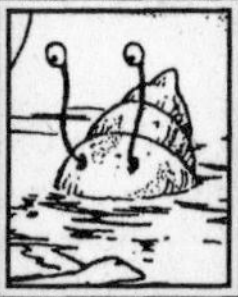 Biting Clam	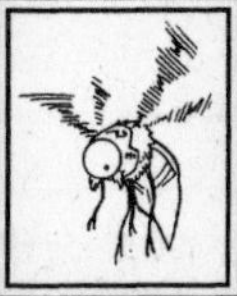 Pen Barry

ぜつ 絶 EXTREME	きょく 極 POLE	ほね 骨 BONE	こう 鋼 METAL	くつ 窟 CAVE
A few monsters do not belong to any of the nine other categories. They have special abilities and are very rare.	These monsters live in extremely cold climates where snowstorms rage. Taking advantage of their bodies of snow and ice, they launch freezing attacks.	These monsters are composed of bones or fossils. They have low defensive power and crumble easily. However, they can resurrect themselves repeatedly.	Since their bodies are made of metal, these monsters have extremely hard shells. They repel every Buster attack.	These monsters live in volcanic areas or caves. They're good at operating in the dark and will attack people who wander into their habitats.
Sample Monster	Sample Monster	Sample Monster	Sample Monster	Sample Monster
? ?	? ?	? ?	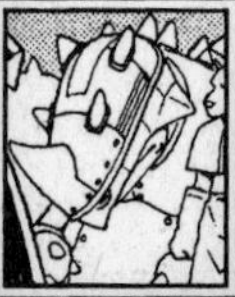 Ironrhino	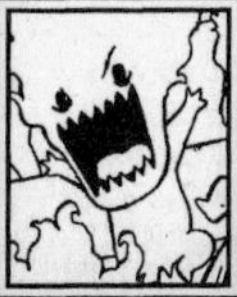 Odo-Odo

BITING CLAM

BOG

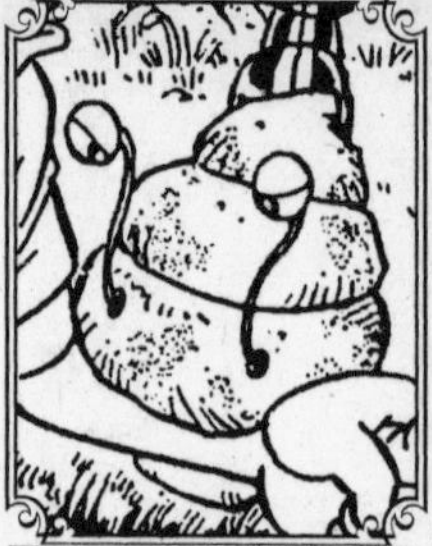

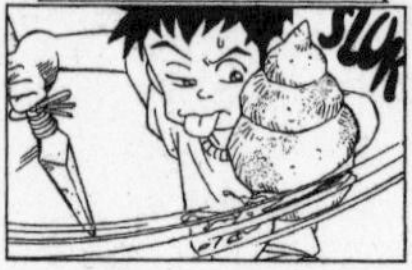
SLUK

▲The very first monster Beet defeated.

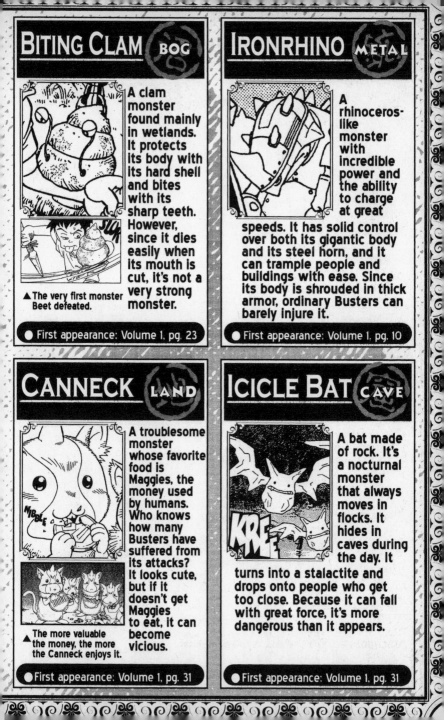

A clam monster found mainly in wetlands. It protects its body with its hard shell and bites with its sharp teeth. However, since it dies easily when its mouth is cut, it's not a very strong monster.

● First appearance: Volume 1, pg. 23

IRONRHINO

METAL

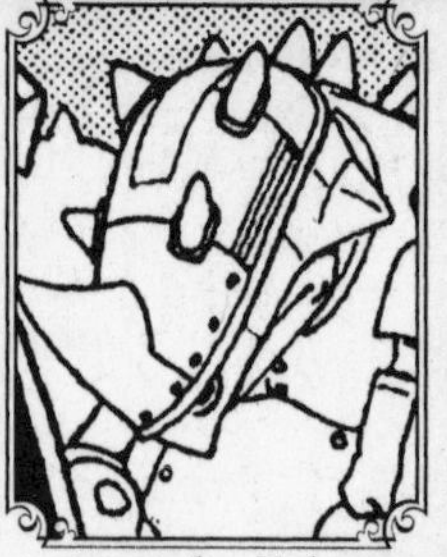

A rhinoceros-like monster with incredible power and the ability to charge at great speeds. It has solid control over both its gigantic body and its steel horn, and it can trample people and buildings with ease. Since its body is shrouded in thick armor, ordinary Busters can barely injure it.

● First appearance: Volume 1, pg. 10

CANNECK

LAND

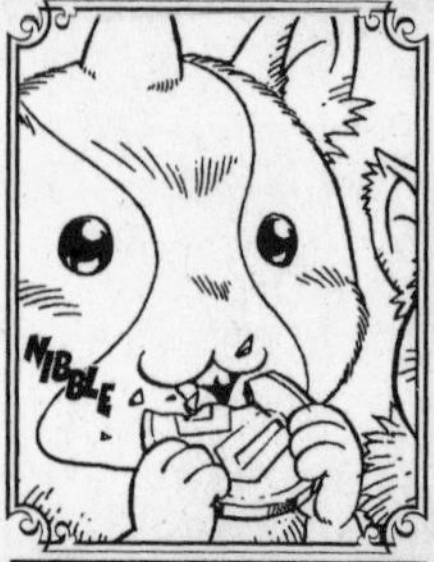
NIBBLE

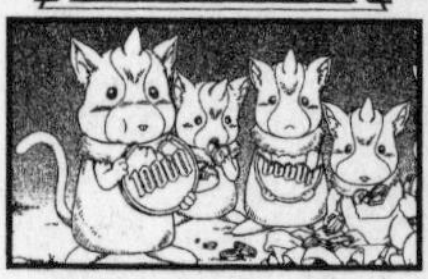

▲The more valuable the money, the more the Canneck enjoys it.

A troublesome monster whose favorite food is Maggies, the money used by humans. Who knows how many Busters have suffered from its attacks? It looks cute, but if it doesn't get Maggies to eat, it can become vicious.

● First appearance: Volume 1, pg. 31

ICICLE BAT

CAVE

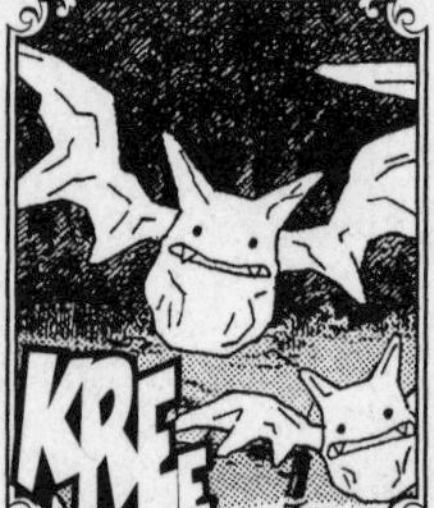
KREE

A bat made of rock. It's a nocturnal monster that always moves in flocks. It hides in caves during the day. It turns into a stalactite and drops onto people who get too close. Because it can fall with great force, it's more dangerous than it appears.

● First appearance: Volume 1, pg. 31

HOUND SOLDIER (LAND)

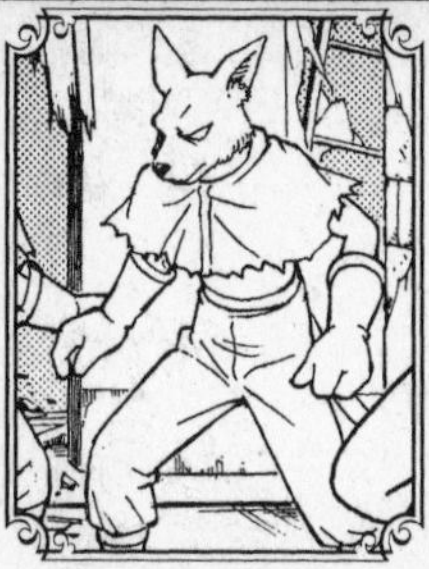

A beast-man with a wolflike appearance and great fighting ability. It can act alone, but it's best when fighting in a pack. It's intelligent and can handle many different duties. Many Vandels keep a Hound Soldier as a personal assistant.

● First appearance: Volume 1, pg. 35

KODA MANBO (WOOD)

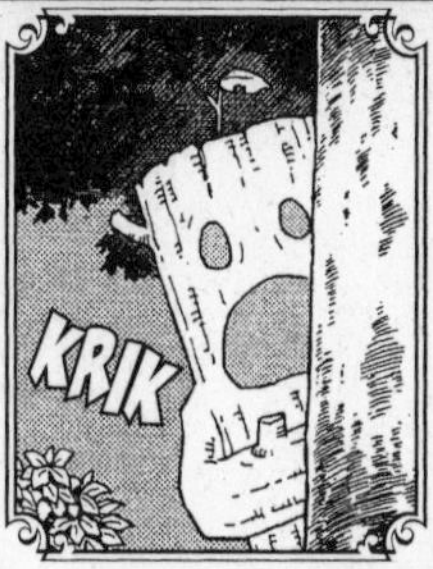
KRIK

A monster that makes mysterious sounds deep in the forests, leading travelers astray. It's the weakest of the Wood monsters, and it hardly ever hurts humans. Because of this, Vandels can purchase these monsters for next to nothing. It takes nutrition through its feet.

● First appearance: Volume 1, pg. 31

AQUA DOG (BOG)

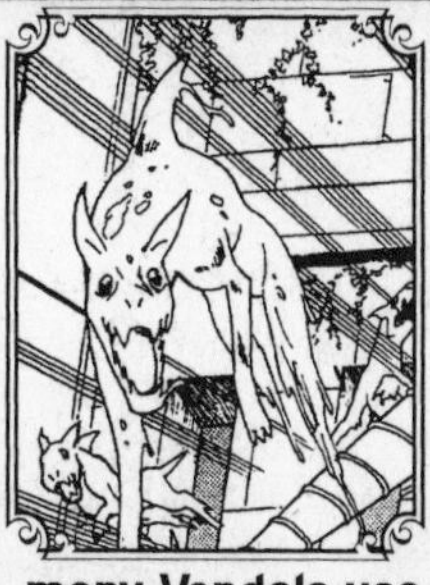

A dog-type monster whose body is made of water. Because Aqua Dogs are fierce and highly athletic, many Vandels use them as guard dogs in their castles. Although an Aqua Dog isn't very strong, it can move quickly along the surface of water. It can be very dangerous if encountered in a swamp or bog.

● First appearance: Volume 1, pg. 80

DRAWMAN (BOG)

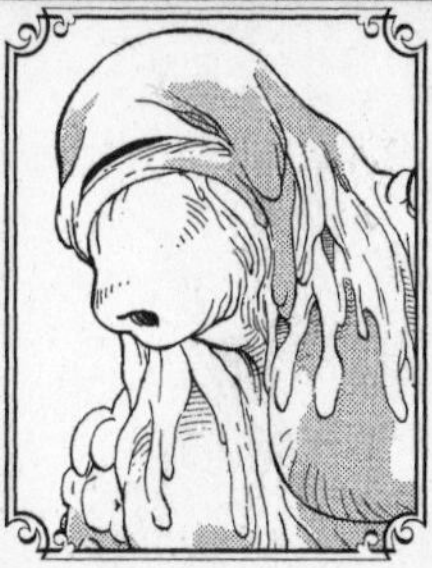

A monster that can disguise itself as a human. It has high-level shapeshifting skills, to the point that ordinary people can't tell it apart from a real human. Busters can recognize a Drawman by its distinctive oily smell.

It's ▶ good at blending into the crowds in a town and acting in secret.

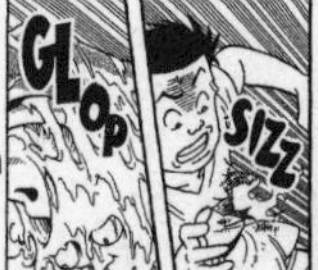
SIZZ
GLOP

● First appearance: Volume 1, pg. 74

DRAWMASTER BOG

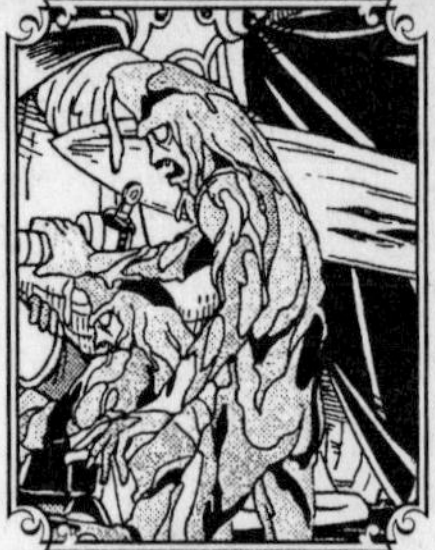

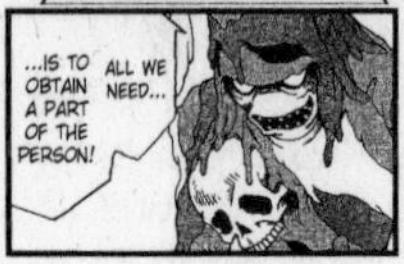
ALL WE NEED...
...IS TO OBTAIN A PART OF THE PERSON!

▲ Not even Busters can detect this high-level disguise.

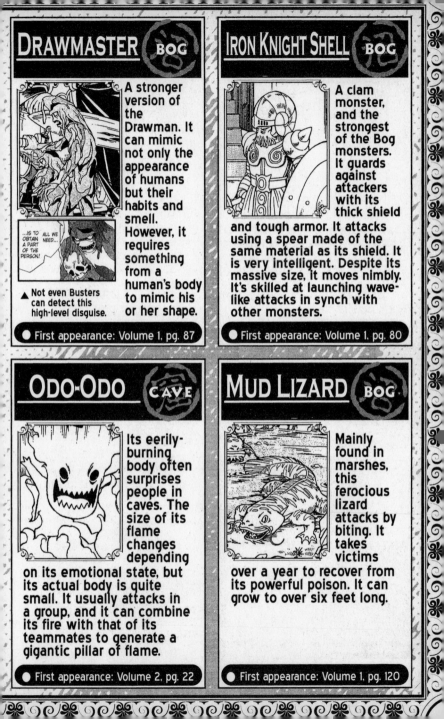

A stronger version of the Drawman. It can mimic not only the appearance of humans but their habits and smell. However, it requires something from a human's body to mimic his or her shape.

● First appearance: Volume 1, pg. 87

IRON KNIGHT SHELL BOG

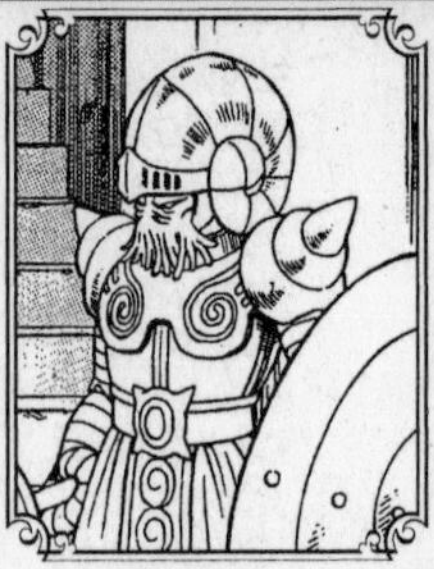

A clam monster, and the strongest of the Bog monsters. It guards against attackers with its thick shield and tough armor. It attacks using a spear made of the same material as its shield. It is very intelligent. Despite its massive size, it moves nimbly. It's skilled at launching wave-like attacks in synch with other monsters.

● First appearance: Volume 1, pg. 80

ODO-ODO CAVE

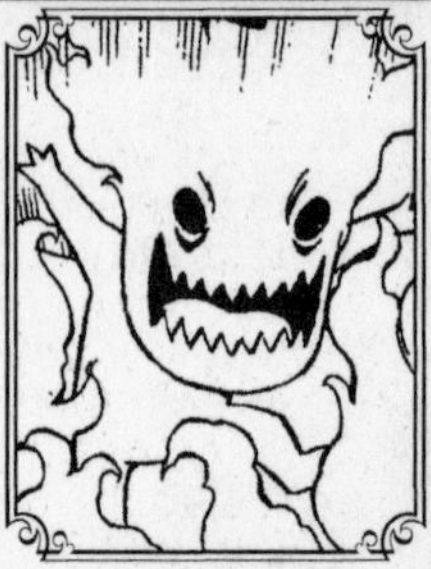

Its eerily-burning body often surprises people in caves. The size of its flame changes depending on its emotional state, but its actual body is quite small. It usually attacks in a group, and it can combine its fire with that of its teammates to generate a gigantic pillar of flame.

● First appearance: Volume 2, pg. 22

MUD LIZARD BOG

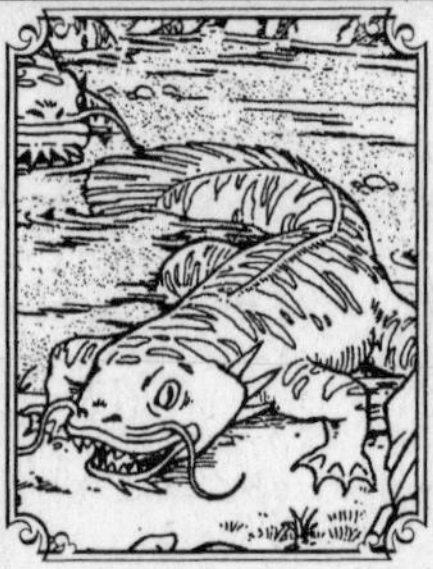

Mainly found in marshes, this ferocious lizard attacks by biting. It takes victims over a year to recover from its powerful poison. It can grow to over six feet long.

● First appearance: Volume 1, pg. 120

HOUND KNIGHT LAND

A stronger version of the Hound Soldier. It is exceptionally strong and intelligent and is capable of making tactical decisions in battle without losing its head. It carries steel knives in both arms. It is also characterized by its skill in hand-to-hand combat, in which it makes good use of its knives.

● First appearance: Volume 2, pg. 23

KNIGHT SNIPER CAVE

A monster that flies through the sky on enormous wings. Although it has high-level grappling skills, its main weapon is a special gun it carries. The horn on its head works as a radar transmitter, which not only helps it when shooting, but allows it to make tactical moves in the dark.

● First appearance: Volume 2, pg. 23

HAZAN
BELTORZE'S FAITHFUL RIGHT-HAND MONSTER

In response to Beltorze's demand for "a strong monster who won't be a burden," the Dark House of Sorcery created this henchman by strengthening a Hound Knight. His fighting ability is equal to a Vandel's, and he is intensely loyal to Beltorze.

▼▶ Hazan emerged unscathed after fighting five Knight Snipers. Having been strengthened by Dark House of Sorcery, he is exceptionally powerful. He also has a cool intellect and can carry out spying duties.

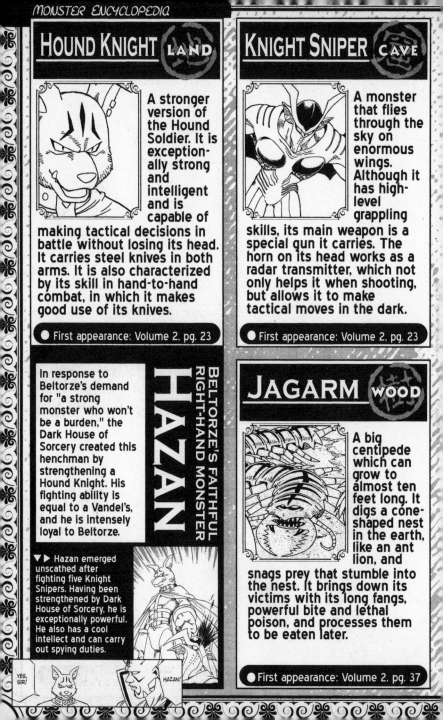

YES, SIR!

HAZAN!

JAGARM WOOD

A big centipede which can grow to almost ten feet long. It digs a cone-shaped nest in the earth, like an ant lion, and snags prey that stumble into the nest. It brings down its victims with its long fangs, powerful bite and lethal poison, and processes them to be eaten later.

● First appearance: Volume 2, pg. 37

PEN BARRY (WOOD)

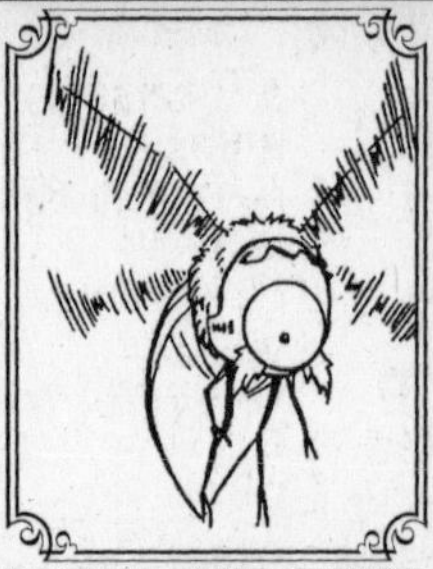

An insect-type monster that can draw anything it sees on paper. Its drawings are extremely accurate. It is often used to spy on enemies.

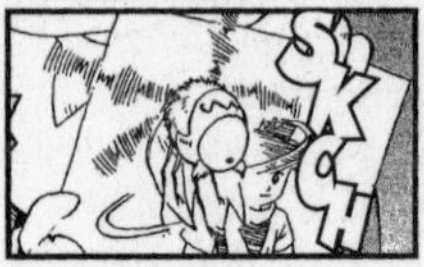

▲It can reproduce objects accurately and in detail.

● First appearance: Volume 2, pg. 65

GIANT BEETLE (WOOD)

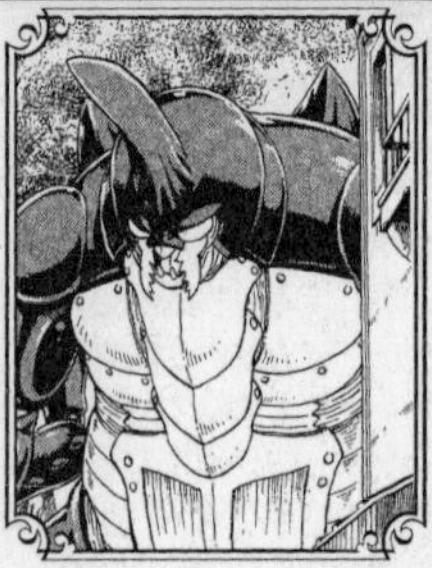

An enormous monster that can grow to over 16 feet long. Despite its flexibility, it has a very hard outer shell that can repel any direct attack. It is known to be extremely greedy, and will eat not only humans, but other monsters, like Jagarms.

● First appearance: Volume 2, pg. 42

GRINEED'S MINION DANGOWL

Dangowl is a strengthened version of a Protector Bug. The Dark House of Sorcery gave him the ability to understand language, allowing him to become the chief henchman of Grineed, the Clever Honcho of Deep Green. He is a perfect example of a monster that works faithfully as a personal steward.

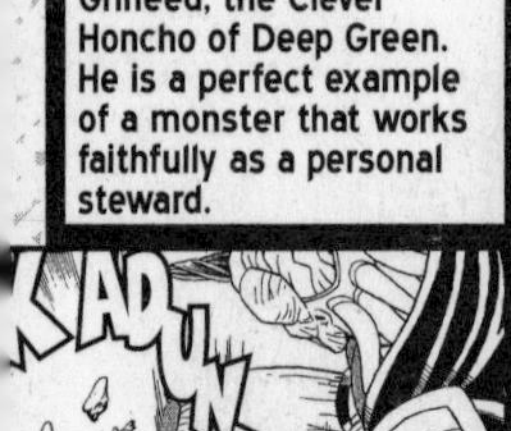
KADUNK

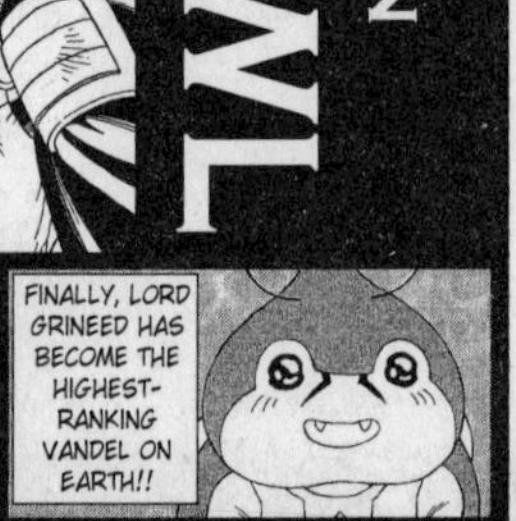
FINALLY, LORD GRINEED HAS BECOME THE HIGHEST-RANKING VANDEL ON EARTH!!

▲ Calming Grineed's rage was one of Dangowl's key duties.

PROTECTOR BUG (WOOD)

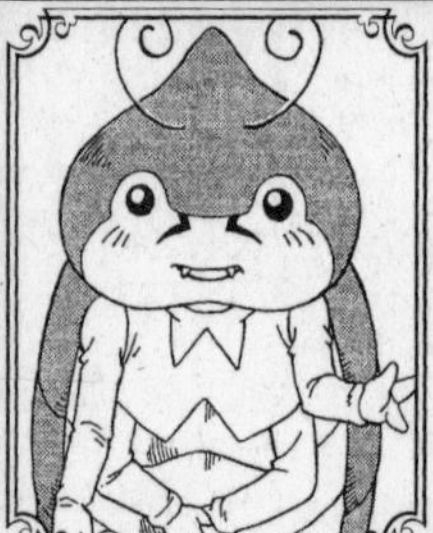

A monster with a tough outer shell on its back. It defends itself by curling up like a pill bug, which allows it to endure a powerful direct strike. However, its stomach is soft and vulnerable, so it can easily be harmed while uncurled. Because of this, it remains in a ball shape when attacking Busters.

● First appearance: Volume 2, pg. 65

CRIMINAL TORCH

WOOD

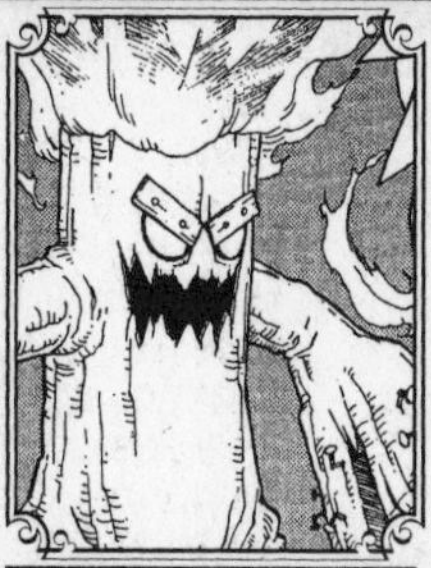

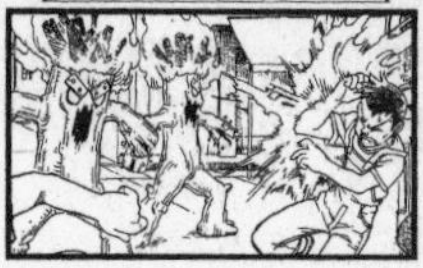

▲ It attacks in packs, burning down villages.

A wood monster in which resides the hate-filled soul of a criminal executed by crucifixion. It attacks by shooting jets of fire from its head. If killed, it can resurrect itself immediately once its fire is relit.

● First appearance: Volume 2, pg. 102

SHAGGY GIRL

?

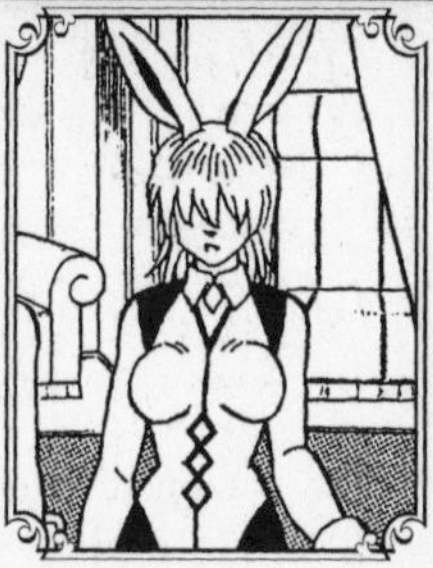

A monster whose responsibility is to guide visitors through the Dark House of Sorcery. She works for Shagie, the Chief of the House. Her bunny-girl appearance makes her popular with visiting Vandels. Her fighting ability is unknown, but she has an encyclopedic knowledge of monsters.

● First appearance: Volume 2, pg. 71

RIVER WHALE

WHIRLPOOL

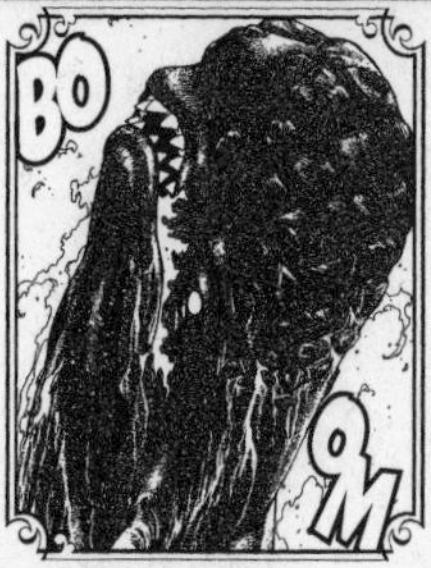
BO
OM

An enormous whale-shaped monster that can swallow even a Long-Necked Devilfish in a single gulp. Its skin is hard. Its head is steely and strong and can easily destroy rocky outcroppings along the river bottom. Only its belly is vulnerable to attack. It is known to be long-lived, with an average lifespan of over 200 years.

● First appearance: Volume 4, pg. 9

LONG-NECKED DEVILFISH

WHIRLPOOL

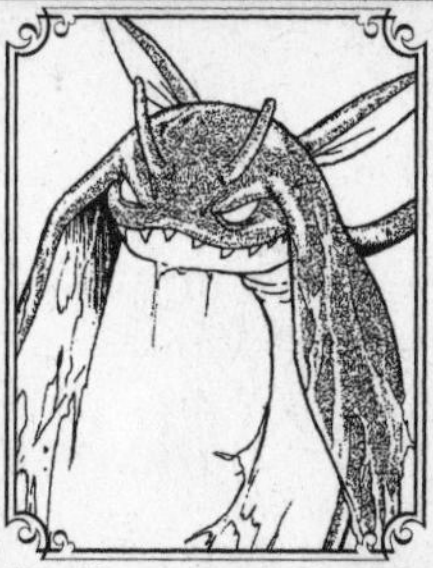

A gigantic, long-necked beast with the head of a devilfish. It lives in the Big River of Ledeux. Upon finding prey, it attacks in a school. It's ferocious, devouring even the bones of its prey. If one Long-Necked Devilfish is killed, the smell of its blood will drive the others into a frenzy, causing them to attack even more fiercely.

● First appearance: Volume 3, pg. 187

BLACK SMOKY CICADA — WOOD 樹

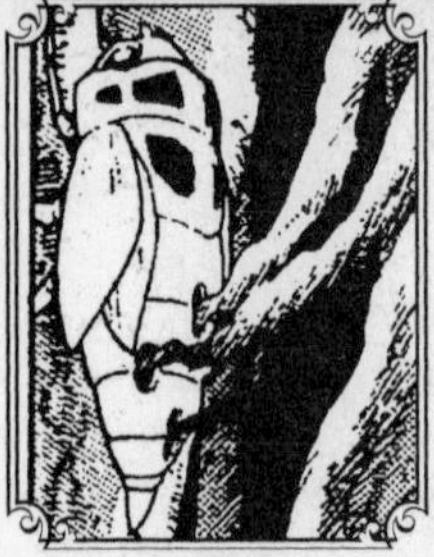

A huge cicada with four holes on its back that release black smoke, polluting the atmosphere. It mainly lives on bark and produces smoke inside its body. It lives ten times as long as a normal cicada. However, when threatened, it behaves just like an ordinary cicada--fleeing the area as it scatters its excretions.

● First appearance: Volume 4, pg. 56

TORYUPUS — WOOD 樹

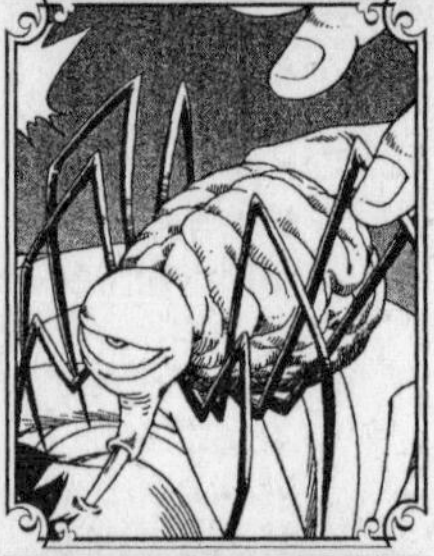

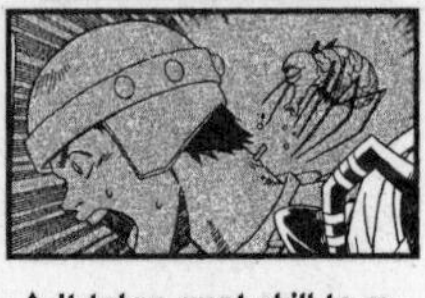

▲It takes great skill to remove the Toryupus safely.

A monster that can control a human by inserting the needle in its mouth into the human's spinal cord. If one tries to separate the monster from its victim by force, the needle will penetrate the spinal cord, killing the human.

● First appearance: Volume 4, pg. 20

BLACK SMOKE BUG — WOOD 樹

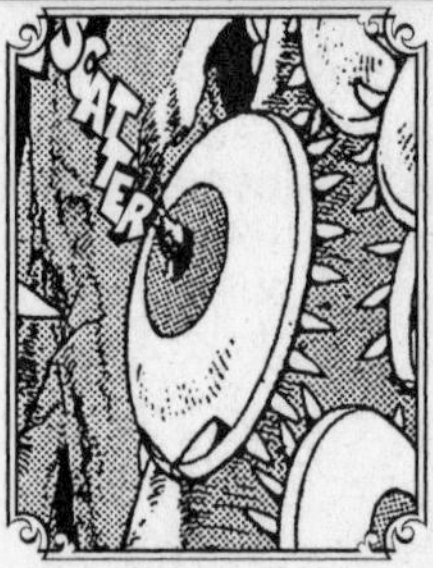
SCATTER

A monster with circular body and nine pairs of legs. Just like the Black Smoky Cicada, it releases black smoke to darken the sky. It does not have wings and can move only by crawling along the ground. However, it can move quickly and deftly on its numerous legs. Even a trained Buster can have trouble dealing with its unpredictable moves.

● First appearance: Volume 4, pg. 56

HUNDRED EYED BUPRESTID — WOOD 樹

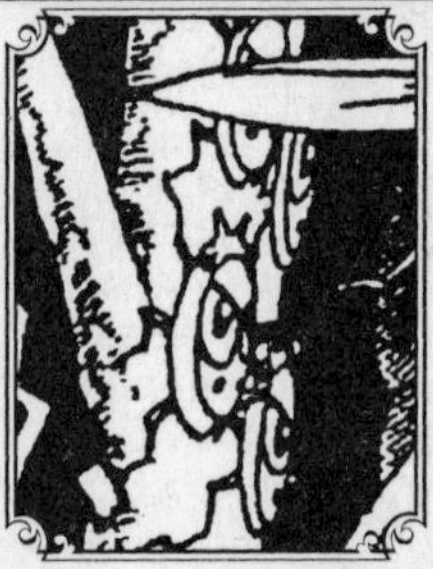

An insect-type monster that eats wood. It has a big appetite and multiplies extremely rapidly. It has hardly any offensive or defensive power. Using the eye-like patterns on its back, it defends itself by distracting the enemy. The wings inside its shell shine in rainbow colors. Many Vandels find them charming.

● First appearance: Volume 4, pg. 56

MEGA DRAGONFLY — WOOD

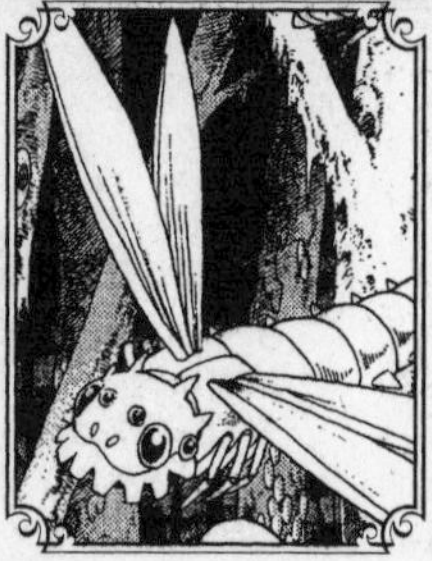

A giant dragonfly that boasts the fastest flight speed of the insect-type monsters. The needles at the tip of its body are filled with a nerve poison, which it uses to attack enemies. It also has powerful teeth, allowing it to occasionally feast on insect-type monsters with hard outer shells.

● First appearance: Volume 4, pg. 56

MEGA TOMBA — WOOD

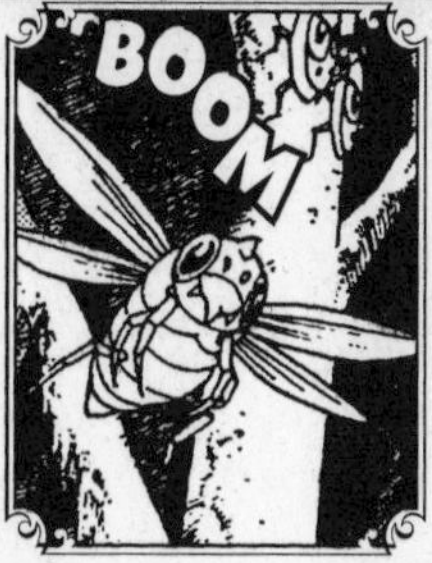
BOOM

A big insect-type monster that lives in wooded areas. It mainly lives off leaves and sap, but it occasionally eats small animals. The horn-like protrusion on its head works like a highly sensitive sensor, helping it escape from its enemy and capture its prey. It is extremely fierce and territorial.

● First appearance: Volume 4, pg. 56

BORM — WOOD

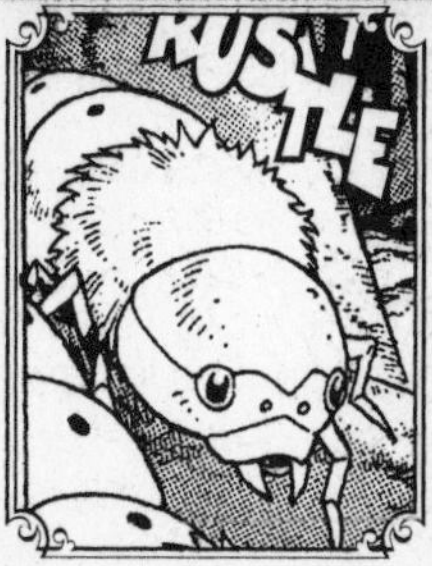

The larval form of the Mega Dragonfly. It usually lives near watery areas, such as lakes and bogs, but it sometimes heads to wooded areas in search of food. It is known to remain in its larval form for an extremely short period of time; it transforms into an adult within a week. Like the Barm, the Borm never turns into a pupa.

● First appearance: Volume 4, pg. 56

BARM — WOOD

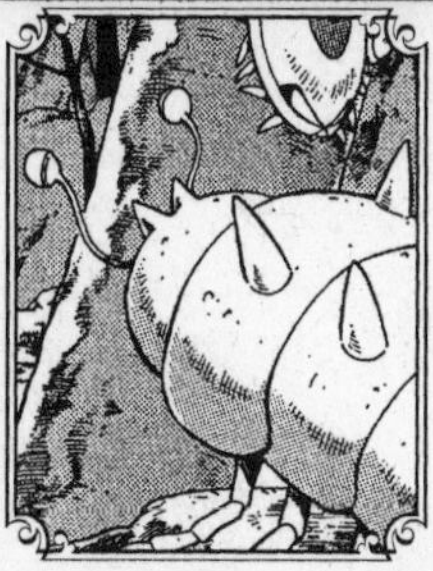

The larval form of the Mega Tomba. It's over twice the size of the adult. It can shoot out its eyes and move them independently. It uses this power to observe enemies while hiding. The thorny protrusions on its back work not as a threat but as a weapon.

● First appearance: Volume 4, pg. 56

GURUME ANT WOOD

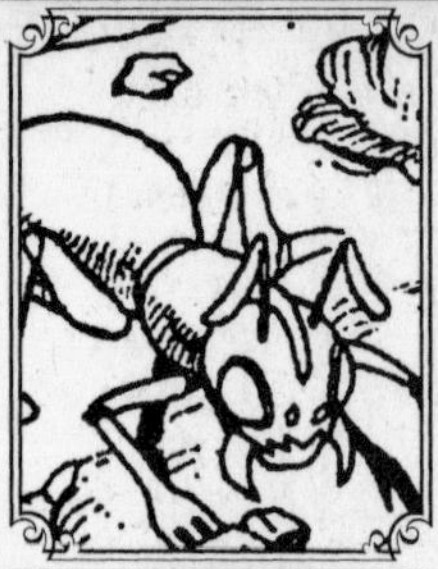

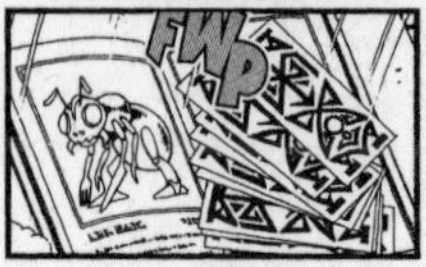
FWP

▲ It can multiply to five times its original number in merely a week.

A termite-like monster that gobbles up everything from trees to stone walls. Although its name is derived from the word "gourmet," it does not have discriminating tastes. It is also known for its ability to multiply very rapidly.

● First appearance: Volume 4, pg. 57

CHIMNEY STINKBUG WOOD

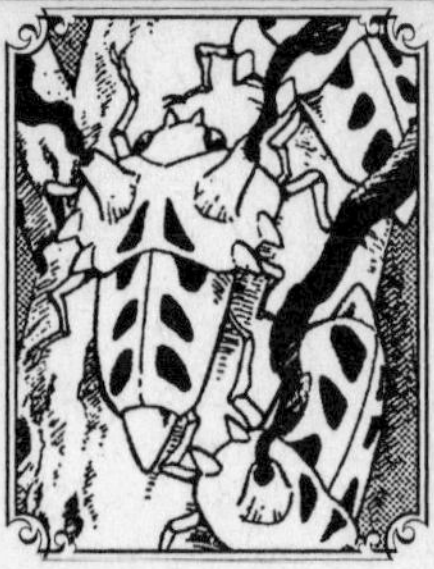

A monster that endlessly blows black smoke from the two chimneys protruding from its back. It lives mainly in wooded areas, but it's not uncommon for it to multiply around towns or cities. In addition to the smoke, it spurts out a foul smell when touched, just like an ordinary stinkbug.

● First appearance: Volume 4, pg. 56

MEDIUM BEETLE WOOD

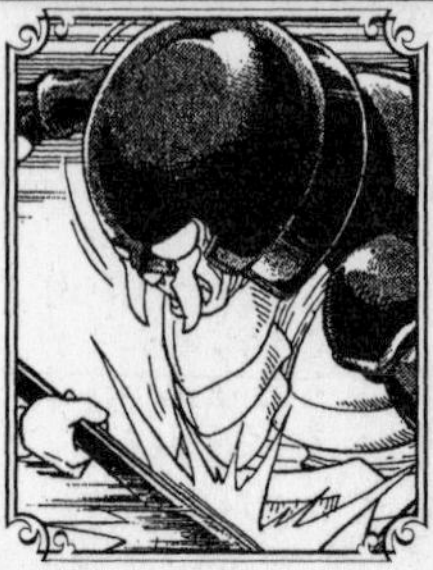

After the Small Beetle completes its first stage of life, it turns into a Medium Beetle. The Medium Beetle is slightly bigger than an adult human. Armed with monstrous strength, it can pull down trees and deflect attacks with its tough outer shell. It requires about half a year and an enormous amount of food to complete this stage and transform into a Giant Beetle.

● First appearance: Volume 4, pg. 60

FLY COMMANDO WOOD

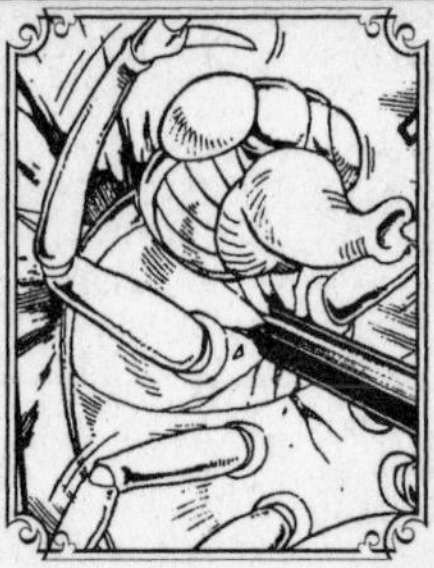

A giant fly that grows to human size. Its saliva contains a component that quickens decomposition; after it sucks sap from a tree, the tree rots and dies. It is attracted to a smell from a specific fruit, and people can use this trait to capture and exterminate it.

● First appearance: Volume 4, pg. 60

SAMNYOUL — WOOD

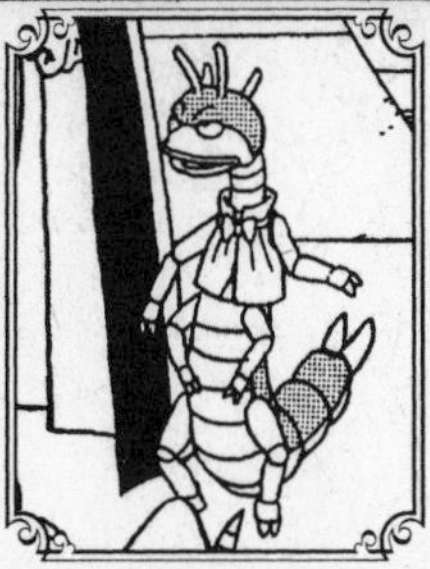

A monster with scissor-like blades on its tail. It uses these blades in battle and when building its nests. Grineed made one of these into a henchman named Ugo.

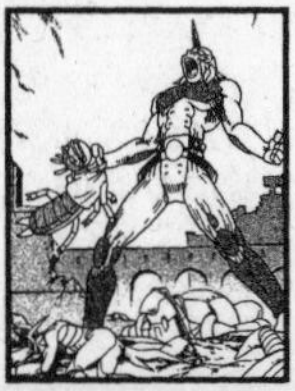

▲ Ugo was a faithful steward of Grineed, but...

● First appearance: Volume 5, pg. 73

GREAT MONSTROUS BUTTERFLY — WOOD

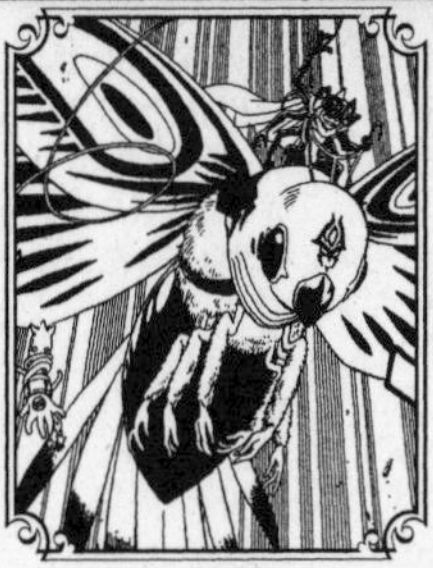

A massive butterfly with a wingspan of over 16 feet. Because of its giant size, Vandels usually use it for long-distance transportation rather than battle. It has a fierce temperament, and a special mask needs to be placed on its head before it can be tamed. The scales from its wings can cause hallucinations in humans who breathe them in.

● First appearance: Volume 4, pg. 108

LAND ANEMONE — WOOD

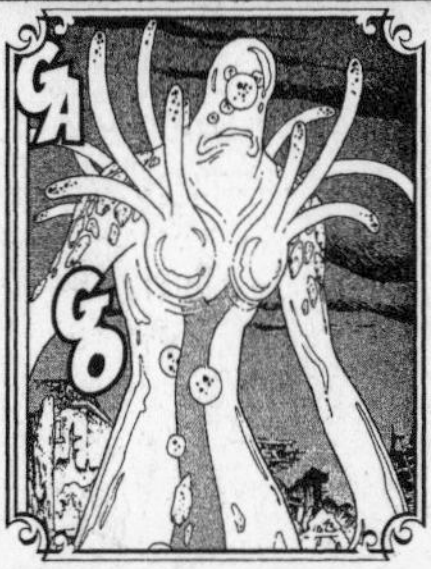
GA
GO

Land Anemone Offshoots can merge into this huge form. It goes without saying that the full Land Anemone is bigger and stronger than the individual offshoots. To fight them, Busters need both high-level skills and a well-thought-out attack strategy.

● First appearance: Volume 6, pg. 17

LAND ANEMONE OFFSHOOT — WOOD

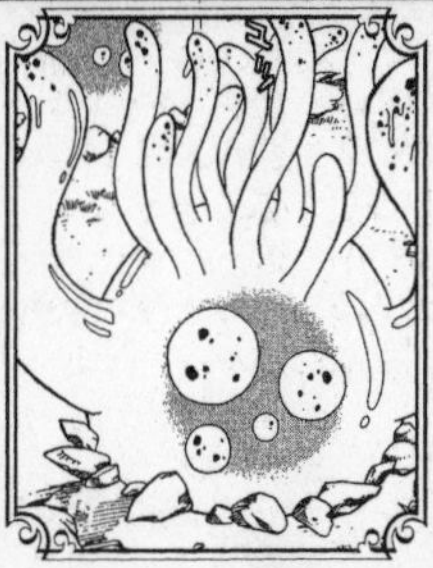

A monster with soluble body fluids that lives underground. At one time, it was popular among Vandels to use Land Anemones to destroy towns by sending them to lay their eggs inside the town gates. These offshoots can split into infinite numbers when attacked.

● First appearance: Volume 5, pg. 165

Warship Tortas — SAND

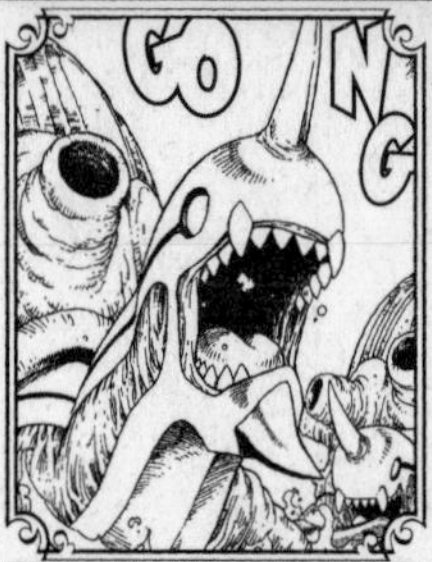

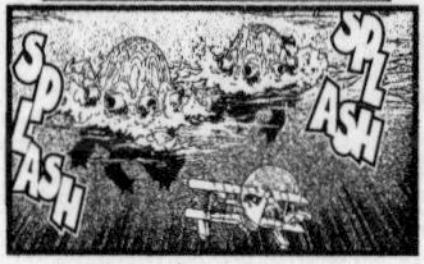
SPLASH
SPLASH

▲It can attack both the land and the sky.

A giant tortoise, active on both land and sea. It has eight large-caliber turrets on its shell, which it fires relentlessly at its enemies. Its battle power matches that of a large warship.

●First appearance: Volume 8, pg. 55

Hover Fish — WHIRLPOOL

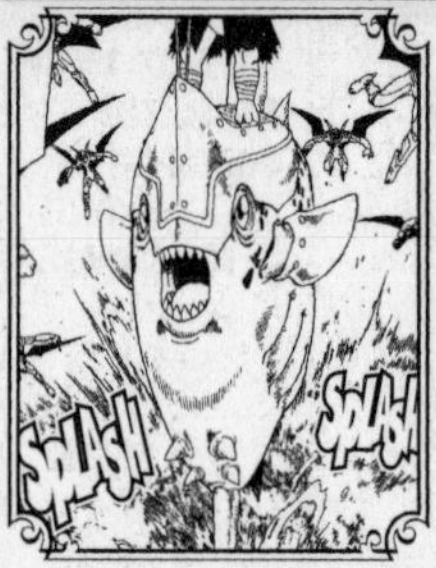
SPLASH
SPLASH

A sea monster that spurts pressurized air from its belly, allowing it to move above the ocean like a hovercraft. Like the Great Monstrous Butterfly, it's mainly used by Vandels for transportation. By skimming the surface of the water with its belly, it can gain propulsive energy and cruise at high speeds.

●First appearance: Volume 7, pg. 181

Rodina's Lovable (?) Pet Cynthia

This Margtin is the pet of Rodina, a seven-star Vandel. To satisfy its endless appetite, Rodina always carries a mysterious sack of food.

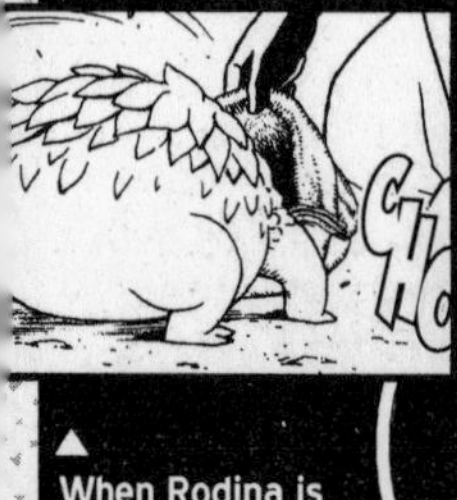

▲When Rodina is holding it or it's eating, it folds the protrusions on its back.

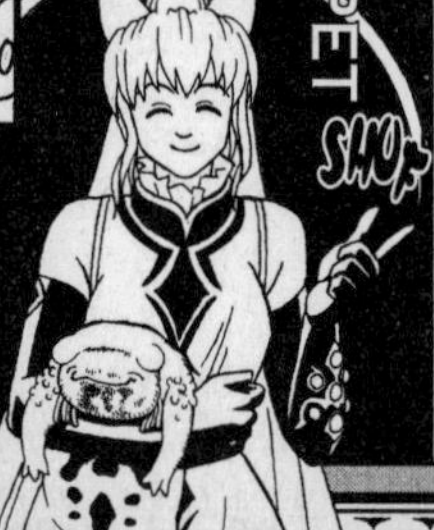

Margtin — WHIRLPOOL

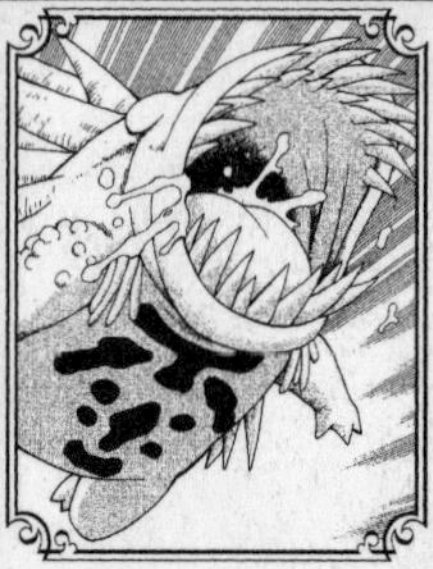

A monster with a bottomless appetite, way beyond its small size. It can crunch up anything in its sharp teeth, but it prefers fresh human flesh. This, along with its fierce personality, makes it a threat to humans. It's nearly blind, but can use its highly developed sense of smell to capture its prey.

● First appearance: Volume 9, pg. 9

BUILD ANT

WOOD

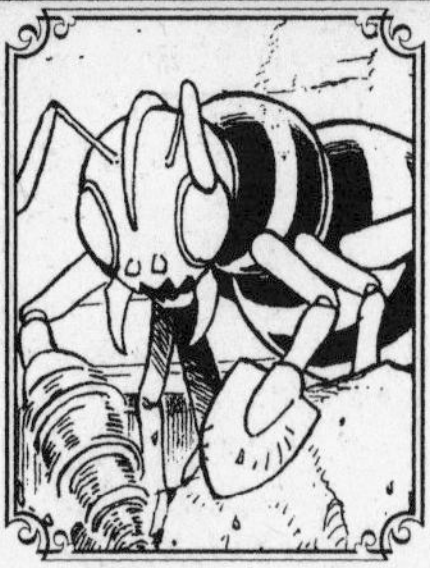

An ant-type monster equipped with a drill and shovel. It builds Vandels' castles and fortresses. Once the Build Ant is given a blueprint, it works without rest until the building is finished. It always works in a team of ten. Because it works quickly, it's very expensive for a Vandel to buy.

● First appearance: Volume 9. pg. 86

RED COPPER SOLDIER

LAND

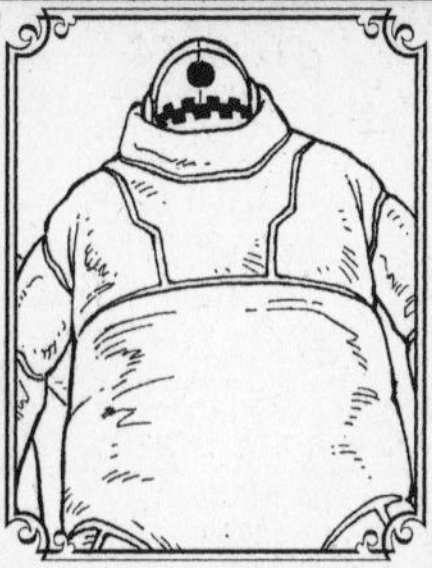

A soldier made of a copper alloy that contains some gold and silver. It is used in many capacities, including launching attacks and defending bases. Although it has no fighting abilities beyond a direct strike, its blow is powerful, and it can destroy the gates that protect towns. Despite its appearance, it can move nimbly.

● First appearance: Volume 9. pg. 17

Have you enjoyed all these monsters and their charms, despite their evil natures? Even more dangerous monsters will appear before Beet and the others in the future!

BLUE FIRE HORSE

LAND

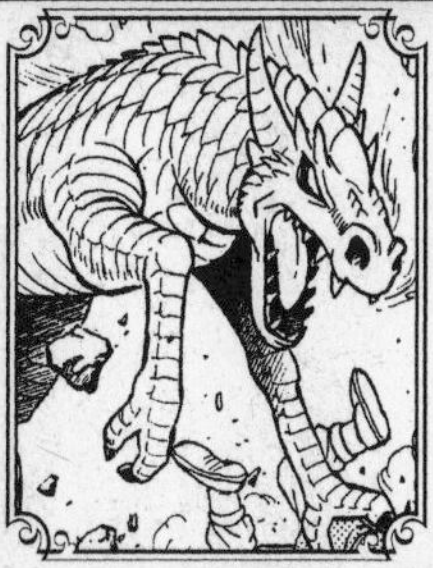

A horselike monster that breathes blue fire, which is much hotter than ordinary fire. Anyone engulfed in its fire will be consumed in an instant without pain. It has an alligator-like mouth and tail, which it uses to attack.

● First appearance: Volume 9. pg. 122

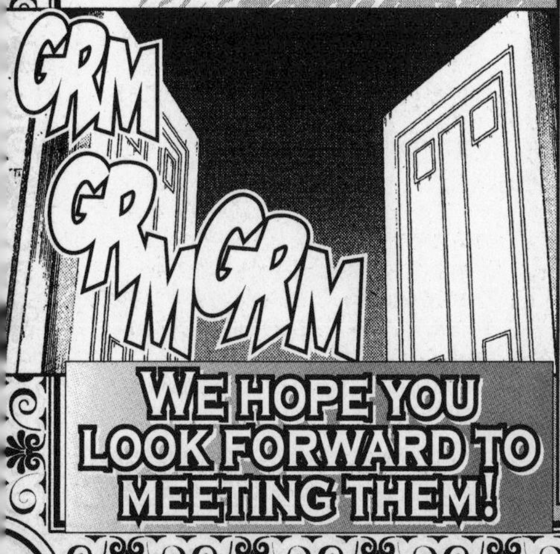
GRM
GRM
GRMGRM
WE HOPE YOU LOOK FORWARD TO MEETING THEM!

Coming Next Volume...

With Slade on their side, the Beet Warriors are ready to take on the world's toughest Vandels...or so they think! When the battle for Bekatrute gets hot and heavy, Beet and his friends decide to stop the invasion at its source by taking down Garonewt. But that means traveling to Garonewt's palace, which is stuffed to the gills with deadly monsters. And Garonewt himself sees Beet as just another pawn in his evil game. Can Beet destroy Garonewt...if it means letting Cruss die?

Available in October 2006!

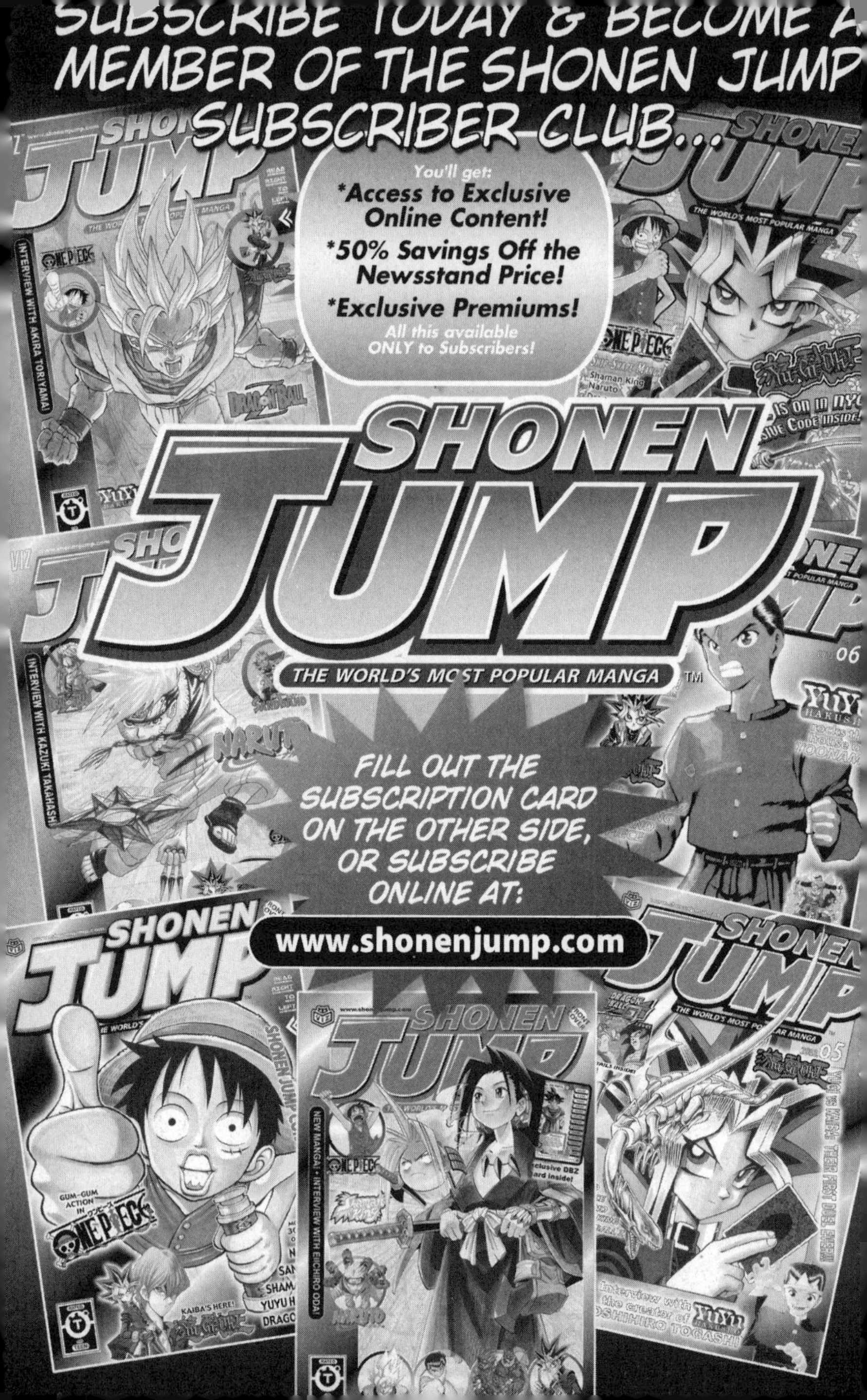
SUBSCRIBE TODAY & BECOME A MEMBER OF THE SHONEN JUMP SUBSCRIBER CLUB...
You'll get:
*Access to Exclusive Online Content!
*50% Savings Off the Newsstand Price!
*Exclusive Premiums!
All this available ONLY to Subscribers!
SHONEN JUMP
THE WORLD'S MOST POPULAR MANGA ™
FILL OUT THE SUBSCRIPTION CARD ON THE OTHER SIDE, OR SUBSCRIBE ONLINE AT:
www.shonenjump.com